W9-BDA-617

The Victor Book of

SYMPHONIES

COMPLETELY REVISED AND ENLARGED
TO INCLUDE 138 SYMPHONIES

by Charles O'Connell

SIMON AND SCHUSTER · NEW YORK · 1948

ALL RIGHTS RESERVED
INCLUDING THE RIGHT OF REPRODUCTION
IN WHOLE OR IN PART IN ANY FORM
COPYRIGHT, 1934, 1941, 1948, BY CHARLES O'CONNELL
PUBLISHED BY SIMON AND SCHUSTER, INC.
ROCKEFELLER CENTER, 630 FIFTH AVENUE,
NEW YORK 20, N. Y.

SECOND PRINTING

MANUFACTURED IN THE UNITED STATES OF AMERICA
BY KINGSPORT PRESS, INC., KINGSPORT, TENN.

MT
150
.025
1948

For Robin

39512

Publisher's Preface

The first edition of The Victor Book of the Symphony *was published in 1935, since when it has become one of the most popular and widely used books on music ever written. In the revised edition of 1941, many works were added and material on modern composers was brought up to date.*

In the past ten years, however, it has become increasingly evident that sooner or later this excellent handbook to the entire orchestral repertoire would have to be enlarged a great deal more. For so popular has orchestral music become in the United States, and so familiar is the standard repertoire, that no one book could hope to treat adequately in one volume all the symphonies, concertos, overtures, tone poems, etc., that our audiences have come to know and to love.

For this reason it was decided some years ago to enlarge and completely revise the old book once more—this time into three volumes. One volume—the present—was to be devoted exclusively to works strictly in the form of the symphony. Its title indicates this salutary exclusiveness. A second volume (published some months ago) was to be devoted exclusively to the concerto, and was called the Victor Book of Concertos. *A third will treat all other orchestral works, like overtures, suites, symphonic poems, etc., while a fourth will take up ballet music.*

This expanded program has enabled the series to be far more comprehensive than the old Victor Book of the Symphony *could hope to be by itself. Thus, whereas the old book offered discussions of forty-nine symphonies, Mr. O'Connell includes in the present volume no fewer than a hundred and thirty-eight. And whereas the old book had room for only nineteen concertos, the* Victor Book of Concertos, *by Abraham Veinus, takes up one hundred and thirty works. Both new books also find space for many hundreds of musical examples.*

Most of Charles O'Connell's original discussions of those forty-nine symphonies have been retained intact in the present volume, with only minor changes where more recent scholarship has turned up interesting new facts or interpretations. Mr. O'Connell has, in addition, supplied all the new discussions, and done them in the same enlightened, popular fashion.

Other long-admired features of the old book have also been retained and revised where necessary—the biographical introductions, the section on the orchestral instruments, etc. They are particularly valuable because Mr. O'Connell has been able to write for the record-buying public, from the point of view of a widely experienced symphonic conductor, and one who has had many years of experience directing and supervising the actual production of phonograph records.

The third book in the series is at present being prepared for the press by Mr. O'Connell; and it is the hope of the publishers that, whereas the original volume served as an excellent handbook, the new series of three books will serve as a veritable encyclopedia of orchestral music for the many millions who now listen to it habitually at concert halls, over the radio, and on records.

TABLE OF CONTENTS

The Victor Book of

SYMPHONIES

A Note on the Modern Orchestra
AND ITS INSTRUMENTAL COMPONENTS

IN THE ancient Greek theater, the *choros* (dancers and vocalists) occupied an allotted space between the players and audience. This space was called the *orchestra*, and would correspond to the orchestra pit in the modern theater, except that it was not depressed below the level occupied by the audience. Early in the nineteenth century it became customary to refer, in theatrical parlance, to the group of musicians who occupied this space, rather than to the space itself, as "the orchestra."

The first instrumental groups known as orchestras included, usually, instruments of the lute type (from which our mandolin and guitar are descended); the family of viols; harpsichords or similar percussion-string instruments; and sometimes small organs. Orchestras were first used almost exclusively as support for vocal music; in fact, the development of the violin can be directly traced to the need for a high-pitched viol to accompany the higher voices in musical-dramatic productions.

Growing use of the orchestra emphasized the shortcomings of orchestral instruments, and brought about their improvement; consequently a tendency to give the orchestra more prominence is noticeable in compositions of the period (1650–1700), and finally composers of importance began writing music for instruments alone. Bach and Haydn were among the most important early composers of purely instrumental music—the former with suites and concertos, the latter with his symphonies. The orchestra which includes in its repertoire Haydn's symphonies today may have as many as one hundred and twenty members (though not all would be used in a Haydn symphony); Haydn's orchestra would have about eighteen men. It would include players of the violin, viola, cello, and contrabass, or bass viol; two each of flute, oboe and bassoon, horn and trumpet; and perhaps the orchestra would boast also a pair of kettledrums.

Mozart introduced clarinets and trombones as regular voices of the orchestra, and Beethoven established almost all the present-day orchestral instruments as members in good standing. In the C minor Symphony (the Fifth) he created a sensation by the sudden introduction

1

of the trombones at the beginning of the fourth movement; and he used piccolo and contrabassoon with great effectiveness.

Almost constant improvement in the orchestral instruments gave Wagner, Brahms, and Tchaikovsky inviting opportunities for colorful orchestration, and they, with all composers of the romantic period, took advantage of such opportunities. No one has ever surpassed Wagner in the brilliance, variety, and significance of his orchestral color. Not satisfied with certain instruments, he redesigned them (the Bayreuth tuba, for example) to produce the precise tone quality he wanted. He was the first, and remains one of the few composers, to write intelligently for the modern harp, and his use of modern valved brass instruments is unsurpassed in effectiveness. The orchestration of Brahms is of course entirely different, darker, and warmer than Wagner's, but rarely as brilliant. Tchaikovsky's is perhaps of a quality halfway between the two.

The development of certain instruments, and the acceptance of others as standard orchestral instruments, helped to increase the size of the orchestra. Theoretically, there should be no more than one instrument of each "choir" in the orchestra: one violin voice, one clarinet, one flute, and so on. But, because all instrumental voices are not of the same power and sonority, a balance must be effected by adjusting their relative numbers; and because composers often, nowadays, write orchestral parts so elaborate that each must be divided among several instruments of one type, the orchestra has grown steadily larger. Furthermore, concert halls have increased in size, necessitating more orchestral power, and we have at last arrived at an orchestra of 100–120 men, which seems large enough for most modern concert halls, yet not too large to be perfectly responsive and flexible.

The symphony orchestra is made up of four groups, or choirs: the strings, woodwinds, brass, and percussion, or *batterie*. The strings include about eighteen first and sixteen second violins; ten to fourteen violas; eight to twelve cellos; eight or ten basses; one or two harps. (Very rarely more harps are used, although Wagner requires as many as six!) The woodwind usually includes two flutes, two piccolos, three oboes, one *cor anglais* or English horn, three bassoons, one contrabassoon, three clarinets, one bass clarinet, and sometimes a contrabass clarinet. The brass choir is composed of three or four trombones, four trumpets, four to ten or even twelve horns, and tuba (sometimes bass tuba or helicon). The *batterie* comprises the drums (timpani or kettle-drums, bass and military drums, tambourine, Chinese drum, and sometimes others); tam-tam or gong, celesta, glockenspiel or orchestra bell; tubular chime, castanets, xylophone, and triangle, together with any other special percussion instruments which the composer may require. The work of the *batterie* is divided among several men, who sometimes play other orchestral instruments as well. The timpanist, however, devotes his entire attention to his own special instruments.

STRINGS

VIOLIN : The violin is the soprano of the string choir, and in some respects the most important instrument of the orchestra. It is capable of a wide range of emotional expression, and of considerable dynamic scope; its tone is of a character that makes it blend well with any other tone in the orchestra.

Range of the Violin

In its present form the violin is the result of a long period of evolution—a period which ended in the superb instruments of the great sixteenth- and seventeenth-century Italian makers. The first "true" violins were made in Italy by Gasparo da Salò (1540–1609), and his instruments were used as models by succeeding makers. The city of Cremona was the seat of the most famous school of violin makers, and it was there that Andrea Amati started the line of artisans whose name in a violin makes it priceless. His grandson, Nicolo Amati (1596–1684), not only made some of the finest violins *in use today*, but was the teacher of Antonio Stradivari, greatest of all craftsmen in this difficult and subtle art. Other makers whose instruments remain priceless, often musically and always intrinsically, were those of the Guadagnini and Guarnerius families.

Any one of these names authentically appearing in a violin makes it exceedingly valuable. That is not to say that modern instruments are necessarily inferior, or that ancient ones are invariably fit for use. It is highly questionable that anyone, unless an impossible combination of musician, antiquarian, and student, could distinguish by the ear alone a Stradivarius from the finest of modern instruments. The value of a Cremona violin is often factitious, or fictitious. There is no miracle, especially and exclusively available to the viol family, which excepts them from the deterioration of age and use; and there is no reason why duplicates of them, executed by a first-class modern violin maker, should not have an equally beautiful quality of tone. This is a statement that will shock many violinists and merchants; the fact remains. The superiority of the Cremona instruments is probably due, not to the ridiculous supposition that a secretly formulated varnish gives them their tone, but to the fact that they were made with endless patience and loving care. Intelligent and persistent manipulation of the sound post of a string instrument will have more effect on the tone than any rare wood, any secret varnish in the world. Furthermore, while a Heifetz can make any violin give out beautiful sound, an amateur fiddler can make a "Strad" sound like a leopard cat in agony. It would seem, therefore, that the player has considerable influence on the tone of even a famous instrument.

The violin bow is a direct descendant of the aboriginal weapon. Its present form was determined by François Tourte (1747–1835), many of whose bows are in use today. The arc is usually of a wood called Pernambuco; the hairs are from a horse's tail, bleached white, and rubbed with resin to increase their friction against the string.

The violin is tuned to the tones G, D, A, and E. The G string is a wire-wound string, and gives the violin its most powerful and deepest tones. The other strings are of "catgut"—actually made from the intestines of sheep, or, more often, of steel. They are of varying degrees of brightness in tone, the most brilliant, of course, being the E string which sometimes is made of steel. The effective range of the violin is about three and one-half octaves, from G below middle C. Higher tones can be produced, but they are neither agreeable nor effective.

A great variety of utterance is possible. Singing passages, smooth and unbroken; sharp, crisp, detached notes, at almost any speed; ethereal harmonics and warm, full, sonorous G-string tones—all are at the command of the capable player. Octaves and, to a limited extent, chords may be played on the violin; when two notes are played at once, the device is called "double-stopping." Brilliant effects are achieved by various methods of bowing: *spiccato* by playing rapidly a number of detached notes in one stroke of the bow; *saltando* by bouncing the bow on the strings; *vibrato* by vibrating the *left* hand from the wrist as the finger presses against the string; *col legno* by playing with the wooden part of the bow; *tremolo* by rapidly repeating the same note with short up-and-down strokes of the bow; *glissando* by sliding the left hand along the string while bowing with the right. Trills, mordents, and other musical decorations are all easily effected on the violin.

Harmonics are very high-pitched sounds, components of the normal tone of the instrument but normally almost inaudible. They are made conspicuous by stopping off the fundamental tone, and causing the string to vibrate in segments. This the violinist accomplishes in one of two ways. He may lightly press upon the strings at their "nodal" points (the points between the segments in which all vibrating strings move), thus interfering with the vibration of the string as a whole and bringing the segmentary vibrations into prominence. The sounds thus produced are called "natural" harmonics. The player may, instead, press strongly on the point of the string which will give the required pitch, and with the fourth finger touch lightly on the new nodal point of the "shortened" section of the string. He thus produces "artificial" harmonics, stronger but less agreeable in quality than "natural" harmonics.

VIOLA : The viola is the contralto of the string choir. It is somewhat larger than the violin, and in size as well as musical relationship occupies the place between the deeper-toned cello and the brilliant violin. Its strings are slightly thicker than violin strings, and the two lower ones are wire-wound. Its tone is sonorous, but, solo, not always agreeable. As supplying a tonal mass of great importance to the orchestra, the viola is highly necessary and desirable, but as a solo instrument it has little appeal, except in the rare cases wherein music intelligently written for it is played by a Primrose or a Tertis.

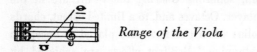

Range of the Viola

The viola in modern orchestra has received much more attention than formerly. The few outstanding artists who play this rather ungrateful instrument have done much to redeem it from the curse of being the resort of unsuccessful violinists, and many modern composers assign to it such music as will bring out to the full its latent possibilities. It is capable of all the technical effects of the violin, and is tuned one-fifth lower—C, G, D, A. Its range is slightly less than that of the violin—about three octaves.

CELLO : The violoncello is the baritone of the orchestral string choir. It is a development of the ancient viola da gamba (knee viol), which was once the bass member of the string family, and was played with the instrument held between the knees, much as the cello is today. Violoncello is a rather cumbersome way of saying "little big viol," which is what it means, so commonly the instrument is called cello.

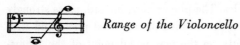

Range of the Violoncello

It is tuned an octave below the viola, and its longer, thicker strings, and the larger body of air vibrated by them, produce a darker but more sonorous and agreeable tone. It encompasses three and one-sixth octaves; it can be manipulated in practically all the tricks of the violin, but not so rapidly. Its tone is warm, vibrant, masculine; the cello is often assigned a singing role in the orchestra, for that reason. In masses of tone the cello is one of the orchestra's most effective instruments, and while its voice is not the most powerful, it can be the most conspicuous and perhaps the most expressive in the string ensemble.

The cello bow is shorter and heavier than that of the violin, and the bow and left-hand technique are entirely different.

DOUBLE BASS. This is the bass of the string choir—a giant vio-
CONTRABASS: lin more than six feet high, and, from the point
of view of the physicist, as inefficient as it is big. The tone of the contrabass, though exceedingly deep and rich, is quite weak in relation to the
size of the instrument and the energy required to play it; nevertheless,
the ten or twelve basses in a symphony orchestra supply a wonderfully
rich and deep tonal foundation, perceptible no matter how powerfully
the rest of the orchestra is playing.

Range of the Double Bass

The contrabass has certain physical peculiarities which differentiate
it from the other viols, and establish its relationship with the oldest
instruments of the viol type. It has sloping, rather than rounded, shoul-
ders; a flat instead of a swelling back, and an exceedingly high bridge.
The bow, also, shows traces of its origin, and more than any other bow
suggests the huntsman's weapon.

The contrabass is tuned in shorter intervals that the other string instruments; otherwise the player, unless his hand were unnaturally large,
could not span them. Therefore, the tuning is in fourths—E, A, D, and
G. It sounds an octave lower than its notes are written. Occasionally a
five-string bass is used, a C string being added to give lower bass notes.
Despite the size of the instrument, most violinistic effects can be performed, but of course not nearly at the speed of the violinist. The tone
is full, deep, sonorous, and resonant, and only to a very limited degree
can it be used solo. Occasionally, however, for weird or comic effects,
conspicuous and even solo passages are given to this instrument. The
most famous of all is the strange utterance of the basses in the scherzo
of the Beethoven Fifth Symphony that suggested to Hector Berlioz the
gambolings of elephants. Serge Koussevitzky, the eminent conductor of
the Boston Symphony Orchestra, is a virtuoso of this Gargantuan violin,
and has played solo in public as well as for phonograph records.

HARP: More than three thousand years ago, a court painter was commanded to decorate with murals the battlements of an ancient Egyptian city. In the procession of figures he limned on the everlasting stone, some bore musical instruments, several of which are distinctly recognizable as harps.

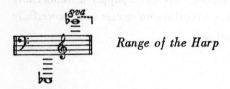

Range of the Harp

The harp is one of the oldest and most romantic of musical instruments. It was known well to the Jews of Biblical times; indeed, David is remembered as a harper and singer. No doubt he wooed a lady as easily as he soothed a troubled prince, with the assistance of his plangent strings; for the harp gives wonderful background to the voice. We often associate the harp with the Irish bards and minstrels—indeed with the Irish race itself; not entirely without reason, for the harp is the only musical instrument regarded as a national symbol, and represented in a national flag. As a matter of fact, the harp has a more intimate connection with the ancient Jews, and was known and widely used in Europe long before Ireland heard it. The painted vases of the ancient Greeks reveal the harp in use, and the troubadours, the minnesingers, and the bards of Northern Europe brought it to the western shores of that continent. Soon it was adopted by the Irish, the Scotch, and the Welsh, and during the reign of Henry VIII was incorporated in the national insignia of Ireland.

The harp, until the beginning of the eighteenth century, had been little improved over its primitive ancestors. To be portable, it had to be limited in size and weight, and consequently in the number of its strings. Chromatic intervals—tones lying between the whole tones (the white keys on the piano)—could not be played, because to tune the harp chromatically would require too many strings. About 1720 a transposing pedal was invented; it would raise all the strings, simultaneously, a half tone. Ninety years later, Sebastien Érard, founder of the French piano house "Érard," developed the double-action harp, employing pedals that would shorten the strings instantaneously, raising them either a half or whole tone, and making it possible to play in all keys.

The modern concert harp is usually tuned in the key of C flat; it has seven transposing pedals, each pedal affecting all the strings of the same name. Thus, the C pedal affects all the C strings, the D pedal all the D's, and so on. When all the pedals are pressed down halfway, the harp is tuned in C major; if they are depressed fully, the instrument will play in C-sharp major. Naturally, the agility of the harp in passing from one tonality to another is somewhat limited by its mechanism, and the powers of the human hand likewise impose handicaps. It is, therefore, not easy to write intelligent and effective music for the harp.

It is curious to note that this, one of the most ancient of instruments, would win the approval of the most radical modernist architect or designer, for the reason that in its structure it is almost purely functional. The slender Corinthian column that is characteristic of the conventional model is a hollow pillar of great structural strength, which serves not only to take a large part of the strains generated by the taut strings, but also encloses the rods connecting the pedals with the tuning mechanism. The gracefully curved neck, lovely as it is, nevertheless is a purely structural form, determined entirely by the varying length of the strings. It, too, has a double purpose; it serves as a base for anchoring the strings, and conceals the transposing mechanism. The sound box is the third member of the triangle; through it pass the strings to their lower extremities, and it resonates and reinforces their tone.

The tone of the harp is rather weak, nor is it susceptible of much variation in color. In the orchestra it is used with beautiful effect, nevertheless; in accompanying solo passages for other instruments, in adding a certain luster to the orchestral texture, and, more rarely, as a romantic solo voice. The lower and middle strings have, in the hands of a skillful player, a warm and lovely tone, unassertive yet by no means inconspicuous in orchestral passages of moderate dynamic intensity. The upper strings have a brilliant but ephemeral tone, which because of the relative inflexibility and shortness of the string is resonated but briefly and weakly. The range of the harp is five octaves; its music is written exactly like that of the piano. The arpeggio, a chord in which the notes are played rapidly in succession rather than simultaneously, derives its name from that of the harp; it is the characteristic utterance of the instrument.

The orchestral harpist must be a musician of the first rank, possessed of an infallible sense of pitch, great digital dexterity, deftness in the use of the pedals, and poise under all circumstances.

WOODWINDS

FLUTE: The flute is a descendant of what is probably the oldest and simplest wind instrument—a hollow reed. Somewhat more proximately, it is related to the syrinx of ancient Greece, from which the vocal organ of the bird is named. It has always been a highly respectable instrument; a cultured Greek youth regarded flute-playing as a necessary and polite accomplishment, and one reads of yearning nineteenth-century bachelors occupying themselves with the instrument when not otherwise engaged.

The beak flutes, recorders, and flageolets of the sixteenth to nineteenth centuries were the ancestors of the present instruments. They were played vertically, however, and not transversely, as is the orchestral flute of today; in their range, tone, and agility, they were not materially different from a ten-cent tin whistle. In 1832, Theobald Boehm invented a keyed flute which greatly facilitated performance, extended the possibilities of the instrument, and gave it the use of the chromatic scale. We owe the modern flute almost entirely to Boehm's improvements.

Range of the Flute

The range of the flute is approximately three octaves. Its tone in the lower register is warm, smooth, and rather dark-colored; as it proceeds up the scale the tone becomes much more brilliant, and in the highest register is keen and penetrating. Incidentally, the player does not blow *into* his instrument, but *across* a hole in its side called the embouchure. He thus agitates the column of air within the flute, and this air column is the vibrating body which produces the tone. The highest notes are produced by overblowing (blowing harder than normally), together with changes in the shape of the lips.

The flute can produce a great variety of effect. It is used in important melodic passages as well as in brilliant, decorative figures; its agility is amazing, its tone almost always discernible in the orchestral fabric. It is capable of exceedingly rapid scale passages, but not normally of a true glissando—an effect which, in the orchestra, is confined practically to the string instruments and trombone. It is almost always used in the accompaniment to the most ambitious efforts of coloratura sopranos, in which the intent is to compare (or is it to contrast?) the agility, tone, and intonation of the voice and flute. This is invariably unfortunate for the voice.

PICCOLO: In Italian, *piccolo* means "diminutive," and the piccolo of the orchestra is essentially a little flute. It is half the size of the flute, it is played in much the same manner, and it can sound an octave or more higher than its larger brother. It ranges through about three octaves, with a tone which at any pitch is exceedingly brilliant and, in its uppermost register, piercing to the point of unpleasantness.

Range of the Piccolo

Composers use it for quaint and fantastic effects, as well as for applying a penetrating point and glitter to heavy masses of orchestral tone.

OBOE: The oboe, in recognizable form, dates back to the days of ancient Greece and Rome. To the Greeks it was known as the aulos; the Romans called it tibia, a name which survives today in an organ stop of woodwind timbre. In Shakespeare's stage directions we encounter the word hautboy, a corruption of two French words meaning "high wood." The oboe might be called the lyric soprano of the woodwind choir. Its tone, especially in its upper range, is bright, penetrating, reedy, or almost of flutelike brilliance, yet always with a very vocal quality that is peculiarly poignant and moving. The lowest tones are round and reedy, with almost a contralto timbre.

Range of the Oboe

The oboe is a sectional, conical tube of wood (cocus, rosewood, or ebony) pierced with holes and fitted with a key system not unlike that of the flute. It is equipped with a double reed, the vibrations of which generate its tones. Its range encompasses two and one-half octaves. Very little wind is necessary to make the instrument speak, and for this reason extended phrases are quite possible. The player is more concerned with holding back the breath than with great blowing power, but he must be able to "feed" it to the instrument with absolute evenness, under absolute control.

The oboe is exceedingly agile; it is capable of brilliant decorative figures as well as fluent and sustained melody, and its versatility makes it one of the orchestra's most important voices. Its very distinctive and incisive tone, "green" and bittersweet, keeps this instrument always conspicuous in the ensemble, and makes it an interesting contrast with other instruments.

COR ANGLAIS This remarkably named instrument is neither [*English Horn*]: "English" nor a horn. It is, actually, an alto oboe, with certain modifications which alter the characteristic oboe tone in both pitch and quality. It has been asserted that the *cor anglais* is a descendant of the old English hornpipe, and that the French, perceiving its value and putting it to work, called it "English" horn. This explanation accounts for the "English," but not for the "horn."

Range of the English Horn

Certain early reed instruments were bent in the middle, forming an obtuse angle; *anglais* might therefore refer to "an angled horn." Regardless of the origin of the name, however, the instrument is an oboe of larger size, lower pitch, and darker tone color. Its bore is conical, and the exterior lines, instead of ending in a slightly flared bell, expand into a roughly spherical bulb, open at the lower extremity. It is this hollow and open bulb which largely determines the curiously dark and almost nasal quality of the tone.

The English horn has a compass of about two and one-half octaves, some German-made instruments having one or two notes lower than the French. The key-and-fingering system is identical with that of the oboe, but the *cor anglais* is pitched five tones lower than its soprano relative.

Nearly everyone knows the lovely *cor anglais* solo in the "Largo" of Dvořák's symphony "From the New World." Many of us, however, have had the misfortune to become acquainted with this poignant melody only as the basis of the banal and tasteless mock spiritual "Goin' Home." The persistence of this emasculate sentimentality on radio programs has not increased the effectiveness of the original melody when it appears, in its proper symphonic setting, on the air; yet, played by a really great executant on the *cor anglais*, its haunting and melancholy beauty can be a memorable thing.

Another famous and exceedingly beautiful passage for English horn is the main theme of the second movement of the César Franck symphony. At the first performance of this work one critic dismissed it breezily for the very reason that the English horn is used in it. Franck was first to employ this instrument in a symphony, and the profound commentator, with true French logic, decided that since no symphony had used the English horn, no work which did use it could be a symphony.

Wagner used this beautiful orchestral voice, as he used every instrument, with singular effectiveness. The unaccompanied solo for *cor anglais* occurring in the third act of *Tristan und Isolde* is a striking example.

OBOE D'AMORE: This instrument, though not frequently used in the modern orchestra, was important to the orchestra of Bach's time, and is found occasionally in modern works and in contemporary orchestrations of the music of Bach. It is tuned a minor third below the oboe and its range is relatively of the same extent. In appearance it much resembles the English horn, having the more or less spherically shaped bell which by surrounding the final opening of the instrument imparts a veiled and mystical quality to the tone. The instrument is keyed and played like the English horn.

CLARINET: The ancestors of the clarinet were the reed instruments in common use (1600–1700) and known variously as chalumeaux, shawms, and schalmeis. These names are all derived from the Latin *calamus*—a reed. The word clarinet comes to use through the Italian *clarino* and English clarion, a small and high-pitched trumpet which the clarinet, or clarionet, eventually succeeded.

Range of the Clarinet

The clarinet is a single-reed instrument. Its bore is cylindrical rather than conical, and the tube is about two feet long, terminating in a slightly flared bell. The range and agility of the instrument were tremendously improved when, in 1843, the Boehm key system was applied to it. The modern instrument has a range of more than three octaves.

If the oboe is the lyric soprano of the woodwind choir, the clarinet is the dramatic. Its tone varies definitely and markedly in different sections of its range. The lowest section is dark, sonorous, and reedy—sometimes melancholy and weird; the middle register is notably weaker and less colorful, and the higher is remarkably clear, bright, and polished.

The saxophone, a poor but close relation of the clarinet, is not regularly a member of the orchestra, but its use in modern music is frequent and often effective. It was invented in 1840 by Adolphe Sax. Like the clarinet, it is played with a single reed in a chisel-shaped mouthpiece. Unlike the clarinet, it has a conical bore, a relatively large and upturned bell, and is made of brass. It is made in many sizes, from tiny soprano to grotesquely large and clumsy bass. Maurice Ravel uses it conspicuously in his effective orchestrations, and Debussy composed a charming Rhapsodie for Saxophone and Orchestra.

BASS CLARINET: A clarinet long enough to produce real bass tone would be too long for convenience; consequently, the bass clarinet is doubled on itself, to bring its length into reasonable limits. It resem-

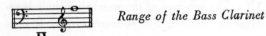 *Range of the Bass Clarinet*

bles, somewhat, a large saxophone. Its tone is more powerful, less reedy, more sonorous and round than that of the clarinet, and extends through a range of about one and a half octaves. Its lowest tones are remarkably big and heavy, closely resembling certain pedal tones in a great organ.

BASSOON: The bassoon is the lowest-voiced member of the woodwind group. It is a collateral descendant of the same ancient instruments from which springs the clarinet, though there is little resemblance between them. Low-pitched notes are a function of the length of the vibrating body. To achieve the low notes of the bassoon, length is necessary, and primitive forms of the instrument were from six to nine feet long. For convenience in playing, the pipe was doubled upon itself and joined together in a block of solid wood. The imaginative Italians saw some resemblance, then, to a bundle of sticks, and gave the instrument the name *fagotto*—faggot.

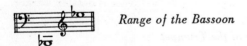 *Range of the Bassoon*

True intonation is difficult for the bassoon, and great skill is required to make it deliver its possible effects. It is, nevertheless, capable of considerable agility and rapidity in its various expressions, and because of this, plus a certain weird, dry quality of tone in certain registers, it is often assigned comical parts, and has won a reputation as the clown of the orchestra. This is a little unjust, for the bassoon is also capable of warm and sentimental expression, of utterances passionate and sad. It is an exceedingly versatile instrument, and has been employed regularly in the orchestra since the time of Handel and Bach. Its tone blends so well with that of certain other instruments that it is frequently used to fortify other groups, notably the cellos. Its range is usually somewhat more than three octaves.

CONTRABASSOON: The sub-bass of the woodwind choir is essentially of the same type as bassoon, but is much larger. It continues down the scale from the bassoon's lowest notes, and can sound the deepest notes in the orchestral ensemble. Actually about sixteen feet long, it is folded six times, so that its coils stand about four feet from

Range of the Contrabassoon

the floor. In addition to carrying the bassoon quality farther down the scale, the contrabassoon, in its lower register, has a quality peculiar to itself—it can snore and grunt and growl quite effectively. Ravel makes use of this ability of the instrument by assigning to it, in his *Mother Goose* suite, the part of the Beast in the episode "Beauty and the Beast."

THE BRASS

TRUMPET: The ancestry of the trumpet is most ancient. It originated in the horns of animals, or in certain sea shells, which primitive man fashioned into crude instruments capable of sounding but one

Range of the Trumpet

note. The oldest extant form of the instrument is the *shofar*, the ram's-horn trumpet still used in modern synagogues, and sounded as a formal summons to the congregation on the Jewish New Year.

Metal trumpets were used for military purposes by the ancient Greeks and Romans, and the present form of the instrument had its beginnings even in those early days, when the trumpet was made in coils for convenience in carrying. A shrill and high-pitched trumpet, the *clarino* or clarion, was much used by Handel and Bach, but the instrument escaped from its natural limitations only when, early in the nineteenth century, valves or pistons were provided. These simplified the method of playing the instrument, and made it possible to execute upon it the full chromatic scale.

The present orchestral trumpet is a brass tube about eight feet in length, coiled in a roughly rectangular shape about eighteen inches long. The greater length of the tube is cylindrical, but about twelve inches from the final opening it begins to expand into a bell. The mouthpiece is cup-shaped, and the lips are brought against it with considerable pressure. By manipulations of the tongue and lips, the player can sound his instrument with great rapidity and brilliance. By the use of the mute—a pear-shaped mass of metal or papier-mâché which fits into the bell—a distant and attenuated tone is produced for special, colorful effects.

The natural tone of the instrument, with its golden clarity, its penetrating brilliance, its noble, even defiant quality, is familiar to everyone. In the hands of a really expert player, its tone can be exceedingly expressive, soft and rich and moving. In the symphony orchestra the trumpet is used for a variety of purposes, but of course its principal duty is to add sonority and brilliance to the ensemble. Its range is about two and one-half octaves; the topmost note is the same high C that sopranos boast of. Some jazz trumpeters can force the instrument even higher, unfortunately.

CORNET: Closely related to the trumpet, the cornet is not an orchestral member in good standing. Its tone is smaller and less brilliant than that of the trumpet. It differs from its relative in that its bore is conical rather than cylindrical, and it is much easier to play. The comparative simplicity of its technique accounts for its popularity in small and amateur orchestras, and among juvenile geniuses. It is occasionally used in the symphony orchestra; in Stravinsky's *Petrouchka,* and in the world's noisiest overture—Tchaikovsky's "1812."

FRENCH HORN: Perhaps the most beautiful voice in the brass choir, the French horn is also the most difficult and the most unreliable. Its tone, pitch, and various effects are more dependent upon the skill of the performer, and less upon the mechanism of the instrument, than in the case of any other brass instrument.

 *Range of the French Horn*

Its remote ancestor is the hunting horn, often observed in old prints coiled around the body of a mounted man. It is a brass tube about sixteen feet long, with coils and crooks which reduce its linear dimensions to convenient size. The bell of the horn is relatively quite large, and into it the player frequently inserts his hand for the purpose of raising or lowering the pitch, and producing muted or "stopped" effects.

In the crude early horns the tones produced were limited by the audible harmonics of the natural, or fundamental, tone of the open instrument. Then it was found that other notes could be sounded by altering the length of the column of air within the horn, by putting the hand into the bell. Later, crooks, or extra pieces of tubing, were devised; these, when inserted, also changed the length of the instrument and consequently its pitch. Finally, the horn was equipped with valves, which made it possible to play the chromatic scale.

The tone of the horn is normally rich, full, and sonorous; sometimes powerful and majestic, sometimes dreamy and mysterious. Muted, it can acquire a singularly sinister character, or a faint and luminous quality that composers have been quick to make use of. It is so intractable and inflexible that rapid or ornate passages are seldom given to it, though Beethoven and Wagner wrote swift passages for horn which only the top-flight players can execute. Romantic melodies are more commonly assigned to the horn; otherwise, it serves as powerful support in ensemble passages. The range of the instrument is about three and one-half octaves, its tone changing very considerably from a rather hoarse utterance at the lower extreme to a singularly smooth and mellow brilliance in its highest notes.

TROMBONE: In classical English literature we encounter occasionally the word "sackbut." This is a corruption of a Moorish word meaning "pump," and was applied to a brass wind instrument closely resembling the modern trombone. In Middle Western America, when the town band flourished, it was a great distinction to play the "sliphorn." The trombone, then (to be neither pedantic nor provincial), is a brazen tube about nine feet in linear length, doubled on itself to about half that length; by means of a sliding, U-shaped tube, the length and therefore the pitch of the instrument can be altered. It encompasses two and one-half octaves, and is the tenor of the brass ensemble.

Range of the Trombone

The tone is broad, free, and noble, when uttered naturally; it can be exceedingly powerful and sonorous, but the instrument is likewise capable of very soft speech. Various interesting distortions of the tone can be effected by the use of mutes. The trombone is the only orchestral instrument, excepting the strings, capable of a true glissando—a continuous glide through a group of notes. Because the pitch is determined by the position of the slide and the player's lips and breath pressure, the trombonist must have an acute sense of pitch, and the ability to arrive instantly at the correct note without "feeling" for it.

The trombone is sometimes used as a solo instrument, but is most effective in massed effects, where its rich and organlike sonority can produce an atmosphere of majesty and power.

BASS TROMBONE: There is a bass trombone, closely resembling the other instrument of the family, but with a larger bell and with different intervals in the slide positions. Its tone is deep and powerful, but not so smooth as that of the tenor trombone. The development of the

Range of the Bass Trombone

tuba tended to displace the bass trombone in the brass choir, but Wagner brought it again into prominence, and modern composers require it frequently.

TUBA: The tuba is the sturdy bass of the brass choir. There are several sizes and types, but most commonly used is the B-flat tuba. It is a flaring (conical bore) tube of brass, approximately eighteen feet long, expanding to a large bell at its final opening. It is coiled to convenient size. The modern instrument is equipped with four valves, or pistons, making it capable of playing the chromatic scale, and giving it, despite its grave and sonorous tone, a surprising agility. Throughout its range of a little over two octaves, its voice is powerful and deep. Curiously, in spite of its position in the scale, the tuba is structurally a close relative of the cornet.

    Range of the Tuba

Tubas of various sizes have been used in the orchestra, and Richard Wagner invented a special one for use in the *Ring* operas. It is known as the Bayreuth tuba, from the Wagnerian theater in that town. The Bayreuth tuba is a pygmy compared to the giant instruments used in military and jazz bands, and occasionally in the symphony. The giant type, which is often seen coiled about the body and towering over the head of the player, is a true tuba, though often known as "helicon," or "sousaphone."

The name tuba, and that of an ancestor of this instrument—the "ophicleide"—survive in the modern pipe organ as designations of pedal stops.

PERCUSSION INSTRUMENTS

BATTERIE: Any instrument which is made to sound by striking, beating, or shaking is a percussion instrument. The piano, for example, though not a member of the orchestra, is a percussion instrument, while the harp, its close relative, is not. Instruments of percussion are the descendants of the most primitive sound-making apparatus. The chief function is to produce and accent rhythm, and rhythm is the most primitive musical impulse. It was natural, therefore, that they should come first, in chronological order, of all musical instruments.

The aggregation of percussion instruments in the orchestra is usually called the *batterie*—things that are struck. Most important of these are the

TIMPANI: Timpani, or kettledrums, achieve their importance chiefly because of the fact that they are capable of definite and intentionally variable pitch. Their Oriental ancestors consisted of a skin stretched over a hollow gourd. The modern instrument is a bowl of copper,

 *Range of Timpani Tuned to Tonic and Dominant, Key of F*

pierced by a small hole at the bottom, and topped with a tightly stretched calfskin. Early symphonic writing calls for but two timpani, which were tuned to the tonic and dominant tones of the key in which the music was written. (*Do* and *sol.*) Hector Berlioz, whose orchestral extravagances are historic, considered a work in which eight pairs of timpani were to be used! Commonly, three to five kettledrums are required; they vary in pitch according to their size and the tension of the drumhead. When three are used, they are generally tuned to the tonic, dominant, and subdominant (*fa*); others are tuned as the exigencies of the music may require.

Notwithstanding their essential simplicity, the timpani are capable of considerable variety of effect, and require great skill and musicianship on the part of the player. A single portentous utterance can be like a clutching hand at the throat; a long crescendo roll suggests terror, and yet the same instrument can impart a rhythmic accent of delicacy and grace.

The pitch of the kettledrums can be altered—indeed, often must be— almost instantaneously while the orchestra is playing. This requires the player to have an uncannily accurate sense of pitch and ability to concentrate, and deftness in handling the pedal and tuning screws, by which the drumhead is tightened. The kettledrum has a range of about half an octave.

Various types of sticks are used, varying from hard to very soft, according to the quality of tone required. The head of the stick is a ball which may be of sponge, felt, rubber, or wood. Sometimes a soft and dull effect is made by covering the drumhead with a loose piece of cloth. Tremolo, staccato, and other effects are produced by skillful players of timpani.

SIDE, SNARE, OR MILITARY DRUM: Essentially, the snare drum consists of a shallow cylinder of brass (or wood), closed at either plane surface by a head of parchment, under tension. Across the lower head, cords of catgut are stretched, so that when the drum is struck they vibrate against the parchment, causing the familiar sharp, crisp rattling effect.

The sticks, of wood, have small round heads, and by an expert player can be manipulated with startling rapidity.

The snare drum is of indefinite pitch but brilliant in tone. It is used as a rhythm-accenting instrument, though occasionally it is given dramatic significance, indicating suspense; or to imitate certain unmusical sounds.

BASS DRUM: The bass drum is nothing more than a greatly enlarged side drum. It is made of wood or metal; its pitch is indefinite but very low, and because of the great body of vibrating air enclosed in it, its tone is exceedingly resonant and quite powerful. Unless muted by a covering of some kind, it will also resonate the notes of other instruments, even while it stands untouched. It is played with a softheaded stick. Its note is audible in the loudest orchestral ensembles, and though it is cumbersome and awkward to play, it contributes very powerfully and effectively to rhythmic effects. It is used also for imitative and nonmusical sounds.

TAMBOURINE: The tambourine is a miniature drum with a single head. It consists of a hoop of wood, over which is stretched a parchment. In the rim of wood are inserted small metal disks, which vibrate when the instrument is shaken or struck. It is of extreme antiquity; we find it pictured in Egyptian, Assyrian, and Greek mural paintings. It seems to have come to us through the Orient and Spain, and is usually associated with Spanish music. It is played by either striking with the hand, or shaking, or both in combination.

CHINESE DRUM: A wide wooden hoop, over which is stretched pigskin—usually gaily painted. A curiously dull and nonresonant sound, of indefinite pitch, is produced when the drum is struck with a hardheaded stick. It is used only occasionally in the symphony orchestra, but has become popular in the jazz band for pseudo-Oriental effects.

CASTANETS: Always used in pairs, the castanets (Spanish *castagna*, chestnut; the wood from which they were made) are hollow shells, clapped rhythmically together, and giving a sharp, clacking sound invariably associated with the dance music of Spain and Latin America. For use in the modern orchestra the castanets are made of boxwood or ebony, and sometimes fastened to a handle with strings. Properly shaking the handle gives the characteristic rhythmic clack. Although the Latin peoples of both Europe and America use the instrument extensively, we find its curious sound in many examples of non-Latin music of the bacchanalian type.

CYMBALS: Disks of brass, with a depression in the center of each. They are of indefinite pitch, but have an exceedingly brilliant and powerful tone. To produce this tone they vibrate at the rate of more than 12,000 cycles per second. The musician strikes one against the other with a rubbing motion, or uses the drumsticks on them. Sudden terrifying crashes, long crescendos, single portentous strokes—these and other effects are in the repertoire of the cymbals.

They are of great antiquity, and have come down to us at least from Biblical times in virtually unchanged form. They have greatly increased in size and power, however, and "sounding brass and *tinkling* cymbal" could not have been written of the instruments of today.

TRIANGLE: A steel rod, bent in the form of an equilateral triangle, with one angle open. It is suspended on a string, and played by being struck with a metal stick. It has a brilliant, tinkling tone, of no determinate pitch but of such brilliance that it cuts through the most powerful utterances of the orchestra.

TAM-TAM: In effect, a cymbal of gigantic size, from three to as much as six feet in diameter. It is made of brass, and is of Chinese origin. When it is vibrated by rubbing with a softheaded stick, it gives forth a curious brassy roar, combining both very low tones with the brilliant overtones of the cymbal. When struck with a drumstick, it has a note of terrifying power.

This instrument is vulgarly called a gong, and tam-tam, or tom-tom, is often erroneously applied to the Chinese drum.

XYLOPHONE: A series of slabs of resonant wood, laid out like the keyboard of the piano and similarly tuned. Usually its range is three and one-half octaves. The player uses two wooden mallets to strike the wooden slabs, and tubes suspended under the latter resonate the tone. Xylophone is infrequently used in the orchestra, though Saint-Saëns made it highly suggestive in his *Danse macabre,* and other, older com-

Range of the Xylophone

posers have occasionally called for it. Modern writers of music like its bright grotesquerie.

CHIME: A chime of bells is part of the equipment of every symphony orchestra. The bells are tubes of metal, usually brass, suspended in a wooden frame, and played by striking with a wooden mallet. The player strikes the bell a few inches below the point at which the string supporting it passes through the tube. The chime encompasses two octaves of the chromatic scale. Its brilliant yet solemn tone is familiar.

Range of the Chime

ORCHESTRA   Sometimes called glockenspiel. Essentially the same
BELLS: as the xylophone, except that metal bars instead of
wooden slabs are used as vibrating bodies. The tone is very high, bright,

Range of the Orchestra Bells

and crystalline. The bells are tuned to the chromatic scale, and generally
encompass three octaves.

CELESTA: The celesta looks exactly like a miniature upright piano. It has a keyboard of four octaves, and a piano action which causes
hammers to strike tuned steel plates suspended over wooden resonating
boxes. It has a sustaining pedal which when depressed permits the
sound to continue until it dies from the cessation of vibration. Staccato
effects are produced when the pedal is not used.

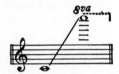

Range of the Celesta

The celesta was not regarded as an orchestral instrument until 1891,
when Tchaikovsky discovered it in the workshop of its inventor,
Auguste Mustel, in Paris. He was thoroughly charmed by the sweet and
delicate tone of the instrument, and straightway wrote a piece for it
("Dance of the Sugarplum Fairy": *Nutcracker Suite*). It is not impossible that the instrument suggested the title of the piece, for the tone is
incredibly sweet, somewhat gelatinous, and can easily become cloying.

Arnold Bax

—————————————— BORN 1883 ——————————————

Arnold E. Trevor Bax, in spite of the somewhat exotic sound of his name, is a native of London and is of English and Irish descent. When he was seventeen years old he was entered at the Royal Academy of Music as a pupil of Frederick Corder in composition and of Tobias Matthay in piano. Five years later he left the Royal Academy for a long sojourn in Ireland. For various periods he lived in the southwestern corner of Eire and during these periods became closely associated with the sophisticated circle of artists in music, letters, and the drama who brought about what has come to be called the "Irish Renaissance." In 1910 Bax lived for a short time in Russia, and from that country as well as from the British Isles drew inspiration for certain of his most effective works.

Most contemporary composers are likely to go to extreme lengths to have their newest works performed, and the means to which they resort in an effort to accomplish this end are occasionally sad, comical, or merely ridiculous. Arnold Bax chose another line of approach with respect to one of his works; and the London *Daily Telegraph* is authority for the assertion that first the composer required utter silence from those who knew of the existence of the completed score of the work. It was his wish that this symphony should neither be performed nor even discussed until his previous symphonies were established in the orchestral repertoire. Had his injunction been observed, it would seem that the performance and the acquaintance of the public with this composition might have been indefinitely postponed, for his earlier symphonies are by no means part of the standard orchestral repertoire and have not achieved the kind of success that establishes a work regularly in orchestral programs. However, Mr. Bax's friends observed his prohibition for more than a year after the symphony in question was completed, when the composer graciously permitted a performance of the work to be given at San Francisco on March 16, 1932.

Bax has written much for orchestra, as well as in other forms. Among the more interesting of his orchestral works are *Festival Overture, Christmas Eve on the Mountains, The Garden of Fand, The Happy Forest;* for the stage he has written the ballets *Between Dusk and Dawn, The Truth about the Russian Dancers,* and *The Slave Girl,* which was written for the lovely and incomparably gifted ballerina Karsavina.

Symphony in E-flat minor

THE symphony in E-flat minor was presented for the first time at a concert of the London Symphony Orchestra, December 4, 1922. The first American performance was given on March 14, 1924, by the Chicago Symphony Orchestra.

The piece we are discussing here approaches popularity more closely than any other of Bax's strictly symphonic works. It differs from his other orchestral pieces in its assertiveness—one might say its surly belligerence; it has a ferocity, and at moments a calculated ugliness which one commentator has, not unreasonably, put down as representative of a "smoldering hatred that is as noble as hatred may be." * It is true that a certain violence and starkness were not unknown qualities in previous works of Bax, but here is something more spirited, more melodramatic, more candidly violent, more deliberately unfriendly than anything appearing in the music of Bax prior to this work. Here his music is like a tragedy without compassion, a drama without a catharsis, a passion without tenderness. One might expect that in the melancholy and less savage slow movement there would be some modification of the composer's ferocity, but such is not the case, for, as Mr. Evans points out, his "grief is as fierce as the anger." The symphony is dedicated to John Ireland.

FIRST MOVEMENT

There is a foreshadowing in the first movement (*allegro moderato e feroce*) of the principal theme in a rather portentous marching figure in

* Edwin Evans in the *Musical Quarterly,* 1923.

the low strings; and after a little the theme itself, a broad and really
aggressive utterance, descends upon the strings and woodwinds.

This arrogant assertion is contrasted dramatically with the implacable
forward drive of the first thematic idea and sweeps to a climax of extraordinary sonority. Certain incoherent cries are torn from the strings
before we come upon the second basic theme of the movement, which is
relatively serene. It sounds like this:

This is music of conflict, of passion, and of rage, a musical conflict in
which the offensive and defensive weapons—the two main themes—are
sometimes frayed and chipped and broken and tossed about in fragments, yet always seem to be repaired and thrust forward again, each
toward its adversary, with renewed strength and swiftness. There are
mysterious interludes, as if the adversary drew off into the shadows
panting and half spent, only to return to the fray with renewed vigor.
The victor is easily identified near the end of the movement, where a
majestic presentation of the opening theme completely dominates the
musical scene.

SECOND MOVEMENT

Bax would be the last person to permit the association of a definite
musical picture, or definite dramatic action, with any of his symphonic
music. It would be difficult, nevertheless, to escape the elegiac connotations of this movement. Mourning can be a matter of resignation to the
inevitable and the acceptance of it; or it can be fierce resentment of a
vital nature toward the necessity and the inevitability of decay and
death. Here the intention of the composer seems to be elegiac only in
the latter sense; and the feeling is externalized at first by means of the
following phrase colored by strings, harps, horns, and trumpets:

Beating upon the irrefragable rock of fate, this theme disintegrates, leaving only its pulsating rhythmic center, over which presently the trombones give out a solemn chorale:

This is the material of which the passionately and violently elegiac movement is fabricated.

THIRD MOVEMENT

The music now is swift and determined. It begins with the brass bringing out a bold idea, buoyant and brave "as an army with banners"; but the real essence of the movement is found here in the cellos:

There is a satellite theme in horns and English horn, which has a certain resemblance to the opening theme of the symphony. The hatred and negation which we may have felt expressed in this music in its first exposition now turn into a kind of bitter, mad frustration, sharp with irony and mordant with sarcasm. Here is a specimen utterance:

The climactic idea of the whole work comes about in an apotheosis of this theme,

but in a broader and more definitely rhythmical version than these
notes can possibly convey.

Ludwig van Beethoven

THERE ARE SO MANY, and such excellent, biographies of Beethoven that there is little need or use, in these pages, for an extended account of his life. He was one of the two or three most important musicians who ever lived, and a story of his life with a just approximation of its importance and influence would fill all the pages of this book.

He was born at Bonn, December 16, 1770. He sprang from lowly and insignificant people. His mother was a cook, his father a drunken musician, who had emigrated from Holland to Germany. His childhood was a succession of miseries. Lessons from a sottish teacher after being dragged, drugged with sleep, from his cot in the middle of the night. Poverty, privation, toil, a loveless life, but never discouragement. The world and the woes that man makes cannot extinguish the divine fire. Recognition came to him finally.

In middle age—in an age when republicanism was treason—he dared to be republican even while he commanded the support of courtiers and princes. When to be liberal was to be heretic, he lived a large religion of humanism—without disrespect to established orthodoxy. When perfumed aristocrats eyed askance his stodgy figure, grotesque manners, absurd garb, he snarled and flashed and played the pettiness out of them. Too great to be ignored, too poor to be respected, too eccentric to be loved, he lived, one of the strangest figures in all history. Passionate in his loves and hates, ruthless toward opposition or criticism of friend or enemy, always in love and never married, ever honorable and never chivalrous, tender in sentiment and Rabelaisian in humor, simply thinking sublime thoughts, that was Beethoven!

Tragedy followed him like a hound. He became deaf and his last years were lived in a whirling void of silence. Silence!—while from within he drew the sounds that all the world has loved to hear, and he of all the world should first have heard! Romantic, humorous, tragic man!

More than a decade of decades has passed since Beethoven, starting up from his sickbed, shook his fist at the frowning skies and died. His grave in the Währing cemetery, hard by the resting place of Schubert, was marked simply with his name, and with symbols of immortality. He lives today in some of the most wonderful music ever penned by mortal hand.

Symphony No. 1 in C major

"This," remarked Hector Berlioz, with a kind of impatient and contemptuous toleration, "this is not Beethoven." Indeed it is not the Beethoven of the Third, Fifth, Seventh, and Ninth Symphonies. You will not find in it the giant that strides across the pages of the *"Eroica"*; you will not feel in it the naked passion, the blazing power of the deathless Fifth, nor the intoxicating rhythms, the arrogant virility of the Seventh. And the heaven-storming Ninth was separated by many years and radical spiritual change and development from the First.

This symphony will certainly not provide a dramatic thrill for the casual listener—though one would be unresponsive indeed not to enjoy it in a calmer fashion. The greatness of this work can be appraised only by considering it against the musical background existing at the time of its first performance, in April, 1800. That is not to say that its charm is exclusively for the scholar and the musicologist. There is musical delight in it for everyone; its chief greatness is, however, in its revelation of the Beethoven that was to be, in its daring, in its originality, and in its forthright vigor.

In 1800 Haydn, father of the symphony, was still alive, and regarded as the great musician of the day. Mozart had been dead but a few years. The former had developed the form of the sonata and the symphony; the latter had brought to these a grace and perfection of finish peculiarly his own. These two composers dominated music of the eighteenth century.

Now came a young man, offering to the public *his* idea of a symphony. It was but natural that he should have been under the influence of Haydn and Mozart, both of whom he admired. Yet he was original enough, and daring enough, to impress upon established and accepted form the print of his own will and thought. Though the symphony has much of the character of the innumerable Mozart and Haydn symphonies, it has more—a ruggedness, a certain vigorous humor, originality in form and in detail, and imaginativeness. In all of these qualities it surpasses anything of Haydn or Mozart—with the exception of the "Jupiter" Symphony of the latter.

Eighteenth-century audiences were much more interested in structural form than in emotional content. Their orchestras would be regarded today as adequate to a private salon, but hardly for the concert hall. Judged by our standards, their music was overdelicate, highly restrained, somewhat "precious." With interest chiefly in, and emphasis upon, line and form, large orchestras and unrestrained emotional outpourings were unknown. Consequently, the power of this music, and the exigent demands it made upon both performer and listener, were shocking to the polite ears of 1800.

But Beethoven revealed himself as a man whose powerful emotions were of a kind that demanded adequate expression through music. He expanded and gave strength to the accepted forms; he regarded them with respect, if not reverence, and he made them serve his purpose. This did not please the standpatters and reactionaries of his own day, who exhibited the antipathy toward innovation that we find among the same class today.

Some of the criticisms of the first performance are interesting. One newspaper had some kind things to say, but complained that "there was too much use of the wind instruments, so that the music sounded more as if written for a military band than for an orchestra." Another critic, nettled by Beethoven's calm disregard for certain musical conventions, said that the symphony was "the confused explosions of the outrageous effrontery of a young man." Notwithstanding much unfavorable comment, the symphony soon became popular, and by the time the Third was produced, the critics, outraged as usual, were pointing back to the First as a model symphony!

FIRST MOVEMENT

One of the disturbing features of some modern music is the use of polytonality (several keys simultaneously) or atonality (no particular key). Imagine then, in 1800, a symphony opening in the key of F, and

within a few measures passing through the key of A minor to G major
to C major! That is what Beethoven the modernist does in the first few
pages of this music. There is a kind of introduction, during which these
strange modulations, and a lovely songlike melody for violins, bring us
in a thoughtful mood to the main body of the movement. Here there is
a marked change in pace and rhythmic feeling, and the violins, softly
but with spirit, give out the principal theme.

The second and contrasting theme appears in the alternating voices of
flute and oboe, shortly after a powerful crescendo has led us to the key
of G major—the related tonality, in which the secondary theme of a
movement in sonata form conventionally appears. The two themes are
worked over in rather conventional style, but with somewhat more contrast in tone color and dynamic effect than was common at the time this
work was composed.

The thematic material is now taken apart with Beethoven's almost
clinical thoroughness. Every melodic possibility is exploited. Thematic
contrasts and combinations, brilliant rhythmic and dynamic effects, and
effective use of orchestral color are employed in presenting the com-

poser's musical thought in various guises. Finally, musical expression derived from the first theme of the movement is used, in conjunction with vigorous chords, as a coda to end this section of the work.

SECOND MOVEMENT

The Beethoven of rough humors and gruff impatience, the Beethoven who dared and startled the world of his day, is more in evidence throughout the second movement of the symphony. It begins conventionally enough—with a melody, sung by the second violins alone; a melody compounded of pathos and wistful humor, a wayward and

charming utterance. Growing from it, and eventually compounding a mass of sonorous and lovely tone, come successively the tones of viola and cello, first violins and woodwind. A second melody is projected; then a brighter phrase, and sustained but softly blown notes of the trumpet. Underneath moves the persistent rhythm of the timpani—the most prominent use of these instruments ever known up to Beethoven's time. Abrupt modulations, sudden and surprising contrasts of major and minor tonalities, sharply etched effects of sunshine and shadow reflect Beethoven's varying humor and his delight in shocking contrasts.

THIRD MOVEMENT

It is probable that modern audiences find more delight in Beethoven's inimitable scherzos than in any other of his symphonic movements. In them we feel abounding vitality, *brusquerie*, mischievousness, and harsh humor that were characteristic of the man. We welcome them particularly when they follow a belligerently and persistently solemn, or melancholy, or overlong slow movement, as they sometimes do.

The third movement of the present symphony is marked "minuet"; the conventional eighteenth-century symphony almost always used a dance form, and most often the minuet, as the third movement. But, though this part of the symphony is in triple time, it is something quite different from the usual third movement of the period. It is swift, it is light, it glints with sprightly humor. It has none of the studied dignity of the minuet, and little of its elegance—but it has life and vigor. In the

later symphonies Beethoven frankly abandoned the minuet as a conventional third movement, and designated it as "scherzo." The present portion of the First Symphony is the ancestor of all his scherzos.

Two melodies, contrasted in form and in orchestral color, are the basis for the minuet proper. There are sudden modulations, mischievous moments of suspense, interesting contrasts of instrumental voices, and always a merry and urgent rhythm moving this charming music. The "trio," beginning with sustained chords in woodwind, is in a more restrained but still humorous mood. The minuet proper returns to end the movement with energetic gaiety.

FOURTH MOVEMENT

A purely technical analysis of this or any other symphonic movement is not pertinent to the purpose of this book. The musician does not need it, the layman does not want it. Except for its vigor, and the violent contrasts, dynamic and rhythmic, which mark it as characteristically Beethoven's, the music is not essentially or vitally different from many another preceding work. This is not disparagement. Neither Beethoven, nor any lesser man, can be original in every detail. If the music followed a pattern which had been exploited again and again, that is not to say that it offered nothing new. The structure was an established one, but the texture is Beethoven's. One can appreciate it with the ears, taking in sounds and rhythms; not with the eyes, examining a mass of words.

The chief subjects of the movement are easily identified and located. There is an introduction, adagio, the main feature of which is a series of ascending passages, first of three notes, then of four, finally of five. After some hesitation, the music moves suddenly into an allegro, and the first theme of the movement, animated and bright, follows at once.

Underneath it moves a scale passage, its marked staccato character easily identifying it.

It is interesting to note the effect of climax which Beethoven, with the economy of means forced upon him by the orchestra of his day, is able to achieve. We sense climax upon climax, each of which actually employs virtually the entire resources of the orchestra. The psychological effect wrought by the composer in the suddenly contrasted passages, played piano, is tremendous, and each peak of power seems higher than the preceding. Presently we come upon a brilliant utterance, boldly put forward by horn and woodwind. The bright scales of the opening section return, and with a succession of chords less long-winded than is common in Beethoven symphonies, the movement ends.

Symphony No. 2 in D major

To WRITE music at any time is a rather trying occupation. To have been a composer of Beethoven's day seems, at this distance, to have been particularly difficult. The poor musician of 1790, or thereabout, had an exciting game to play, and woe betide him if he did not play according to the rules. Formality was the thing, and the composer who could write strictly to a form, and still avoid using someone else's melodies, was pretty sure to be regarded as successful. The matter of expressing a large and noble feeling, in a large and noble way, was not the point at issue.

It will be remembered that Beethoven was one of the first composers who broke the bonds imposed upon his spirit and his inspiration by the musical conventions of his time, and in many of his pages shouted a song of himself which in a sense paralleled the "barbaric yawp" of Walt Whitman. The nine symphonies were not, however, a numerical progression toward this freedom. Curiously, the first, and from then on all the even-numbered symphonies, conformed more closely with the classical mold than did the odd-numbered, which certainly to modern ears are the most exciting.

This symphony was written during the year 1802. It was one of Beethoven's many years of depression, but there is little trace of his despondency in this music. He was in love, which is misery enough for anyone. His health was bad, and the measures taken to relieve it were worse than the disease. His deafness was acute, and seemed to be aggravated by his other physical disorders. Beethoven felt that death was near, and tried to resign himself to it. Some of his greatest work was still before him.

The symphony was first performed in Vienna, April 5, 1803. Surely the Viennese love music, for at this same concert, which began at six in the evening, they listened not only to this symphony, but to the First, the C minor Piano Concerto, and the oratorio *The Mount of Olives!*

FIRST MOVEMENT

In listening to the early Beethoven symphonies, and particularly to all the even-numbered ones, we, like his own audiences, must to some extent observe the rules of the game. We must not expect the emotional content of the greater, later symphonies; we must not expect the rich orchestral color that Brahms gives us, or that we find even in the Bee-

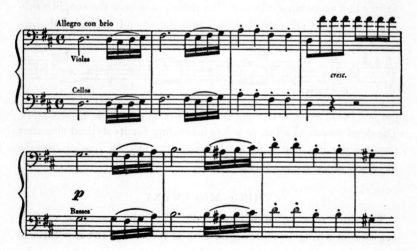

thoven Fifth, Seventh, and Ninth; we, too, must regard form and structure as of paramount interest.

There is an introduction, rather brief, but embodying three well-defined themes. The first is in full orchestra, with the thematic melody in the woodwind. The second is brighter and more powerful, with sweeping scales and emphatic chords at its conclusion. The third, with descending triplets in the strings, quickens and involves the whole orchestra.

The main body of the movement now follows, with the principal subject proposed by cellos and basses. The movement is strictly in form, so, watching for the conventional second theme, we come upon it, in rather definitely marked rhythm, stated by clarinets, and answered by powerfully bowed strings. The two themes are developed elaborately and characteristically, and a long coda, deriving its basic material from the first theme of the movement, brings it to a conclusion.

SECOND MOVEMENT

If Beethoven was hedged about with conventions which sometimes restrained him in his expression of the larger passions, he could and did make of his slow movements utterances of the most pointed eloquence. The present section is no exception. It has a pure lyric beauty that remains serene and undisturbed, however distracting the musical figures that accumulate about it. The strings announce the songlike subject, and indeed are entrusted also with the second and third themes,

the last being somewhat more brisk and cheery than its predecessors. The development of all three is less interesting for its stylized character than for the fact that it never obliterates the melodic line or disturbs the mood of the themes themselves.

THIRD MOVEMENT

The term "scherzo," which means, literally, a jest, was first applied, not without wit, to an extravagant kind of love song. The conventional third movement of a symphony was in the form of a minuet, but Beethoven injected so much vigor and swift rhythm into his third movements that, though in ¾ time, and three-part form, they could not be called minuets. He applied to them the term scherzo, as indicating their light and playful character.

There is a naughty flippancy in this scherzo, and it is refreshing after the stiffness of the first and the quiet plaintiveness of the second movement. A light and animated subject, alternately played forte and piano, is presented in changing rhythms and modest orchestral colors. The trio, or middle part of the movement, gives us a bright little melody, repeated with considerable ornamentation.

FOURTH MOVEMENT

The fourth movement, though highly developed, is saved from the weighty dignity of many final movements by its engaging rondo form. Its lightness made Hector Berlioz, that indefatigable student of Bee-

thoven, suggest that here was a second scherzo in the symphony. And he added his delighted comment on the distribution of the theme in fragments among the orchestral instruments, with the consequent variety of tone color. Reference to the term rondo in the Glossary of Music Terms, beginning on page 547, will make clear the structure of the movement.

Symphony No. 3 in E flat ("EROICA")

BEETHOVEN the democrat, the human, the believer in and champion of human rights did no violence to his convictions when he dedicated this symphony to Napoleon. He believed sincerely that that autocrat was possessed by motives springing from a humanistic creed akin to his own. When on May 18 in 1804 Bonaparte accepted the title of Emperor, Beethoven, his democratic soul outraged by the annihilation of his conception of the man, ripped the title page from his just-completed manuscript, and with imprecations dashed it to the ground. Later, when the work was published, the title, translated, read, "Heroic symphony, for the celebration of the memory of a great man."

However great the hero who might be celebrated in this noble music, it would further illuminate him. In majesty, brilliance, and power; in breadth and depth of feeling; in sheer magnificence, it ranks among the musical masterpieces of all time. Into it Beethoven poured his own superb vitality, so that it lives and moves powerfully; his own conception of a hero, so that it speaks nobly; his own genius as a musician, so that it appeals universally.

One of the curses that has fastened itself upon music is the habit of the scholars and the sentimentalists of attaching to musical works imaginative and usually farfetched titles, in most cases never heard of by the composer, and usually ridiculously unfitting. The teachers of music appreciation have been the most serious sinners in this respect, and have begotten in the minds of the young and the musically innocent more perverted ideas than sound ones. It is a pity if people who, for one reason or another, have not had time to acquaint themselves with the delights of music must be led to it under false pretenses. Music, strictly speaking, cannot tell a story. It does not mean anything that can be expressed in words. It cannot paint a picture. Often it can fortify and make more vivid our impressions and recollections of persons and events and things; often it accompanies and increases the emotional effect of dramatic action. When so intended, the composer almost invariably lets us know in advance. In nine cases out of ten, such titles as "Moonlight" Sonata, and "Spring Song," and "Raindrop" Prelude are expressions of the cheapest kind of musical sentimentality, and no importance whatever should be attached to them.

The *"Eroica"* comes by its subtitle legitimately enough, but musical commentators have not been content with the name Beethoven himself gave it. They must find cryptic meanings and illustrations in its four unintegrated movements—in the movements which, by their varying character and unusual sequence, have so puzzled and worried academic minds for more than a hundred years. The many contradictory interpretations urged by various commentators in themselves establish their futility. Dismiss from your mind every consideration but that of pure music, of moving, living sound that transfers to you an emotional state; do not seek for hidden meanings, for musical illustrations, for tone pictures. Beethoven was eloquent in but one language—the universal language of music. In the symphony he speaks, in *his* language, of the qualities, of mind and heart, he finds in the ideal hero. Be content with this. What this music, or any music, means to another is not of first importance to *your* hearing of it; let it impress *you* as it will. You will be uplifted, and thrilled, and happier by the experience.

FIRST MOVEMENT

The two-fisted Beethoven asks attention in no uncertain way—and gets it—with the two swift, staccato, and powerful chords with which the symphony begins. Now he goes directly to his subject, and deep in the choir of cellos, we hear, somewhat tentatively but clearly, the basic theme of the movement. A few moments later, boldly and with elastic vigor, it is put forth by horns, clarinets, and flutes in octaves.

Here is a straightforward theme, not unmilitary in its simple intervals like those of a trumpet call. Yet, simple as it is, Beethoven has constructed about it a towering edifice of sound that moves; sound that surges and flows and beats against one's consciousness with terrific power. Here and there the theme, in one or another of the many voices of the orchestra, appears and dominates all the elaborate developments of itself. It is like a principle of living, which, though seldom explicitly stated, directs and can be detected in a man's every action.

After the first presentation of a contrasting theme, divided among the woodwinds (oboe, clarinet, flute) and violins, both ideas are magnificently developed. The musical quotation above is but the merest germ of

the mighty ideas which the composer now projects through the orchestra, and which culminate in a succession of vigorous and impatient thrusts of tone. Sometimes we feel that the music has departed far from the simple affirmation which was urged at the beginning as the basic thought of the movement—yet always with a sudden influx of light Beethoven shows clearly the imminence of that idea. Let it come, as it does, in the virile voices of cellos and basses; let it breathe gently in the rounded mellow tones of the horn; let it speak incisively in the penetrating accents of the woodwind; it is still the same simple utterance, and the source of all the life and power of the movement.

SECOND MOVEMENT

One may look upon Death as the inevitable, and regard it unemotionally. One may see it as the frustration of the noble impulses and heroic designs which lying Life encourages one to feel and to undertake, and therefore resent it, bitterly and impatiently. And, finally, one may regard Death as the unreasonable, inexorable taking-off of one beloved —and weep.

Here in the second movement of the symphony—which Beethoven himself entitled "Funeral March"—is a curious combination of the latter two attitudes toward Death. The significance of the music cannot possibly be misconstrued. That agonizing slow beat can be only the terrible rhythm of the march toward the grave which figuratively the audience makes behind the body of Beethoven's hero—and makes, literally, with every passing interval of time.

Presently the music expresses more of what we might regard as the hero's own attitude toward Death. We recall, from the first movement, the power, the activity, the restlessness and ruthlessness there expressed; here, in spite of the slow rhythm, we feel an impatience, a resentment toward Death, the one enemy, the one obstacle, that cannot be

overcome. The theme that began the dreadful march, although first presented softly and sadly, sometimes is uttered with vehemence, as if to elbow aside the mournful musical creatures that move along with it. Then, in a voice which of all orchestral sounds can be most tearful— the oboe—comes the melody, sad and lovely and resigned, to answer the sullen mutterings of the bass. Later, another very beautiful and important theme is given to the strings.

This movement is too long. Someday, a conductor daring or foolhardy enough will make intelligent revisions that will shorten it by several minutes. The critic will be aghast, the purist will rage, the Beethoven-worshipers will cry "sacrilege," but the music and the audience will benefit. It does not require twenty minutes and more for Beethoven to establish and sustain the mood he wishes to achieve here—unless, someone may argue, he wishes to achieve boredom, and distinct discomfort in the least dignified portions of the anatomy. The basic ideas of the movement are repeated endlessly, nor is there sufficient variety in orchestration, or in thematic treatment, to justify the prodigious and tedious length of this movement. It must be confessed that there are some few conductors who can make it seem less long than others, and for these we give thanks and leave the music as Beethoven wrote it.

THIRD MOVEMENT

The electric vitality of this wonderful scherzo, coming as it does upon the heels of a funeral procession, has puzzled the musicologists for a hundred years and more. Why, they ask, should a movement of this obviously joyous character follow hard upon the melancholy preceding movement? Perhaps the sardonic Beethoven could give a reasonable answer; no one else has ever done so. Certainly the swift vigor that comes mysteriously into being with the opening notes of the movement is a striking contrast to, and a mighty relief from, the solemnity of the dirge. That is sufficient for musicodramatic purposes.

The thematic elements hardly require illustration. A rustling in the strings, lightly played but full of energy and swiftness, grows to a merry tumult of colorful sound, and the wonderfully elastic rhythm urges the flying strings along their tangled way. The trio is one of the delights of Beethoven's music. A subject for the horns, very like a hunting call, and, if played strictly in tempo (which it rarely is), fiendishly difficult for those unreliable instruments, leaps upward and outward from the orchestra and is presently answered by the whole band. Wistfully the horns repeat their engaging utterance, and there is for a moment a note of pathos in the responses of the other instruments. But then the sudden fierce joy of the opening part of the movement returns and sweeps all other thoughts before it in a powerful climax.

FOURTH MOVEMENT

The final movement of the symphony is a triumph. It leaps into being with a most brilliant passage for all the strings, growing in sonority as it approaches the lower ranges of the instruments, and resting, finally, on a series of mighty chords in full orchestra. Then comes the pronouncement of the theme, presented in the simplest possible way— plucked, note by note, from the strings of violin, viola, cello, and bass. On its repetition, a curious effect of echo is brought about when the woodwinds (flutes, clarinets, and bassoons in unison) imitate each note of the strings, half a measure behind them.

There is, after the forceful and vivacious first utterance of the movement, something dark and ominous in this chief theme, yet its developments are of the most triumphant brilliance. Later on, we shall find it extraordinarily combined with a new and brighter musical idea. To illustrate the combination of both themes, we borrow the convenient condensation appearing in that excellent work *The Standard Concert Guide,* by George P. Upton and Felix Borowski. Here it is:

The themes once stated in their entirety, the remainder of the movement is devoted to an exhaustive exploration of the tonal and contrapuntal possibilities that lie within the simple thematic sentences. Every
instrument of the orchestra, it would seem, presents its version, against
contrasting utterances from the rest of the ensemble. Always we feel a
growth toward a certain climax, and a gathering of the orchestral forces
for a final triumphant effort.

This climax comes very suddenly and with gigantic power in the
final section of the movement. The capacity of the main theme of the
present movement for further enlargement seems to have been exhausted; there is a transitional period during which you will hear, now
subtly, now boldly presented, thematic material from the preceding
movements; then, involving all the orchestra's thunders, the moment
toward which the composer has been moving relentlessly from the very
beginning of the symphony arrives in a blaze of splendor and a magnificence too overpowering for words.

Symphony No. 4 in B-flat major

THE history of the Fourth Symphony reveals, incidentally, some phases
of the character of the composer that the more sentimental biographers
and incense burners are wont to ignore. Continually pressed for money,
because of his own debts and those contracted by relatives, Beethoven

was sometimes harassed into certain dealings with his publishers and others that cannot be described as precisely ethical.

Count Oppersdorf, at the time a warm admirer of the composer, a lover of music and a man wealthy enough to maintain a small symphony orchestra at his castle, commissioned Beethoven to write a symphony for him. In this year, 1806, Beethoven was absorbed in the production of the Fifth Symphony, but with a commission at hand, he laid it aside and devoted himself to work on the Symphony in B-flat major, published, eventually, as the Fourth. He dedicated it to his patron, and, later, received a respectable sum of money for it. It is related, in Thayer's biography of Beethoven, that "he did not send the Count the score, as was the custom, for exclusive use during a fixed period, but turned it over to Lobkowitz for performance, being in urgent need of money; a year later, he substituted the Fifth for the Fourth and accepted from Count Oppersdorf a hundred and fifty florins in March and two hundred in June for it, without delivering it; this sum being, it may be presumed, a bonus for the larger work, the Count having asked for something employing an unusual apparatus. This symphony was also withheld in the end, for reasons which are not known, and Oppersdorf had to content himself with the mere dedication of the Symphony in B-flat originally designed for him." We can readily surmise why Count Oppersdorf and Beethoven had no further relations!

The first performance of this work was at a concert given for the benefit of the composer, March 15, 1807, with Beethoven conducting, of course.

FIRST MOVEMENT

About the time this music was written, Beethoven seems to have been in love with the Countess Therese von Brunswick; he was even given evidence that his sentiments were returned. Because of this circumstance, there has been a disposition on the part of many commentators to assume that the gay spirits that move almost always in this music are a reflection of Beethoven's happiness in his affair with the Countess, and his delight in their engagement. To listen to the music, however, is to remain unconvinced of this theory. Joyful it is, to be sure, but it is hardly the kind of joy one would expect from the mercurial Beethoven,

successful in love. When that man's deepest emotions were stirred, they
were not expressed in music of this type, where the composer returns to
the style and the formality of the earlier symphonies. There is something pretty, and sweet, and light in this music; there are even stylized
and derivative things. The aroused Beethoven rarely resorted to such
moderate and conventional devices in expressing himself.

Whatever lies back of this music, or whatever its history, we are immediately concerned with how it sounds. It sounds happy, and ingratiating, and complacent. It never approaches the sublimity of the *"Eroica"*
that preceded nor the Fifth that followed it. But it is Beethoven in a
happy mood, taking joy in his own craftsmanship, and consciously producing a very lovely and perfect thing.

The strings have a strange downward phrase, against an organ point

in woodwind, at the beginning of the adagio opening section of the first
movement. The contemplative suggestion of the introduction does not
endure for long, and presently the movement proper, with its vivacious-
ness and lightfooted rhythm, its clowning bassoon and delicately bowed
strings, comes into being. The thematic material is developed in quite

conventional, but utterly charming style. There is a crescendo in the second section of the movement which Berlioz finds as important and compelling as that famous one which leads from the scherzo to the finale of
the Fifth Symphony. Simultaneously there are interesting suspensions
and modulations, and the rollicking mood of the opening part of the
movement suddenly returns.

The curious simplicity of the long scale passage in the strings, the persistent use of the timpani, and the gradual accretion of orchestral forces toward the end of the movement are features of decided interest.

SECOND MOVEMENT

There is a wonderful tenderness and feeling of peace in the lovely melody which, after a brief introduction in strings, Beethoven assigns to the first violins as the principal theme of the movement. No less sweetly

do the woodwinds intone it. And yet, in spite of the placid atmosphere, there is a quiet intensity here that seizes very deftly and firmly upon the emotions and the imagination; and when, toward the end, the timpani take up, as a solo, the tonic and dominant that we heard in the introductory figure, the atmosphere of tenseness, of melancholy and perhaps of foreboding, envelops all, and remains a little while.

THIRD MOVEMENT

The minuet deviates somewhat, but not importantly, from the classical style.

It is somewhat more playful, and less dignified, than some classical symphonic movements in the same form. But it is beautifully clear and simple in structure, in melodic outline, and in its characteristic well-marked ¾ rhythm. The middle section, or trio, moderates the tempo somewhat, and places more accent upon melody than upon rhythm.

FOURTH MOVEMENT

The final movement achieves even more of gaiety and sprightliness than we have yet heard in the symphony. The violins open the festivities with a gay figure in sixteenths, which sets the pace and establishes the brisk rhythm of the movement. There are occasional rowdy outbursts—

the kind of *subito* interjection of seriousness, or of drama, in which Beethoven frequently and delightedly indulged. His good humor, however, persists to the end, where the concluding measures suggest a serio-comic denouement.

Symphony No. 5 in C minor

HERE is the potent and concentrated and ultimate distillation of the genius that was Beethoven. This symphony is compounded of all that was the essential man and the essential music. Incredibly condensed and powerful, the forces that moved this strange and wonderful man are here focused upon and welded into one superb structure. The godlike, yet so human, rages that possessed him; the tenderness and warmth that sometimes radiated from him; the wry and wicked and harsh humor that flicked and stung like scorpions; the superb courage, the impatience, and finally the heroic and unreasoning defiance that breathed hotly from so many of his utterances—all are here, stripped of concealment, of ornament, and of craftsman's device. All are here, in this mighty, this comprehensible and human music.

There is in the world music of more sophistication, but there is none that so surely makes itself understood. There is music magnificently employing orchestral resources Beethoven did not know, but there is none that speaks more powerfully. There is simpler music, but none that, so naked and shameless, so clearly and with such terrible intensity, exposes the tempests and the triumphs of the human soul. Shaken by a frenzy that must have demented a lesser man, Beethoven nevertheless restrains, within a beauty and symmetry of form, the passions in whose fire this music was begotten, and perhaps it is this restraint, this iron hand that the composer lays upon himself, that most commend this music. For we are all hedged about by the tricks and trials of fate, by the disciplines and necessities of living; in uttering so superbly his very self, within self-imposed restraints, Beethoven speaks for all of us—as we should want to be.

We cannot, nor do we need to know, what passions moved the composer in this music. The sentimentalists would have you believe that it reflects the rise and fall of his amorous fortunes. No wholly rational being could draw such a conclusion from this ruthless, blazing, cosmic music. In the broad sense, this is not an expression of one man's thought or feeling. This is the utterance of a tormented and puzzled and cynical and hopeful—and finally triumphant humanity. This is the voice of a people, of a world, pitiful and puny, yet bearing within it, as the peasant may bear the seed of a potentate, the elements of final greatness.

This music lay gestating in the mind of Beethoven for many years. His papers reveal the nascent idea as early as 1800, when he was concerned more immediately with the formal and derivative, the almost adolescent early symphonies. It seems to have been performed for the first time at a concert in the Theater an der Wien, Thursday, December 22, 1808. The conductor was Beethoven. The "Pastoral" Symphony was also performed at this concert. When we consider the relative popularity of the Beethoven symphonies today, it is difficult to understand why Beethoven himself chose the *"Eroica,"* and not the Fifth, as his favorite. (The Ninth was not yet in existence.) For surely the Fifth has a more powerful, direct, and universal appeal to human nature than any other great music in existence.

Think of Beethoven as he was, and you will not approach the Fifth Symphony in awe. Perhaps that will come later, with fuller understanding. Nor will you, if you think of the man's intense humanity, turn aside from this music as a problem to be solved. Though you may be weary of today's interminable round, you will never look upon it as one more of life's enigmas. No, it is simple. It is clear as morning light. There is no one so poorly versed, or so experienced, in the magic art of music, who does not come under its spell. It is the expression of a vigorous, vital, manly man, whose introspection revealed in himself, to himself, some of the meanings of life. He is able by his art to communicate his thought and feeling to you. Listen.

FIRST MOVEMENT

It must be admitted that, while Beethoven left no "program" for the symphony—it needs none!—he did give us a clue to the significance of that brutally powerful phrase which opens the movement, and which, explicit or implicit, can be discovered as the vitalizing thought through all four movements of the work. "*So pocht das Schicksal an die Pforte,*" he said. ("Thus fate knocks at the door.") But this was some time after the symphony had been written, and may have been an afterthought, or an idea that occurred at the moment. It is not unreasonable, and has infinitely pleased the musical romanticists. If a motto be needed for the symphony, this one, the possibility of which, at least, was admitted by Beethoven himself, will do as well as any other. For this harsh and powerful utterance is as persistent as fate, and as almighty in this music. It shall be noted further.

At the opening of the movement, this subject is thrust at us by all the strings and the clarinets; on its sudden and climactic expansion, the whole orchestra puts it forth with violence. It is quoted in its simplest form:

From these four notes a towering and active and raging organism of tone is swiftly erected, and the mercilessly dynamic and dominating character of the principal theme is established. Its driving force is suspended on a powerful chord, and after the horns more gently suggest it in an altered guise, we can note a brief but lovely musical thought, spoken through the strings and woodwind in a pensive dialogue with itself.

And in this movement gentleness and grace are battered and defeated and crushed into silence by the awful force and frequency of the assaults of the first four-note phrase. Distorted and driven and exhausted, the sweet, sad protestings of the second theme finally disappear, and

Beethoven turns loose, in violent chords, the orchestra's mightiest forces, that relent, it seems, only from exhaustion. The oboe, a lonely and tearful voice, raises a piteous cry, but seems only to provoke new torrents that rage swiftly through the strings. Once again the placid and comforting voice of the horn gives pause—and yet once again the impetuous strings return to sweep resistlessly through the orchestra with the ever-present and fateful utterance that is peculiarly theirs.

The bitterness and violence of this movement have no parallel in music. The sheer power that moves it, the utter logic and inevitableness and finality of this music, almost remove it from the manipulations of the conductor; given instruments and knowing hands, it plays itself. Many a conductor has found that there is but one interpretation—Beethoven's—and *that* one speaks, rudely and clamorously and sufficiently, for itself. This is an utterance of the supreme and ruthless ego, momentarily frustrated but unconquered, and it does not brook interference.

Toward the close of the movement comes that superb passage, still in the deadly rhythm of four notes, in which a perverted version of the gentle theme, once so diffidently sung by the violins and woodwind, is presented, noticeably in the flute, and mocked with brutal imitation by the whole string section. What marvelous antithesis! What demoniac humor!

There is no gentleness or peace, or even conclusive triumph, at the end. Only the violent presence of the dominating theme, uttered with such vehemence as the orchestra, until now, has not known. And on two chords like mailed fists raised against the skies, the movement ends.

SECOND MOVEMENT

It is not easy, at first glance, to be convinced that the lovely song which is the opening and the basis of this movement is rhythmically related to the harsh and intolerant theme of the preceding section of the work. Here cellos speak with warm sentiment; here all is gentleness— gentleness that can, to be sure, grow into intensity, but never to violence. Yet, in exhibiting the persistence of the dominant motive of the symphony, Beethoven has with uncanny insight and subtlety incorporated into the suave cantilena of the cellos certain rhythmic elements of the first movement's chief theme. Here is the theme of the cellos:

Dolce is Beethoven's indication of the manner in which this lovely melody is to be played. Analyze it, and conceive it as played with the natural accents somewhat exaggerated, and you will see that the accented notes fit precisely the rhythmic form of the first movement "motto."

Violas and cellos, with the latter dominating and the basses supplying a soft pizzicato accompaniment, sing their song undisturbed, even when an answering but mournful cadence descends from the woodwinds. A new and more somber thought is projected by the clarinets and bassoons, and here again the persistence of the four accented notes recalls dreadfully the knocking of fate. The orchestra seems to grow impatient with this persistence, and a swift-growing crescendo draws out a powerful and downright protest, culminating in a fiercely vigorous note almost torn from the deep-voiced basses. But even here, a rhythmic analysis shows the ubiquity of the central thought of the symphony.

The deliberate compactness and density of this music happily prevent a slow movement too long drawn out—as sometimes happens, it must be

admitted, in Beethoven's works. The variations—which form this movement assumes—have the charm of variety in color and treatment, yet
with fundamental unity and coherence. The composer makes no effort
to exhaust, absolutely, their remotest musical possibilities, but rather
selects from those possibilities the particular versions which seem most
fittingly to disclose his emotional state.

Here the emotional condition, if not absolutely one of serenity, is at
least continent and stable. The restlessness, the impatience, the abandoned passion of the preceding section are quite gone, and only at the
end is there an outburst to suggest that violence and ruthlessness are
not dead, but only sleeping.

THIRD MOVEMENT

Furtively from the shadowed regions of the basses' and cellos' lowest
strings comes a mysterious, an ominous, and suggestive utterance. It is
but a breath of tone, a premonition. Its intimations do not disturb the
gentle and tentative responses of the upper strings, or of the woodwinds, and as the phrase is repeated we are still uncertain of its import:

And here is the reply:

There is a pregnant pause, and a lingering on the last note of the
woodwind. Then suddenly, in the most arrogant voice of the horn,
comes this suggestive warning:

Almost at once, the whole orchestra is involved in this bold assertion,
with intonations of defiance and power. But note, note the rhythm: it is
the rhythm of the summons of fate! That four-note phrase, almost with

the same significance as in its first awesome appearance! Is fate now to be triumphant or conquered? Can that wickedly stubborn thought be overcome?

The answer is laughter. For life is grotesque and bitter, and full of contradictions and denials and unreason; and we know no escape but to laugh. And that we may inwardly laugh, bitterly or wholesomely as we may, Beethoven invents for us and presents to us a dance; an astonishing grotesque choreography for those cumbersome and serious giants of the orchestra, the great contrabasses. So are serious men made fools.

And he makes the orchestra, willing or not, join in, until finally, when it seems convinced of the harmlessness of the recent warning of the horn, and rises to a peak of high good humor, he brings it to earth again. Insinuatingly the plucked strings, with hysterical assistance from the woodwind, timidly echo what lately was the bold proclamation of the horn, and Beethoven makes of the orchestra a single plangent instrument. Gone now are the powerful phrases of strings that rocked perilously for a moment in the upper ranges, and then plunged with ever-increasing power and confidence into the gloomy terrain of the bass. Gone the golden glints of trumpet and of horn. Now all is fearful and fervid and furtive; now suddenly there is all but silence.

But it is not silence. One can all but hear the sound of heavy breathing in the faint note of strings, held pianissimo against the throbbing of timpani, throbbing in that grim and awful rhythm that has never ceased since this music began. But now it changes, it falters, it comes more quickly but still mysteriously and far away. Without the slightest change in color or in power of tone, with nothing but an alteration of rhythm and, later, flickering interjections of the strings, Beethoven effects a marvelous clearing of this overcharged atmosphere. Suddenly there is a feeling of great joy to come; suddenly there is a fiercely brilliant crescendo, and finally a golden blaze of tone from the whole orchestra.

This extraordinary transitional passage is one of the most thrilling

things in music. The hypnotic spell exerted by the long-sustained pianissimo; the low thunders of pulsing drums and curious flickerings of the
strings, like summer lightning; and then, like a great shout of triumph
impossible to restrain, the sudden bursting forth of the brass—all these
combine in a sublime and powerfully moving effect that has no parallel
in music.

FOURTH MOVEMENT

Beethoven reserved for this outburst the trombones, which take the
lead in the first pronouncement of the movement:

Depth is added by calling upon the contrabassoon; brilliance by the
inclusion of the piccolo. Later, in another subject, the coloring of the
orchestral texture is altered, but not its exuberant spirit. The clarinet,
joined by violas and cellos, has this happy phrase:

These are the chief materials out of which Beethoven weaves the
glowing fabric of this wonderful music. Here is joy that seems almost
delirious; here, after the humors and questionings and communings of
the previous music, is exaltation beyond restraint. What if, in the midst
of this frantic rejoicing, comes the recollection of the summons of fate,
or of the bitter laughter that once seemed the only answer to that dreadful knocking? It serves only as a new point of departure for an exploration of the happy possibilities of the present movement, and by contrast makes them happier and more wonderful.

Perhaps it is possible, after hearing and thinking upon this music, to
reflect that fate, after all, is but the composite and the resultant of all
the diverse forces of life, of all our own deliberate acts; and to come to
the realization that "we ourselves are heaven and hell." When fate
knocks too persistently at the door, perhaps this music, and the sublime

thoughts of the great man who spoke through it, will disarm that dreadful visitor and rob him of his terrors.

Symphony No. 6 in F major ("PASTORAL")

THE "Pastoral" Symphony was first performed in 1808, and probably had been composed, for the most part, during the early months of that year. In it Beethoven departed radically from the fundamental idea of his music up to that time, in that the symphony seeks to represent, to a certain extent, a story and a picture. Therefore, it would seem to come perilously close to what we know as "program music," although an intimate examination and study of it places the "Pastoral" in a quite different category.

Beethoven was probably the first to attempt quite so frank a depiction of nature, through an extended composition. Imitations of the sounds of nature were probably no great novelty—and Bach had inserted an instrumental imitation of the crowing of a cock into music descriptive of the Passion of the Saviour. The entire "Pastoral," however, relates to a country visit and to country scenes and incidents— and involves the imitation of several varieties of bird songs.

FIRST MOVEMENT
"The awakening of serene feelings on arriving in the country"

That Beethoven should create one great musical work under the inspiration of nature was perhaps inevitable. Though his ancestry was Dutch, nevertheless he was a German of the Germans in his passionate love of nature, of birds and brooks and growing things, and in the naïveté and ingenuousness of his response to them. To walk by himself in the woods, to sit in the crotch of a favorite tree and sketch his musical ideas, to be out of doors at every opportunity were to him the acme of happiness.

The "Pastoral" Symphony is not, actually, the story in music of a journey into the woods. It is rather an expression, in music, of the spirit of nature, and the feelings aroused in one by communication with nature. To call the symphony "program music" is to slight the music and belittle the composer. True, here and there we encounter more or less literal details—but these only in sufficient number, and with sufficient emphasis, to center our attention on the sights and sounds that engendered the feelings expressed in the main body of the work.

The sweet cool moist airs of "incense-breathing morn" envelop the opening measures of the first movement . . . like a scarcely felt zephyr, barely stirring dew-laden leaves, yet awakening drowsy birds and all but silent flutterings among the trees. It is significant that here, in a

passage that is anything but showy, the composer should have written in double counterpoint (a musical device: the simultaneous presentation of two distinct melodies) in order to gain an effect of pastoral simplicity! Yet precisely that effect *is* achieved, because the complicated polyphonic figure springs with utter naturalness from under the Beethoven hand. It was the tongue in which he spoke; its mechanical and technical complications were as nothing to that musical-mathematical mind. The result is, to the ear, an utterance naïve, free, natural, infallibly expressive of what it seeks to convey; to the mind, it is at the same time a wonderful and perfect synthesis of sounds.

The blithe spirit aroused by arrival in the green countryside persists throughout the movement. It teems with life and vigor—yet it is the mist-veiled vitality of springtime. There is no heaven-storming climax, no imperative summons of the orchestra's mighty sonorities, but rather an impelling growth and vigor as subtle, as mysterious, and as inevitable as the force that pushes a spearhead of grass above the fresh brown earth.

Beethoven's brook is a placid and clear stream, gently flowing, rippled by the lightest of breezes, and mirroring an unshadowed sky. Overhead, branches, bud-burdened, sway in a smooth untroubled rhythm; they might have been willows, bending lovingly over the calm waters, and as lovingly touching the waters' shining bosom. Strings give forth

the main thematic ideas, with strings, again, in the sweeping but not obtrusive rhythm that accompanies the chief subjects.

Presently the woodwinds—what poetry, what significance in that name at this juncture!—sing the melody. Again, a second theme is un-

folded in the string section, but briefly; cellos below and clarinets above
repeat it, while in a kind of duet, bassoon and violin deliver themselves
of a kindred melody. Occasionally a sweetly dissonant trill, high in
strings, or perhaps in the woodwind, ruffles the placidity, as if some
swooping bird had touched in flight the polished bosom of the waters
with tiny claw or plumed pinion.

Nor are the birds wholly imaginary. Here Beethoven indulges in a
literal touch—explicitly indicated in the score. After a mild little climax, there is a brief hush, as of the anesthetic warmth and stillness of
midday; then, quite clear, quite suggestive, come the calls of birds. The
trill of the flute is the song of the nightingale; the little figure in repeated notes, for the oboe, is the thin and pensive piping of the quail
. . . and the cuckoo call of the clarinet is unmistakable. But not even a
birdcall disturbs the sweet complacence in which the movement ends.

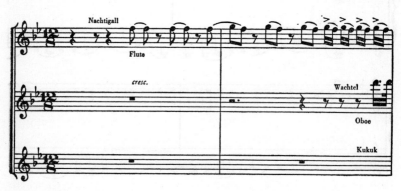

THIRD MOVEMENT
"A jolly gathering of country folk"

Now the woodland wanderer comes upon a merry group of country-men, in a holiday revel. The music is obviously and inescapably dance music; the tune, one that might have been born in the misty history of

Erin, for Irish it is, even to the very characteristic ending. Its first cadence is sounded in strings alone; the flute, bassoon, and oboe join in the answering phrase. It is dainty; it is light; it is appealingly simple and naïve in rhythm and in melodic line.

After this theme is somewhat developed, a new one, more song than dance although in the same gay rhythm, appears in the solo voice of the oboe—suggesting, we may remark without irreverence, a quaint little German folk tune * that every schoolboy knows. The tune gathers

to itself new color and strength when it is given, after a space, by the mellow horn. Now a new rhythm, heavyfooted, rather slow, like peasants in a rude dance, keeps the music moving with a kind of uncouth grace. And again, the original merry tune returns, the entire first portion of the movement being repeated.

Storm and Tempest

But suddenly (third section of movement) a new voice, agitated, fearful, crying a dread warning, appears, to send the merrymakers scurrying for cover. Black clouds, pregnant with lightning and with rain, are driven swiftly across a frowning sky. Trees groan and bend in agony under the first onslaught of whistling winds . . . a blinding bolt rends the heavens . . . the very earth quakes under the concussion of

* A doggerel about a dachshund.

thunder. And then the rain . . . keen shining lances driven into the warm sod . . . a fierce storm, but swiftly over. Hardly have the first signs of its waning fury appeared, before we hear music expressing a religious thankfulness. The first timid bird lifts up his tiny song, a shepherd plays upon his pipes, and the sun shines once more.

In this section of the symphony some interesting presentiments of later Beethoven music are discernible—notably, during the storm scene, certain passages later employed, almost as they stand in the score, in the composer's overture to *Egmont.*

FOURTH MOVEMENT
"Gladsome and thankful feelings after the storm"

The shepherd's song, and the quasi-religious sentiment expressed at the conclusion of the storm scene, form the basis for the construction of the fourth movement. The music broadens tremendously; the once almost playful rhythm takes on an impulse of deep and solemn feeling; and yet the simple and straightforward spirit of the music is never for a moment lost. An occasional brief trill recalls the tremors of the terrifying storm . . . but the solemn joy of the movement is scarcely disturbed, and it proceeds in a splendid elaboration of the basic elements of tranquillity and thankfulness.

The variations built up on the basic material are more than representations of it in ornamented style; they are truly *developments* and elaborations, springing from the intrinsic musical possibilities of the themes themselves. And still, throughout its complications, there is in the movement the same delightful clarity and candor that distinguishes the symphony as a whole.

The climax, at the end, is not effected by the commonplace burst of sonority and brilliance, but rather by a gradual subsidence of the orchestral forces, during which the most careful listening will disclose, against the scales that appear in the violins, violas, and (doubled) in the cellos and basses, a faintly blown reminiscence of the basic theme of the movement, sounded upon the muted horn. Sturdy Beethovenesque chords end the movement and the symphony.

Symphony No. 7 in A major

THE Seventh of Beethoven's nine symphonies was written during one of the composer's more and more frequent periods of spiritual travail. His deafness was daily growing worse; a love affair had but recently been broken off, and the political situation, in which Beethoven was always interested, was not at all reassuring.

These circumstances perhaps helped to solidify certain traits in the character of the composer which had been developing for quite some time. The symphony reflects them. It is touched with the boisterous, often crude humor of its author; it is not without a mordant bitterness, yet a bitterness, penetrating as it is, that is never precisely pessimism, and certainly never despair.

Beethoven himself, despite his increasing deafness, conducted the first performance of the Seventh, from manuscript, on December 8, 1813, at the concert hall of the University of Vienna. It is interesting—and refreshing—to note that notwithstanding the composer's difficulty in hearing, and his often ill-timed and sometimes absurdly exaggerated gestures, the symphony was received with acclaim.

FIRST MOVEMENT

The magnificent introduction to the movement presents the themes very clearly indeed. The first comes at the very beginning, separating itself, in the thin voice of the oboe, from the mighty opening chord. As it slowly progresses, in long elliptical phrases, the full orchestra

emphasizes its periods with powerful chords. Presently the strings intone ascending scales in crescendo, the basses alone holding aloof from these until the apex of their power is reached. Now the second theme of the introduction, again in the penetrating voice of the oboe, sounds rather sadly and wistfully, but the orchestra derives from it figures of tremendous breadth and power. In the midst of this development comes a sudden pause. A nervous flicker of string tone . . . an impatient ejaculation from the full orchestra . . . tentative, hesitating reduplicated notes in the upper woodwind . . . and suddenly the main theme of the movement proper appears in the silken tones of the flute.

Now we begin to perceive the reason for designating the Seventh as the "dance symphony," for this quaint little theme, so soon to be the foundation for a vast and infinitely varied structure of tone, is unmistakably imitative of a folk dance. In fact, it resembles rather strikingly certain cadences of "The Low-Backed Car," an Irish tune of considerable age, and almost a perfect old-fashioned jig.

The many different forms into which this theme is molded by the genius of Beethoven are really amazing in their constantly renewed variety and shifting orchestral color. Somber touches there are, indeed —as if Beethoven, instead of feeling the bitter and gruff humor which pervades the symphony generally, became suddenly and acutely conscious of his woes . . . and the revel of tone and color is on again with perhaps an almost ecclesiastical chord thrown in like a pious grimace, now and then.

Toward the end there is a new burst of revelry . . . an occasional curious hesitation, as if the composer distrusted, momentarily, his ability to remain keyed to sardonic humor, and stood undecidedly on the brink of melancholy. But there is fierce vehemence and power at the end.

SECOND MOVEMENT

The second movement happily falls short of being a funeral march. The suggestion is powerfully present; yet, hear it through and you decide that now Beethoven is serious rather than sad, philosophical

rather than pessimistic. The first theme, ushered in by a somber chord
in the horns and woodwind, is gloomy and ominous, but the counter-

theme, though still in the minor mode, lends a brightening touch of
hopefulness. There is always a gleam of light in Beethoven's darkness.

With rigid economy of material, the composer achieves in the second
movement certain amazing contrasts. The softly stepping basses suggest
an atmosphere of mystery . . . solemn portent . . . lowering clouds
of woe . . . and yet almost the same figure, assigned to the brighter
ranges of the string section, is bright with hope, vehement in exhorta-
tion, passionate in pleading. The rhythms of the two themes—one persistent and strongly marked, the other fluent and flexible as a stream—
are oddly contradictory, yet fitted together as perfectly and as wonderfully as the angular and refractory fragments of a mosaic are brought
together to form figures of gracious curve and motion.

There are further contrasts—in color and tonality as well as in
rhythm. Note, for example, the appearance of the third theme of this
movement. It is introduced shortly after the beginning of the third

section of the movement. Note, too, the fascinating fugal treatment at
the close of the second section.

As the movement draws to a close there is a slowly pervading light.
The original themes are glorified and sublimated in the mysterious
tones of the horn and in the floating unreality of the upper woodwind
ranges . . . a final daring touch of grotesquerie in the plucked notes

near the end . . . and at last an unexpected alteration in accent that brings the movement to its conclusion.

THIRD MOVEMENT

Beethoven was famous for his playing of slow passages at the piano, and his expression of himself in a similar style through the orchestra is equally distinctive. But, hearing certain of his scherzos, such as the present movement, it is sometimes difficult to perceive why the distinction should have been made in favor of the more stately and dignified andante and adagio movements.

For here are wonderfully vigorous and elastic rhythms; rugged gaiety, sustained exuberance and expression of the most fundamental joys of life, all of which contribute to the construction of music which in its own way is quite as moving, quite as expressive and impressive, as the soberly melodious slow movements. Grant that the mood of Beethoven was more often sad than joyous; the joyous mood, when it does come, is none the less truly Beethoven!

The first theme opens the movement. It approaches wildness almost

as closely as Beethoven could, yet underneath it is possible to see the perfectly ordered structure. Brilliant orchestral color is freely applied, especially when fragments of thematic material are repeated in different sections of the orchestra. Superb climaxes develop with the ascending scales . . . and suddenly the swift scales are reversed to give a new effect.

Perhaps the most striking contrast is effected about the middle of the movement, however, when the boisterous opening section is repeated, in tones of ethereal delicacy, yet with every original detail of accent and phrasing perfectly imitated. It is dreamlike, reminiscent—or like seeing through the mist of years some beauty once beheld in all its vivid, glowing splendor.

The contrasting theme, as will be remembered from the preliminary discussion, is much slower, and rather solemn. We hear it in a combination of clarinet, bassoon, and horn, with the last most prominent: and

against it is poised a long-sustained note of the violins. Later the theme is presented in a similar figure, but with most of the orchestra intoning it against the long quivering flame of tone put out by the trumpet.

The second division of the movement reveals development of the themes so clearly posited in the opening section. As the end is approached a prayerful spirit is breathed gently into the music . . . only to be elbowed roughly aside by the violent chords in full orchestra that bring the movement to a close.

FOURTH MOVEMENT

The powerful opening chord in the string section is answered and reduplicated even more powerfully by the remainder of the orchestra . . . again the same figure . . . and with scarcely a pause the wild dancelike first theme leaps into dynamic life . . . a bacchanal indeed!

Here the "dance symphony" reaches its apotheosis. Here the fundamental, the primal source of all music—rhythm—holds complete sway. There is an almost savage, primitive joy in these measures; a fierce exaltation of the purely physical that could be expressed only through rhythm, which more closely than any other element in music approaches and appeals to the physical. It is almost impossible for any human being to remain motionless through this movement!

One does not, now, give that rapt attention which might have been demanded by the second movement, or by any of Beethoven's more serious melodies. No: here we become, whether we will or no, a part of the rhythm created and driven along by the composer, conductor, and orchestra; something involuntary, something deep within us, leaps and moves to the headlong abandoned onrush of this music.

The second theme, which appears after less than half the first division of the movement has been played, is almost as bacchanalian and contagious as the first, and it leads to even wilder revels. But suddenly, near the end there is a mysterious change, so subtly effected that we are scarcely conscious of the means employed. The original subject reappears, now in the tender, tremulous accents of the flute, infinitely gentle, pensive, yet still touched by joy. It is but a bit of byplay, an aside, a highlight, a momentary distraction, and the wild dance goes on until the end.

Symphony No. 8 in F major

THERE seems to have been a curious ebb and flow in the inspiration, the power, and the moods that were Beethoven's. The Eighth Symphony, charming as it is, no more represents the mature and full-statured Beethoven than does the First. The heroic proportions and valorous spirit that distinguished the Third, the fierce and godlike rages of the Fifth, the vigor and bacchanalian abandon of the Seventh—there is little of any of these qualities to be discovered in the Eighth, nor is there much that could be regarded as evidence of the forthcoming Ninth and last of the symphonies. Perhaps these even-numbered symphonies were the result of the sheer urge to create that certainly drove Beethoven in every waking hour; and perhaps the incidence of the creative urge, and of material out of which to fashion his creature, were not simultaneous. Beethoven had, nevertheless, so mastered the form and the medium that even such habitual workings of the spirit, as exhibited in the present symphony, take on the aspect of masterpieces.

Beethoven was perhaps too concerned with troublesome and unmusical things, when this music was written, to abandon himself thoroughly to his inspiration. His deafness, already a handicap in his profession, was beginning to prey upon his mind. His brother, Johann, had involved himself in an affair with the landlord's daughter, and the hot-tempered Beethoven rushed to Linz to take the matter into his own hands: so successful was he that the result was precisely what he had wished to prevent. His brother married the girl. There is something at once droll and pathetic in Beethoven's hotheaded and tactless interference in his young brother's love affairs. Although he loved ladies of quality, he was none too discriminating in his own amours—he died of an affliction rarely contracted from respectable individuals—yet he rushed incontinently to prevent a liaison, not to mention a marriage, between his brother and a girl of the servant class.

However disturbing these circumstances were, they did not prevent Beethoven from completing, during the year 1812, the Seventh and Eighth Symphonies; a trio for piano, violin, and cello; a sonata for violin and piano, and certain less important works. The Eighth Symphony was not performed, however, until more than a year later. It was first presented at a concert in Vienna, on Sunday, February 27, 1814. A little more than thirty years later it was played by the Philharmonic Society of New York, in November, 1844. It was not favorably received at its first performance, nor has it ever become a favorite to rank with certain others of the immortal Nine. However, the overfrequent playing of the favorites has the advantage of turning attention, ultimately, to the less-known symphonies, and for this reason, perhaps, the Eighth is appearing more frequently on symphonic programs. It is worthy of frequent hearing, and certainly repays in pleasure the most careful attention.

FIRST MOVEMENT

The rugged directness, amounting to *brusquerie*, that so often marked Beethoven's "company manners" is reflected in the bold and unheralded proclamation of the chief subject at the very outset. It is played in full

orchestra, and vigorously, in downright ¾ rhythm. The violins succeed with a brief delineation of a graceful swaying figure, broken by a hesitant pause, and taken up then by woodwind (bassoon). The somewhat dessicated tones of this instrument insinuate themselves into the melodic pattern of a second theme, introduced by the violins, and presently emerge in the brighter company of oboe and flute, with a restatement of the second theme.

The movement follows, in the main, the conventional pattern of the sonata form. With the exception of a few notable features, the entire work harks back to the earlier Beethoven—the derivative, exploring, but still form-bound Beethoven. For the stylized development section of the movement, Beethoven selects as basic material the swaying violin figure mentioned above, combined, at times, with the first few notes of the principal theme. A powerful restatement of this chief theme, delivered by basses and bassoons in their most assertive tones, is the most conspicuous feature of the formal recapitulation. To end the movement Beethoven indulges in one of those long and reluctant codas that comes close, at times, to arousing impatience. It is as if the composer, having discovered a pleasing idea, was loath to let it go. But a final version of the first theme signals the end of the movement.

SECOND MOVEMENT

In consistency with the formal character of the symphony, the second movement appears in one of the nearest related keys—the key of the subdominant, B-flat major. Contrary to convention, however, the second movement is the scherzo, though not so marked in the score; and there is no directly contrasting slow movement.

This is the shortest symphonic movement in the Beethoven literature —and one of the most charming and graceful. In it we find an ingratiating and finished and gently humorous quality which can only be described by that outmoded and misused word "elegance"; yet it has strength and vitality and energetic action. Berlioz remarked that the movement is so complete, so logical and final, that it seemed to have "fallen from heaven into the brain of its author, and to have been written at a sitting." But this is the art that conceals art, for an examination of Beethoven's sketchbooks and papers has shown many sketches which ultimately found their development in this movement.

The opening theme is of interest, not only in its charming self, but because it is identical with a little "round" which Beethoven composed extemporaneously at a dinner given for him by some friends. Among the guests was Mälzel, good friend and inventor of the tyrannical metronome. Beethoven, with rare but charming graciousness, imitated with staccato notes the ticking of the inexorable metronome in the little round, or canon, which he called *"Ta, ta, lieber Mälzel."*

The opening theme is presented by the strings, with woodwind accompaniment. It is full of geniality and good humor. The theme, and

the movement as a whole, are a dangerous temptation for the conductor who wants to make an "effect." There is a distinct inclination for the music to get out of hand, and, if it is taken too fast, Beethoven's effect is completely destroyed. A metronome on the conductor's stand would be an excellent idea, in some cases; though, on the other hand, there are conductors who beat time just as regularly and automatically.

The second subject, even gayer than the first, presently succeeds, and the whole movement, brief though it is, creates a delightfully happy and friendly atmosphere.

THIRD MOVEMENT

Here is a conventional symphonic minuet, the characteristic third-movement form of Beethoven's earlier years. It is rather curious that, unless seized by some fury quite beyond the bounds of conventional expression, Beethoven could turn to the devices of the purists and the formalists, and beat them at their own game. Even here, when he wrote more or less to a pattern, the composer exhibits elements of the power and individuality and imagination that set him so far above his contemporaries. The minuet of Beethoven has vigor in its rhythm. There

is nothing mincing about it. A lovely melody springs from the assertive rhythm established in the first two measures. The violins sing it, and the serious bassoons imitate them a bit later. The trio, or middle part of the movement, is developed mostly by a pair of horns and solo cello; later, the clarinet has pleasant and melodious things to say. The third section of the movement is identical with the first.

FOURTH MOVEMENT

There is nothing in the preceding movements to prepare us for the outburst of force that occurs in the final movement, except that, in so far as we are already acquainted with the composer's mercurial temperament and his love of violent contrasts, we might have been led to expect something serious and potent in the closing section of his work. Where all has been grace and lyric loveliness and quiet humor, we now find Beethoven drawing a sweeping and vigorous circular tonal pattern; a formal, yet free and almost boisterous gesture in which he asserts his more usual self. Roughly, the movement is in rondo form. The very simple opening theme is developed into a forceful and eloquent expression. Prompted by the violins, the full orchestra in a vigorous forte

asserts the primary musical idea. A second theme is also given to violins, then to woodwinds. The structure of the movement is so beautifully clear that to follow the thematic material through its development is, in spite of the moving pace and constant accessions of orchestral power, a fairly easy matter.

There is a concluding section of considerable length, derived for the most part from the two principal themes. The symphony ends in an atmosphere of healthy and vigorous gaiety.

Symphony No. 9 in D minor with Choral Finale on Schiller's "Ode to Joy"

IT IS not improbable that Beethoven set about the work of composing this mighty symphony with a conscious effort to surpass even himself. He had been collecting material for it during a period of years, and when finally he applied himself to the task, he seems to have been seized with a demoniac energy and power, and an influx of inspiration that expanded him to his full stature—and at the same time exhausted him. For in this music Beethoven finds the orchestral instruments, and his own superb knowledge of their powers, insufficient; he turns to the human voice for the final expression of the cosmic thought and emotion that surged within him.

The scholastic musician has argued for years about the merit and propriety of including, as climax, a chorus in the finale of this symphony; about the status of this chorus—whether, indeed, it should be regarded as an integral part of the symphony, having its real origin and justification in what has preceded it, or as merely an incident, a dramatic device. The latter opinion seems untenable, in view of the references to preceding themes made in the last movement, as well as their comparison there with the theme of the *Ode to Joy*. Furthermore, it can be suggested, at the risk of being regarded as flippant, that in the final movement Beethoven made no real departure from "absolute" music, because, in the first place, he treats the voice quite like an instrumental group in the orchestra; secondly, because the vocal parts are so written (and so badly written, from the singer's standpoint) that the words become unintelligible, and the *Ode to Joy* has no significance except that expressed through tone, through rhythm, and through melodic line. Which is quite sufficient.

It is not to be supposed that Beethoven's literary taste was of the most discriminating; yet it has always seemed highly questionable that the symphony, after its marvelous setting forth of the whole gamut of human joys, could settle upon so gaudy and vague and verbose an outpouring as Schiller's *Ode* as the ultimate expression of Beethoven's thought and feeling. It is more reasonable to believe that the vague references to human brotherhood and world embraces touched the great heart of the composer, and supplied to him an idea of greatness and of universality and humanity. For he was always the democrat, a man essentially "of the people"; he could always be excited by an idea that seemed to promote equality and brotherliness.

So, it is not a symphony on Schiller's poem; the poem is but a vehicle for drawing in the voice, the most expressive of all musical instruments. What the voice says is, in performance, neither important nor intelligible; its rhythms and intonations, not the words of the poem it sings, drive Beethoven's thought into our consciousness.

The symphony was first performed on May 7, 1824, in Vienna. Beethoven did not conduct, but sat in the orchestra, following with a score, and vigorously beating time for his own benefit. When the work was finished, he was still beating time, and one of the chorus, noting his actions and knowing the reason for them, touched him and turned him toward the audience that he might *see* the applause. He had been deaf for twenty years.

FIRST MOVEMENT

There is a feeling of striving, of discontent, of mysterious confusion and restlessness in the music here. Beethoven seems groping for some utterance that will completely express him. It is a musical parallel to the mental agony of searching for one certain word that persistently evades utterance, though it is clearly in some remote and, for the moment, unresponsive brain cell. Fragments of melody are snatched hastily from the strings—and suddenly these fragments fly together, miraculously like pieces of a shattered sculpture, and the bold and joyful theme of the movement is shouted bravely forth by the full orchestra.

The music is full of the brusque impatience, the brutal power that has been exhibited but once before in the symphonies—in the Fifth; but here is another kind of passion. There is a lift and a manly joyousness in this music that is far removed from the stark agonies of that deathless utterance. This is the joy of living, not the tragedy of life. And, without any alteration of the character or spirit of the movement, without important mutations of the theme, that joy is explored in detail; in a succession of strong yet melodious developments. There is hardly ever a recession of the driving force that moves this music, except when, occasionally, a reflective little song in woodwind gives pause; and toward the close of the movement, where the orchestra finally wins back, after moments of soberness, through a labored but powerful progression, to a final mighty pronouncement of the principal theme of the movement. For once we are spared the lingering farewells that so often marked Beethoven's conclusions; here all is powerful and sure and downright. All has been said that can be said on this theme, and so Beethoven leaves it.

SECOND MOVEMENT

The beauty of musical form is not always evident to those who have not been forced, by one circumstance or another, to study it; nor is it necessary, always, to listeners whose joy in music is, as it should be, primarily sensuous. The beauty of the fugued treatment of the second movement is, however, so clear and perfect that no one can escape it. Not only are its contours exquisitely symmetrical and rounded, but it is informed with a rare and irresistible rhythm, with tonal color and contrast, with a high-spirited and at times almost rowdy vigor that seize and shake the most phlegmatic.

There is a brief introduction, and then the subject is incisively projected by staccato violins:

Strings, staccato

Various strings, horn, woodwind, bass enter upon and experiment with this lightfooted and rollicking theme, building to climax after climax, with ever-growing assertiveness. Timpani, with a powerful rhythmic figure, renew the vigor of the orchestra when it would seem to flag. For melodic contrast, there is a sweet little theme, the melodic line of which actually has an ecclesiastical turn, but, as it is played *vivace*, seems like a bucolic parody of a hymn tune:

This is the trio of the scherzo; the succeeding and final section is structurally similar to the first, but in it Beethoven derives from the orchestra new and shrewdly mixed tone colors. There are small fragments of melody, and near the end, the second theme reappears briefly; but it is elbowed roughly aside by the violent chords that close the movement.

If the first movement suggests the subjective joys of maturity and strength and vigorous manhood, we may imagine that the second presents the endless round of worldly pleasures—the cycle of superficial things with which man distracts himself, and which, ultimately, brings him back to the point from which he departed. There is an intimation of Beethoven's impatience and dissatisfaction with this kind of pleasure, in the impatient chords that terminate the movement; later we shall see that actually he was seeking a different kind of joy.

THIRD MOVEMENT

Everyone who knew Beethoven well enough to leave us some word of the master has commented with admiration, with astonishment, at his skill in improvisation, in transposition, and sight-playing; but all conclude with tributes to the poetry of his playing in slow passages. Sir George Grove, the great English commentator, writes that it was not brilliance and technical skill in Beethoven's performance at the piano, but the "loftiness and elevation of his style, and his great power of expression in slow movements, which, when exercised in his own noble music, fixed his hearers and made them insensible to any fault of polish or mechanism." The adagio movement of the Ninth Symphony illustrates the composer's singular felicity in music of such a mood.

Bassoon, clarinet, oboe, and strings intone the introduction, and then in the most silken tone of the violins the moving subject of the movement is exquisitely sung:

The music suggests a curious mixture of feelings. Complacence, passionate yearnings, wistful melancholy—all have their expression here; there are even echoes from the church. We can heartily agree with Hector Berlioz, when he wrote of this movement, "If my prose could only give an approximate idea of them [the melodies of the movement] music would have found a rival in written speech such as the greatest of poets himself would never succeed in pitting against her."

The serenity of the first song of the strings is presently altered, and we come upon another theme, with a change of rhythm, of tonality, and of emotional plane. This, in violin and viola, is deeper and more intense:

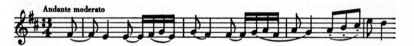

What joys did Beethoven contemplate here? Those of peace, perhaps; or those of assured and sanctified love. The variations erected over these themes do not disturb their essential quality, but seem like new and sometimes less solemn aspects of the prevailing thought. Toward the end of the movement the calm atmosphere is somewhat disturbed by prolonged pealings from the brass, but the long-drawn note of the trumpet fades once more into tremulous string tones, and the wood-wind, the horns return in their mellow mysterious beauty.

FOURTH MOVEMENT

It is in the fourth movement of the symphony that Beethoven's music reaches that sublime altitude where with a single farther step it must of necessity become vocal if it is to say more than the wordless instrumental voices say. That additional step is, of course, taken. But first there is a period of preparation, of reflection, of consideration and anticipation.

A wild discordant cry bursts from the orchestra; a succession of descending, then ascending chords, nervous and impatient, is driven forth in all its voices. A recitative passage for the basses foreshadows an injunction to the rest of the orchestra, which presently we shall hear in articulate form. But it is understood now, as it were, by the orchestral instruments. Their dissonant utterance comes again, but there is a pause, and, after the repeated adjuration of the basses, the orchestra briefly explores the preceding thematic material for some ultimate pronouncement, big and expressive enough for utterance of the mad exaltation that is presently to come. It is now that we hear and feel the surge of the great underlying conception of the work beating against the barriers of inarticulate music. The opening measures of the preceding movements are searched for even the germ of the final joyous expression; they are searched in vain, and the orchestra vigorously rejects them. There is a soft and distant voice in the cellos and basses, a voice that grows stronger in its uplifting and unadulterated joy; yes, this is the word, the phrase, the ultimate pronouncement that Beethoven sought. Stronger it grows, until it is put forth right valiantly. It is the hymn to joy:

Now the other strings take up the joyous strain, and now the full orchestra. Yet once more comes the terrible dissonance of the opening measures, and the impatient chords, but now a voice of authority speaks. It is not the wordless voice of an orchestral instrument but a vigorous baritone in a kindly command: "O friends, no more these discords! Let us raise a song of sympathy, of gladness. O Joy, let us praise thee!" Here is the moment toward which the entire work has been striving, and now the voices dominate even the orchestra. To happiness is added jubilation, and a fever of exaltation in which the greathearted Beethoven reaches out to embrace the world.

BARITONE SOLO, QUARTET, AND CHORUS *

Freude, schöner Götterfunken,
  Tochter aus Elysium,
Wir betreten feuer trunken,
  Himmlische, dein Heiligtum!
Deine Zauber binden wieder,
  Was die Mode streng geteilt;
Alle Menschen werden Brüder,
  Wo dein sanfter Flügel weilt.
Wem der grosse Wurf gelungen,
  Eines Freundes Freund zu sein,
Wer ein holdes Weib errungen,
  Mische seinen Jubel ein!
Ja, wer auch nur eine Seele
  Sein nennt auf dem Erdenrund!
Und wer's nie gekonnt, der stehle
  Weinend sich aus diesem Bund!

Freude trinken alle Wesen
  An den Brüsten der Natur;
Alle Guten, alle Bösen
  Folgen ihrer Rosenspur.
Küsse gab sie uns und Reben,
  Einen Freund, geprüft im Tod;
Wollust ward dem Wurm gegeben,
  Und der Cherub steht vor Gott.

Praise to Joy, the God-descended
  Daughter of Elysium!
Ray of mirth and rapture blended,
  Goddess, to thy shrine we come.
By thy magic is united
  What stern Custom parted wide,
All mankind are brothers plighted
  Where thy gentle wings abide.
Ye to whom the boon is measured,
  Friend to be of faithful friend,
Who a wife has won and treasured,
  To our strain your voices lend!
Yea, if any hold in keeping
  Only one heart all his own,
Let him join us, or else weeping,
  Steal from out our midst, un-
    known.

Draughts of joy, from cup o'er-
    flowing,
  Bounteous Nature freely gives
Grace to just and unjust showing,
  Blessing everything that lives.
Wine she gave to us and kisses,
  Loyal friend on life's steep road,
E'en the worm can feel life's
    blisses,
  And the Seraph dwells with God.

The alternations of quartet and chorus bring constantly new and more intense variations in the theme of joy, from the lovingly entwined melodies in the vocal cadenza of the quartet to the sturdy assertions of male voices alone. Beethoven introduces not only variations of the

* The English translation is that of Natalia Macfarren, and is generally used in American performances. It is published by Novello & Co., Ltd., London (New York: The H. W. Gray Company, Agents).

melody but also of rhythm and tempo and texture of the music, using at times certain sections of the chorus, at others various combinations of chorus, quartet, and soloist; and finally, in the most exuberant vocal outburst in music, he asks of the whole ensemble the delirious, the frantic, and almost unsingable closing passages. One wonders, especially during the inferior choral performances which are so much more frequent than good ones, if in evaluating this music we have not been too much swayed by its spectacular qualities, or even by a feeling of relief and congratulation if the chorus actually does sing always "in time and in tune." If we did not know the complete sincerity of Beethoven, it would be possible to think that here he "doth protest too much"; that such frenetic, such almost insane jubilation, on so abstract a concept, cannot be real. We can only conclude that Beethoven felt in it something quite beyond the rather banal and pretentious verbiage of the poet, something even beyond the powers of his own music. And so, we can but give ourselves up to the excitement, the joyous madness of this symphony, and allow it to move us as it will.

The remaining portions of the choral parts are appended:

Freude, schöner Götterfunken,
  Tochter aus Elysium,
Wir betreten feuer trunken,
  Himmlische, dein Heiligtum!
Deine Zauber binden wieder,
  Was die Mode streng geteilt;
Alle Menschen werden Brüder,
  Wo dein sanfter Flügel weilt.

Praise to Joy, the God-descended
  Daughter of Elysium!
Ray of mirth and rapture blended,
  Goddess, to thy shrine we come.
By thy magic is united
  What stern Custom parted wide,
All mankind are brothers plighted
  Where thy gentle wings abide.

CHORUS

Seid umschlungen, Millionen!
  Diesen Kuss der ganzen Welt!
  Brüder! über'm Sternenzelt
Muss ein lieber Vater wohnen.

Ihr stürzt nieder, Millionen?
  Ahnest du den Schöpfer, Welt?
  Such' ihn über'm Sternenzelt!
Über Sternen muss er wohnen.

O ye millions, I embrace ye!
  With a kiss for all the world!
  Brothers, o'er yon starry sphere
Surely dwells a loving Father.

O ye millions, kneel before Him,
  World, dost feel thy Maker
    near?
  Seek Him o'er yon starry sphere,
O'er the stars enthroned, adore
    Him!

CHORUS

Freude, schöner Götterfunken,	*Praise to Joy, the God-descended*
Tochter aus Elysium, etc.	*Daughter of Elysium, etc.*
[AND]	[AND]
Seid umschlungen, Millionen!	*O ye millions, I embrace ye!*
Diesen Kuss der ganzen Welt,	*With a kiss for all the world,*
etc.	etc.

Ihr, stürzt nieder, Millionen,	*O ye millions, kneel before Him,*
Ahnest du den Schöpfer, Welt?	*World, dost feel thy Maker*
Such' ihn über'm Sternenzelt!	*near?*
Brüder! Brüder!	*Seek Him o'er yon starry sphere,*
Uber'm Sternenzelt	*Brothers! Brothers!*
Muss ein lieber Vater wohnen.	*O'er the stars enthroned, adore*
	Him!

QUARTET AND CHORUS

Freude, Tochter aus Elysium,	*Joy, thou daughter of Elysium,*
Deine Zauber binden wieder,	*By thy magic is united*
Was die Mode streng geteilt;	*What stern Custom parted wide.*
Alle Menschen werden Brüder,	*All mankind are brothers*
Wo dein sanfter Flügel weilt.	*plighted*
	Where thy gentle wings abide.

CHORUS

Seid umschlungen, Millionen! etc.   *O ye millions, I embrace ye!* etc.

Symphony in C major ("JENA")

SCHOLARS and particularly musicologists, who are so preoccupied with
what is old and obscure, are never so happy as when they discover
something new. Most frequently the unearthing of a forgotten, obscure,
or discarded musical work is followed by realization of the fact that
its creator had good reasons for discarding or forgetting the work or
allowing it to fall into desuetude. An exceptional case is, of course,
the Bach *St. Matthew Passion*, resurrected by Mendelssohn; or the
Schubert B Minor Symphony. On the other hand, we have the Schumann Violin Concerto, "discovered" with great *réclame*, the performance of which by Yehudi Menuhin was preceded by noble fanfares,
and was succeeded, for obvious reasons, by its complete abandonment
as a part of the standard violin repertoire.

The authenticity of the "Jena" Symphony of Beethoven is certainly debatable, at least on historical grounds. The Herr Doctor Professor Fritz Stein announced in 1911 that he had unearthed a previously unknown symphony by Ludwig van Beethoven. Dr. Stein professed to have found, two years previously in manuscript form in the archives of the *Academic Concerts* in Jena, a work in symphonic form and of symphonic dimensions—a symphony in C major, also surnamed "Jena." The complete account of Dr. Stein's researches and conclusions was published in 1911 editions of *Zeitschrift der Internationalen Musik Gesellschaft*.

By inductive reasoning it is possible to arrive at the conclusion that this symphony is authentically Beethoven. No score has ever been discovered, but there was a complete set of parts, some of which revealed the name of Beethoven, some of which definitely stated that the work had been written by Beethoven ("par Louis van Beethoven"), and most of the parts were quite obviously in Beethoven's handwriting. The chemical composition and watermark of the paper indicated definitely that the work was written not later than the end of the eighteenth century. The most conclusive evidence, however, lies in the fact that in many passages the work reveals the style of Beethoven. It is true that a good part of the music suggests Haydn or Mozart more strongly than Beethoven, and one critic went so far as to analyze and proportion the work as " six-eighths Haydn, one-eighth Mozart, one-sixteenth Beethoven, and one-sixteenth a composer in the manner of Schubert."

Indeed, if the work had been presented as having been written by an imitator of Mozart or of Haydn, a shrewd observer might not be inclined to argue, and yet there are phrases and even basic ideas wholly worked out which seem so characteristically Beethoven that on reflection one can hardly doubt the authenticity of the work.

FIRST MOVEMENT

One must not look to this symphony for the heroics of the Third, the conflicts, humanities, and triumphs of the Fifth, the Dionysiac ecstasies of the Seventh, or the grandeur of the Ninth. This symphony, if it is Beethoven, is the formative, tentative Beethoven, owing much to Haydn and Mozart but nevertheless depending for its vitality on a quality that must have been Beethoven. There is a rather pretentious, not to say pompous, introduction that suggests the imminence of important matters, but what follows is rather conventional eighteenth-century music, expertly developed and worked out. The movement is in fairly strict sonata form and notable rather for its form than for any positive element of greatness. Perhaps its most conspicuous feature is the employment of scale figures contrasted against a pleasant but not extraordinarily distinguished melodic figure. The Haydn formula is rather rigidly observed.

SECOND MOVEMENT

The second movement materializes a certain contemplative quality which Beethoven often brought to his music. It is developed from a phrase strongly suggestive of a sentimental German song called *"Steh' ich in finstrer Mitternacht"* ("At Midnight I Watch at the Window"). There are some interesting and, for Beethoven, quite radical dissonances, swiftly followed by their conventional resolution. The thematic material is treated with various orchestral colors and even with tentative variations.

THIRD MOVEMENT

The derivative quality of this music is perhaps more evident here than anywhere else in the symphony. It is cast in the conventional minuet form *à la* Haydn, and though in truth it varies from the norm in that it lacks the primness and dignity of a conventional Haydn minuet, neither does it exhibit the rough treatment that Beethoven so often in the great nine symphonies applied to this form. There are two themes and the conventional trio.

FOURTH MOVEMENT

The final section of the symphony, apart from being exceedingly grateful to the ear, is interesting because it presages in some details the later Beethoven—particularly in the use of the wind instruments and in the building up of climax by means of orchestral rather than purely dynamic means. The first theme is projected by the strings, and then what amounts to an orchestrated crescendo—a crescendo built by adding instruments rather than by increasing the force of any particular instrument—is built up under the thematic material. The movement is quite formal and stylized and, apart from the purely sensuous pleasure that lies in listening to it, it is more distinguished as a premonitory echo of the Beethoven that was to be than as a particularly great or unique piece of music in itself.

Hector Berlioz

<hr>

1803-1869

<hr>

THE GREAT MUSICAL romanticist Hector Berlioz was born near Grenoble, December 11, 1803, the son of a country doctor. His father wished that Hector should succeed him in the medical profession, and the leanings of the lad toward music were severely frowned upon; for to the practical doctor music was a frivolous diversion, not to be considered as a career. Berlioz therefore had few opportunities to pursue the art in his boyhood. He was nineteen years old before he received any systematic musical training, and even then he gained his point only after disagreements with and financial desertion by his parents.

In 1822, Berlioz was enrolled at medical school in Paris. His lack of interest, and a horror of the dissecting room, made him decide definitely and finally in favor of a musical career. He so informed his parents who, after vainly pleading and threatening, cut off their support. He was admitted, after private study, to the Conservatoire. During seven years at this famous school, Berlioz was almost continually in conflict with his teachers; for their academic point of view and methods irked him, and like so many gifted with great facility, he left weak places in the structure of his musical development by taking what he thought were "short cuts," and by contempt for certain fundamental rules which, however dull and perhaps senselessly applied by his teachers, were nevertheless necessary for rounded and full artistic attainments.

In 1830 the composer won the Prix de Rome, but after staying eighteen months in Italy on this scholarship he returned to Paris. In the following years he became known and admired the length and breadth of Europe—except in Paris, where perhaps the fact that he wrote for the symphony orchestra rather than for the exploitation of pretty girls and not necessarily pretty singers at the Opéra had something to do with the tardiness of the French public's response.

When music failed to pay his way, Berlioz turned to journalism, and wrote with an eloquent and effective pen. To his *Memoirs* we owe many a priceless sidelight on music and musicians of his time. He was a musical megalomaniac—we still have them—and suggested orchestras of as many as four hundred and sixty-seven instruments, to be used with a chorus of three hundred and sixty voices; four chorus masters, and two assistant conductors, one for woodwind and one for percussion, who were to take their cues from the conductor-in-chief, Hector Berlioz.

He had a positive genius for orchestration, notwithstanding some fantastic ideas such as the above. He was the first composer really to exploit the full tonal resources of the symphony orchestra, and the standard instrumentation of the orchestra of today owes much to him. He was not among the greatest of composers, but certainly is among the most entertaining.

Symphonie fantastique
[*Episode in the Life of an Artist*]

MUSICIANS, unlike novelists, are not often given to writing, consciously, autobiographies in their compositions. Richard Strauss did so deliberately in *Ein Heldenleben;* Beethoven perhaps wrote vital chapters of his life in the Fifth, and elsewhere; but no one else, except the incorrigibly romantic Hector Berlioz, has given a detailed, literal, and candid exposition of his emotional life. He was a man of fantastic imagination, of powerful passions, of undoubted genius. His one satisfying means of expression was music, and when the central fact of his life—or at least what he took to be the central fact—resulted in heartburnings and tragic disappointments, music was his refuge, his release, his "escape mechanism."

The *Fantastic Symphony* was written as the outgrowth of Berlioz' mad passion for the celebrated Irish actress, Harriet Constance (Henrietta) Smithson. It was played for the first time, at Paris, December 5, 1830. The ambiguous suggestions of the final movement can be accounted for by Berlioz' bitter and almost insane grief when calumnious stories as to the character of Miss Smithson came to his ears. He revised this movement, but the music remains. The composer made handsome apologies for crediting evil report about his lady, and, three years after the symphony was first performed, they were married. They were not happy.

When the score was published, Berlioz inserted a preface which constitutes adequate comment on the significance of the music. Following is the translation, by Harriet Bret, which is printed with the French version by Berlioz in the edition of the symphony published in 1900 by Breitkopf & Härtel:

Program of the Symphony

"A young musician of unhealthily sensitive nature and endowed with vivid imagination has poisoned himself with opium in a paroxysm of lovesick despair. The narcotic dose he had taken was too weak to cause death, but it has thrown him into a long sleep accompanied by the most extraordinary visions. In this condition his sensations, his feelings, and his memories find utterance in his sick brain in the form of musical imagery. Even the Beloved One takes the form of a melody in his mind, like a fixed idea which is ever returning and which he hears everywhere. (This recurring melody, or *idée fixe*, which typifies the Beloved One, is first heard in the allegro, in C major.)

FIRST MOVEMENT
Dreams, Passions

"At first he thinks of the uneasy and nervous condition of his mind, of somber longings, of depression and joyous elation without any recognizable cause, which he experienced before the Beloved One had appeared to him. Then he remembers the ardent love with which she suddenly inspired him; he thinks of his almost insane anxiety of mind, of his raging jealousy, of his reawakening love, of his religious consolation.

SECOND MOVEMENT
A Ball

"In a ballroom, amidst the confusion of a brilliant festival, he finds the Beloved One again.

THIRD MOVEMENT
Scene in the Fields

"It is a summer evening. He is in the country, musing, when he hears two shepherd lads who play, in alternation, the *ranz des vaches* (the tune used by the Swiss shepherds to call their flocks). This pastoral duet, the quiet scene, the soft whisperings of the trees stirred by the zephyr wind, some prospects of hope recently made known to him, all these sensations unite to impart a long unknown repose to his heart and to lend a smiling color to his imagination. And then She appears once more. His heart stops beating; painful forebodings fill his soul. 'Should she prove false to him!' One of the shepherds resumes the melody, but the other answers him no more. . . . Sunset . . . distant rolling of thunder . . . loneliness . . . silence. . . .

FOURTH MOVEMENT
March to the Scaffold

"He dreams that he has murdered his Beloved, that he has been condemned to death, and is being led to execution. A march that is alternately somber and wild, brilliant and solemn, accompanies the procession. . . . The tumultuous outbursts are followed without modulation by measured steps. At last the fixed idea returns, for a moment a last thought of love is revived—which is cut short by the deathblow.

FIFTH MOVEMENT
Witches' Sabbath

"He dreams that he is present at a witches' revel, surrounded by horrible spirits, amidst sorcerers and monsters in many fearful forms, who have come together for his funeral. Strange sounds, groans, shrill laughter, distant yells, which other cries seem to answer. The Beloved Melody is heard again, but it has lost its shy and noble character; it has become a vulgar, trivial and grotesque dance tune. She it is who comes to attend the witches' meeting. Riotous howls and shouts greet her arrival.

"She joins the infernal orgy . . . bells toll for the dead . . . a burlesque parody of the *Dies Irae* . . . the witches' round dance . . . the dance and the *Dies Irae* are heard together."

The orchestration of the symphony, as usual with Berlioz, is heavy and at the same time brilliant. There are moments of poignant beauty—and of outrageous bombast; also according to the characteristic Berlioz. Under the first heading comes the lovely pastoral duet of oboe and horn, in the third movement; under the latter, the abandoned outbursts of the "Scene of the Sabat"—the fantastic Black Mass celebrated in the final movement. The gross burlesque of the *Dies Irae,* a hymn for the dead in the Requiem Mass of the Roman Catholic Church, is an effective trick which Berlioz was neither the first nor the last to employ. Among the unusual directions for playing the music are these: four timpani are to be played separately by four musicians (third movement); bass drum is to be set on its side and played with kettledrum sticks by two players (last movement).

The *idée fixe* in its entirety is reproduced here as a matter of interest. This theme appears in every movement of the symphony. Its treatment is often highly symbolic, as can be noted in the fourth movement where it is cut off—even as a last thought of one's beloved—by the death stroke. In the fifth and last movement, the treatment is even more programmatic. Here the young musician pictures himself as dead . . . and attending the "Witches' Sabbath." He is "in the midst of a frightful group of ghosts, magicians, and monsters of all sorts, who have come together for his obsequies." There are groans, laughter, howling, shrieks . . . and then suddenly "the Beloved Melody is heard again, but it has lost its shy and noble character; it has become a vulgar, trivial, and grotesque dance tune." It seems to mock him as it is squeaked out by an E-flat clarinet, later assisted by a piccolo. And then at the close, the *Dies Irae* develops into a wild fantastic orgy. You can readily visualize the young musician, writhing in a cold perspiration on his bed, as his drug-distorted mind pictures this terrible scene. It is a notable bit of orchestral programmatic composition—the material that serves to link Beethoven and his pure classic subjectivity with such a titan as Wagner in whom we have the objective carried to its very zenith.

39512

Symphony, *Romeo and Juliet*

MORE than one composer has attempted to collaborate with Shakespeare. It would be difficult to establish a claim that any have succeeded, if one looks upon Shakespeare qua Shakespeare, with the possible exception of Verdi and his *Otello;* but the greatest of English dramatists, and perhaps of all dramatists, has moved more than one composer to great and passionate and dramatic utterance. Berlioz' *Romeo and Juliet,* motivated though it was by the composer's sensitive, almost hysterical, responsiveness to Shakespeare's play, stands by itself as a musical work of the highest dramatic force, passionate intensity, and musical eloquence.

It has been noted here that Berlioz was for a long period fiercely enamored of the Irish actress Henrietta Smithson, whom he pursued for years with all manner of solicitations, commands, and entreaties, until he had so confused and beglamored the lady that she finally consented to marry him. The marriage soon became a burden to them both. Madame Berlioz was insanely jealous. She interfered with her husband's career, insulted his friends, accused him of many and gross infidelities, and finally sought escape from her unhappiness in liquor. There was no taming of this shrew, and the marriage disintegrated. Berlioz never forgot the love that he had once known, though the object of it had probably in twelve years ceased to excite his passion or compel his abject adoration.

Curiously enough, Berlioz began this work at a most unhappy moment in his marital relations, but apparently he could completely abstract himself from the immediate present and refresh at least the spirit of the sweet madness of his youth. Twelve years intervened between Berlioz' first love for Henrietta and the composition of the *Romeo and Juliet* symphony; yet his passion, perhaps purified by adversity, burns in this music as incandescently as it ever could have burned when he pursued and won his actress.

One can easily understand the motivation of this music if one remembers the fascination which the plays of Shakespeare had for the composer, with particular reference to the fact that in 1828 Berlioz had witnessed a performance of Shakespeare's *Romeo and Juliet,* with

Smithson naturally playing Juliet. He had previously seen *Hamlet*, which was quite overpowering, but in his own reminiscences he tells us himself what happened to him at the performance of *Romeo and Juliet*:

"Ah, what a change from the dull gray skies and icy winds of Denmark to the burning sun, the perfumed nights of Italy! From the melancholy, the cruel irony, the tears, the mourning, the lowering destiny of Hamlet, what a transition to the impetuous youthful love, the long-drawn kisses, the vengeance, the despairing fatal conflict of love and death in those hapless lovers! By the third act, half suffocated by my emotion, with the grip of an iron hand upon my heart, I cried to myself: 'I am lost! I am lost!' Knowing no English, I could grope but mistily through the fog of a translation, could see Shakespeare only as in a glass, darkly. The poetic weft that winds its golden thread in network through those marvelous creations was invisible to me then; yet, as it was, how much I learned! An English critic has stated in the *Illustrated London News* that, on seeing Miss Smithson that night, I said: 'I will marry Juliet and write my greatest symphony on the play.' I did both, but I never said anything of the kind. I was in far too much perturbation to entertain such ambitious dreams. Only through much tribulation were both ends gained."

It is said that Nicolò Paganini, the fabulous Italian virtuoso of the violin, was consulted by Berlioz as to the nature of the next work he should undertake. Paganini, we are told, declined to advise the composer, although he might have been in a position to do so, for he had just presented Berlioz with a grant of twenty thousand francs. Berlioz apparently believed that Paganini had provided this money, although from what we know of the character of the Italian master this seems improbable; and indeed the whole story is apocryphal.* The work was written between January and September of 1839 and performed in November of that year at the Conservatoire. Berlioz conducted, with an orchestra of one hundred and sixty and a chorus of ninety-eight. The performance was a prodigious success, despite the snarls of some of the critics, one of whom asserted that Berlioz "did not understand Shakespeare" and that the fabulous web of tone which we know as the "Queen Mab" scherzo reminded him of the "operations of an imperfectly oiled squirt." In the audience was a young composer named

* Yet the score is dedicated to Paganini.

Richard Wagner, who, at the time, asserted that the music took him by storm—yet it is of record that Wagner later described the *Romeo and Juliet* symphony as made up of "piles of rubbish heaped up among the most brilliant inventions." The first complete performance in America of the *Romeo and Juliet* symphony was given by the New York Symphony under the direction of Leopold Damrosch, April 8, 1882.

Berlioz himself has left us a clear statement of his artistic purposes in creating this music. In the preface to the score he writes:

"There should be no doubt about the character of this work. Although voices are frequently employed, this is not a concert opera, a cantata, but a symphony with chorus. If song occurs in the beginning, it is for the purpose of preparing the mind of the hearer for the dramatic scenes, in which sentiments and passions should be expressed by the orchestra. It is, moreover, to introduce gradually in the musical development choral masses whose too sudden appearance would do harm to the unity of the composition. Thus the prologue, in which, after the example of the prologue by Shakespeare himself, the chorus exposes the action, is sung by only fourteen voices. Later is heard, behind the scenes, the male chorus of Capulets; but in the funeral ceremonies women and men take part. At the beginning of the finale the two choruses of Capulets and Montagues appear with Friar Lawrence; and at the end the three choruses are united."

The symphony is divided into three sections, each subdivided. Complete performances of the work are rare because of the difficulties and the large orchestral and vocal forces required. Excerpts, such as the "Love Music" and the "Queen Mab" scherzo, frequently appear on orchestral programs. A notable performance, complete, was given under the direction of Arturo Toscanini at the concerts of October 7 and 9, 1942, of the Philharmonic-Symphony Society of New York, with Jennie Tourel, mezzo-soprano, Jacques Gerard, tenor, Nicola Moscona, bass, and the Westminster Choir under the direction of Dr. John F. Williamson. The program for this occasion informs us that Mr. Toscanini wished to have included in the notes the rather arrogant comment which Berlioz himself makes in the score at the head of the section "Romeo in the Family Vault of the Capulets." Here is a free translation: "The masses have no power of imagination. Consequently music which is imaginative has no power to move them. The section which follows is an example, and I am inclined to believe that it should be omitted, unless it is performed for a sophisticated group thoroughly familiar with Act V of Shakespeare's tragedy as interpreted by Garrick. . . . Such a situation might happen once in a hundred times, and, in view of the exactions of this symphony upon the conductor, it would seem advisable to have a moment of silence after the funeral of Juliet, and then move to the finale."

The symphony has its own program, text, and outline and requires little in the way of description or analysis. The first section, with its music of conflict, is obviously intended to suggest the quarreling between the houses of Montague and Capulet. The second section presents Romeo first in lonely despair in the Capulets' garden, and later as he intrudes upon the festivities in the home of his beloved. The final subdivision of Part Two of the symphony is the famous "Queen Mab" scherzo. Meanwhile, the tenderest episode of the whole work occurs in the lovely scene, the theme of which is sung with tender sentiment and passionate expression by horn and cellos. The third section of the work embraces the obsequies of Juliet, Romeo in the mausoleum of the Capulets, and the pitiful aria of good Friar Lawrence, as well as the powerful finale. It is interesting to note that, as originally performed, the finale was regarded as brutally abrupt; later the composer appended the coda which appears in the 1857 edition and is used today.

Leonard Bernstein

BORN 1918

L EONARD BERNSTEIN, one of the most talented of the younger generation of musicians in America, was born in a New England mill
town, Lawrence, Massachusetts, in the startlingly recent year of 1918.
He attended Boston Latin School and Harvard College, where music
was his major pursuit. At Harvard he studied music with Edward Bur-
lingame Hill, A. Tillman Merritt, and the distinguished American composer Walter Piston. He was graduated from Harvard in 1939 and
pursued his musical work at the Curtis Institute, where he worked at
composition with Randall Thompson, conducting with Fritz Reiner,
and piano with Isabella Vengerova.

After learning the rudiments of conducting from Fritz Reiner, Bernstein worked for several seasons at the Berkshire Music Center under
the direction of Koussevitzky, where he has of recent years been a member of the faculty and has conducted some of the public concerts as
well as the American premiere of the opera *Peter Grimes* by Benjamin
Britten. He was also assistant conductor of the New York Philharmonic-
Symphony for one season and, in an emergency, conducted with notable
success the concert of November 14, 1943. He has been intimately connected with the New York City Symphony as its permanent conductor,
and has been guest conductor with many of the major symphony orchestras in this country and abroad.

Among his most successful compositions are two ballets, *Fancy Free*
and *Facsimile,* and he has to his credit also a sonata for clarinet and
piano, a cycle of songs, the score of the musical hit *On the Town,* and
the very interesting symphony *Jeremiah,* which was cited by the New
York Music Critics Circle as the finest new symphony by an American
composer to receive its *première* in the season of 1943–44.

96

Symphony, *Jeremiah*

THE lamentations of Jeremiah are among the most eloquent passages in all Holy Writ. The prophet must have been, in addition to a prognosticator of the shape of things to come, a passionate lover of his home town, Jerusalem, for his most poignant utterances are reserved for his weepings over that ill-fated ancient metropolis. These are of the substance of Hebrew liturgy and, rather oddly perhaps, constitute the essence of one of the loveliest and most touching ceremonies of the Roman Catholic Church—the Tenebrae. This service is seldom observed except in a cathedral church, for it requires a choir of priests which could not be assembled elsewhere. While the priests' choir intones the lamentations of Jeremiah, the lights are put out one by one until all have been extinguished, whereupon, the fire laws notwithstanding, the congregation departs in darkness and silence; but on the third night the ultimate darkness is succeeded by a strange commotion behind the high altar occasioned by the priests' choir smiting their breviaries with bare hands, the noise symbolizing the rending of rocks and earth as Christ arose from the sepulcher. The whole ceremony is not unlike a religious version of the Haydn "Farewell" Symphony, succeeded by a strange kind of applause.

It is hardly necessary to suggest that Bernstein's treatment of the lamentations of Jeremiah is somewhat different from that in the Roman Catholic liturgy. The music is by no means orthodox, either musically or ecclesiastically speaking. Yet, through the skill of the composer, it establishes the atmosphere of the orthodox Hebraic and tells its tragic story in potent terms and eloquent phrases. The symphony *Jeremiah* was given its first performance by the Pittsburgh Symphony Orchestra in Pittsburgh on January 28, 1944, with the composer as conductor. Perhaps the most authentic comment upon the work, aside from that of the omniscient critics, would be provided by the notes supplied by the composer to the Pittsburgh Symphony program edited by William E. Benswanger and repeated in the program of the Boston Symphony Orchestra, which is in charge of the erudite John N. Burk:

"In the summer of 1939 I made a sketch for a Lamentation for Soprano and Orchestra. This sketch lay forgotten for two years, until in the spring of 1942 I began a first movement of a symphony. I then realized that this new movement, and the Scherzo that I planned to follow it, made logical concomitants with the Lamentation. Thus the Symphony came into being, with the Lamentation greatly changed, and the soprano supplanted by a mezzo-soprano. The work was finished on December 31, 1942, and is dedicated to my father.

"The Symphony does not make use to any great extent of actual Hebrew thematic material. The first theme of the Scherzo is paraphrased from a traditional Hebrew chant, and the opening phrase of the vocal part in the Lamentation is based on a liturgical cadence still sung today in commemoration of the destruction of Jerusalem by Babylon. Other resemblances to Hebrew liturgical music are a matter of emotional quality rather than of the notes themselves.

"As for programmatic meanings, the intention is again not one of literalness, but of emotional quality. Thus the first movement ("Prophecy") aims only to parallel in feeling the intensity of the prophet's pleas with his people; and the Scherzo ("Profanation") to give a general sense of the destruction and chaos brought on by the pagan corruption within the priesthood and the people. The third movement ("Lamentation"), being a setting of poetic text, is naturally a more literary conception. It is the cry of Jeremiah as he mourns his beloved Jerusalem, ruined, pillaged, and dishonored after his desperate efforts to save it. The text is from the Book of Lamentations 1:1–4, 4:14–15, 5:20–21. An approximate translation follows:

> "How she sits desolate—
> The city once so full of people;
> She is become as a widow!
> So great among the nations,
> Princess among the provinces,
> She has become a tributary!
> She weeps, she weeps in the night,
> And her tears are upon her cheeks;
>
> "There is no comfort among all her lovers;
> All her friends have betrayed her,
> They have become her enemies.
> Judah is exiled through affliction
> And great servitude;

She dwells among the nations,
She finds no rest;
All her pursuers have overtaken her
In the narrow passes.

———

"Jerusalem has sinned, sinned greatly. . . .

———

"They (the sinful priests and prophets) wandered
Like blind men in the streets,
Polluted with blood,
So that their garments could not be touched.
'Depart, unclean,' men cried to them.
'Depart, depart, touch us not!'

———

"Lord, wilt Thou forget us forever?
How long more wilt Thou forsake us?
Turn us unto Thee, O Lord. . . ."

Georges Bizet

ALEXANDRE CÉSAR LÉOPOLD BIZET was born in Paris, October 25, 1838. His godfather nicknamed him "Georges," and as Georges he is known to the world at large. Both of his parents were musical, and the child was but four years of age when his mother began giving him instruction upon the piano. Like other infant prodigies an absorbing musical interest dominated his existence, and he showed little liking for normal childish play. His greatest enjoyment was sitting crouched outside the door of his father's studio listening intently to the vocal instruction that went on inside. When he was about eight years old his father desired to begin the lad's musical education in earnest, and was astonished to learn how much the boy already knew. A retentive memory and an innate musical intelligence had mastered many difficulties for the youth. When the father took the boy to the conservatory, his extreme youth appeared a barrier, but his fund of knowledge so completely won the admiration of the members of the committee of studies that he was admitted, and in six months had taken the prize for *solfège*.

Zimmermann, teacher of counterpoint at the conservatory, was in poor health and about to retire when the talent of young Bizet came to his attention. He became so interested in the boy that he made an exception in his case, and took him as a pupil. Bizet's scholastic career both in musical science and as an executant at the piano was meteoric. He played with a brilliance of technique, and could with gentle or intense finger pressure lift a melody from its accompanying harmonic intricacies in a way that charmed his hearers. His teachers said of him that he was a "remarkable virtuoso, a fearless reader, and a model accompanist." His ability to arrange at sight for piano the most difficult orchestral score drew admiring comment from the great Berlioz himself.

When Zimmermann died, Bizet studied composition with Halévy, whose daughter he later married. Halévy welcomed him and said that he was already fit to participate in a contest for the Grand Prix. His youth, however, militated against him, and even though he waited before submitting a composition, the jury awarded him only a second prize. Another coveted prize which he won before his twentieth year entitled him to a three-year sojourn in Rome at government expense, after which Bizet returned to Paris. Here he found himself confronted with the hardships which beset so many young musicians—chiefly, to nourish the body while the soul clamors to create. Bizet was obliged to meet the cost of living by giving piano lessons, writing transcriptions, and arranging orchestrations, when he would have liked to devote his entire time to composition. Opportunity eventually came to him when a patron of the arts made a gift of 100,000 francs to the Théâtre-Lyrique. This fund provided for a commission to compose an opera to the libretto of *The Pearl Fishers*. Bizet was intensely interested in the theater, and put every effort into the work. His opera, *The Pearl Fishers*, won the prize, and quickly was followed by the colorful *L'Arlésienne* music, incidental to Daudet's drama. The opera *Carmen*, now so popular, was unsuccessful at its first performance in 1875. The composer died three months later at Bouvigal, near Paris.

Symphony No. 1 in C major

WHEN a major work by a major composer becomes lost, destroyed, or forgotten, there is usually good reason for it. This is particularly true when a work of the composer's youth disappears, for often in his mature years the artist is ashamed of his early work. Bizet's symphony was written in 1855 when the composer was seventeen years old and a student at the Paris Conservatoire, but the work did not achieve a hearing until 1935, when it had lain in obscurity and desuetude for eighty years. Anyone who hears it must be grateful to Felix Weingartner, who conducted the premier performance at Basel, Switzerland, February 26, 1935.

One does not, even after hearing or studying this delightful music, associate Bizet with the three great B's of music, and certainly not with either of the two—Beethoven and Brahms—who stand in such eminent places among composers of symphonies. Perhaps neither Beethoven nor Brahms would claim musical kinship with the composer of *Carmen* and of this symphony, but there was another master who might have felt artistic sympathy with Bizet, and that is Mozart. This music is brilliant yet suave, exciting, excited and urbane, calculated, assured, sophisticated, deliberately and consciously charming. It is a musical miniature marvelously detailed, colored, and polished. It is neither obvious nor subtle but has an engaging quality of naturalness artfully contrived that resists analysis and in effect needs none.

FIRST MOVEMENT

In structure, and to some extent in harmonic treatment, the first movement of the symphony owes something to Beethoven and something to Mozart. It would be surprising indeed if a composition by a seventeen-year-old boy written in the year 1855 were completely free of such influences; but this seventeen-year-old boy asserted his own originality and brought to bear upon his work an instinct for elegance, a delicate sense of comedy, a deftness and logic of orchestration that were particularly his own. The principal subjects of the movement are quoted:

SECOND MOVEMENT

The second movement is filled with a tender melancholy. The mournful song of the oboe over an accompaniment by violas pizzicato establishes a reflective, introspective mood which, though occasionally and momentarily disturbed, colors the movement from beginning to end. The opening melody is as follows:

THIRD MOVEMENT

The third movement is alive with a fine, vital vigor, high good humor that is nevertheless disciplined, proportioned, and exquisitely neat. It derives its motive power from this theme played *allegro vivace*:

FOURTH MOVEMENT

In the final movement the scholar can very probably detect in embryo certain ideas which the composer later employed in his matchless score, *Carmen*. The swift pace and vigorous rhythms do not exclude certain delightful melodic elements, the most persistent and perhaps the most charming of which runs as follows:

And the movement ends with a final dash of high spirits.

Alexander Porphyrievich Borodin

ALEXANDER PORPHYRIEVICH BORODIN was the illegitimate son of a prince of Imeretia. In his boyhood he showed a decided leaning toward the two subjects which later became the absorbing interests of his life: music and science. At nine years of age he had already attempted to compose, and at thirteen had produced a concerto for flute and piano. His mother, who gave him every educational advantage, had set her heart upon a medical career for the boy; and when he was sixteen years old sent him to the St. Petersburg Academy of Medicine. Here he remained for six years, for, unlike Schumann, who studied but had no interest in law, Borodin found his medical work entirely congenial. Despite the fact that it took the major part of his time, he managed to hear and even participate in the performance of a great deal of music. His interest was more profound than a mere drawing-room devotion, and led him to study seriously to improve his deficiencies in the technique of composition.

Two years before his graduation from the medical school Borodin served in a military hospital for a period during which he became acquainted with Mussorgsky, then a young subaltern in the army. They met occasionally at the homes of superior officers and Borodin was impressed with Mussorgsky's outspoken ideas on the subject of nationalism in music, for up to that time his experience had brought him in touch with little other than the western classics.

Graduating in 1858, he spent the next few years on an extensive scientific tour which took him to Italy, Austria, Germany, and France. The result was that his musical interests were dominated by Western European ideas, which persisted until the friendship with Mussorgsky was resumed. This occurred when Borodin's appointment as assistant lecturer at the St. Petersburg Academy gave him greater leisure to devote to his art. Mussorgsky introduced him to Balakirev, who was at the time deeply immersed in projects for his Free School of Music, founded to spread the teachings of nationalism and intended to counterbalance the cosmopolitanism of the newly established conservatory headed by the great Rubinstein.

It was not long before Borodin's conversion to nationalist aims was effected. He studied composition under Balakirev, and began his first serious composition, his Symphony in E-flat, which, because of interruptions for the scientific activities he pursued until his death, took him five years to complete. The second, in B minor, was written during the years 1871–77.

It is curious to note that the Soviet government, recently dedicating a monument to Borodin, honored him not for his music but for his medical services to the Russian people.

Symphony No. 2 in B minor

THE charm of the B minor Symphony lies largely in its intense national character. It is as though medieval Russia peered through its magnificent measures. When it was performed in London in 1896, the London *Telegraph* published this note:

"It contains scarcely a theme that can on any ground reasonably be referred to classic sources. Every important melody is of an Eastern cast, and some of the subjects were derived, one might suppose, from the Middle Asia celebrated in his symphonic poem (*"Dans les Steppes de l'Asie centrale"*) . . . an idea supported by frequent repetition of brief phrases in the manner long recognized as characteristic of Oriental art. But the most curious feature in the work is the presentation of such music strictly in symphonic form. The Russian composer does not use even legitimate opportunities of freedom. Having chosen his model, he respects it and, so to speak, compels the 'fiery and untamed steed' of the Ukraine to figure in the limited circle of the *haute école*. The effect is curious and interesting, especially at moments when the composer seems to have difficulty in keeping his native impulses from getting the upper hand. Thus the leading theme of the first *allegro*, a phrase of eight notes, haunts nearly the whole movement, chiefly by simple repetition. A second subject does appear at proper times, it is true, but comes in apologetically and departs speedily, hustled by the aggressive eight notes. Using a big orchestra, Borodin employs color with Eastern lavishness, and exhausts his resources in *tours de force* of various kinds, seeking, perhaps, to counteract the effect of a certain thematic monotony.

FIRST MOVEMENT
Allegro

The symphony begins with a statement of the main theme—an impassioned utterance that impresses itself indelibly upon the imagination—a kind of motto that shines through the fabric of the entire movement. Syncopation in the brass section alternating with majestic chords for woodwinds and strings suggest, by their very repetition, the ideas of great strength and barbaric power.

A second subject is lyrical in style, and of great beauty. It is introduced by the cellos, taken up by the woodwinds and upper strings, and is then welded into the texture of the movement. Here the usual development section gives way to a colorful orchestration in which the motto is repeated in turn by clarinet, bassoon, and oboe in a manner characteristically Oriental. Drums introduce a new rhythmic figure above which trombone and trumpets sound the main theme. This is later proclaimed in unison by woodwind, brass, and strings with an insistence that is forceful and vigorous.

SECOND MOVEMENT
Scherzo

The brilliant scherzo is in the key of F major. The most striking feature of this sparkling movement is the rapid repetition of a single note in the horns, which persists at terrific speed almost throughout, and offers the horn player an opportunity for both distinction and exhaustion. Dazzling outbursts of woodwind and pizzicato strings leap like showers of sparks. A startling effect is a recurring syncopated passage, one of many curious and effective rhythmic elements in this fascinating movement. Gradually the agitation subsides, and in striking contrast is heard a haunting melody of the solo oboe. Other woodwinds and horns continue the flow of melody, which is developed in broader version by violins and cellos just before a return to the shimmering prestissimo with which the movement opened.

THIRD MOVEMENT
Andante

A clarinet solo with harp accompaniment introduces this movement. The horn sings the chief melody, and it is one of melting tenderness. For a little space there is a distinctly Oriental color and movement in the music, and then a sudden fortissimo precedes a third subject. This is developed to a powerful climax. The movement ends with the clarinet phrase which began it, while the horn answers dreamily, and the pianissimo roll of drums accentuates the deep tranquillity of the whole.

FOURTH MOVEMENT
Finale

The chief motive, which is heroic in character, is announced by the upper strings. Almost at once there follows a fiery development, a tonal flame that rages madly through the orchestra, only to subside to a rich glow like a distant reflection of what has gone before. The clarinet announces a second subject which is repeated in the bright tones of piccolo and oboe and later bursts out with the fervor of a glorious hymn. Trombones re-establish the mood of the first movement, after which the second melody of the finale is heard, this time in the entire string section, and then in the splendor of the full orchestra.

Johannes Brahms

1833-1897

CLIO, MUSE OF HISTORY, must have smiled as she recorded in the life of Brahms no tale of poverty and woe, but rather a goodly span of years, placid and happy. Few of the great composers were untouched by misery; few, therefore, possessed the mild and equable disposition that Brahms concealed beneath a gruff exterior, and few escaped the unhappy circumstances which, when recalled, reproach us for our indifference to the great ones in our midst.

Brahms was a musician by heredity. Several generations of his ancestors had been directly concerned with music; some made their daily bread through their skill in that divine art, and Brahms in early childhood revealed a gift that his elders neither could nor would neglect. He studied willingly and earnestly as a child; with bold initiative and relentless application as he grew older in years and in his chosen avocation.

Fortune favored him. He attracted the attention of Joachim, the greatest violinist of his day, and through Joachim, the interest of Liszt, than whom no greater pianist, possibly, has ever lived. Through Joachim also was arranged a meeting which was to have a most important effect upon Brahms' career—that is, the meeting with Schumann, who as editor of an important musical journal and as a composer of eminence was in a position to forward the ambitions of the young Brahms, and did so most willingly. Had the introduction of Brahms' music to the world been engineered according to the ideas of a modern "publicity agent," they could scarcely have attracted more attention. From the first notice by Schumann, every published work of Brahms was the occasion for widespread discussion. That this was not invariably favorable did not detract from its effect in bringing the composer into prominence.

Still fortune was kind. Brahms received a commission as director of music at the court of a German prince, just when he needed the experience, the leisure, and the financial rewards that only such an appointment could give.

He lived calmly, happily, and successfully. Attending the obsequies of Clara Wieck Schumann, pianist and wife of the composer, and tireless propagandist for Brahms' own music, he contracted a cold which aggravated a chronic ailment and resulted in his death on April 3, 1897, at Vienna.

Symphony No. 1 in C minor

BRAHMS approached the task of writing for the symphony orchestra with great seriousness, and with a consciousness of the importance of the work, the dignity of it, and the exactions which it makes of the composer. He was a musician of mature powers, of established merit and fame, before he undertook the composition of his First Symphony. He realized that even genius must attain the stature that is achieved only after years of experience, experiment, and thorough comprehension of the smaller musical forms, before asking of itself the exigent requirements of the symphonic form. He knew his own powers—though rather diffidently seeking the approval of others whose musical opinions he valued; and the result of his accurate self-estimate, his patience, his sincerity, and his magnificent talents is the C minor Symphony—the greatest "first" symphony ever written. Mature, finished, plethoric with melody and with orchestral color, as vigorous and vital as Beethoven, as songlike as Schubert, as perfectly formed as Bach—and as subtle as Brahms!—this wonderful music, though it is the first symphony from the hand of Brahms, represents the genius of the composer in its most splendid development.

The First Symphony was completed in September, 1876, and was first performed, at Karlsruhe, two months later, on the sixth of November.

FIRST MOVEMENT

The introduction is like the drawing of a huge and magnificent curtain, rich with gold and ornament, sweeping slowly apart to reveal behind it the fierce swift movements of drama. Thirty-seven measures of glowing and sonorous tone, moving slowly and with ever-growing might

and majesty toward its inevitable climax. Portentous beatings of timpani, measured and powerful and determined, support strings and
woodwinds moving in contrary and circuitous paths toward a single
vehement and final thrust as the climax of the introduction is attained.
Now there are fragments of melody, poignant phrases of flute and oboe
and violin, and a subsidence of the great powers of the orchestra as we
approach the beginning of the first movement proper.

Now the expectancy, and the marvelously developed emotional stringency of the introduction are justified, for the movement leaps into
flaming vitality and clashing dramatic contrasts from its very opening
note. From this apparently simple subject the composer develops a

throbbing and vital organism, full-blooded and muscular and agile; a
concourse of sound that almost seems to leap and to shout, to defy and
encourage, to warn and to command. There are brief moments of reflection, almost of tenderness, yet always urgent rhythms permit no dwell-
ing upon gentleness. Sometimes a plucked note or two, like the curious
trifles that provoke conflicts, seems enough to arouse the orchestra from
its breathless pauses, and to send orchestral antagonists off again to new
clashes of tone.

Toward the end of the movement there is a wonderful instance of
Brahms' amazing rhythmic sense, and his fondness for odd and conflicting internal impulses in his music. Strings against the whole orchestra
contest with swiftly growing vehemence for possession of a fragmentary
theme, and the resulting double simultaneous syncopation creates a
vivid and almost visible effect of a short fierce struggle. Strings are vic-
torious, though the bassoon joins them even when the thematic fragment
has been torn from the mouths of the woodwinds; then the violins themselves abandon it, and are given instead a sad and lovely and reflective
melody which presages the end of the movement. At the close a warm
and enveloping wave of tone waxes great and wanes, and is swept, finally, into silence by the single note plucked from the strings.

To mention a Brahms symphony today is to provoke inevitable questions. "Why did his contemporaries think him dull? How could his music have been called an exhibition of 'sullen asceticism'? How could an American critic, in 1878, pontifically declare of this symphony that 'it will not be loved like the dear masterpieces of genius'?"

Today we know that Brahms ranks among the very first musicians of all time. His symphonies—especially the C minor—are astonishingly popular, ranking in public esteem with the best and most famous of the Beethoven nine. The explanation probably lies, first, in the reluctance of most of us to accept what is new and different, and secondly, in the charm exerted by anything which, though familiar, continually exhibits new items of interest and pleasure.

These reasons may at first glance seem contradictory; they really are not. Prior to 1926, the Brahms symphonies did indeed appear in the repertoire of every first-class orchestra, but like much else in the orchestral library, they were endured rather than enjoyed by a large section of the public. The sudden popularity of the C minor can be traced directly to its recording by the Philadelphia Orchestra. It happened that electrical recording, then in its earlier stages of development, was thoroughly successful for the first time, in this particular work. The records were used all over the world for demonstrating the possibilities of the new recording and of electrical phonographs. Their power, clarity, and fidelity, so greatly surpassing anything before known in recorded music, amazed everyone who heard them—and incidentally made the hearers pretty well acquainted with this music! The greater frequency of the Brahms First on orchestra programs from this period to the present was probably the result—and naturally the other three symphonies, though never winning the popularity of the First, began to have more frequent hearings. The recording removed the symphony from the class of unfamiliar things, and, because it made repeated hearings possible, established the music in that little group of precious things which become dearer and richer with the years.

SECOND MOVEMENT

The dramatic intensity, the vigor, and nervous animation of the first movement now give way to a dreamy and contemplative mood, touched with melancholy. It is a gentle, not a passionate melancholy; it is a mood that might have been born of calm observation of life, with its inevitable disappointments, griefs, and futilities. Here is an acceptance of things as they are, the bitter and the sweet, the sad and joyous, and all the mercurial conditions of existence; with sober reflection upon them.

There is no introduction, and the principal theme is the first lovely melody you hear—conspicuously in the first violins.

We have not long to wait for the entrance of the second theme, a song equally beautiful, pensive, and longing, in the singularly poignant voice of the oboe. It rises, lonely and trembling, from the closing cadence of the first full expression of the chief subject.

In the strings, once more, sounds the antithetical phrase, soaring aloft in the clearest and loveliest tones; a pulsing rhythm lies beneath, vitalizing and urging onward the dreamy melody. Strings and woodwind bear the burden of the movement. Sometimes they are used in contrasting tone colors; sometimes one supports and colors the other; always there are new and fluent and fascinating derivations from the themes, and mutations of timbre and harmony. The final expression of the thematic content of the movement is given to the solo violin, doubled with a solo horn, this lyric passage occupying almost the last fourth of the movement. To the end, above the mysterious tones of the horn and the accompanying harmony in the orchestra, we hear the eloquent violin pour forth its passionate utterance, starlike and bright even against the full sweep of the orchestra; and its more delicate tones hover, like a disembodied voice, over the very final chord.

THIRD MOVEMENT

In only the Fourth of his symphonies did Brahms exhibit a movement of such robust playfulness as to justify calling it a scherzo. In the present work the third movement is indeed lively, and graceful; it has touches of a gentle and whimsical humor. But it is by no means the wry humor of a Beethoven, nor the bitter and sardonic grin that sometimes leers from the pages of Tchaikovsky. It is rather as if Brahms, the childless lover of children, smiled upon their quaint conceits.

The movement begins with the theme, given to the sweet and unassertive voice of the clarinet; a theme much like a children's folk song, gracefully moving above a pizzicato accompaniment in the cellos, and reinforced, first by a detached phrase in the violins and violas, and then, gently and softly, by the string and woodwind choirs.

Presently there is a new theme, subordinate in importance, but temporarily affecting both a rhythmic and modal change in the music. Imperceptibly, however, the first theme returns, but now almost concealed beneath decorative figures of great delicacy and beauty. Then comes the second important theme, in woodwind voices, rather lively and with a graceful, swinging rhythm that motivates most of the remainder of the movement. Here it is:

Here, perhaps, is the rotund and bearded Brahms gravely shaking a warning finger at some mischievous child, and as the little song of the first few measures once again returns, the warning gesture, by its transfer to smooth and warm utterances by the strings, becomes a caress. The final word of the movement is given to a graceful phrase of the second theme, most ingeniously worked into the lustrous musical pattern in the last subsiding measures.

FOURTH MOVEMENT

Had he written nothing else, the man who evoked this music from his mind and heart must have won proud place among music's immortals. Surely this movement is one of the sublimest utterances human ears have heard. It is here that words most ingloriously fail, and reverent silence should be the only comment. The human tongue knows no speech to encompass in words this expression, this outpouring of passion and of exaltation, this magical evocation of power and beauty. Here, surely, no one needs words to help him know and feel the poignancy of that first awful cry that is torn from the orchestra; nor the tragedy, so terrible in its dramatization by the furtive and fateful progress of the plucked low strings, that ends in the violins' brief delirious confusion; nor the strange and wonderful metamorphosis by which madness becomes philosophical complacence, and complacence becomes exaltation.

The first phrases sweep through the orchestra, and then pizzicati steal secretively up from the depths of the bass; then mount, more swiftly and more boldly, until with a final feline leap they reach and entangle the whole string section. Above chromatic mutterings of the violas and cellos, other orchestral voices sadly lament. Again the fearsome progression, as of the footsteps of a menacing beast, moves through the plucked strings, and now not only the woodwind answers but also strings in deliriously whirling figures, flying like wind-blown leaves before fierce gusts of tone from below. At the vertiginous pinnacle of this mad interlude comes a terrifying roll of the timpani, which not only climaxes the scene but ends it. Then like a breath of sunlit spring air we hear a calm and lovely song blown softly and sweetly from the horn. And again it comes, cool and silvery now in the voice of the flute. Close upon its ending there sounds, in warm complacence, the soothing and heartening "choral" theme which later will arise to dominate the orchestra with heaven-storming power.

The theme given out, first by horn and then by flute, aroused tremendous interest when this symphony was first played in England, by the Cambridge University Musical Society. If you hum it to yourself, just as it is written, it will probably seem familiar:

But if you make a very slight change, it will be even more familiar—for you hear it from half of the chiming clocks in the world. It is the famous "Cambridge Quarters":

At the English performance just mentioned, many hearers believed that this curious resemblance between the theme and the tune of the striking clock at Cambridge was no accident; that Brahms deliberately wished to pay a compliment to his Cambridge audience. As a matter of fact, there is no reason for believing the similarity to be other than a coincidence.

There are richly scored phrases derived from the horn call, and presently, after an instant's pause as if for breath, the orchestra plunges into that magnificently high-spirited song which is the essence of the movement—a song which, first presented in the warmest tones of the strings, sweeps vigorously along and in a few measures erases from memory the terrors and the awe of the introduction.

It was here that the enemies of Brahms found—since they were looking for it—evidence that he had looked to Beethoven for his material; it was precisely here, also, that his friends found proof that he had surpassed Beethoven. The first and casual hearing of this passage, with its bounding vigor and joyousness, does indeed suggest certain moments in the Ninth Symphony, but it is not possible for a reasonable person to believe that the resemblance is more than mere accident.

Comparisons between this movement and the choral finale of the Ninth Symphony might, however, be undertaken for reasons other than a slight resemblance of themes. Sometimes it is difficult to escape the conclusion that Brahms accomplished here what Beethoven sought and failed to do in the Ninth. In this music Brahms, employing only those forces natural to his medium, accomplishes a magnificent proclamation of joy and exaltation which has, perhaps, no parallel, no equal in music. In doing so he works calmly, confidently, sanely, and beautifully. With the sublime complacence of a man who knows his powers, who knows that they are adequate to his concept and to his work, he builds a mighty paean of joy that seems utterly natural and convincing and unconstrained. Leaving out for the moment the question of the complete originality of the central theme, certainly Brahms' treatment of it is original, various, brilliant, logical, satisfying; and Brahms is never frenetic, never shrill.

It must be admitted that in introducing a chorus in the last movement of the Ninth, Beethoven did violence to the unity of the symphony as a work of art. It can scarcely be denied that the vocal parts themselves, for the most part, are written with complete indifference to the limitations of the human voice and breathing apparatus. Beethoven's inevitable resort to the variation form, worn threadbare by himself and others, and not particularly appropriate in this choral music, cannot be adduced as evidence of originality. And, to many hearers, even though they love the music, the Ninth Symphony choral finale is frantic and unconvincing. Nor does the use of a definitely second-rate poem as the theme of the movement make it much more persuasive, unless we consider that Beethoven's choice of the verses was dictated not by their literary excellence but by their references to human brotherhood—an ideal always close to the heart of the composer.

There is no occasion here, of course, for an extended discussion of the relative merits of Brahms and Beethoven. The spectacular features of a performance of the Ninth, however, have so frequently distracted attention from its obvious faults as absolute music that occasionally it is helpful to withdraw a moment from its undeniable impressiveness and to consider it coldly. Informed and unbiased musical opinion would probably rank the Brahms C minor above the Ninth, and the growing popularity of this work seems to indicate that the joy expressed by the broadly intelligent, cultivated, civilized Brahms is more certainly sincere and convincing than Beethoven's wildest outbursts.

Brahms uses that wonderful, elastic, electrifying melody as the basis for a long and marvelously elaborated development; a development that explores every musical possibility of the theme, and builds slowly but certainly toward a magnificent climax. There is a constant growth in dramatic intensity, involving reminiscences of early themes of the movement, and suggesting an atmosphere of keen anticipation and suspense. At the moment when one might think that the uttermost limits of power have been explored by the orchestra, the choral theme bursts forth in glowing tones, the orchestra's brazen voices dominating all with their mightiest powers:

Once more wild rhythms leap and bright colors flash; a mighty chord is built of a bold descending figure in the brass, and the end comes on a single long-drawn conclusive chord of noble simplicity.

Symphony No. 2 in D major

THE epic breadth and grandeur of the C minor Symphony (the First) was never again approached in the four works composed by Brahms in this form. Well might he have exhausted himself of heroic utterance in that matchless music; and so, in succeeding works, other moods, not less impressive or attractive, engross him. Therefore, in the four symphonies, we have more variety of intent and content than can be found in any other group of symphonies by any one composer.

The Second Symphony is perhaps the best introduction to the orchestral music of Brahms. Its content is full and rich enough for the most exigent, but its structure is very clear, its moods not too subtle or exacting. Though not without moments of somberness, it is generally lyric and sunny, occasionally even playful. Melodies in profusion sing through these measures and remain unforgettably in mind, while to satisfy those for whom music must produce a thrill by rhythmic and dynamic power, there is the brilliant fourth movement.

The symphony was performed for the first time by the Vienna Philharmonic Orchestra, December 30, 1877, under the direction of Hans Richter. Brahms had tantalized his musical friends with obscure or misleading information about the character of the music, and with his customary modesty had even denied the work the name of "symphony" in his jesting comment on it. The very day before the performance he wrote that "the orchestra . . . play my new symphony with crepe on their sleeves" . . . and added ironically, "It is to be printed with a black border, too!" How relieved must have been his admirers to hear this glowing and happy music!

FIRST MOVEMENT

Over the shadowed figure of the basses the horn romantically dreams

upon the first theme. Presently violins suggest a swaying melody, not of profound thematic importance, but leading eventually to the yearning song of the cellos which is to be developed as the second basic idea of the movement. Woodwinds (flutes) are attracted to this flowing melody, and present their own version in answer to the strings. Upon the basis of the melody the composer develops a firm and sonorous tonal fabric, through which runs always the bright strand woven by violins, cellos, and basses, enlivened by occasionally irregular conflicting rhythmic impulses.

The structural lines of the movement, in spite of the descending transitional phrase which now appears in the flute, are tending upward; and it is possible to visualize the music as forming itself into a strongly defined, a sturdy, and symmetrical pyramid. The apex is reached in the development of the principal theme, which is now elaborated in a series of colorful derivations, increasing always in interest and animation, and gradually drawing upon more and more of the orchestral resources. Yet always there is a beautiful and fascinating clarity, the progress of each instrumental voice somehow seeming independent, yet vitally related to that of its fellows. Alternately powerful and gentle utterances presage a return of the underlying theme in its explicit form, and the music, guided by the wandering horn, gradually descends from the peak of its powers into a placid valley, filled with sunshine and contentment.

SECOND MOVEMENT

It is curious to discover that Brahms, though we know him to have been a dissembler of his inmost thoughts and feelings except in music, regarded himself as "not at all a sensitive person," and "absolutely without nerves or sympathy." It requires only a single hearing of the restrained yet passionate song of the cellos and the violins, in the first few measures of this movement, to convince us otherwise. The music is

grave, but warmed and intensified by a tenderness and intimacy, and by suggestions of secret pain; and it speaks with a directness and shrewd poignancy that few sensitive listeners can resist. This is the utterance, not of a confirmed and neurotic and hypochondriac sufferer, but of one who from a calm yet not remote philosophical eminence observes the woes of humanity, little and great, and grieves for them. Other slow movements in the Brahms symphonies are tender and touching, but nowhere else does Brahms reach so surely into the vast profound of human feeling.

Detaching oneself momentarily from the emotional significance of this music, it is interesting to note the beautifully formed contours and development of the music. After the presentation of the first theme, it is given in a kind of imitation, by horn, oboe, and flute; and a second idea is brought forward by the strings, and later elaborated in woodwind with still another melody moving against it through the cellos and violas. The melodic possibilities of this material having been thoroughly explored, the movement, remembering for a moment the theme that brought it into being, closes in serenity.

THIRD MOVEMENT

The journeyings into the profounder depths of the human soul are too recent for Brahms to burst forth, immediately, into a classical scherzo; so he introduces, at the beginning of the movement, rhythmic and melodic ideas occupying a happy middle ground between the pathos of the preceding movement and the playfulness that is presently to come. The oboe has a bewitching little song, half wistful and half gay, accompanied by cellos pizzicati. Other woodwinds likewise discourse upon this theme, and it establishes a mood at once questioning and hopeful.

With a sudden change of tempo the strings, in a crisp and elastic rhythm, are given the delightful presto. All questionings are at once answered, all doubts resolved; here is delicate merriment, here is frolic, here is joy. There are interludes of thoughtfulness, and of reflection, as when the woodwinds suggest a serious moment, and the oboe insinuates its pristine pensiveness. The reply is a sturdier assertion of the motive of the presto.

But there is a sudden appearance of darker orchestral colors, and the idea of the presto, which seemed about to be developed as the dominating spirit of the movement, is ultimately discarded for a return to the first plaintive theme. Violins and flutes and oboes are attracted to it, and in this mood the movement closes.

FOURTH MOVEMENT

The finale of the First Symphony, after its awesome and portentous introduction, brings us into a mood which asserts a profound, a vigorous, and vital optimism.

The present movement is concerned with joy, too; but with a lighter and more brilliant, a more vivacious and unreasoning gladness. The headlong rush of the violins ushers in a period of what seems, emotionally, a period of complete abandon; yet one can observe that Brahms

achieves this freedom within the confines of strict form. Hanslick, the noted Viennese critic, concedes that this movement is "always agreeable," and suggests that "Mozartian blood flows in its veins." One would rather believe that the life fluid which courses through this music is thicker and stronger stuff than any that ever circulated in the delicate tissues of Mozart's music. In its formal finish it can be compared with the work of the older master; but scarcely otherwise.

The development of the chief themes, both of which are first projected by the strings, is highly elaborated, yet the spirit of the music is never lost in these tangles of academic form; on the contrary, it seems to grow in power and emphasis as the music moves along. The concluding section reaches new peaks of exaltation, of almost frantic high spirits; powerful chords, underlined by syncopation, bring new powers to bear; brilliant brasses lend point to the orchestra's declamations, and resounding chords establish a triumph at the end.

Symphony No. 3 in F major

THE earliest critics of the Brahms symphonies proved their own diminutive stature when, to them, the grandeur of the music was obscurity. The coldness with which Brahms was once received was not only the result of his daring to be different; it was not merely the traditional public reluctance to accept something new. It was, in fact, inexperience with music conceived on so mighty a scale that called forth the solemn dicta that Brahms was "heavy," recondite, obscure, esoteric.

For no one before Brahms had built the symphony into such a gigantic structure. No one had conceived a pattern at once so broad in outline and so exquisite in detail. Nor is this a reflection upon the masters who had gone before. There can be no belittling of a Beethoven Fifth, which gains its end by a fundamental simplicity, an almost brutal straightforwardness, an emotional exhibitionism that constitute a musical portrait of the great soul in which that immortal music was born. But when such a work as, for example, the Beethoven Fifth was the *summum bonum* of symphonic music to the critics of Brahms' day, it is scarcely to be wondered at that Brahms' own Third, with its subtlety, its poise, its mellow warmth, its autumnal richness, and its sunset glory, should fall upon uncomprehending ears.

Ease of comprehension is certainly no criterion of excellence. Half the joy of beauty is in the discovery of beauty, and though in our day we enjoy, at first hearing, a Brahms symphony, it is because we inherit, so to speak, a degree of musical sophistication. The joy of discovering new and personal beauty in this music is nevertheless still ours; and we profit by the mistakes, and avoid the pitfalls, of our musical forebears. One of the chiefest charms of the music of Brahms is its endless revelation of new and unsuspected loveliness; of hidden perfections, adumbrated to our perceptions even after the tenth and the fiftieth hearing.

That the music, or, more accurately, the charm and beauty of the music of Brahms often defy words is no indication that they are obscure. On the contrary, if words could adequately describe the loveliness and the significance of music, there would be no need of music. Music is a language, universally comprehensible, which expresses things beyond words. It is a communication, between composer and listener, of an emotional state. Words fail. Music, intelligently conceived and executed, never fails. The child, the savant, the poor, the ignorant, the rich —all can grasp in some degree its significance; and it is only when words come between composer and hearer that music may be confused, uncertain, obscure.

FIRST MOVEMENT

The Brahms Third has been interpreted, at one time and another, as a musical picture of Hero and Leander; or of Shakespeare's Iago! or as having a recherché moral significance as of the eternal struggle between good and evil. None of these conceptions has any valid basis; they are but products of individual imaginations, reactions of individual human entities, thrust into history solely because of the importance of the persons who experienced them. As in the case of any "pure," subjective music, your own intellectual and emotional response to the symphony must be the ultimate criterion by which you will judge it.

The majestic opening chords have much more importance in the music than would at first appear. Major and minor, bright and somber, they indicate an emotional state disturbed by conflict. They have still a further purpose, musically, for after a few bars you will perceive them again, not in woodwind, as at first, where they dominate the orchestra, but in the bass, supplying a somewhat ominous suggestion.

The main theme of the movement sweeps downward in the strings immediately following the two broad opening chords. There is a contrast-

ing, upward-moving figure in the woodwind, and then, just before the second principal theme, occurs a phrase that might have been transplanted bodily from the groves of the Venusberg itself. Wagner lay

stricken at the time this symphony was written, and it has been suggested, rather inappropriately, perhaps, that in this surprising echo of
the song of the Venusberg sirens, Brahms paid tribute to the dying
Wagner. In view of all circumstances, the suggestion is incredible.

Now comes the second theme, almost like a lullaby in its gentle sway,
in the voices of clarinet and bassoon. The strings urge onward a brisk

rhythm; details of composition and orchestration now cluster about the
broad basic lines of the movement. The gentle second theme darkens
when it is given to the somber voices of the heavier strings; the first
theme, similarly treated, is almost completely disguised.

Where now is the electric brilliance in which this theme once flashed,
cleaving its way through great masses of orchestral tone? Scarcely have
we time to wonder what darkling cloud has enshrouded the music, when
the theme appears again, with all the brightness and vigor of its first
coming. Now the basic material of the movement grows to the fullness
of its splendor under Brahms' wonderful development. Now the firm
basic structure of the movement supports the masses of detail that disclose it, not merely as a finely articulated skeleton, but as a vital principle determining the form and significance of the movement itself.

SECOND MOVEMENT

If there is serenity in the second movement, there is also passion, intense though restrained; if there is ingenuousness, there is, too, a sub-

tlety, an ingeniousness not to be disregarded. The main theme is, of course, the lovely song of the woodwind, like a hymn for little children, that opens the movement. It is as if a great organ played gently . . . but the answering cadence is not the white and passionless voices of children, but a deep and tremulous yearning utterance of the strings. Yet more poignant, more pleading, is the voice of the oboe that in solitary eloquence pierces the masses of tone that encircle it.

There are countless embellishments and mutations of the main melody, yet in all its wanderings, in all its guises simple or obscure, it yearns and is unsatisfied. Presently, after the lowest reaches of the strings have been explored, the woodwinds (clarinets, bassoon doubling) suggest a comforting thought. And again, the strings bring forth a still brighter figure, carried on, now, alternately by wood and strings.

Brahms is often calm, serene, placid . . . but dullness has no place. The rhythms of this movement could hardly be described as turbulent, and yet there is conflict. Is it aimed to accent the pervading calm by contrast—or by disturbance to prevent a monotone in the pattern of the movement? Who knows . . . and what matter? Here is a delicate and skillful thing, but one of a thousand details that make Brahms . . . *Brahms!* Listen attentively, and you will detect the faint rhythmic clashing of three notes in strings against two in woodwind.

And yet, there is always a wonderful unity, rhythmic and melodic. It can hardly escape you: note, for example, toward the close of the movement, the appearance of a subject in the woodwind against the figured accompaniment of the strings and the chorded brass. What is it but the candid opening theme, subjected to a slight rhythmic mutation that makes it seem to grow naturally and logically from what has preceded it?

THIRD MOVEMENT

The third movement of a symphony is, traditionally and technically, a dance movement. With Brahms, whose love and understanding of the Hungarian and gypsy dances is one of the traditions of music, such a movement would be inevitable. But the use of a dance form in the symphony antedated Brahms, of course, by many a year. The minuet of the

Mozart symphony, the scherzo of Beethoven, were handy devices which the composer bent to his purpose of expressing a humor not exactly compatible with the more serious musical forms. And thus a composer of today, if in his symphony he placed a fox-trot movement, would be perfectly justified by all canons of technique, by tradition and convention.

It is not to be inferred, however, that the dance movement necessarily is frivolous, trifling, or lacking in depth. It need not even be happy. The *passacaglia*, the saraband, and other dance forms were at least serious; the minuet, stately; the polonaise, solemn.

Do not, therefore, expect this third movement, although it exhibits certain dance-suggestive rhythms, to be of a character at odds with that of the main body of the work. True, the movement is contrasted, and deliberately so, with the others; but not to the extent of dissipating the spirit of calm and mellow joy that vitalizes the work as a whole.

The cellos sing the dance song that is the chief theme of the move-

ment . . . sing it without prelude as this section of the symphony opens. Then, when one would naturally expect a second and perhaps a brighter theme, the same song is transferred, with a gain of emotional content, an even more pensive suggestion, to the violins. Still later, when the appearance of a new motive seems inevitable, an even more mournful projection of the theme is effected in woodwind voices—flute and oboe, doubled. Yet there is a certain vitality, a determined forward motion, a rhythm strangely at variance, in its persistence and gentle insistence, with the emotional potency of the melody itself.

Presently a brief pause, a tentative mutation of harmony, and the second theme finally does appear. It seems to have a certain diffidence, a hesitation . . . yet its rhythm is definite, its tonal coloring (in flute, oboe, clarinet, bassoon) rich and pervasive. The cello, below, proceeds in a figure of its own, and occasionally a gently blown horn adds to the luminous tone of the woodwind choir.

There is a transitional passage of singing loveliness, and now the horn, in no uncertain tone, duplicates the song of the cellos at the opening of the movement; the oboe repeats the former part of the violins. Color is applied with a generous hand; the melodic elements of the movement are reviewed in various guises, and there is, finally, a tentative and hesitating approach to the figure described in the preceding paragraph. Suddenly the mood vanishes, that motive is never re-created, and the movement quickly, but gently, ends.

FOURTH MOVEMENT

The Brahms of the fourth movement is indeed that mighty Brahms of the C minor (First) Symphony. Here is the opulence of orchestration, the overwhelming power, the invariable certitude, the virility and vitality of that noble music. But here there is more: there is more of poise, more of the feeling of achievement. For beyond the triumphant note one senses the warm soft flow of peace—a rich autumnal peace. The goodly harvest is gathered; the day is done; a golden western light flows over the world in splendor, and dies . . . in splendor.

Strings and bassoon, not loudly, but with the vigor and emphasis of restrained power, give us the first theme in strong and perfect octaves.

Woodwind enriches the harmony, and then, a powerful and sonorous phrase, half military, half of the cloister, is ushered in by the horn and pronounced by strings and woodwind. An almost savage pronouncement of the horn grows directly from this phrase, and there is a period of further elucidation of the first theme. The dynamic range is extended; there are exigent demands upon the orchestra's power, but another ominous utterance of the horn presently restrains the spirit of abandon. The fierceness of attack relaxes temporarily, until the violins presently whip the vast pool of sound into a new frenzy.

Strangely, this new burst of energy is devoted to the solemn, almost ecclesiastical subject we heard not long after the movement began. But one more climax, one more terrific burst of energy, one more upward surging of all the orchestra's mightiest powers, one more stentorian warning in the brass—and the twilight begins, gently and all but imperceptibly, to fall across the scene.

There are no words, there is no need of words, to describe this music in its last moments. The glow of a mighty presence pervades it. The magnificent complacence of a great spirit broods comfortingly above it, resolving all doubts and questionings in the serenity, the peace, the spiritual satisfaction of its close.

Symphony No. 4 in E minor

BRAHMS' Symphony in E minor was first performed in 1885, published during the following year, and played for the first time in America by the Symphony Society, in New York, in December, 1886. Brahms was uncertain of the merit of the work, and in fact seems to have been generally depressed both during the months of composition and the first few performances, which he himself conducted. It is said that, just prior to beginning work on the Fourth Symphony, he had studied diligently, and had been deeply impressed by Sophocles' tragedy *Oedipus*, and perhaps there is something of the grief and terror of that awesome work in certain portions of the symphony. That is not to say that it is a symphony of gloom or melancholy. It is always thoughtful, sometimes philosophical, occasionally gay; never morbid, never depressing.

FIRST MOVEMENT

Always it seems strange that Brahms ever could have been considered cold and pedantic, intellectual rather than emotional, forbidding and heavy. True, after the sometimes thin and effeminate prettiness of Mozart, the mellifluous facility of Schubert, the stark simplicity and ruggedness of Beethoven, music conceived so magnificent in outline and so elaborate in detail as the music of Brahms often is must have lacked the power to evoke a spontaneous reaction from the casual listener. The music lover, the concertgoer of today, however, is perhaps more sophisticated. Each year of musical history, each composer who has come and gone, has widened and deepened musical background, sharpened musi-

cal perception, refined musical discrimination. And though Mozart and
Schubert and Beethoven lose nothing through the years, the sophisticated and occasionally abstruse Brahms finds today an audience more
receptive, more appreciative and sympathetic than he knew while he
lived.

The very opening phrases of the first movement draw us into a moving current of music—music that seems to have begun nowhere, music
of which we suddenly, not shockingly, become conscious. The theme is
cast in a figure much like a dialogue, strings questioning, woodwind

answering. A pleasant rustling in the accompaniment, gradually growing more prominent, suggests the general current of life, with life's insistent questionings and half answers persistently intruding. There are
wild calls on the horn, and the second important theme appears as a
fragmentary melody in the cellos, with the curious dominating character invariably assumed by a melody when it is laid in the bass . . .
but an upward sweep presently carries it into the higher, more penetrating, yet less commanding voices of the lighter strings.

The movement proceeds not in the strictly academic sonata form but
as a series of episodes and climaxes, unified into a perfect whole more
by their emotional significance than by any interrelation of structure.
The second section of the movement, for example, opens much like the
first, but with a sense of uncertainty achieved by the slight variation of
the questioning phrase with which it began. The wild phrases of the
horn which once before have briefly appeared return with more emphasis, and are elaborated at such length as to give them momentary
dominance. The questioning phrase of the beginning is again presented,
now in a solemn light, and still without definite answer.

A climax greater than the several preceding climaxes of the movement develops in the final section of the movement . . . a spirit almost
warlike grips and moves the music until its final insistent questions are
put down under the emphatic chords and beatings of the great drums
in the closing measures.

SECOND MOVEMENT

Horns, then the bassoons, oboes, and flutes put forth a tentative tentacle of tone, a delicate tendril that presently fastens and fashions itself into a lovely melody woven of dreams under a summer sun.

In writing a simple melody, the composer reveals his greatness, if any he has. The little man can command the bravura effect, can evoke the orchestra's mightiest thunders, but only the great achieve the sheer simplicity which because it is simple and elementary touches our deepest and most vital sensibilities. This achievement is frequent in the music of Brahms, and is notably accomplished here.

Gone are the feverish questionings, the inadequate answering, the strife, the tumult, and the overbearing power of the first movement. Now all is bright, placid, warm, restful. If there is a hint of sadness, it is of that pleasant melancholy with which comfortable age regards the time-softened memories of restless youthful years. The melody flows over the almost imperceptible disturbances of plucked strings, but there is growing emotional stringency; presently you feel a new and more passionate impulse, the strings giving it expression above a woodwind and horn accompaniment. Still another and more powerful motive, strings echoing woodwind with emphasis. And yet the movement has reached no definite and permanent emotional plane . . . its melodies, vagrant as they are, touch lightly the wellsprings of feeling.

At the very moment when we feel that the errant spirit which animates the movement *must* alight and reveal itself fully, we come upon an agitated passage in which the strings' most moving accents are called forth, briefly but powerfully. Now we know that the former wanderings were as the strange succession of fantasies that come in illogical procession through a sleeper's subconsciousness. Now they are revealed, as it were, in the hard light of full awakening . . . lived over . . . and presently dismissed with a smile.

THIRD MOVEMENT

A joyous outpouring of vigor and vitality, a happy command of the orchestra's full forces in a jolly tune that surely had its genesis in some wild peasant dance . . . thus the third movement (*allegro giocoso*: lively and joyously) of the symphony springs into being. The chief theme is in the opening bars, and throughout the first few minutes you will hear it in a variety of tone colors; in its original form, and curiously inverted; in the bass and in the tenor voices of the orchestra.

Then, a little later, the same theme in a quaintly distorted form partakes of the character of a pious supplication, perhaps in mockery, perhaps in atonement for its former exuberance. But not for long . . . for a new figure, as bold and as gay as the first, elbows aside, as it were, the faintly ecclesiastical utterance. Never again through the movement can the bright spirits be restrained, and they rush on through all the orchestra's choirs to a swift and vigorous climax.

FOURTH MOVEMENT

It was characteristic of Brahms' quiet daring to use, for the finale of his symphony, an ancient dance form—the *passacaglia*.* It has been remarked that in this instance the judgment of the composer was open

* A *passacaglia* is an ancient dance form, the musical beauty of which attracted the attention of composers of serious music. A *passacaglia* is musical construction consisting essentially of a ground bass and variations. A ground bass is a note or phrase—in the *passacaglia* always extending two, four or eight measures—upon which series of harmonies and variations are built. In this form the ground bass may appear either in bass or treble; it is generally rather solemn in character, and its musical treatment is extremely elaborate. The *passacaglia* is closely related to the *chaconne,* or *ciaccona.* J. S. Bach made notable use of these and other ancient dance forms in his organ compositions. Brahms first introduced the *passacaglia* into the symphony.

to question, for if anywhere in the symphony clarity is essential, it is in the finale. The *passacaglia* is not a simple form, and in the hands of a composer less lucid in his musical expression than Brahms is in this instance, it might have meant the popular failure of his work.

Even if it were necessary deliberately to abstract one's attention from the magnificence of the finale as a whole, in order to follow the structural elements of the *passacaglia* form, the effort would well be repaid. But such a mental abstraction is not necessary. A listener knowing nothing, and caring less, about form and construction will be charmed, will be gripped and moved by this magnificent music. The musically initiated will be conscious, without effort, of both the technical structure and the musical beauty of the movement.

The first eight measures of the movement give us the ground bass of the *passacaglia*. It is sounded mightily in the brass and woodwind, and its first ornamentation appears immediately when on a repetition of the

theme it is contrasted with pizzicato strings. Again, it runs counter to a distinctly new and flowing melody far above it. Now the basic theme comes itself into the treble range, and through all versions, through all variations appears a definite growth, a working toward a climax— a form within a form.

And this growth is felt even when it appears in the diffident accents of the flute, wherein an increasing of emotional tenseness replaces that of dynamic effect. The same is true of the subdued choir of brass that presently intones a solemn phrase . . . a phrase replaced in a moment by the basic theme itself, put forth in powerful brazen accents by the same instruments that lately spoke so gently.

And once more as the final section of the movement begins, the brass with even augmented power blares forth defiantly against the acid commentary of the strings, the same potent utterance. Yet with each recurring emphatic statement of the theme, one feels there is a reserve, a something left unsaid, a something which *is* said finally, in gorgeous counterpoint and intoxicating rhythm, in the closing measures of the symphony.

Anton Bruckner

1824-1896

ANTON BRUCKNER, one of the most important composers of the last hundred years, was born at Ansfelden, not far from Linz in upper Austria. He was musically trained from childhood, first by his father, the village schoolmaster, later and more formally by teachers in Vienna and elsewhere. As a mere child he was accomplished both as organist and composer, and in later years held important posts as teacher, lecturer, and concert organist. His early life was made difficult by poverty, but such material trials were as nothing compared to the succession of disappointments and persecutions he experienced in his middle and later years. Chief of the disappointments was the coldness and bigotry which Viennese musicians exhibited toward his music, and the incredible difficulties, not only of getting an appreciative audience, but of persuading anyone to play his works.

Bruckner composed much music for the church, several important choral works, a notable string quartet; but it was his eight symphonies that eventually established him as a composer ranking in the same group with the greatest of the nineteenth century. The argument has been advanced that Bruckner's music is too strongly derivative from that of Richard Wagner; to which the Brucknerite counters with evidence that many of the passages apparently Wagner-inspired were actually written *before* the Wagnerian music from which they were supposed to derive. It is a fact, however, that Bruckner had a profound reverence for Wagner, both as man and musician. Wagner, in turn, was profoundly touched by this devotion, and, as for Bruckner's achievements as a composer, he had this reckless statement to make: "I know of only one who may be compared to Beethoven, and he is Bruckner." (Gabriel Engel: *The Life of Anton Bruckner*. Roerich Museum Press, New York.)

The friendship and admiration existing between Wagner and Bruck-

134

ner were not altogether a benefit to the latter. Out of his adoration for
the composer of the *Ring* operas, Bruckner had written his Third, sometimes called his "Wagner" Symphony, in which he actually quotes, ver-
batim so to speak, passages from Wagner. At the time, the enmity between Wagnerites and anti-Wagnerites was incredibly bitter. Bruckner
succeeded in antagonizing both; the one group by daring to write, as
they thought, like Wagner the almighty; the other, by afflicting them
(*sic*) with more Wagnerian music. But Vienna did not like Bruckner,
regardless of his Wagnerian references, and when at last his Third Symphony was performed, under his own direction, by the Vienna Society
of the Friends of Music, the audience, headed by a director of the Conservatory, first laughed, and then departed; and before the music was
finished there were not more than ten people left in the parquet. Among
these ten was Gustav Mahler, devoted disciple of Bruckner, who attempted to console the heart-broken composer, but in vain.

In spite of cruel disappointment, Bruckner continued working at his
symphonies and was almost finished with the last movement of the Sixth
when Hans Richter, the great conductor and admirer of Wagner, discovered the long-finished but unplayed Fourth, or "Romantic," while
visiting the composer. He admired it immediately and determined to
play it at the first opportunity. It was a magnificent success. Bruckner's
musical fortunes improved, everywhere but in his own country, from
that day onward. It is of passing interest to note that his Third Symphony was played in New York, under Anton Seidl, December 6, 1885,
some months before Vienna would listen to the composer. But he was
not without able protagonists, among them Karl Muck, Arthur Nikisch,
and Theodore Thomas.

Toward its close, this life that had seen so much of personal tragedy
was made happy and serene; it was even enlightened by a few belated
and innocent love affairs with young girls, whose proximity always
seemed inspiring to Herr Bruckner. These came to nothing. The aging
composer had honors heaped upon him; in them he rejoiced, and with
them, his work, and the faithful ministrations of a scolding but devoted
maid servant he lived out his days. Brahms, against whom his friends
had often tactlessly opposed him, stood outside the churchyard at the
funeral, muttering sadly of his own approaching end; Hugo Wolf, an-

other neglected genius, was refused admittance because he was not a
member of the societies whose representatives filled the church. The
body of Bruckner was taken to the old church of St. Florian, where he
had so often made music, and it was laid to rest under the great organ
that had served him so well.

Symphony No. 3 in D minor

ANTON BRUCKNER, like so many of those who elect to live by the art of
music, had his share and more than his share of misery during his life.
It is something of a relief to record that the Third Symphony at least
came into being at a time when the composer's poverty and unhappiness were at their minimum—indeed, at a period during which some
of his ambitions were realized and there was promise of happier years
ahead. In 1867 Bruckner succeeded to the post of professor of organ,
counterpoint, and composition at the Vienna Conservatory, a position
which gave him time and opportunity for composition and at the same
time a degree of security which left his mind and creative impulse free
to operate in his chosen field. Some years later he was named professor
of musical theory at the University of Vienna, and the circle of his admirers continually expanded. The musical intelligentsia, or at least that
part of it which had not been committed to the music of Brahms, found
in Bruckner's music something quite rare and wonderful, and the fact
that Richard Wagner also admired Bruckner's work did him no harm.

It was during this period of relative success—1873—that the Third
Symphony in D minor came into being. No sooner was it finished than
the composer hurried with the manuscript to Bayreuth seeking the approbation of Wagner. Apparently he was successful, for the present
symphony bears on its flyleaf the dedication "To Master Richard Wagner, in deepest reverence." Wagner's approval took a curious form.
Sometime before the "Meistersinger" was produced as an opera, Wagner
permitted Bruckner to include the finale of the work as a part of a concert program which the Austrian composer conducted at Linz. The first
complete production of "Meistersinger" did not come about until several years later.

The Third Symphony of Bruckner was played for the first time anywhere at a concert of the Society of the Friends of Music in Vienna, December 16, 1877. Bruckner himself conducted his work, though the remainder of the program was directed by the regular conductor of the Friends of Music, Dr. Josef Hellmesberger. Following that occasion there were two revisions of the symphony, and it is the final one, published in 1889, which is played today. In this score Bruckner contents himself with an orchestra of conventional size and instrumentation: woodwinds in pairs, four horns, three trumpets, three trombones, tympani, and strings.

FIRST MOVEMENT

Bruckner's is "musicians' music." The meat upon which a musician feeds is music, and if it is solid fare, tasty and nourishing, he cannot get enough of it. No symphony can be too long if it is profound, if it is honest, if it is done by the sure hand of a master craftsman, if it satisfies the canons of construction and style. Bruckner's symphonies fulfill these specifications, which helps to explain why they are sometimes difficult for the average listener to assimilate but a joy to the serious and thoughtful player and student. As the music of Bruckner is more and more frequently played, as it becomes integrated with the symphonic repertoire, it loses whatever forbidding qualities it might have had for the amateur and takes on much of the substantially satisfying and gratifying qualities that we have long since found in Bruckner's contemporary (and to a certain degree, rival), Johannes Brahms.

There is no story to be told, no picture to be limned, no heroic mood of exaltation or melancholy to be exploited in this music. It is music *per se*, music subjective and abstract, vital and richly colored. It is simply declarative rather than hortatory. Its persuasiveness lies in its logic rather than in any wildly emotional appeal. It convinces by an almost reticent sobriety rather than by tearing a passion to tatters. There are some, but few, moments of *Sturm und Drang*; still less of the turgid harmonies and over-complicated ideas which the composer's involved mental processes sometimes produced.

There are four preparatory measures in the strings, and presently the first part of the main idea on which the movement is constructed is delivered by the trumpet, which manages to be emphatic and gentle at the same time.

This part of the symphony is of more than ordinary interest because of the harmonic developments which circulate about a long organ point * on D held in the cellos and basses. When the second part of the main idea is eventually delivered by the full orchestra very powerfully, it follows this line:

And now again the composer employs the difficult but effective device of an organ point, now on A.

The second and contrasting theme of the movement is voiced by the violas and horn accompanied by a melodic figure in the upper strings. The thematic idea follows:

From this point onward the development of the movement takes place in formal style, in the course of which the basic ideas are analyzed, dissected, developed, and once more synthesized and re-presented.

SECOND MOVEMENT

Here is ingratiating music, grave but not melancholy, songlike and simple. The strings alone issue the first statement of the basic theme, which runs its sober course along this line:

* Organ point: a tone sustained in one voice while a variety of melodies or harmonies are played in the other voices; sometimes called a pedal point.

There is some growth of sonority, a well-marked change of pace, and the introduction of new but subsidiary material; but as the movement closes there is a return, at least by implication, to the opening mood and melody.

THIRD MOVEMENT

It has been mentioned here that there is no possible program, no reference to the material world, in this music. Yet one of Bruckner's warmest admirers and most profound students could find in the present movement reminders of a "bird's concert, in a lovely hour by fish pond and forest, after sunset." Surely this is German romanticism at its worst. True, there is a pastoral quality in this charming movement, and parts of it approch the common ordinary waltz, as, for example, this passage in the first violins with accompaniment pizzicato from the lower strings:

But even later on when woodwinds chirp so merrily it would require imagination of the most sentimental type to find anything resembling a bird's concert.

FOURTH MOVEMENT

Here if anywhere the music become declamatory as the most powerful voices of the orchestra give out this sonorous statement:

This attitude does not persist for long in the music, however, and it becomes even more persuasive, though less powerful, when we hear the kind of double simultaneous theme put forward by strings and horn:

This material is developed to almost heroic dimensions and the movement ends in sonorous majesty.

Symphony No. 4 in E flat ("ROMANTIC")

THE wheel of fortune turned violently for Bruckner when, on February
20, 1881, this lovely music was first performed, at Vienna, under the
devoted guidance of Hans Richter. Here was the first adequate performance of any of his symphonies, and listening to it was a spellbound audience, which, after each movement, compelled the diffident composer to
appear and bow to the applause. The symphony had been completed
almost seven years before; but Bruckner had revised it in 1878; and
the scherzo, the famous "hunting scherzo," had been inserted, though
it had not been a part of the original score.

After the first performance, the overjoyed composer rushed to Richter, and, embracing him, cried, "Take this"—pressing a coin into his
hand—"and drink a glass of beer to my health!" Richter, it is related,
wore the coin on his watch chain ever afterward.

The music of Bruckner is massive and mighty. At the risk of offend-
ing his active and admirable champions, it might even be said that at
times it is over-elaborated and by no means simple of comprehension.
The latter is not urged as an objection, but as a statement of fact.
Though more·and more lovers of music are coming, with each succeeding season, to a better understanding and appreciation of such music as
this, it must be admitted that Bruckner's works are not easy to assimilate, nor is there any way for the layman to develop an appreciation of
them except by repeated hearings. Such notes as logically come within
the compass of this book must therefore extend only to a general and
condensed impression of the work.

FIRST MOVEMENT

Gabriel Engel, in his valuable *Life of Anton Bruckner,* says in connection with the subtitle of this symphony, "There seems little doubt that the detailed 'program' or symphonic plot communicated to his circle of friends by Bruckner was a post-analysis influenced by no other than Wagner, who had even published a rather fantastic pictorial description of Beethoven's Ninth. It is at any rate silly to dilly-dally over the fitness of its details; for the 'Romantic' has so clear and effective a tale to tell that it has become the favorite vehicle for the introduction of Bruckner to a new audience. That the composer did not regard the program seriously is evident from his remark concerning the Finale: 'And in the last movement,' said he, 'I've forgotten completely what picture I had in mind.' The work possesses, however, an unmistakable unity hitherto without precedent in absolute music, for all four parts spring from the main theme, in the first movement. So logical and masterly is the development of this theme in the course of the work that the climax is not reached until the closing portion of the Finale."

This theme is slowly evolved out of the material with which the movement opens. The strings establish the tonality of the movement with a restrained pronouncement of a chord in E major; and almost at once the close-knit fabric of the music becomes discernible. Against the strings, a horn projects a call, and the imitative figures in the woodwind, based on this proclamation, are presently identified as the first theme. The second important thematic idea is sung by violas and later by cellos, against another and harmonizing melody of the same contours, voiced by the violins.

The entire movement is developed with regard to structural formality, and in the final passages, the theme which appeared at the beginning is vigorously recalled.

SECOND MOVEMENT

If by "romantic" we mean sentimental, then the second movement is the section which establishes most firmly the subtitle of the symphony; but if we choose to use the word in a somewhat musical sense, then any movement except the first could justify it, for the second, third, and fourth movements are rather free and unconventional in form. Mr.

Philip Hale, the always illuminating author of the Boston Symphony Orchestra program notes, describes this movement as "a sort of romanza built in three themes. The first is given out by the violoncellos; the second is a cantilena for violins, the third for strings and woodwind in full harmony."

There is, to be sure, nothing difficult of comprehension in this lovely and often lyrical movement; and if the song of the violins, in the second theme, does not carry conviction and significance to any sensitive heart, then no explanatory comment can aid it.

THIRD MOVEMENT

This is the famous "hunting scherzo" so enjoyably featured in the revised version of Bruckner's score. Always happy in writing for the horn, the composer here assigns to that versatile, if unreliable, instrument a series of characteristic calls which form the basis for the movement. The outlines of the movement approach the conventional, but the development of the thematic material is elaborate and free. The middle section, or trio, reveals a contrasting mood in moderated time and less emphatic rhythm. Then the bright hunting horn returns in the concluding section.

FOURTH MOVEMENT

Modeling almost as tangible as that of the sculptor is revealed in the fashioning of the fundamental musical idea of the movement. The phrases of the horns are joined and molded, and developed from their soft beginnings into a bright sentence stated by trumpets; then the whole orchestra drives forth the theme in an aggressive pronouncement. Now the whole orchestra is vitalized, and the texture of the music, though temporarily thinner, is brighter and more intricately woven. It grows simultaneously in sonority and elaboration, and arrives, after extended development, at a conclusion of magnificence and grandeur.

Symphony No. 5 in B-flat major

THERE is something suggestive of the slowness and inevitability of a glacier's movement in the manner by which Bruckner's symphonies came into being, achieved their final form, were ultimately given performance and now, so many years after his death, are moving with the same titanic power and mountainous slowness into the accepted repertoire of the symphony orchestra. The present work, sometimes subtitled "Tragic," occupied the composer during a period of several years. Upon its completion in 1877 Bruckner put it aside and a year later undertook to revise it. He never heard it performed, which perhaps was "tragic," for when it was first played on April 8, 1894, Franz Schalk conducting, the composer was too ill to attend the concert. He was then seventy years old. The first American performance of the work was given by the Boston Symphony Orchestra, Wilhelm Gericke conducting, December 27, 1901.

It has been remarked elsewhere that Bruckner's music is less easy of assimilation than some. It is rather curious that this symphony, though technically quite complicated indeed, is not so difficult of comprehension as certain other works of the same composer. Somehow the horizontal motion of this music helps to give it a clarity and vitality which are not always evident in the massive, the perpendicular, and monumental contours of the preceding "Romantic" Symphony and other works of Bruckner. Here too are symmetry and balance, thesis and antithesis: a questioning phrase almost always is associated with an answering one, an assertion always has its reply, a theme, its countertheme. Indeed, the richness and clarity of the counterpoint is perhaps the most distinguishing characteristic of the Fifth Symphony. Another factor which tends to emphasize the clarity and coherence of this work is the employment in the various movements of thematic material common to them all.

FIRST MOVEMENT

The introduction, adagio, establishes a melancholy, or at least contemplative, mood which is not essentially altered although it is strongly vitalized by the main section of the movement which follows it, allegro. Not even the introduction can be overlooked for thematic material. One of the important musical ideas appears almost at the beginning, in the somber voices of bassoons and violas supported by pizzicato scales in the low strings. There is a declamatory statement from woodwind and

strings in unison; then the chief theme of the introduction in the assertive trombones and glowering bassoons. There is some elaboration of
this idea with another thematic fragment in counterpoint above it; and
then we are led into the first movement proper. We are very soon informed by clarinets, violas and cellos of the basic idea of this movement. A contrasting subject, more leisurely in its unfolding, develops in

the string choirs pizzicati (the extensiveness with which Bruckner uses
the plucked strings in this work has suggested to some a title for it—the
"Pizzicato" Symphony). Now succeeds a great orchestral song of the
keenest emotional fervor and of somewhat happier significance than
the music which surrounds it. This long and lovely melodic line is handled, for the most part, in the first violins, whose tone is colored and
enriched by the voices of clarinet and flute, doubled in unison and in
octaves. The entire treasure of thematic ideas now having been exposed,
it is thoroughly, clearly, and beautifully developed into a melodic and
harmonic structure of impressive solidity and clear outline.

SECOND MOVEMENT

Again plucked strings support an introductory theme delivered by
the oboe, the accompanying figure recalling the use of a similar device

in the introduction of the first movement. A curious detail here is that
the melody is in $4/4$ time while the accompaniment is in $6/4$.

THIRD MOVEMENT

As the third movement begins, we find a striking instance of the thematic coherence of the work as a whole in that the basic idea of the

third movement scherzo is really a transformation of the pizzicato figure from the second movement, now in triple rhythm instead of the previous ⁶⁄₄. In writing the scherzo and the finale of this work, Bruckner
appears to have abandoned his customary leisurely habits, although
there is nothing to indicate that the movements were done in haste. The
scherzo, incidentally, was the second movement in the order of composition, the adagio having been written first, then the scherzo, then the
finale, and the first movement not until more than a year later.

FOURTH MOVEMENT

Structurally the fourth movement is somewhat complicated, although
aurally it does not seem so. Considerable use is made of thematic ideas
drawn from the introduction to the first movement, and also from the
first movement proper; and the fugal treatment is masterly. The main
theme of the first movement seems to be the note on which Bruckner
reaches his most triumphant climax, and we hear it given out in the
brass after a kind of chorale played by a separate stage band composed
of three trumpets, three trombones, four horns, and a tuba. Bruckner,
incidentally, directed that this band be separated from the main orchestra and raised on a platform behind it. This is seldom practical in the
concert hall, although it is sometimes done.

Symphony No. 7 in E major

BRUCKNER was fortunate enough to have as first interpreter of this noble work the distinguished conductor Artur Nikisch, who presented it in
Leipzig in 1884 only a few months after its completion. The symphony
was dedicated to Ludwig of Bavaria, who, perhaps through the influence of Richard Wagner, was well disposed toward Bruckner, as toward
the Titan of Bayreuth. The orchestration of the symphony is somewhat
unusual in that it employs, along with the usual strings and wind instruments, no less than four tubas and contrabass tuba. A recording of
the work made some years ago by the Minneapolis Symphony Orchestra under Eugene Ormandy brought about the presentation of the medal
of the Bruckner Society (the famous Kilenyi medal) to Mr. Ormandy
and to the then musical director of RCA Victor.

FIRST MOVEMENT

This music, like all of Bruckner's orchestral works, is highly subjective, and it is no more possible here than elsewhere to read into it anything beyond what the composer says in notes and bars and staves. It will do no violence to the spirit of the music, however, to suggest that it moves in an atmosphere that is deeply, if only implicitly, religious. We know that Bruckner was a man of profound devotion; we know his association with the organ and with the church; and we know something of his beliefs and convictions. There is no such religious celebration here as one finds in the "Reformation" Symphony of Mendelssohn; there is no such specific reference to the church; yet here music seems to serve the spiritual expression of a mind and heart that were in an almost medieval sense believing and devout. Here the talents of a musician are put at the service of his religious faith as if, like the Jongleur de Notre Dame, the composer had dedicated his act, however unworthy, to the God who had given him his talent. The basic impulse of the first

movement is found at the very beginning, incomplete but definable, and it grows in power and intensity with constant accretions of tone until it reaches a climax of resounding sonority. A contrasting idea is then pre-

sented in the woodwind, accompanied softly by restrained harmonies in the brass. The development is involved but nevertheless directed by the formal logic which generally characterizes a Bruckner first movement. There is a mighty crescendo and climax at the close.

SECOND MOVEMENT

Here is a hymn of heroic proportions. Sonorities suggestive of organ tone present the solemn tune which is the foundation of this movement.

A succession of melodies, all warmly sonorous, all grave and all beautiful, extend the movement to its climax, and at the end there is a remembrance of the beginning.

THIRD MOVEMENT

Even in this scherzo, which basically is motivated by a light-hearted and heavy-footed dance rhythm, the suggestion of the religious influence is not lacking. For centuries the dance was a part of church ceremonial, and the character of the music of this movement suggests such innocence and almost a crude choreography. The secondary theme of this movement, on which the whole middle section is based, is worthy of particular attention since it is one of the most beautiful Bruckner ever set to paper.

FOURTH MOVEMENT

The organist speaks again in this movement, both in the quasi-ecclesiastical character of the melodic elements and the great sonorities in which they are revealed. There are, again and again, echoes from the organ loft, with flashes almost of ecstasy superimposed upon the solemnities of the thematic material. The movement is rather formally developed but with great variety of orchestral color and remarkable dynamic contrasts. The climax comes in a kind of apotheosis of the second theme, yet the last thought that the composer leaves with us is the same one which he introduced at the beginning of the movement.

Symphony No. 9 in D minor

PERHAPS no music that we know has been the subject of more controversy or the object of more propaganda than the music of Anton Bruckner. Fierce feuds, often involving considerable personal bitterness, raged about this music, though the composer held himself aloof from them; and to this day there is still controversy, though it involves no personal animosities, and there is active and sustained propaganda for the music, carried on by the Bruckner Society of America. Johannes Brahms could not and would not have been a member of the European section of this Society, for it was he who said, "Bruckner? That is a swindle which will be forgotten a year or two after my death . . . after Wagner's death his party naturally had need of another pope, and they managed to find no better one than Bruckner. Do you really believe that anyone in this immature crowd has the least notion what these boa constrictors are about?" Hugo Wolf would have been welcomed into the Bruckner Society, however, for his remark, as exaggerated as that of Brahms, would well qualify him: "A cymbal crash by Bruckner is worth all the symphonies of Brahms with the Serenades thrown in." Contemporary debaters are more temperate, contemporary conductors are more receptive, contemporary audiences more patient than those of Bruckner's own time. Indeed, some of Bruckner's music was played in our country before Vienna ever heard it, and at the present time, largely because of the authority and prestige of Bruno Walter and the enterprise of Eugene Ormandy, certain symphonies of Bruckner, and of Mahler too, are finding their way into the standard orchestral repertoire.

There has been a controversy regarding this particular symphony, but this had to do not so much with its merit as with its authenticity. When the composer died he had not finished the Ninth Symphony, or at least had not composed a fourth movement. The exact condition in which the work stood at that time was not widely known; and the work was not performed until seven years later, in February, 1903, when Ferdinand Loewe, one of the most vigorous protagonists of Bruckner's music, played the symphony for the first time. It was no secret that Loewe had done some rearranging of the work, presumably necessary, and because of its unfinished condition it was assumed also that the Loewe edition was consonant with the composer's thought as manifested in his score. To many critics there was something curiously un-Brucknerish in the Ninth Symphony. No one seriously doubted its authenticity, however, until certain musicologists decided to examine the *Urtext*. Here, to their astonishment, they found that Loewe had drastically altered and perverted the music, distorted or inserted thematic material, reversed or canceled dynamic contrasts, conventionalized the harmony, and committed other varieties of musical mayhem. The investigators found that, excepting the lack of a fourth movement, the music was by no means unfinished. Anyone unterrified by the formidable title which the musicologists Haas and Orel gave to their work may study *"Anton Bruckner: Sämtliche Werke Vol. 9 Kritische Gesamtausgabe im Auftrage der Generaldirektion der Nationbibliothek und der Internationalen Bruckner Gesellschaft herausgegeben von Robert Haas und Alfred Orel."*

The discovery of the original version of the symphony, together with the persistence with which conductors chose to play the Loewe version, led to an interesting and possibly unique concert at which both versions were performed before a qualified audience in an effort to determine which was the more convincing as authentic Bruckner. The music was played by the Munich Philharmonic Orchestra conducted by Siegmund von Hausegger.* In the judgment of virtually all hearers, the unretouched, if incomplete, score was vastly superior and the International Bruckner Society decided that "because of the overwhelming impression made by the original version at its first performance, the Ninth Symphony, in the exact form in which it was left by the master, should no longer be kept from the musical world."

The Loewe version of the Ninth was performed in this country for the first time at Chicago under the direction of the late Theodore Thomas in 1904. The original version was presented in New York in 1934.

Unfinished though it is, this symphony is of heroic proportions, and for the most part quite leisurely, even occasionally lethargic, in its movement. It required years for Bruckner to accomplish it. He began work on it, apparently, in 1887, and at the time of his death in 1896 the work was only three-fourths completed, though he had worked nine years on it. Unsympathetic souls might say that it requires almost as long to play it.

FIRST MOVEMENT

Not a single theme, but a complex of themes is made the basic material upon which Bruckner lays the design of his massive music. There is a long introduction, based on a straightforward idea projected by the horns against a translucent background of tremulous strings. After

* It is interesting to observe that a recorded version of this symphony by the Munich Philharmonic Orchestra conducted by von Hausegger is available on Victor Records.

some mutation this idea is temporarily abandoned for a lighter and brighter one put forward by the violins as follows:

Various other short thematic elements are introduced, and upon the last of these a climax of impressive proportions is erected as a prelude to the most important idea in the movement—a very powerful, even noble utterance poured forth *fortississimo*.

These are the basic elements of the movement. These constitute the raw material out of which the composer weaves an orchestral texture, luxurious, high-piled, and thick, but brightened by masterly touches of instrumental color. The realization of the movement comes about at a leisurely pace, and the hearer has plenty of time to study its detail.

SECOND MOVEMENT

The second movement is a scherzo. It is curious, perhaps, that Bruckner, who has so often been berated for the length and tediousness of some of his music, was nevertheless most appealing in rapidly moving music, although even his scherzos are often too long for their material and as insistent and repetitious as an oration by Hitler. The present movement should not be described quite so harshly, however, though the whole first section, which is rather long to begin with, is repeated in its entirety.

THIRD MOVEMENT

The final movement—not, however, a finale—is one of the profoundly introspective and somewhat melancholy utterances that occur frequently in the music of Bruckner. It is wonderfully melodious, built on the broadest lines, moving almost languidly, and utterly devoid of any kind of excitement except the inner spiritual response that all beautiful things must elicit from those sensitive enough to perceive them. This music paints no picture, tells no story except in its revelation of the workings of a noble, thoughtful, and articulate soul.

Ernest Amédés Chausson

CHAUSSON was one of the rarest of musical spirits; a man of wealth and sophistication, who, giving up a lucrative and more or less respectable profession—the law—devoted himself and his sensitive discerning gifts to the pursuit of art. Like an obedient French son, Chausson studied for and was admitted to the bar because of his parents' wish that he do so before devoting himself exclusively to music. He was in classes under Massenet when, at the age of twenty-five, he entered the Conservatoire at Paris. The teaching of Massenet did him little good, and certainly aroused no enthusiasm in him. Fortunately, César Franck was also on the staff of the Conservatoire at the time, and perhaps sensing in Chausson a modesty and hatred of ostentation as well as musical gifts somewhat similar to his own, the kindly Franck took the young composer into the little group of students who believed in and surrounded him, and for three years Chausson sat at the feet of the master.

The French preoccupation with music for the opera and the stage, combined with Chausson's own lack of assertiveness and confidence in himself, probably account for the fact that his music was long neglected by the public. The music itself is not of a type which would normally impress the French musical public. It is rarely dramatic, never flamboyant; and it was suspected of Wagnerian influences. Strangely enough, it was the great German conductor Arthur Nikisch who helped bring Chausson's music to an appreciative public; later Ysaÿe, the Belgian violinist, and Colonne, the distinguished French musician, helped the good work along.

Chausson's standing as a composer was improving with rapidity when his unfortunate death occurred. He was riding a bicycle on his estate at Limay, and losing control of the machine, coasted rapidly downhill and crashed into a stone wall. He died of a fractured skull.

Symphony in B-flat major

THE French are, as a people, often credited with a love of logic, a certain emotional volatility, an ingrained respect for form. If we concede these virtues, it is not easy to understand why this music was so difficult to establish in the favor of the French public. It has the logic of a syllogism, the symmetry, the deft emphasis, and the formally disciplined emotional appeal of a Ciceronian oration and, in addition, the cunningly woven, glowing colors of a Gobelin tapestry. Yet the French public would have none of it for a long time, though certain French musicians appreciated it and asked for it the attention of all who would listen. It was brought to this country by Vincent d'Indy in 1905, while he was guest conductor of the Boston Symphony Orchestra—though the first American performance was given at Philadelphia. It was one of Chausson's last major works, dating from 1890, which makes it two years younger than the César Franck symphony, and it antedates by seven years the composer's death. The music was dedicated to Henry Lerolle, a famous painter and an intimate of Chausson.

The resemblance between this symphony and the D Minor of Franck, in some details, is quite obvious and certainly no more accidental than similar resemblances in the works of other admirers of Franck, such as d'Indy, Dukas, and Saint-Saëns. The symphony in elliptical, circular, or, as it has come to be known, cyclic form was successfully established by César Franck, and his followers were quick to perceive its logic, its opportunity for employing reminiscence to reinforce emotional impact, its unity, grace, and strength. Beyond the employment of the cyclic form, the fastidious craftsmanship, and certain minor details of orchestration, resemblance between this music and the Franck symphony ends. In melody and harmony, in thematic invention and development, the work is characteristic of its composer and of no one else. It has been aptly said of Chausson's music that it "is saying constantly the word '*cher*.' His passion is not fiery. It is always affectionate, and this affection is gentle agitation in discreet reserve." One may not always agree with this dictum insofar as the present music is concerned, for there are climaxes and passionate utterances of notable power and intensity;

there are evocations of orchestral power that approach the limit of the instruments' reserves, but they are always controlled, directed, and managed with superb finesse.

FIRST MOVEMENT

This symphony, like Franck's, begins with a grave introduction, and it is well to remember the thematic basis of this section—heard in the clarinet, horn, and lower strings—for the cycle of the symphony begins exactly here, and this particular idea will have more importance later. In the first movement proper two basic ideas are presented and are developed in rather formal manner, but with fascinating interplay of color accomplished by a surprising variety of instruments.

SECOND MOVEMENT

Chausson's second movement employs an English horn and so did Franck's; there the resemblance between the two movements ends. There are two chief melodic elements and several subsidiary ones, all of them sung by the orchestra with restrained passion—sometimes by the strings, sometimes by a combination of the English horn and clarinet, sometimes in the wooing voice of the horns. One of the really impressive climaxes of the symphony is developed out of these melodies, but the movement ends quietly.

THIRD MOVEMENT

The third movement, like the first, has a rather brief introduction notable for the vigor of its utterance and the swiftness of its pace. The basic idea is realized by the dark-voiced basses, and echoed in the upper strings. Intimations of a further thematic idea are insinuated; its full version finally appears in the voice of the oboe. This material is expanded in a series of long crescendos accomplished not only by increasing the power of each instrument but by adding, with remarkable deftness, one instrument after another—a treatment which not only extends the possible duration of a crescendo but appears to increase its final power. There is a wonderful peroration, in which the very opening bars as well as much subsequent material of the symphony are beautifully articulated into a resounding finale.

Carlos Chávez

CHÁVEZ is certainly the most widely known and beyond any doubt the most enterprising of Mexico's musicians. He has been absorbed in music since childhood and had written a symphony before he was out of his teens. Music in Chávez's adolescent years did not fare so well in Mexico, but its renaissance in that country possibly began when, in 1921, the state commissioned Chávez to compose a genuinely Mexican musical work. This resulted in the creation of a Mexican ballet called *El Fuego Nuevo* (*The New Fire*), a work which philosophically at least was the outgrowth of the revolution in Mexico, which began in 1910 and perhaps is not yet complete.

This ballet, as well as his first string quartet, established Chávez as a musical force of no mean importance. He traveled and studied for several years prior to 1930, and on his return to his native Mexico became Director of the National Conservatory, Chief of the Department of Fine Arts, and Conductor of the Symphony Orchestra of Mexico. The difficulties of the last-named position were such as to break the heart of a lesser man, for the conductor practically was required, among other things, to show his violinists how to hold a violin. The undaunted Chávez, however, made a fine orchestra of his willing, eager, but untutored personnel. Perhaps the happiest circumstance in Mr. Chávez's life was his meeting with Leopold Stokowski and the enthusiastic support and opportunities which Stokowski gave him. Stokowski presented, and presented magnificently, Chávez's best-known and finest work, the ballet *H.P.*, and saw to it that Chávez had opportunities to conduct the best orchestras of the United States.

Sinfonia de Antigona

ALTHOUGH this music does not follow the conventional pattern of the symphony and is rather recklessly free in style, the composer insists that "it is a symphony, not a symphonic poem." It was synthesized from incidental music written by Chávez for a presentation in Mexico of Sophocles' tragedy *Antigone*. Mr. Chávez, in a rather cryptic comment on the music, discloses that it was suggested by the tragedy; that it is not programmatic in that "the character of Antigone, her self-confidence, defiance, heroism, and martyrdom, are expressed by the symphony as a whole, not successively." He goes on in a still more cryptic vein to say that "the most elementary musical materials serve for this music, which could not be grandiloquent. Bare and elemental, it could not be expressed by laconic strength, just as what is primitive is reduced to its elements because it is primitive."

The theme at the beginning of the symphony is emphatically of interest as it is sung by the English horn:

But it is not the principal theme of the movement, which occurs considerably later on. The basic musical idea is proposed by the solo oboe joined by other woodwinds. It goes like this:

A contrasting theme, on which the development of the first part of the symphony is based, is given to the violins in ⅔ time:

Observing Mr. Chávez's disclaimer of any program for this symphony, it is difficult to make any contributions to the listener's understanding other than to indicate the basic musical ideas which go into the texture of the work. The basis for the whole work is found almost entirely in the quotations given here, plus an idea which motivates the slow section of the work, and is assigned to the bass flute, proceeding as follows:

The whole tissue of the brief symphony develops out of these ideas.

Sinfonia India

ALTHOUGH this work is not as self-conscious and conventional as the *Sinfonia de Antigona,* it is perhaps a more valid, genuine, and spontaneous art work. It politely bows to the sonata form, which is the only justification for regarding it as a symphony, but it is earthy and indigenous, honest and Mexican, which cannot be said of all of Chávez's music. Here too Chávez uses native Mexican Indian melodies, and they would be difficult to find in any other of his important works. He uses, too, a certain number of Mexican Indian instruments, particularly among the percussion. It may be interesting to trace out on the piano the several important Indian or mestizo melodies upon which Chávez bases this short but finely wrought work. Here is an important melody that occurs in the first part of the symphony and which is a tune common among the Huicholes, a Mexican Indian tribe:

The contrasting theme is a pleasant melody indeed, taken from the folk music of the Yaqui Indians of the state of Sonora:

You will notice too, after the above themes have been somewhat exploited, an arresting pronouncement of the horn out of which develops another melody of the Sonora Indians, which goes as follows:

And in the finale of the symphony one finds a forthright melodic idea which Mr. Chávez heard among the Indians living along the Gulf of California:

On this melody the climax of the symphony is based.

Vincent d'Indy

1851–1931

V INCENT D'INDY lived through a period which saw the rise and decline of more than one musical reform and revolt. It is astonishing, somehow, to find that he was a veteran of the Franco-Prussian War, knew Liszt, Brahms, Franck; and was present at the first performance of Wagner's *Ring* operas; yet lived through the World War I, knew the music of Stravinsky and Ravel and Schönberg, and, it seems, left us only yesterday.

The composer was born at Paris, and died there. As an obedient son, he studied for the bar at the wish of his parents, though his musical inclinations were strong. His father was not unsympathetic to music, and played violin himself; on the death of his mother, d'Indy was entrusted to the care of his grandmother, who was an excellent musician and taught him much. He became a member of an orchestra, playing timpani; later won an appointment as a chorusmaster, and finally studied under César Franck at the Conservatoire. He was not satisfied at the school, and became a private pupil of Franck.

In 1905, d'Indy was invited to conduct a series of concerts in America, with the Boston Symphony Orchestra. He accepted, and appeared in Boston, Philadelphia, Baltimore, Washington, and New York, playing many of his own works with conspicuous success. The composer wrote a number of books, among them a life of his friend and teacher, César Franck; a biography of Beethoven; and technical works on music. He composed much chamber music, as well as choral, and some beautiful things for the piano.

"His attitude toward his art," remarked the late Lawrence Gilman, "was almost priestly in its elevation; yet he was richly human and tender—exerting, when he chose, a passionate and far-sweeping eloquence. He was a warm colorist whose sense of design was unfaltering; a poet whose discourse betrayed, at its best, an unforgettable nobility."

Symphony for Orchestra and Piano
on a French Mountain Air

VINCENT D'INDY was a perceptive, discriminating, and fastidious artist, appreciative of the particular beauties of music other than his own and yet relatively uninfluenced by anything but his own artistic convictions. Though it is possible to find in his music tendencies that reflect the romanticism of his time, it is likewise possible to point out a stylistic purity amounting to austerity. He was an artist of patrician taste with sufficient confidence in himself to be himself. If there is any definite influence exercised by any other composer upon the music of d'Indy, it is that of his master, César Franck, and here only to the extent that the cyclic form developed by Franck, because of its rounded symmetry and inevitable logic, appealed to d'Indy's orderly and disciplined thought processes.

FIRST MOVEMENT

The piano part in this symphony is of such importance as thoroughly to justify the inclusion of the instrument in the title of the work; yet while the piano is most important of all instruments in the orchestra, it is still part of the orchestra, integrated with it, and at no time does the music suggest such a relationship between piano and orchestra as one finds in the concerto. The piano here is an orchestral color, albeit a very dominant one, and technically the part requires the services of an artist of virtuoso stature; but this part is never really detached from or independent of the orchestra. Nor must one expect, in a proper performance, to find the piano standing out in relief against the mountainous orchestral tone.

The French mountaineer song on which most of the symphony is thematically based presents itself almost at the beginning, sung with pensive accent but rather lively rhythm by the English horn. Fragments of it are scattered about through the orchestra, and eventually a sweeping melody derived from the mountain song is entrusted to low woodwind and strings, overlaid with the brighter color of the piano's arpeggios. Finally the melody is stated boldly by the piano itself, and here we have a clear revelation of the basic material from which virtually the entire symphony is constructed. Nor is the second and subsidiary theme less clearly enunciated. It comes after a bit in a rather bizarre tone color compounded of piccolo, horns, and harp, animated by an accompaniment in the strings and decorated by broken chords from the piano. There are instrumental dialogues and debates, always in freshened colors and intensified dynamics, and a climax as spectacular as a snow-capped mountain, glittering with flashing passages for woodwinds, harp, and piano.

SECOND MOVEMENT

What is meant by the cyclic form is once again evident at the beginning of this movement, which opens with the piano in a little tune the derivation of which can easily be perceived since it is a variant of the mountain song upon which the entire symphony is based. A new series of elaborations of this melody now develops with kaleidoscopic changing of orchestral colors and the development of varying and unexpected rhythms.

THIRD MOVEMENT

If anywhere in this symphony a certain programmatic significance could be discerned it would be in the third movement, where the atmosphere of gaiety, the riotous orchestral color, and excited rhythms could readily suggest a festival of mountain folk. Still it is possible to observe the little song, in its various mutations, which is the germinal idea of the entire work. There are short periods of a recurring sober mood with some references to the second movement, and many to the theme of the first; but the movement and the symphony end in great good humor.

Symphony No. 2 in B flat

IT IS curious to recall that Vincent d'Indy, whose music we are accustomed to regard as rather precious and perhaps more than a little obscure, derived his musical impulses from the great men of his time whom we have considered as rocks of solid conservatism, whose works have become classics of the contemporary orchestral repertoire. D'Indy studied with such people as Marmontel and Lavignac; he sought out and knew Johannes Brahms; he solicited the acquaintance of Duparc, who dutifully introduced him to Richard Wagner; later on he importuned the attention of César Franck, with whom he studied at the Conservatoire and later as a private pupil.

We in our country are inclined to forget that, musically speaking, we knew d'Indy rather well. We are also likely to forget that he was partly of Negro origin. We should remember that he has given to the world of music something in almost every form of music and, in addition, was a teacher whose influence has been by no means inconsiderable. He was keenly interested in ancient music, particularly that of the church, and we have to thank him for many transcriptions and revisions of music of this type. As a lecturer he was interesting and informative; as an editor he exhibited a discriminating taste and profound musicianship, and we must thank him for intelligible editions of the works of Monteverde, Rameau, and Gluck. We should venerate his memory also for the magnificent concerts that he gave to us in the United States in 1905 and again in 1921. The symphony which we have under observation was first performed in America in a concert of the Philadelphia Orchestra December 31, 1904; it was heard again under the direction of the composer at a concert of the Boston Symphony Orchestra on December 2, 1905, and a few days later at a concert of the Philadelphia Orchestra as well as at subsequent concerts of the same orchestra in Baltimore, Washington, and New York. Unquestionably the most notable concert of all these was that at which d'Indy appeared as guest conductor of the Chicago Symphony Orchestra December 30 and 31, 1921, when he played not only the Second Symphony but three other works of his own composition: the prelude to *Fervaal*, *"La Queste de Dieu"* from *La Légende de Saint-Christophe*, and the *Variations Symphoniques, Istar*.

FIRST MOVEMENT

At the risk of being redundant, one must point out that this symphony, like almost all of those by musicians who have studied under the beneficent influence of César Franck, is cyclic in character—which is to say that the entire work is ultimately derived from a single germinal idea presented in its many metamorphoses, subjected to many an emotional variant, but underlying almost every movement of the whole work. This is not to say that the basic theme of the work is every now and then baldly and boldly presented to the listener in its pristine form. On the contrary, the underlying idea of this or any symphony in the cyclic form is often suggested or presented in fragmentary form or merely intimated, yet at the same time it must and does vitalize the whole work, movement by movement. One must recognize that in the cyclic form there are two ways of giving vitality and reality to the motif that makes the symphony go. One is broad, frank statement of the thematic idea; the other is the use of derivations, perversions, and mutations of the thematic idea which nevertheless leave it recognizable.

In this instance there is an introduction of some dignity which in its rather devious way presents two musical ideas which, as we shall see, form the whole basis for the symphony. The first is clear and obvious and bold and strong, presented by the lower strings with the assistance of the harp:

The second of the two musical ideas which vitalize the symphony will be heard in the wind instruments with the melodic line most clearly stated in the flute:

These two ideas are exploited to a considerable degree and then the first movement proper, the vitalizing element of which is the second theme quoted above, gets under way with its basic idea stated boldly by the solo horn.

From this point onward the development is perhaps conventional, but marvelously decorated with the warmest and most brilliant colors of the orchestra. Unless one cares to follow a score measure by measure, note by note, there is little point in outlining the various mutations, translations, transpositions, and other devices employed by the composer to exhibit the ideas that grow out of the basic theme. Having detected in

its germinal form the basic idea of the movement, one will certainly experience no difficulty in watching its agglutinations, simplifications, developments, and translations throughout the movement.

SECOND MOVEMENT

The composer indicates that the movement should be played not too slowly. Just about at the time when one begins to wonder where the nexus between this movement and its predecessor may lie, a development of the secondary theme of the first movement presents itself first in the bass clarinet, and then in the strings. There is a livelier and more vital section involving both harp and strings, pizzicati, and then a highly interesting motif derived ultimately from the first theme of the symphony. It looks like this:

THIRD MOVEMENT

One of the most interesting details of the third movement is the thematic idea presented with a certain straightforwardness by the solo viola accompanied by its companions among the lower strings. This ingratiating song of the viola is not so far removed in character from the

Modéré

mf très simplement

Viola

folk song, and perhaps is vaguely reminiscent of some of the mountain airs which d'Indy on more than one occasion incorporated into his music. Even when interrupted by the wind instruments, particularly the horn, this nostalgic song continues obscurely. Here there is a temptation to romanticize, for surely this music sets free the imagination and encourages the sentimental. One's reaction to this music is as one chooses. The scholar can and may find in it the perfection of form and the sure-handed skill that marks the master craftsman. Those who see in music the beauty and conviction of human emotion will likewise find satisfaction here; but perhaps this music will be most ingratiating to him who can listen to music objectively, weighing and evaluating both its formal structure and its emotional content; and in balancing these, this listener at least will not be disappointed.

FOURTH MOVEMENT

The fourth movement, which is expected to be played in a very slow tempo and in $\frac{4}{4}$ time, is basically derived from thematic material introduced in the preceding sections of the symphony. Here is perhaps the final justification of the so-called "cyclic" style of symphonic writing, and yet here too d'Indy does violence to a canon of polyphonic music—to wit, a fugue is always lively, always complicated, always a *coup*, at least for the composer. Here the fugal treatment is first of all slow, if not to say labored; it is not involved and though it sounds very impressive it is actually quite simple in structure. Fundamentally this lumbering fugue is based on a subject which you will hear in the low strings and sounds like this:

Lent ($\quarternote$=56)

sfz   *p*

Developments of this figure lead to a superb climax not only of the movement but of the whole symphony, which the composer marks, not inaptly, *Lent et largement chanté.* Somehow out of all the self-conscious derivations, mutations, and cyclical seekings of the symphony, the composer evolves at this moment a period of grandeur and magnificence rare indeed in music, and particularly in music of the French school. Here the orchestra really sounds forth as only a great orchestra, adequately instructed by measures and notes and rests and bars and accents, can sound forth; and the final bars of this movement justify with their swift pace and tense vigor all the laboriously correct, perfect, and even beautiful measures that have gone before. It is as if in the final measures the composer really appreciated the material that had fallen to his hand, and he builds of them a noble and towering edifice of tone.

Antonín Dvořák

1841–1904

ANTONÍN DVOŘÁK was born on September 8, 1841, the son of an inn-
keeper of Mühlhausen in Bohemia. His father had destined him to
succeed to his estate, but, as the inn dispensed music as well as hospi-
tality (through the offices of the bands of itinerant musicians who occasionally played for the entertainment of villagers and guests), something stirred within the boy, and, perhaps before he realized it, he had
set his heart upon the precarious career of a musician instead of looking to the complacent comfort that was no doubt assured the proprietor
of a village caravansary.

On his own initiative the boy Dvořák persuaded the village schoolmaster to teach him to play the violin and to sing, and presently he was
allowed to sing in the church, and to play, too, on special occasions.
When he was twelve years old, he was sent by his father to Zlonitz, a
town not far from his birthplace, where he was given the opportunity
to proceed in his music under the tutelage of the local organist and the
discipline of an uncle. Here Dvořák's musical education really began;
here he learned the fundamentals of organ and pianoforte playing, musical theory, harmony, extemporization, and other branches of the art.

The elder Dvořák gave the boy permission to go to Prague to study
music with a view toward making it his life work. In October, 1857, he
did so, entering in organ school and barely living on the small allow-
ance which his father was able to give him. Even this soon stopped, and
now Antonín's ability to play upon the violin stood him in good stead,
for with it he was able to keep body and soul together, and, meanwhile,
to join an orchestra; now he was brought in contact with the masterpieces of music, and, as a viola-player later, came under the influence
of the composer and conductor Smetana.

Dvořák probably never dreamed of making his way in the musical
world as a virtuoso; composition was the field which more particularly

appealed to him, and neither hunger nor poverty, nor the lack of the tools of his craft, could prevent his steady laboring in this direction. He was helped by several kind friends, however, and attained sufficient standing as a musician to be judged worthy of the post of organist at St. Adalbert's church in Prague. He accepted this position in 1873, left the orchestra in which he had been playing, married, and settled down to work harder than ever.

Not until he had reached the age of thirty-two did Dvořák come into notice as a composer, although during his years of quiet yet intense labor he had developed greatly. A patriotic cantata was the vehicle which brought to him the attention of musicians, and, fond as he was of the national musical idiom, Dvořák made a striking success of it. His rise to prominence really dates from this event. As a result of it he obtained both more substantial emoluments and the friendship of musicians whose position was already unassailable. Among the latter was Brahms who, as a commissioner appointed to pass upon musical works submitted for a prize of an annual pension, came upon certain duets of Dvořák which fascinated him not only because of their general musical excellence but by their demonstration of the composer's knowledge of Bohemian national musical characteristics.

It was not long before Dvořák became known in England and in America. In 1892 he was invited to accept the post as director of the National Conservatory of New York; he came to America, and held this position until 1895. Returning to his native Bohemia, he became head of the Conservatory of Prague, where he remained until his sudden death on May 1, 1904.

Symphony No. 1 in D major

THIS book makes no effort to trifle with the science of musicology, which is exceeded in dullness only by the science of economics; nor is musical history of great interest to the author or to those who for one reason or another are beguiled into reading the book. Nevertheless, on occasion it is necessary, for the sake of resolving certain confusions, to trespass diffidently upon the arid areas which the musicologist and the historian regard as exclusively their own.

Because we hear only five of Dvořák's symphonies, and of these the fifth most frequently, it is often assumed that Dvořák wrote only five symphonies. The fact is that he wrote nine. Some of the nine are wisely suppressed, not willfully, but by the censorship which time, taste, and judgment combine to impose. Here is a brief chronology which may be of interest to the historically minded: Dvořák's first two symphonies, one in C minor and one in B-flat, were composed in 1865; the third, in E-flat, in 1873; the fourth, in D minor, in 1874; the fifth, in F major, in 1875; the sixth, in D major, in 1880; the seventh, in D minor, in 1885; the eighth, in G major, in 1889; and the ninth, and last, in E minor, in 1893. As finally edited, the sixth symphony, in D major, Opus 60, is now programmed and regarded as Dvořák's First Symphony; the seventh symphony, in D minor, Opus 70, is programmed as the Second Symphony; the fifth, in F major, Opus 76, is regarded as the composer's Third Symphony; the eighth, in G major, Opus 88, is now listed as his Fourth Symphony; and his last work in this form, the famous symphony "From the New World," in E minor, Opus 95, is identified as the Fifth Symphony.

Composers have many qualities in common with creative artists in other fields, not the least of which is, frequently, a marked inclination to denounce and disown the get of their early creative passion. Sometimes the creative artist withholds and restrains his impulse to work in the great forms until he feels that his powers have fully matured. As the art of making a symphony became more sophisticated, it happened more and more frequently that the composer awaited the full blossoming of his talent before undertaking this highly developed musical form. It is remembered that Brahms, with all his "long, long thoughts," did not undertake his first symphony until he was more than forty years old, and Dvořák, though in truth he had written two symphonies by the time he was twenty-five, chose to forget them and, by applying the formula of the survival of the fittest, acknowledged finally but five of the nine symphonies he wrote. Occasionally it happens that the composer is wrong; more frequently it happens that the public is wrong when early works or works which their creator regards as secondary are allowed to relapse into desuetude. The first three symphonies of Tchaikovsky, for example, were all but forgotten until recently Victor, in conformity with its laudable purpose of making all the music of all great composers available in recorded form, brought about both the public performances and the recordings of the Russian master's earlier works in the symphonic form: which, of course, had been obscured by the persistent, and in a sense unfortunate, popularity of the Fourth, Fifth, and Sixth Symphonies. Similarly, the recording company has made available certain symphonies of Dvořák other than the "New World" which, through its popularity, had obscured the virtues of its predecessors. Generally speaking, conductors are unwilling to give to unknown works (except contemporary works) the time and study necessary to an adequate presentation, and only the lure of a recorded performance can persuade our *maestri* to look beyond the certainties of a Schubert B minor, a Dvořák E minor, or a Tchaikovsky F minor to the problematical success of unfamiliar works. The recording company, therefore, is entitled to the gratitude not only of people who are interested in a collection of recorded music, but the gratitude also of the concert public who, were it not for the pressure exerted by the recorders upon conductors, would never hear the less familiar works of the great composers.

Geographically it is a long way from Prague to Glasgow, though not so far from Glasgow to Dublin; but Dvořák managed to traverse this triangle in almost everything that he wrote—and with occasional excursions to the deep south of the United States. In almost all of his music there are certain characteristics common to Czech, Scottish, Irish, and American Negro music. The most notable of these are, first, a kind of innocence in melodic invention; second, a well-defined type of syncopation; third, a type of phrasing which has been defined as the "Scotch snap"—though this particular cadence is common to Scotch, Welsh, Irish, and American Negro music.

FIRST MOVEMENT

One may observe all of these qualities in the very first subject of the first movement of the symphony, which is proposed by the lower strings.

This contagious tune spreads throughout the orchestra and has imposed upon it much of the limitless variety of color, much of the variety of articulation that a modern orchestra makes possible. In contra-

distinction to this ingratiating idea, the second subject is proposed, and this one has a dual character—a kind of Jekyll and Hyde creature, Mr. Hyde being presented first in the warmly colored utterance of horns and cellos:

Dr. Jekyll, let us say in one of his rare sentimental moments, is represented in the song of the oboe which presently follows:

How Dvořák exploits the potentialities of this material is tersely described by Donald Tovey: "The development begins with one of the most imaginative passages Dvořák ever wrote. No listener can fail to be impressed with its long-sustained chords, from the depths of which fragments of the first theme arise until the basses put them together in a dramatically mysterious sequence, which suddenly breaks off with a masterly and terse working up of the energetic auxiliary themes."

The development of a theme by synthesizing its fragments is quite characteristic of Dvořák. Even in this symphony, so long preceding the familiar and always lovely "New World," one can observe the unexpected but logically satisfying sequence in which particles of the thematic material fly together and join themselves, just as the solid elements in a solution suddenly, under the influence of a catalyst, join together in logical, geometrical, mathematical, and perfect form.

SECOND MOVEMENT

The second movement, after a short introduction, reveals a melody quite comparable in its emotional appeal to the famous "Largo" of the Fifth Symphony. The violin choir is charged with responsibility for this lovely song—a theme of a poignant beauty that makes extended comment quite superfluous. A series of almost Schubertian modulations transpires, but these charming mutations lead back inevitably to this appealing song which is the theme of the movement:

THIRD MOVEMENT

The third movement is in rather conventional form but is by no means conventional in content. The abandon of Bohemian folk dancing is the spirit which moves this music. The movement is invested with a fiercely determined happiness; a vigorous, even violent, rhythm that will brook no interruption. Yet it is interrupted for a contrasting moment of tender sentiment—a breathing space sweetly reflective, almost sentimental. The driving rhythms of the opening return and end the episode.

FOURTH MOVEMENT

Energy is the essence of the third movement, but in the fourth it reaches a new, unexceeded, and unexpected degree of intensity. What was a vital pulsation now becomes a driving force, and it is a force not associated necessarily with the dynamic powers of the orchestra but rather with the inexplicable feeling of life and motion which rhythms can create independently of the intensity of sound. As Dr. Tovey aptly remarks, this section of the symphony "is admirably endowed with that quality that is the rarest of all in post-classical finales—the power of movement. . . . Dvořák had the classical secret of movement, which is not a power that can be obtained at the expense of higher qualities, for it is one of the highest." There are two thematic ideas involved in this section of the work, and it is in these that the composer exploits the suggestion of restless motion which gives the movement its life. The first is proposed without overemphasis—in fact, pianissimo—and is heard at the beginning of the movement:

The second, with its remarkable elasticity and verve, comes a little later:

These are developed into a finale of that particular kind of brilliance, achieved partly by the shrewdest kind of orchestration and partly by natural thematic development, which we have learned to associate with the music of the great Czech master.

Symphony No. 2 in D minor

IT IS fashionable, among the cognoscenti, to discount Dvořák as a mere entertainer of the groundlings, or at best as old-fashioned, a minor prophet, a composer who has achieved extinction through popularity. It is true that too many of us know him only through the "New World" Symphony, the "Slavonic Dances," and "Humoresque"; and this is unfortunate because other works of Dvořák bear within themselves both the seeds of greatness and the elements of popularity. His music is almost always alight with incandescent passion, full of singularly touching melody, animated with vital rhythms, and most of all, informed with a spirit that is touched with nobility, moved by conviction, and directed by sincerity.

Laughter and tears are never far apart in Dvořák's music, and the D minor Symphony, while it generally moves in an atmosphere of melancholy or at least of deep introspection, has its surprising contrasts of brief joys and happy incidents.

The first performance of the D minor Symphony came about under the happiest of circumstances and was distinctly a triumph for the composer. The date was April 22, 1885, scarcely more than a month after Dvořák completed it. "The enthusiasm at the close of the work was such as is rarely seen at a Philharmonic concert," said the London *Athenaeum.* The composer had not long before been elected a member of the Philharmonic Society of London and on the occasion of the first performance of this symphony was invited to share the podium with Sir Arthur Sullivan. He conducted a rather curiously contrived program, which included Spohr's "Faust" overture, Beethoven's "Leonore" No. 1, and Mozart's "Don Juan," while Weber's F minor Concertstück was also included with Madame Clothilde Kleeberg in the solo part. There was some vocal music as well. The first performance of this symphony in America was given at New York by the Philharmonic Society January 9, 1886, under the direction of Theodore Thomas. Dvořák evidently felt that in the Second Symphony he had accomplished something of considerable importance. When publication of the symphony was discussed the publisher offered three thousand marks, attempting to justify this rather meager compensation by pointing to the commercial unsuc-cess of Dvořák's first symphony and other works. What he wanted was more "Slavonic Dances," which had been enormously successful both for Dvořák and for the publishers. In the gentlest and firmest way Dvořák wrote that he could not let his publisher have the Second Symphony for three thousand marks but required double that amount. The composer likewise referred to the "Slavonic Dances" and reminded his publisher that they had been highly profitable. Finally he said, "If one regards this from a common-sense viewpoint, reconsidering all that you have indicated in your last letter, it leads to the evident conclusion: that I should compose no symphonies, no large vocal works, and no instrumental music; only now and again perhaps a couple of 'Songs Without Words,' pieces for piano and dances, and goodness knows what other 'publishable' pieces. Well, as an artist who desires to amount to something, I simply am unable to do it!" Dvořák's letter had the desired effect. The publisher paid six thousand instead of three thousand marks for the symphony, and Dvořák promised to write some additional "Slavonic Dances," "if he felt like doing them."

FIRST MOVEMENT

The Slavonic flavor of Dvořák's music is always evident and not least evident in his Fifth or "New World" Symphony, which was intended to be so American. We find it here. We find it in the bright colors, the vigorous and often syncopated rhythms, and the passionate emotional intensity. The first movement is rather formal in outline, but within the framework of the sonata form the composer achieves a very considerable degree of freedom. Basses and cellos initiate the principal subject of the movement low and quietly. This idea is expanded first by the

clarinets and then by other instruments; a short diversion is presented by the violas and then by the upper strings, and finally the first and principal subject is projected in the orchestra's most powerful voice. A short period of restraint brings us to the second thematic idea of the movement, which we hear in the woodwind with murmuring comments

from the strings. Both subjects are extensively developed, and at the end of the movement we are reminded once more of the very same theme that opened it.

SECOND MOVEMENT

A rather stately and songlike theme in the woodwinds with string accompaniment begins the second movement, and this is one of many melodic ideas which the composer employs and exploits in this ingratiating music.

Each movement of this work has a symmetry which often arises from the fact that the composer reminds us of thematic ideas that have gone before and quite frequently ends a movement with a direct reference to the same phrases that opened it. This happens here, and in the first violins, toward the end of the movement, the same thoughtful utterance that opened the movement can be discerned.

THIRD MOVEMENT

The scherzo is a vigorously jolly one. In the first section of the movement the strings have matters pretty much under control, with the first theme assigned to the violins and violas against a countertheme below in the cellos.

The whole first part of the movement is derived from this material. The middle section, for contrast, is given its thematic basis primarily by the woodwind, and the two ideas are explored in a distinctly lighthearted mood. As so frequently happens in the closing bars of a movement, Dvořák recalls the subject matter of the first few measures.

FOURTH MOVEMENT

The warm dark voices of cellos and clarinet establish the mood of the finale with this motif:

There is a second basic idea originally declaimed by cellos and later transferred to brighter instruments, notably flutes and oboes.

The movement is in rather conventional form, although the brilliance and clarity of the orchestration tend to obscure this fact. The two quoted passages form the basis for the entire movement, and their development brings a brilliantly orchestrated and vigorous coda.

Symphony No. 4 in G major

HERE is no epic; here, no gigantic music thundering its message across the world; here no stormy passions, no uncontrollable yearnings bewailed. Here is the musical outpouring of a great yet simple heart moved, one may sense, by the loveliness and wholesomeness of the natural world. After hearing this symphony it is not surprising to find, in almost every comment written about it, the appearance of the word "idyllic" and references to a "pastoral" quality which certainly is evident. One friendly critic referred to Dvořák's musical ideas as "breaking into flower, not like little blossoms lodged in the stony crevices of

an architectural structure, but as the Czech meadows flower, in luxuri-
ant garlands of varied charm and color"; and he speaks of this symphony as "simple, straightforward music, without any pretense at scholasticism." Perhaps a more eloquent but certainly not a more accurate
description of this music could be devised. Its mood is happy; its com-
plexities few; its ideas, spontaneous and uttered with a directness and
simplicity that audiences for many a year have found endearing.

It has often been stated in print that the first performance of this
work was given in England, and indeed the work has been referred to as
the "English" Symphony—a manifest absurdity since it is as characteristically Bohemian as anything Dvořák ever wrote. The performance on
April 14, 1890, by the London Philharmonic Orchestra, Dvořák conducting, was not the first performance, for Dvořák himself had conducted one at Prague some months earlier. As for the unjustified titling
as "English" Symphony, this would hardly be logical from any point of
view, but particularly because the work is dedicated, by means of a line
or two in the original manuscript, "To the Bohemian Academy of Emperor Franz Joseph for the Encouragement of Art and Literature, in
thanks for my election." Perhaps the reference to "English" came about
because of the fact that the symphony was published by an English firm
—Novello—and the first English performance * was conducted by
Dvořák while he was in England to accept an honorary degree from
Cambridge University.

Dvořák, a man of engaging simplicity, was quite overcome, though
pleased by his scholastic honors. He wrote home, with delightful ingenuousness, about the occasion:

"I do not like these celebrations. And when I have to be in one of
them, I am, as it were, on pins and needles. I never shall forget how I
felt when they made me a Doctor in England. Nothing but ceremony,
and nothing but doctors. All faces were serious, and it seemed to me as
if no one knew any other language than Latin. I looked to the right and
to the left, and I did not know to whom I was to listen. And when I realized that they were talking to me, I had quite a shock, and I was

---

* The first performance in America was given by the New York Philharmonic
Orchestra, Anton Seidl conducting, March 11, 1892, and Dvořák himself conducted
the work, before thirty thousand Czechs, at a concert of Czech music at the World's
Columbian Exposition in Chicago, in 1893.

ashamed at not knowing Latin. But when I think of that today, I must laugh, and I think that to compose the 'Stabat Mater' is, after all, more than to know Latin."

FIRST MOVEMENT

The beginning of the movement is innocently deceptive in that the thoughtful and almost melancholy song most conspicuous in the cellos is not, as it might seem, intended to establish a mood for the movement, but rather to supply in advance a contrast with the bright motives that follow. After a change to the major key, there is some birdlike warbling of the flute, a warmly phrased subject for the lower strings, later joined

by the woodwind. The woodwinds presently have a new idea of their

own, beginning pianissimo but developing into a very powerful orchestral climax. There is no strict symphonic development, but there is indeed a plethora of thematic material presented in succession and in contrast rather than in conventional sonata development. A rather whimsical mood is suggested by the frequency and suddenness in changes of orchestral color, rhythm, and modality.

SECOND MOVEMENT

The second movement, like the first, begins rather seriously, and in the reflective phrase projected by the strings we find the basis for the major part of the movement. In the second section of the movement oc-

curs a climax of considerable power, accomplished after a careful and skillful expansion of orchestral forces.

THIRD MOVEMENT

The third movement was looked upon as not only merry, but actually comical, when the Fourth Symphony was first played in New York. Perhaps at that time it was regarded as a breach of protocol to smile at a concert of symphonic music; but Dvořák certainly suffered no such inhibition, and here encourages a gay mood, marked by bright figures that dance through the orchestra in varying rhythms and quickly changing contrasted orchestral colors.

FOURTH MOVEMENT

The shining voices of the trumpets command attention to the begin-

ning of the last movement. There is a strongly rhythmical and dignified subject upon which the composer imposes several ingenious variations. Two interesting additional ideas are put forth, one for flute alone, the other in the clarinets; the first theme returns in a quicker tempo; reference is made, somewhat obscurely perhaps, to the principal subject of the first movement; and the finale builds itself up into a climax of resounding power.

Symphony No. 5 in E minor
[*"From the New World"*]

IMMEDIATE and widespread popularity has accomplished the ruin of many musical works of considerable merit, and for reasons much similar to those which make the brummagem songs and dances of Broadway but the ephemeral efflorescence of our swift and brilliant modern life. They are heard too frequently, assimilated too quickly, and their intellectual content is not sufficient to sustain, for any considerable period, the soul of man, to which all valid music must appeal in order ultimately to survive. It would be invidious to compare a work of a serious and sincere but not highly gifted composer with the titillating trifles of Tin Pan Alley, yet, when elusive popularity attaches its dubious hold to either or both, the reason for the general acclaim and the brevity of its duration is the same in both cases—the paucity of substantial material upon which the spirit can feed.

Conversely, great musical works are only in comparatively rare instances "popular" immediately. Sometimes they win the approval of the more esoteric musical circles at first or second hearing, but usually public approbation must wait upon public assimilation—a process which is slow, labored, rarely complete, and sometimes impossible. Nevertheless, there are a few notable works of permanent value that have been immediately accepted and eventually appreciated even by the public at large. Dvořák's symphony "From the New World" is one of them.

We have almost forgotten the storm of controversy that raged in musical circles following the first presentation of the symphony. It had to do with the manner and degree in which the "New World" was influenced by characteristic American music, that is, the music of the Indian and the plantation songs of the Negro.

Discussions of these matters are not of paramount importance now. The "New World Symphony" has been assimilated into the collective body of musical works which we have come to regard as properly in the repertoire of every symphony orchestra; old prejudices and opinions are forgotten in the extraordinary charm of the music itself. Matured judgment of musicians and music lovers has vindicated the declaration of the composer that he sought not to embody in the symphony a literal version of native American music—assuming that there is such a thing—but rather an interpretation of the spirit of that American music which most closely approaches the folk song.

It is interesting to recall that the symphony was written in America, most of the orchestration being done at Spillville, Iowa, whither the composer had fled from New York in a period of homesickness. Here in this little town was a colony of Bohemians; here Dvořák could feel that he was among his own, could hear his native tongue, and feel contact with those who certainly were his friends. The symphony was written during December, 1892, and the early months of 1893; the last touches were given on May 25, 1893. In the following December, the symphony "From the New World" was given its first performance, in New York City, by the Philharmonic Society of New York, with Anton Seidl conducting and Dr. Dvořák present.

FIRST MOVEMENT

The symphony opens with a brief introduction, the melody assigned to the lower range of the cellos, syncopated, yet with its syncopation almost concealed in the adagio movement, and the smoother descending figure of the viola and the double bass. A placid note of the clarinet, and a more sudden utterance of the horn, the latter drawn out and gradually diminishing, occupy the interval that lies between the first melody and its repetition in contrasting tone colors by flute and oboe. The entire string section, dominated by the cello and the double bass, bursts out in an impatient brief phrase, each repetition answered with equal asperity in the woodwind. In this passionate utterance of the strings lies the first germ of the theme of the symphony, which from this point begins to take form as the plastic but fragile material is strained into one mold and again into another under the pressure of the composer's thought.

A syncopated rhythm has appeared once, and now, more pronounced in the waywardness of its movement, another irregularly accented figure is given to the flute, oboe, and clarinet. Immediately following it, we have the first statement of the principal theme in its most important rhythmic, but not harmonic, form. Now come sudden and vehement chords of the full orchestra, with a swift-rising climax to the beginning of the first movement proper.

The violins carry over the final note of the introduction, and as the movement proper opens, the theme is heard against them in the horn, now in its final rhythmical form and harmonic position. Its first state-

Allegro molto

ment is answered by strings, bassoon, and clarinet in a dainty, dancelike rhythm; again it appears in the attenuated tones of the oboe, in the sonorous voice of the trombone, and in the singing strings. After presentation of the theme in various guises, there is a transition to a subsidiary theme derived remotely from the woodwind's response to the first pronouncement of the chief subject of the movement.

A climax is built upon this plaintive little song, and preparations are made for the presentation of the second important theme of the move-ment—a subject for which the melody of the Negro song *Swing Low, Sweet Chariot* undoubtedly furnished inspiration. The flute, solo against the string section in pianissimo, breathes the pensive yet moving air; later the violins seize upon it more energetically, and presently it is developed into the final climax of the opening section of the movement. Now begins the wonderful development and working out of the rich thematic material.

The horn breathes a dreamy reminiscence of the second theme, a reminiscence immediately translated into present action by the brighter voices of the piccolo and the strident note of the trumpet in a brief canonical figure. Melodically the figure is the same as when first pre-sented, but there is a slight rhythmic change that adds vigor. Now the themes of the movement are assigned to various instruments and appear in the minor, then in the major mode. The elementary ideas are pre-served with clearness and unity, even in contrapuntal passages, chiefly by using the themes in fragmentary and rhythmically altered form rather than by building up harmonic variations of them.

SECOND MOVEMENT

Considered as a complete entity, the second movement, or "Largo," of the symphony "From the New World," is one of the most appealing and best-known pieces of music in all the literature of the orchestra. Its principal melody is generally conceded to be one of the most beautiful solos for the *cor anglais*, or the alto oboe, in all music.

The movement opens with solemn harmonies in the brass and woodwind, brightening in color and expanding in volume as they are thrice repeated. Articulated with the last of this series of chords is a second series, now in all the strings, muted, and in pianissimo. Then begins the languishing melody in the *cor anglais*, the strings, still muted, supplying the lovely, chorded accompaniment. Presently the solo instrument is joined by the clarinet for a few bars; and later by the bassoon for an equally brief space, but the clarinet alone breathes the echo of the final cadence. A vivid contrast in tonal colors is presented after the conclusion of the "song" with woodwind intoning an imitation, in higher, clearer voices, of the opening chords of the movement, the full orchestra joining in a *sforzando* at the close.

The mood is not one of violent emotion, but rather of deep and painful longing without surcease. And so the one outburst of passionate emphasis fades, almost as suddenly as it came, into the pleading, almost tearful voices of the violins, putting forth their version of the chief motive of the movement. Presently the plaint of the first solo instrument comes again, and an impression of the terrible loneliness of the prairies, stretching without motion, sound, or variation, for mile after mile under a blazing sky, is easily suggested.

As the movement proceeds we hear an echo of the song of the *cor anglais* in woodwind, followed by the mysterious, dreamy communing of the horns. As their tones fade, a new melody, more definitely sad yet with added vigor, appears in the flute and oboe, with flutterings of the strings beneath it. The soprano oboe joins the flute in a derivation of this new song, against the secretive pizzicato accompaniment from the double basses, and presently the first version of the subject is repeated with fierce emphasis by the violins, while the contrasted flute puts forth cool tendrils of tone like soothing fingers caressing.

By one of those unexpected modulations which, notwithstanding the fact that we have been utterly unprepared, come smoothly, exquisitely beautiful, and refreshing, the composer leads us from the melancholy minor back into the major mode, this part of the symphony ending on the major triad in the key of C sharp. The sudden shaft of light that strikes into the shadows of the still echoing minors is most ingeniously generated by the mutation of a single note—the sharpening of the middle member of the triad, which brings us into the parallel, rather than the relative major—a Bachlike evolution lighting the close with sunset glory.

Later occurs a striking instance of the use of silence, as the painter would use complete absence of light as an expressive touch; exactly where one would expect emphasis in the phrase, there is a quick fading, a stillness, a terrible voice more eloquent in what it represses perhaps than any sound could be. If music can either suggest or call forth a tear—and it can—here is a wrenching sob, an inward cry that is stifled into silence before it is born. And the song bravely attempts to go on, but only a single note is uttered before hopelessness once more descends. Another broken phrase; then with more firmness and courage the first phrases of the theme are given again, and we come to a lingering close of exquisite beauty. Imperceptibly a wandering figure leads to a return of the opening phrases of the movement—solemn harmonies low in the horn and brass, brightening in their slow approach to a subdued climax.

THIRD MOVEMENT

The paradoxical combination of the whimsical and the somber, the grotesque and the quaint, give to the third movement, the scherzo of the "New World Symphony," a weird, a macabre gaiety that is utterly fascinating. It is animated by an uncommon rhythm—a rhythm which, whether it attracts to itself a considerable section of the orchestra and thus temporarily becomes uppermost in the scheme of the movement, or engages but a small number of instruments, always makes strangely moving impulses distinctly felt. Emotionally, the scherzo occupies a plane seldom touched by any other composer—a kind of middle ground between sadness and exuberant joy; and the combination of melodic factors expressing the one, with rhythmic elements suggestive of the other, is unique and highly effective. Here, too, may be observed the appearance of several characteristics of the peasant and gypsy music of Bohemia—an emotional capriciousness, a certain diablerie that in a moment becomes instead pure sentiment; sudden rhythmic impulses, and the use of melodies very like folk tunes of Middle Europe.

Both the rhythmic and the thematic content of the scherzo are present in embryo in the opening chords of the movement, vigorously spoken by practically the entire orchestra. There is an internal rhythm even in the first chord, effected by the syncopation applied to the entering notes of the timpani and horns; throughout the movement an uncommon rhythmic beat can be felt urging on the sometimes plaintive voices that would linger in the delights of sweet melancholy.

Plucked and spiccato strings maintain the rhythm at the beginning, with woodwinds flickering above, entangled in a little canon that is later adopted by the violins, and which leads to a passage descending and rising again in a swiftly growing crescendo. After the climax the whole first section is repeated, and there is a modulation to the parallel major —effected, it should be mentioned, in precisely the same manner as that at the close of the second section of the preceding movement, by the alteration of a single note. Now comes a lovely little song, a song that would linger on its own caressing accents, but is pressed forward always by the nervous rhythm that moves beneath it in the strings. Flute and oboe, doubled in octaves, sing this melody, with the bassoon shadowing their brighter tones. Presently the theme is heard in the reedy voice of the clarinet divided in octaves, and in its most emphatic statement, it appears in the sonorous cello.

The scherzo presents an opportunity to observe how different from

that of other composers is Dvořák's manner of expressing and amplifying and elaborating emotional values. Sadness often touched him, and perhaps at no time more than during the period occupied by the writing of the present symphony; consequently, its traces will be found frequently in his music. And the very fact that the scherzo—ordinarily abandoned in most symphonic writing to the exploitation of less serious thoughts—is distinctly marked by melancholy, is in itself an interesting comment on both the temperament of the composer and on his music in so far as it is a reflection of his temperament. The circumstances of his birth, his early life and surroundings, the influences to which he was exposed, all contributed to the formation of an intense, sensitive, volatile spirit, quickly and powerfully responsive to external influence of every kind. His music reflects these influences. His life was clouded by sorrow, as is every life, but he knew that there is joy in existence, and it speaks from his music as eloquently as the griefs that are so often assumed to be more productive of poetic eloquence. The temperament of the typical Czech is too full of fiery energy to make a rite of sorrow, and Dvořák could not have expressed with such terrible literalness the intolerable woes of Tchaikovsky, for example; yet when he does tell of spiritual pain, his message is the more vital because it suggests suffering in a living organism—one quickened with the breath of life, one that recoils in wounded surprise from the hurts of life. It is the captivating child of nature who speaks in Dvořák's music, never the weary sophisticate. And the pain is quickly gone.

So the feeling of the second movement is longing and love, but not essentially sorrow; and in the third movement, the close approach to melancholy is checked by a rhythm that leaps with vitality, and turns into weird mirth a thought too pitiful for lodgment in the merry heart.

FOURTH MOVEMENT

Full of vigor and vitality, the major theme of the final movement bursts forth in horn and trumpet after nine measures of introduction quite as forceful as the theme itself. This bold declaration, in marchlike cadence, in its brazen emphasis, its power reinforced by a throng of instruments, suggests the cortege of some lordly satrap, as it moves in heavy dignity and pompous accent to its completion. Decorative figures are added by the strings as the theme is repeated. Its antithetical phrase also is assigned to the strings, speaking, however, not in their frequent flowing cantabile, but in accents of fierce vehemence.

Between the first and second theme a subsidiary motive is now interposed. Strings once more come to the fore, and move in agitation until a single stroke upon the cymbal gives pause to their rapid motion. Here we find the second important theme of the movement, and perhaps the loveliest melody in the entire symphony.

With little prelude to herald it, this entrancing melody, hopeful, yet with a faint suggestion of weariness and grief, arises serenely out of the whirling masses of tone that surround it, and undisturbed by interruptions of the restive violin and the touch of ominous meaning lent by quick strokes of the timpani proceeds gently to its conclusion. Within a few bars the violins take up the strain, altering the serenity of the woodwind to a passionate intensity, as well as presenting a varying form of the song, with an elaborated accompaniment based upon the broad and defiant first subject of the movement. A three-note figure (taken from the old ditty *Three Blind Mice*) is now worked into the texture of the music, and is used as a solid ground bass from which spring several interesting elaborations, finally coming uppermost as the first section of the movement draws to a close. The suggestion of finality contained in this simple group of three notes is borne out as various instruments of the orchestra seize upon it. It passes through the upper strings, and then is suspended imminently in clarinet, oboe, and bassoon; at last, still retarding, one hears it plucked sharply from cello and double bass, quite unequivocally marking the completion of the composer's present thought.

As the present part of the symphony proceeds we shall find in it vivid reminiscences of mottoes from the preceding movements—in fact, there are almost literal repetitions of them. Derivations of the three-note subject that closed the preceding section of the movement appear, flute and oboe giving out the figure with a brilliant trill on its final note. Presently the mysterious voice of the horn presents, in contrast to this item, a form of the bold sentence that appeared as the first important theme of the fourth movement, with an added phrase of less defiant spirit; after a repetition of this subject in various subdued voices, out of the somberness shines the first motive of the second movement, the lovely English-horn melody in almost its original harmonic position, but somewhat altered rhythmically. In the recollection of the themes of the symphony Dvořák goes back even to the first movement, and in a derived form, the syncopated first subject of the opening part of the work now appears, this also in juxtaposition with the bold opening subject of the present movement.

The final section of the movement is devoted practically in its entirety to a résumé of the first themes of the preceding movements, all drawing to a splendid climax in which the first motive of the present movement is given with tremendous force and decision. Statement of this theme, with harmonic suggestions of others, and a last strong but quickly fading chord, bring the symphony to an end.

Whether or not the "New World Symphony" is America's contribution to music has been discussed these many years, and though prejudices of one kind and another have long since expired, there are those who still insist that the work was inspired by American aboriginal and Negro music, as well as many more who assert the complete independence of the symphony from anything that Dvořák found in the music of America. That question will never be decided, for argument never convinced anyone. Nor is there need for either argument or decision; it is much more to the point to appreciate and enjoy a composition that is musically rich, highly original, completely sincere, and which, if it be not America's tribute to music, is surely music's most beautiful tribute to America.

Sir Edward Elgar

1857-1934

EDWARD WILLIAM ELGAR was born at Broadheath, near Worcester, England. He came of pure English stock, his father being a native of Dover, his mother belonging to a yeoman family of Herefordshire. The father was a musician by vocation as well as by avocation. He had a music shop in Worcester, and in his remaining time played the violin in a local orchestra, and was organist of the Roman Catholic Church of St. George. His taste ran to the classics.

Although the elder Elgar recognized his son's talent, he was unable to afford special guidance for him. Apart from a few violin and piano lessons the youth was left almost entirely to his own devices, drudging laboriously to lay the foundation for future musical expression. This struggle for knowledge was an early indication of Elgar's power of self-assertion; a beginning of his march toward a great ideal; namely, the making of music as a pure and sincere medium of self-expression, and the emancipation of British music.

Of distinct benefit to young Edward was the fact that various musical instruments were available to him. For example, he played bassoon in a wind quintet for which he is accredited with having written music. But his greatest successes were with the violin, which led him to positions in orchestras and appearances as a soloist. An important influence in Elgar's youth was his association with the Worcester Glee Club, an organization in which he appeared as conductor, violinist, and piano accompanist. During all this time of interpretative activities, he was busily engaged in composing music. After careful consideration he decided to abandon the idea of becoming a solo violinist, and in 1885 succeeded his father as organist at St. George's in Worcester.

In 1889 Elgar married the daughter of Major General Sir Henry Roberts, and her companionship and sympathetic encouragement were always a source of inspiration. After his marriage he took up his residence in London. Here his reception proved none too warm, but he continued composing, undaunted by the struggle for recognition. He was nearly forty years of age when he produced his now famous cantata *King Olaf*. Later *The Dream of Gerontius*, after a poem by Cardinal Newman, was produced, but it was not until after its enthusiastic reception in Germany, where the favorable criticism of Richard Strauss brought the composer into prominence, that the work became popular in England and other countries.

The production in 1908 of his First Symphony marked Elgar as a master of that musical form, in recognition of which his knighthood of 1904 was augmented by the Order of Merit. From then on his successes were unquestioned. The English people have come to look upon him as their private Beethoven, and although Elgar's music scarcely ranks with that of the great classical masters, it has the charm of sincerity and sound workmanship. The composer's devotion to his purpose of advancing the standards of English music, both in composition and execution, was one of his most admirable characteristics. When he died, early in 1934, England lost a valuable protagonist of her claims to distinction in the field of music; nor is there, at the moment, any indication that Elgar's successor is alive.

In America Elgar is generally known almost entirely by the *Pomp and Circumstance* marches, one of which has been adopted as a patriotic air, and used both in America and England. Unfortunately it is as unsingable as "The Star-Spangled Banner," but we nevertheless often hear public assemblages and other groups struggling with "Land of Hope and Glory."

Symphony No. 1 in A flat

ELGAR'S First Symphony is by no means the best of his instrumental works, although for a considerable period it was by far the most popular, surpassing both his celebrated oratorio *The Dream of Gerontius* and the *Enigma Variations*. Indeed, the symphony had more than a hundred performances during the first year following its *première*— a record that probably could not be matched by a new work by any contemporary composer. The symphony is dedicated to Hans Richter and, like Elgar's other very successful works, was first performed under the direction of that conductor at a Hallé concert at Manchester in 1908. The first performance of record in America, so far as can be ascertained, was given by the Philadelphia Orchestra under the direction of Leopold Stokowski on November 22, 1912.

It is not difficult to discover several reasons why this music has been permitted to lapse into desuetude. It is long, it is prolix, it is pretentious, and its length is entirely out of proportion to the importance of its content. It has neither the spiritual conviction of *The Dream of Gerontius* nor even the rather ponderous yet engaging humor of the *Enigma Variations*. It is certainly of interest to the student of Elgar's music, but its lack of interest to concert audiences generally is reflected in the fact that performances are extremely few and far between. Its most notable features are, first, the impressive theme, which at first is rather sketched than explicitly stated and which appears to be a mere fragment of introduction; it is followed by the main body of the first movement in an indirectly related key and markedly allegro, and yet, by a very ingenious development of the original theme, the music of the first moments of the symphony come to dominate not only the first movement but, to a certain degree, all four movements. Another feature of the symphony which is perhaps of some interest is the fact that in the first movement the composer uses a theme almost unmistakably of Celtic origin—not unlike an Irish reel—and later on employs the same idea, but in tremendously reduced tempo, so that it is metamorphosed into what is almost a dirge. The pious sonorities of the opening bars are presented, by implication or in fragments, and in quite dominating form at the very end.

Symphony No. 2 in E flat

SIR EDWARD composed this music during the years 1910 and 1911 and dedicated it "To the memory of His late Majesty King Edward VII." Inasmuch as by the time the symphony was first played His Majesty was dead, there is also a footnote. "This Symphony, designed early in 1910 to be a loyal tribute, bears its present dedication with the gracious approval of His Majesty the King. March 16, 1911." The work was first performed at a concert by the Queens Hall Orchestra, May 24, 1911, at the London Musical Festival. The first American performance was given by the Cincinnati Symphony Orchestra at Cincinnati under Leopold Stokowski, November 24, 1911.

It is reported that Edward Elgar disliked any programmatic associations with his music, and indeed it is true that most composers profess an abhorrence of program music even when they frequently write it. If Sir Edward expressed an unwillingness to attach any programmatic idea to this symphony, he did not deter his admirer, Dr. F. H. Shera, professor of music at the University of Sheffield, from suggesting a program, and indeed Sir Edward more than once encouraged this very thing, particularly in his *Enigma Variations*, where obviously there is a program at which the composer would no more than coyly hint. Dr. Shera, in his brochure dealing with certain instrumental works of Elgar and quoted by Lawrence Gilman, confesses that "It is tempting to regard the work in the same light as 'A.B.S.' regarded it when, in the program of the Three Choirs Festival in 1929, the annotator wrote: 'Perhaps we may say that the Symphony was planned in 1910 to be an epic of the Edwardian age, and that on the death of King Edward, the second movement was incorporated into the original scheme. But even if this were not the composer's intention, this symphony certainly stands as the epitome of an age marked by a brilliance and splendor which dissolved in a moment on August 4th, 1914.' "

Dr. Shera feels that with the death of King Edward in May, 1910, the period of peace in Europe was approaching its end. He refers to "the uncanny spectral theme" which one will notice, laid in strings and horns muted, in the opening movement and later on in the symphony as well—"the dance of life interrupted by the vision of death. . . . Its real spiritual parentage is found in Holbein, in whose *Dance of Death* we have the same sense of death in life as was expressed by the thought of the skeleton at the banquet or the slave murmuring *memento mori* in the ear of the Roman general borne along in the triumphal car." Perhaps one can find such meanings in this music, and perhaps in effect all music is program music, since music, to be valid and to communicate anything, must transmit to the hearer an impression of something either objective and material or subjective and immaterial.

It is curious, however, that Dr. Shera should go so far afield in reading meanings into this music and should so blandly ignore the possible significance of the lines from Shelley which appear in the score of Elgar's symphony:

> *Rarely, rarely comes thou,*
> *Spirit of Delight!*

Perhaps Dr. Shera overlooked these lines deliberately, out of the difficulty of establishing a parallel between Shelley's "Invocation" and Elgar's symphony. Shelley's poem is, on the whole, an outpouring of melancholy; Elgar's music is prevailingly happy.

To romanticize the music of Sir Edward Elgar is a task a little too difficult for anyone but a Lawrence Gilman, who admired him, or an Ernest Newman, who loved him, or a Dr. Shera, who studied him. Elgar's music is workmanlike, beautifully crafted, and, in a kind of Victorian way, rather shyly romantic in itself and—not at all shyly—grandiloquent. Like the roast beef of old England, it is always sound, solid, and satisfying, though to some contemporary tastes it may seem to require the seasoning of a little more salt.

FIRST MOVEMENT

It is healthful fare for all that. The first movement is not quite orthodox, and not sufficiently unorthodox, to permit us to forget the proper formalities. Rather than two major and unequivocally identifiable themes we have instead two groups of rather fragmentary themes which are contrasted and developed in what, for Elgar, is an excited and almost impetuous manner. The general atmosphere is one of wholesome

good humor and even a lighthanded gaiety at moments; but as the movement progresses the musical firmament becomes somewhat overcast, and from the shadows there emerges eventually the "uncanny spectral theme," the prescience of death in life—a weird effect accomplished by a daring arrangement of dissonant tonalities in muted strings

and percussion. In the closing section of the movement there is a tentative return to the wholesome and vital happiness that we might have noted at the opening—somewhat less exuberant, perhaps, but still full of animation, vitality, and sanity.

SECOND MOVEMENT

The second movement is contemplative rather than melancholy, serene rather than sad. It is constructed simply, or at least with apparent simplicity, out of two very engaging melodies: the first a rather

solemn utterance of woodwind and brasses proposed with the utmost restraint; the second in more penetrating tonal quality (English horn and oboe) but no more assertiveness. These thematic ideas, in a scholarly and by no means ineffective manner, are harmonized and colored in a great variety of ways, but they never lose their gravity, their dignity, their solemnity. Toward the end of the movement there is an interesting reference to the main idea of the symphony, suggested with a certain diffidence by two violas *soli*.

THIRD MOVEMENT

The third movement of the symphony corresponds roughly to the conventional scherzo, although it is not so called in the score; rather, it is called a rondo (presto in C major). Even its heavy-handed humor is engaging, but what is perhaps most surprising is the profoundly sentimental (in the best sense) episode which occupies the middle section of the movement. Throughout this episode, which the strings play with long bows, there is a growth of intensity that develops into a passionate utterance for full orchestra. The mood of the opening is restored as we approach the end of the third movement.

FOURTH MOVEMENT

In referring to the fourth movement of this symphony Mr. Ernest Newman, the distinguished London music critic, pays tribute to Elgar for his consummate knowledge of the art of getting off the stage. Indeed, this is an art—an art akin to the classic peroration of the Roman orator, and, to the irreverent, reminiscent of the story told about the old Negro preacher who, when asked for the secret of his rhetorical success, said it was simply this: "Fust I tells 'em what I'm gwine to tell 'em, then I tells it to 'em, and then I tells 'em what I have told 'em." What Sir Edward intends to tell us is told rather succinctly as this movement begins. It is a rather dictatorial assertion, thrust forward by low winds and cellos. It is emphasized by repetition and in whole or in part occupies a good proportion of the movement. A climax is finally worked out, and we are given time to get our breath before Sir Edward finally tells us what he has already told us by recalling the first theme of the first movement in a broad and unmistakable form. There are momentary upsurges of orchestral power, but the music gracefully and through a series of pianissimo passages retires into silence.

César Franck

CÉSAR AUGUSTE FRANCK, in many respects the greatest of "French" composers, was born at Liège, Belgium, of a family of artists, on December 10, 1822. His father's people were directly descended from a long line of painters who were conspicuous in that art through the sixteenth century. His mother was of German blood. The father, noting signs of talent in his boy, saw to it that he was given adequate instruction in piano, first at Liège, and later at Paris, where the family moved in 1835. Later the young Franck entered the Paris Conservatoire, where he achieved notable success and prizes in pianoforte, organ, and composition.

It was at this time that Franz Liszt, one of the greatest virtuosos of the piano in musical history, was startling Europe with his performances, and winning for himself fame and wealth. The elder Franck was ambitious for his talented son, and hoped that he too might, by diligent work and shrewd management, achieve a parallel success. César, naturally modest and retiring, did not regard this idea with any noticeable eagerness, and thereby incurred parental disapproval. He further complicated matters by bringing into the strait-laced Franck family, as his wife, a famous young actress of the Comédie Française. His marriage was the last straw, and he was obliged to leave his father's household, and maintain himself as best he could by giving piano instruction, and later, on his none too generous income as an organist. In 1858, however, fortune smiled upon him, and he was appointed to the post of organist at the fashionable church of Sainte-Clotilde. His success here was marked—so much so that he was retained in the position until his death. What is more important, the organist's position gave him time for composition.

As organist, Franck's extraordinary skill, both in executing the works of the masters and in improvising his own, amazed and delighted his auditors; but his compositions were appreciated by few while he lived. Not until he was almost ready to die did the bigoted musical public of Paris, fascinated by composers of more obvious merits, permit him a really notable success.

Franck certainly was one of the most lovable of the great composers. He was possessed of a curious and engaging and naïve candor, and at the same time of a deep spirituality and gentleness that endeared him to all who knew him. His innocence and sincerity were conspicuous characteristics. When the D minor Symphony was first played publicly, the family were naturally interested, and when the composer returned home from the concert, they eagerly asked if it had been a success— meaning, of course, to ask if the audience had applauded and received it well. Franck smiled his beatific smile, and rather absently answered, "Oh yes, it sounded beautiful, just as I thought it would."

The composer was a devout Catholic and deeply mystical; the brooding and spiritual beauty of his music, especially of the improvisations with which he so sweetly filled the echoing nave of Sainte-Clotilde's, caused it to be said of him that he "conversed not with men but with angels."

Notwithstanding his Belgian and German ancestry, Franck is justly regarded as a French composer. His training was almost exclusively French, and in his personal sympathies he was definitely and enthusiastically a Frenchman. Indeed, shortly after the war of 1870, during which he had been as anxious and disturbed as anyone because of the precarious condition of France, he became a French citizen. His compositions, in their meticulous attention to detail and their perfection of form, in their clarity, unity, and logic, are characteristically French. Finally, his was the influence that helped to develop the golden period of French music during the late nineteenth and early twentieth centuries, when such men as Pierné, Ropartz, Lekeu, Chausson, Duparc, Bordes, and d'Indy—all pupils of Franck—brought new vitality and significance to French music.

Franck did not leave a great quantity of music, if that is important. The trying circumstances that beset him practically all his life made composition difficult, and under such conditions the amount, not to mention the quality, of his work is really extraordinary. Among the

larger instrumental forms, he wrote (in almost every instance) only one of each variety; but in every case that one is a masterpiece. The Symphony in D minor, the Quartet in D major, the Piano Quintet in F minor; the Violin Sonata in A major, the Symphonic Variations for Piano and Orchestra, the Prelude, Choral, and Fugue for piano, the Chorals for Organ, the oratorio *Les Béatitudes*—all are masterpieces in their genre.

César Franck was never a robust man, but the quiet routine of his life and the shining happiness of his inward being helped to prolong his days. One day in 1890 he was injured in an omnibus accident while on the way to the home of a pupil. Though apparently he recovered, the injury nevertheless resulted in complications which caused his death a few months later, November 8, 1890.

Symphony in D minor

IN SPITE of Franck's satisfaction on hearing the first performance of his only symphony, it must be recorded that neither orchestra nor audience regarded it very highly. The public first heard the work at the Paris Conservatoire on February 19, 1889. Had the orchestra's opinion been regarded by the management, the work would not have been performed at all—and it must be remembered that this was no ordinary orchestra, but one made up then, as it is now, of professors and distinguished students of orchestral instruments, and therefore given to strong sentiments and emphatic expression of them. The enthusiasm of the conductor, M. Jules Garcin, at length prevailed, and the concert was given. The public, however, remained either uncomprehending or openly hostile. Vincent d'Indy, a pupil of Franck, in his biography of the composer describes the attitude of the audience:

The subscribers could make neither head nor tail of it, and the musical authorities were much in the same position. I inquired of one of them—a professor at the Conservatoire and a kind of factotum of the committee—what he thought of the work. "That, a symphony?" he replied in contemptuous tones. "But, my dear sir, who ever heard of writing for the English horn in a symphony? Just mention a single symphony by Haydn or Beethoven introducing the English horn. There, well, you see—your Franck's music may be whatever you please, but it will certainly never be a symphony." This was the attitude of the Conservatoire in the year of grace 1889. At another door of the concert hall, the composer of *Faust* (Gounod) escorted by a train of adulators, male and female, fulminated a kind of papal decree to the effect that this symphony was the affirmation of incompetence pushed to dogmatic lengths.

Of course this was but one more instance of the curious inability of most people to accept with open mind and heart anything that differs from the conventional. It has happened before, in music; it happens with each succeeding season, and it will continue to happen as long as human nature remains what it is. Nevertheless, we are still, in these days, puzzled by it, especially when we consider the extraordinary popularity of this symphony, its wealth of tender and beautiful melody, its drama, its conflict of mind and spirit, its opulent tonal color. The French say that to understand all is to forgive all. Since we think we have come to understand this music, it is possible that, unlike Franck's contemporaries, we can forgive daring and originality and even honesty of purpose that disregards all else.

FIRST MOVEMENT

The mystic cycle of this symphony begins with the strange and fateful question that has troubled the spirits of so many men of music. Down in the deep and gloomy recesses of tone where only the great basses can speak, we hear, softly and portentously, the wondering phrase—a phrase that Beethoven wrote, almost identically, as the question "Must it be?" in one of the last quartets *; that mighty Wagner used with dreadful significance in the titanic *Ring* tetralogy; that even the facile and superficial Liszt found occasion for, in *Les Préludes*.

This curious, doubting, and soul-wearied question is the emotional basis of the whole symphony. Throughout the present movement, it is asked by almost every voice of the orchestra, in almost every possible accent; persuasively, piteously, impetuously, hopefully, and almost

* Quartet in F major, Op. 135.

despairingly. Even at those moments when it seems temporarily banished from the composer's heart, we can almost always find it lurking secretively, buried under more suave and happier utterances; but it is there, leading us with the music through mysterious mazes of distracting loveliness. There is neither escape nor answer. The bittersweet tones of descending woodwinds and strings do not satisfy this persistent questioning, nor is there more than momentary comfort in the lovely song of the strings, coming from pale ethereal heights to warm low soothing utterances. Tremulous flights of tone, again in the strings, suggest the beating of caged pinions; and they beat in vain. Sudden fortissimo chords upraised like barriers against flight, and now the strings together project, with new and stronger emphasis, the questioning motto of the movement. Swift modulations to new tonalities only bring more intense and passionate expression. Yet there are moments when tentative answers to the tormented soul-questioning of the theme begin to appear—moments of such rare and diaphanous and unearthly beauty as to snatch at one's heart and stop one's breathing. There is the piteous half answer of the flute, and the hopeful contemplation of the solo horn, intimating the quiet and the peace that may come. What storms rage through the music thereafter do not banish the faint glimmerings of ultimate glories, and even the relentless and magnificently powerful final utterance of the questioning theme, at the end of the movement, ends upon an exalted major chord that promises ultimate triumph.

It seems somewhat beside the point to disintegrate, even in words, the lovely plastic material of which this music is made. Its structural features are discernible, if not obvious; and despite the multitude of musical elements contained in it, its unity is extraordinarily perfect. Students will doubtless observe the frequency with which Franck resorts to the contrapuntal device of the canon; his modulations to remotely related tonalities; his expansion of the characteristic first-movement form to dimensions adequate to the thought he wished to convey; and the importance given the third theme. The cyclic form, by which the movements are thematically connected, and the logical development and unity of the symphony thereby tremendously enhanced, was not of course original with Franck except in the sense that, even when employed by Beethoven in the Ninth, it was not used as effectively, nor with such intimate union of thematic ideas.

SECOND MOVEMENT

The English horn, in the hands of an undistinguished player, can be exceedingly disagreeable. Its tone is susceptible of many subtle variations in quality, and not only technical ability but keen musical taste and discernment are necessary equipment of the instrumentalist if the beautiful possibilities of this curious oboe are to be realized. Franck, with his acute sense of color, must have heard, or must have had an ideal of, the perfect executant upon this instrument, for in the present movement he has created for the *cor anglais* one of the loveliest melodies ever written for it. But this is a dangerous movement, and a dangerous melody, for a conductor can, by incorrect tempo, either sentimentalize or despiritualize the music and the theme, while the solo player, by unsympathetic phrasing or an ill-chosen reed, can pervert and destroy the essential beauty of the melody.

Harp and pizzicato strings suggest the outlines of the theme as the movement begins. At the seventeenth bar the solo voice of the English horn enters with its exquisitely melancholy song, its brooding tones shadowing the somber theme with rich dark brilliance. A thought upon this theme reveals that it is remotely derived from the fateful and persistent question that moved throughout the whole first movement; and as the music now grows in contemplative spirit, it is as if that old interrogation were taken up and considered in a new and more philosophical light.

The pizzicato strings and harp continue, for a space, in the accompaniment. Presently violas add a poignant countermelody of their own; clarinet and horn in unison continue the theme, and as the flute adds its brighter and more hopeful voice, the cellos are drawn to the countertheme.

Here is one of the loveliest moments in symphonic music—and curiously, one which most commends the symphony to us today, though it was a particular affront to the listeners at the first performance. Why do we love this music so much? To the senses it is a delight—but our senses can be delighted often and variously, and Franck was not the first to use the instruments that sing to us here. It can only be because, in this symphony, there is revealed to us a deep and kindly and lovable spirit, a spirit that strained against the doubts and futilities and disillusionment of this world, and who, while giving expression to the struggles that raged—despite his placid exterior—within his great and simple soul, is able also to lead us to glimpses of a light beyond the world.

There are flights toward that light as the movement progresses—flights of swift muted notes, like the beatings of thousands of invisible wings, coursing the misty upper airs in clouds of vibrant color and life. Incredibly we find that even this will-o'-the-wisp figure is remotely derived from the eternal question of the first movement—notwithstanding its soaring hopefulness. The meaning seems clear: out of eternal questioning, someday comes an answer; out of living, life.

What if, presently, the fluttering pinions droop, and the sad song of the English horn returns? There has been a moment of pellucid light; there has been a gleam of something from afar, and now the music moves more certainly, with more vitality, toward the coming vision. That vision is not beheld, for the present; yet there are clear intimations of the direction from which it shall come in the slow ascent of luminous tones arising from the harp.

While the symphony is formally divided into three movements, the second movement is actually a combination, an intimate joining, of two distinct sections, the latter of which could very logically be regarded as the scherzo of the work. This part begins following the first abandonment of the theme introduced by English horn, and opens with the fluttering motive of the strings and the answering cadence of the woodwinds. The rhythmic pattern of the two sections changes temporarily with the introduction of the second theme, which would establish a new mood and movement, but the intimate connection of the themes, and the significance with which they are contrasted, weld them together in such a way as to lead the composer to unify them in a single movement. As a matter of fact, it is not difficult to imagine how the composer, if it had suited his purpose, could by transitional passages have joined the entire symphony into a single movement. The sequence of moods is so natural and logical, and the thematic unity so perfect, as to make such an achievement perfectly possible in theory.

THIRD MOVEMENT

Why music in a major tonality suggests happiness, and in the minor conveys varying degrees of melancholy, must be an interesting matter for speculation by the psychologist. True, it does happen that gay sentiments are sometimes transmitted through music in the minor mode, yet there is usually a wry or macabre quality in such gaiety. It is likewise true that the major keys can hold within themselves music that is sad. But in all these exceptions, rhythm has an influence too; and the fact remains that a single chord in the major seems bright; in the minor, depressing.

The very first brief chords that usher in the theme of the third movement change the entire atmosphere. At once there is brightness; at once, hope and good spirits. The theme that follows hard upon the opening chords sustains these happier feelings, and replacing the melancholy, the philosophical, and pensive, and at times almost despairing significance of the music, there comes a feeling of wholesomeness and vitality and energy as welcome as a cool and sunlit breeze. Indeed, there is something breezy in the soft-spoken but vigorous theme as cellos and bassoons announce it. It is wonderful that—as yet—no creator of fox trots has discovered it. It is a cheerful and ingratiating tune, with syncopation all ready-made, and nothing but reorchestration necessary to make it the masterwork of a Tin Pan Alley genius. Adopted by the violins, and punctuated vigorously with elastic syncopations, it swiftly becomes an exultant song. There is a swift diminuendo, and then softly from the brass comes the solemn yet joyous second theme—the choral like utterance of triumph that is to climax the movement and the sym-

phony. "Here," says Leopold Stokowski, "César Franck seems to come from his church into the sunlight and life of his friends outside." And Ropartz, in his critical comment upon this music, asks, "What is there more joyous, more sanely vital, than the principal subject of the finale, around which all other themes in the work cluster and crystallize? The symphony is a continual ascent toward gladness and life-giving light, because its workmanship is solid, and its themes are manifestations of ideal beauty."

All the other themes do cluster and crystallize about this noble proclamation of the brass—and indeed gradually efface its first utterance as they recall the troubled past, and intrude themselves, at times to the point of domination, into the texture of the present movement. But there is power in the basic thought of this movement, and remembrances of the doubts and sorrows of what has gone before are presently thrust aside with almost hysterically joyous cries. Once more the great choral theme is proclaimed by full orchestra, and then there is a recession of orchestral light, and a period of contemplation. There are meditations of the woodwind, and anxious questions of the strings; yet again comes the once melancholy subject of the second movement, but now gloriously transmuted into a great song of gladness; now bravely shouted forth in brazen voices and joyously trembling strings.

The dark past with its misgivings can now be reviewed as some dreadful night that is gone, some fevered imagining driven away by the coolness of sanity and newborn day, and as final uncertainties are overcome, and perceived as definitely in the past, the great choral theme, after a passage of joyous frenzy, projects itself in glittering blades of tones from the whole orchestra. All evil and all doubt at last done away, we see "the vision splendid."

Reinhold Glière

BORN 1874

B OTH MUSICALLY and chronologically, Glière occupies an important place between the extreme moderns who are now his contemporaries, and the last of the great nationalistic Russian composers. He was born at Kiev, and educated at Moscow Conservatory, where he studied composition under Taneiev and Ippolitov-Ivanov. He was a brilliant student, and won a gold medal for composition in his graduation year. He lived in various European cities, but the disturbances incident to World War I prevented a permanent residence until finally he returned to Russia, where he was appointed head of the Kiev Conservatory. He made a distinguished success of what seemed a hopeless task, bringing the school through a series of troubles to a position of security and importance.

Glière has maintained his standing with Soviet government and people; his ballet, *The Red Poppy*, is at present one of the most popular musical works heard in Soviet entertainment centers.

Symphony No. 3 in B minor ("ILIA MOUROMETZ")

THIS symphony, of prodigious length and enormous interest, has for its theme and inspiration a group of ancient Russian folk tales, concerning a hero not entirely legendary, who may have lived during the twelfth century. This was Ilia Mourometz, a man of infinite valor and strength, who feasted and fought on a grand scale, was converted to the Christian faith, and is supposed to have become, eventually (and in no flippant sense), ossified.

Glière inserts, as a foreword to his score, the following story, the basis of the symphony, in Russian and French:

I.

In the ancient days when the benign Prince Vladimir reigned, there lived a peasant's son named Ilia Mourometz. This young man, for thirty

206

years, had strangely remained motionless in a sitting posture: until one day two wandering strangers, who were really gods, came and cried to him, "Arise and go! You are fated to be a famous and powerful hero!" Ilia arose inspired, and went forth into the lovely countryside. He took a great horse, worthy of a hero, and set out to find a kindred spirit, the great knight Sviatogor. This giant was so huge that he was restricted to the mountaintops of Sviaty Gory, for the land of Holy Russia would not bear his weight. Ilia boldly approached the great one, greeting him respectfully; and they became friends.

The two heroes mounted swift horses, and coursed over the mountain-tops, entertaining themselves with games and trials of skill and strength. They came upon a huge sarcophagus, so deep that when Sviatogor placed himself within it, he could not be extricated; and then he knew that his doom was upon him. But before he died he gave his secrets and his advice to Ilia. Then the dew of death came upon him, and he breathed no more. His powers were transmitted to Ilia, who leaped upon his charger and took the highroad to the great city Kiev. His gigantic steed took lakes and rivers at a bound, and the swish of his tail razed cities.

II.

In a dark woodland there lived the ferocious Solovéi the Brigand. The road to the seven towering oaks beneath which lay his stronghold was dangerous—slippery and guarded by barriers. This villainous fellow could send forth sweet cries, like a nightingale, or ferocious, bloodthirsty bellowings; he was strong enough to lay forests low, and to crush the unhappy men who might be beneath the trees. He kept three enticing maidens, who played with heaps of gold and silver and jewels, and enticed the unwary with gifts. As Solovéi hears the tread of Ilia's mighty warhorse, he roars with rage and sends out his seductive birdsong. Ilia answers the summons with an arrow of incandescent steel from his unerring bow. The glowing dart pierces the right eye of Solovéi the Robber; and he falls prostrate on the damp ground. Ilia lashes the unhappy giant to his stirrup leather, and drags him away toward the palace of Vladimir, the prince.

III.

Vladimir is holding revelry with the heroes and the nobility. Ilia comes before the great gate of the palace, and commands the wounded and captive Solovéi to give forth his cries and his birdsongs. The cowed brigand obeys; the walls and the roof of the palace tremble, the heroes and the noblemen fall—all except Vladimir, and even he is shaken. Then Ilia beheads the cowering Solovéi, and the grateful Vladimir acknowledges him as hero, and gives him the seat of honor at the princely table. Vladimir's guests salute Ilia as brother.

IV.

In Orda, the land of gold, there arose the chieftain Batygha the Wicked and his pagan host, so numerous that the breath of their horses obscured the sunlight like a cloud, so villainous that their very odor suffocated a Christian. But Ilia Mourometz at the head of his twelve warriors advanced against them defying them; and battled for twelve days. Then a warrior, huge and terrible as a mountain, detached himself from each of the opposing forces, Ilia Mourometz on one side, Ouda-laya Polyenitsa on the other. They rushed together, and in the first encounter neither was injured. Then each seized the other's horse by the mane; still neither was unhorsed. They dismounted and wrestled on the ground. From evening until dawn they struggled, and Ilia was thrown to the ground. But from the warm earth he gained new strength, and dealt his adversary such a mighty stroke upon the breast that the man was driven high above the trees of the forest. Ilia seized the senseless form, put out its eyes, chopped off the head, and mounting this grisly trophy on a Tartar lance, bore it aloft before the cheers of his comrades-in-arms.

Seven of Ilia's heroes advanced with him, scornfully shouting, "Where is the celestial army that we so lately overcame?" Hardly had they pronounced the words, when two mighty warriors sprang from the earth. "Advance, then, heroes!" shouted these. "Let us have a trial of strength." The two warriors advanced; Ilia cut them down, but they became four, and unhurt. Ilia butchered these, and they became eight, whole and menacing. All of Ilia's men threw themselves upon the enemy, but these continued to multiply, and the little band of heroes fled toward the mountains. As they approached the towering hills, one by one they were turned to stone. Only Ilia remained—and he too turned toward the heights; he too was suddenly stiffened into motionless stone. And since then there have been no more heroes in Holy Russia. (*Translated freely by C. O'C.*)

FIRST MOVEMENT

The symphony is tremendously elaborated, and its outlines are often covered with a dense, rich layer of orchestral color. Usually the music is not played in its entirety: for practical reasons cuts are made here and there, and even with them, the symphony can be tedious in any but the most expert hands.

The movement proper is preceded by an introduction, based upon mysterious suggestions from horn and strings, both muted, and forecasting the thematic ideas of the main body of the movement. There are rhythmic indications of growing excitement in the music, and as the tale unfolds, *cor anglais,* and again oboe with strings, suggest thematic material ripe for development; the chief theme of the movement comes, vigorously and strongly rhythmed, in cellos and bassoons. The introduction to the movement is probably intended to suggest the wandering stranger who galvanized the immobile Ilia into life; the theme of the bassoons and cellos could represent the sturdy fellow himself.

Now there is a considerable period of elaborate development, as we observe the exploits of the protagonist and his development to the stature of hero. There comes a pause; then a resumption of the music in a mysterious atmosphere, and a softly intoned theme for the brass, like a choral—hinting, perhaps, at Ilia's eventual turning toward a very muscular Christianity. All the thematic material is now developed on the broadest lines, and every orchestral instrument is required to present its most gorgeous and striking tones. Interesting use is made of the percussion section.

SECOND MOVEMENT

This section is largely given over to a musical portrait of Solovéi the Brigand. His birdlike warblings are frequently heard, first in flutes and at intervals in other woodwinds. The contrabassoon has a figure which must be the lusty roars of the brutal fellow, and near the end of the movement this becomes particularly terrifying as it is shouted out in the powerful voices of trombones (muted), bassoon, and double bass. But the movement ends with little fierceness, and a gradual retraction of orchestral forces.

THIRD MOVEMENT

Now we observe Ilia at the court of the Prince Vladimir. Gently plucked harp strings suggest the improvisations of a minstrel, and presently a voice—clarinet—is heard, closely followed by flute, in a quick but somewhat hesitant figure. This is the basis for a considerable section of the movement, but there are other, rather fragmentary themes, and occasional references to thematic material from preceding sections of of the symphony.

FOURTH MOVEMENT

Here the composer pictures in music the incredible performances of Ilia on the field of battle—prodigies of valor which are arrested only when the gigantic hero is turned into stone. Ominous mutterings of the drums, both timpani and bass; mysterious utterances of the horns (muted), and strange groanings in the strings, prepare us for a scene of terror and strife. As the battle rages this way and that, the orchestra follows with a fugue based on a powerful theme of cellos and bassoons. Hoarse brasses intrude a fierce warlike note, but references to material from the first movement have a calming effect. Mighty climaxes are yet to be attained, however. In the quieter portions that succeed one of these, we may pause and wonder if the dying brigand had put a curse upon our Ilia, for we hear remembrances of that villain's birdlike cries, and shortly thereafter occurs the awful miracle in which heroic Ilia is turned to immovable stone.

Karl Goldmark

1830-1915

V ERY FEW COMPOSERS whose cases are of record have faced a firing
squad, even though there may have at times been suppressed desires
among their audiences for just such a fate for them. Karl Goldmark,
when suspected of certain political involvements, was arrested and actually dragged out to face avenging rifles, but at the last minute the
interference of a friend and the eventual proof of Goldmark's innocence brought about his release, and he lived for eighty-five long years.

Goldmark was born in the town of Keszthely, Hungary, May 18,
1830, into a family whose greatest riches were happiness and the love
of music. His father was the cantor in the local synagogue but could
not afford to give young Karl a conventional musical education, in spite
of the boy's obvious hunger for music and demonstrated capability
for playing the violin. The local schoolmaster helped as well as he could
and the young composer-to-be responded vigorously. In one way or
another it was arranged that he should go to Vienna to study with
Jansa. After two years with this pedagogue he became a student at the
Vienna Conservatory. During the political disturbances of 1848 the
Conservatory was closed, and Goldmark was suspected of having con-
sorted with rebel elements, and it was for this that he was brought before the firing squad.

In 1850 the composer established himself in Vienna, where he spent
almost all the remaining years of his life. He studied with almost ferocious diligence, and little by little won the attention and respect of contemporary performers, who programmed his works with increasing
frequency. The *Rustic Wedding Symphony,* the opera *The Queen of
Sheba,* and the overture *Sakuntala* were resoundingly successful, and
these works alone have made his name a familiar one throughout the
musical world. He achieved considerable fame in the field of musical
criticism as well as in composition, and through his newspaper defended

Richard Wagner—strangely enough maintaining at the same time a musical friendship with Johannes Brahms. He died in Vienna, January 2, 1915.

Rustic Wedding Symphony

THIS work, so fresh, so ingratiating, so full of innocent charm, does not conform technically with the standard definition of a symphony. The sonata form, in which lies the genesis of a symphony, is not employed, although the conventional four movements in their conventional sequence are here. The first movement is a theme and variations; the second, a kind of orchestrated song; the third, a scherzo without either the vigor or playfulness of the conventional movement in this form; and the fourth movement, a miniature tone poem. All four movements are intended to be descriptive. Each evokes the atmosphere of the Hungarian countryside and employs some country tunes. All are appealingly melodious and clothed in rich orchestral raiment.

The Rustic Wedding Symphony was first performed by the Vienna Philharmonic under the direction of Hans Richter, and with a celerity rare even today an American orchestra added the work to its repertoire less than a year after its *première*, the first performance in our country being given at New York by the New York Philharmonic Orchestra, Leopold Damrosch conducting.

FIRST MOVEMENT

The theme, which the composer calls a march, is discernible almost

throughout the movement, but appears first unostentatiously in the lower strings; nor does it ever assume the assertiveness that one ordinarily associates with a formal march. By employment of variations the composer evokes a variety of moods ranging from bucolic gaiety to tender melancholy, which was precisely what he wished to do in presenting a musical picture of Central European peasant life. The first variation

comes from the horns; the second, from the violins, which are interrupted in their dissertation by virtually the full orchestra vigorously
presenting the lively third variation. In the fourth, the mood changes
and the strings, now in the minor mode, put forth a pensive and sweet
utterance. The more virile basses, associated and sometimes doubled

with the bassoons and contrasted with the horns, bring us variation
number five. Once more in the deep voices of the basses, you can trace
the course of the sixth variation, with both woodwinds and upper strings
fashioning a complicated network of tone in accompaniment. The next
variant is in remarkably free style and quite complicated in orchestration, but its coherence is maintained throughout. Variation number
eight is assigned to violins and various woodwind instruments, with the
melodic line kept shining and clear. In the ninth variation the subject
again descends to the bass with new contrasting melodies interjected by
violins and flutes. The succeeding variant might have been and probably
was inspired by a country dance, with the first violins assuming the part
of very sophisticated country fiddlers. The mood changes for the next
section, and the thematic material is passed around from one instrument
to another, its final appearance being entrusted to the clarinet. A subject
which might be considered a new theme, but which is actually a development of the original basis of the movement, appears in the twelfth variation. It is largely assigned to the woodwinds, with the oboe having the
principal voice, and subsidiary comment in bassoon, flute and clarinet.
The final variation brings a return of the original mood and tempo with
somewhat more emphasis on the bucolic quality of the whole movement.

SECOND MOVEMENT

This tender and delicate music is fashioned chiefly from two perfectly
obvious melodies. The first, heard at the outset, might be a grave ceremonial dance without very marked rhythmic character but with a tenderness and grace that suggest the entrance of the virgin bride and her

attendants. The second is more songlike. Both are too simple, straight-forward and in themselves descriptive, to require extended comment.

THIRD MOVEMENT

Here the music presents what must be a pastoral scene full of soft colors and gentle contours. There are country songs and dances as well as a rural landscape and the orchestra exudes an artful simplicity which, once we have accepted the composer's purpose and program, conveys with superlative skill an impression of those sights and sounds which the composer undoubtedly had in mind.

FOURTH MOVEMENT

One may readily believe that this movement is intended to suggest a tender scene that could have taken place between bride and groom in some secluded spot away from the merrymakers, the noise, and the feasting. Nowhere in his music, not even in the Oriental splendors of his *Queen of Sheba,* has Goldmark achieved such lovely melody, such adept orchestration, such poignant sentiment and dreamy atmosphere. A melody of passionate warmth introduces the movement, continuing

until it is succeeded by a contrasting section wherein the conversation of the newlyweds is suggested in a dialogue between various pairs of instruments. It is significant, perhaps, that the dialogue figures are quite imitative, suggesting the unity and agreement which one may suppose exists between husband and wife—at least on the wedding day.

Howard Hanson

H OWARD HANSON, one of the most distinguished figures in contemporary American music, was born in Wahoo, Nebraska, and is at present living in Rochester. His earliest musical instruction was derived from his mother, and later at the Luther College in Wahoo. His studies were continued in the Institute of Musical Art in New York City, and at Northwestern University, where he obtained his degree. In 1916, when only twenty, he was appointed Professor of Theory at the College of the Pacific in California. Three years later (1919) he became the Dean of the Conservatory of Fine Arts in the same college. His merit as a composer was soon recognized, and in 1921 he received the Prix de Rome. He spent three years (1921–24) as a Fellow in the American Academy in Rome, and, upon his return to the United States, assumed the Directorship of the Eastman School of Music in Rochester, New York.

Howard Hanson has been a vital factor in stimulating interest in American music during the past several years. Perhaps the most noteworthy of his labors in this field has been the inauguration of the American Composers Concerts, in which project he enlisted the support of the Rochester Philharmonic, and the services of ballet groups and soloists. Hanson has also aided American music in many other ways: as Chairman of the Commission on Curricula of the National Association of Schools of Music, as President of the Music Teachers National Association, and as a member of the examining jury for the American Academy in Rome.

Dr. Hanson has also achieved a considerable reputation as a conductor and has led the orchestras of many American and European cities. As a composer, his output is rather large. He has written many songs, and many piano pieces. His chamber music includes a Quintet in F Minor, Op. 6 (1916); a *Concerto da Camera,* Op. 7, for piano and strings (1917); and a String Quartet, Op. 23 (1923). His symphonic creation includes several symphonic poems (*Before the Dawn:* 1919; *Exaltation:* 1920; *North and West:* 1923; *Lux Aeterna:* 1923; *Pan and the Priest:* 1926); a *Symphonic Rhapsody* (1918), a *Symphonic Legend* (1920), a Concerto for Organ and Orchestra (1926), an orchestral Suite from the opera *Merry Mount* (1937), and three symphonies. His First Symphony, the "Nordic" Symphony, was composed in 1922; the Second, the "Romantic" Symphony, in 1930, and his Symphony No. 3 in 1937. Aside from his opera *Merry Mount* (composed in 1932 and produced at the Metropolitan Opera House in New York on February 10, 1933) the "Romantic" Symphony presented here is perhaps the most famous of his works. Dr. Hanson was invited to conduct it, in 1930, with the Augusteo at Rome, which he did with eminent success. In 1933, the work was performed for the first time in New York, by the Philharmonic Symphony, Arturo Toscanini conducting.

Symphony No. 1 ("NORDIC")

ALTHOUGH it was the first work to gain for its composer world-wide attention, it would be a daring commentator who would accept the assertion that Howard Hanson's First ("Nordic") Symphony is either the greatest work that he has written or shall write. It dates from his twenty-fifth year (1921), and Howard Hanson has progressed in many directions and to a notable degree since then. The symphony has, however, a number of distinctions extra to its very notable musical values, among them the fact that it is one of the few works by an American composer ever given a first performance in Europe, and this under the direction of the composer himself. The Nordic Symphony was played for the first time by the orchestra of the Augusteo in Rome. Hanson, who was then a Fellow of the American Academy in Rome, conducted. The first performance in the United States was played by an orchestra with which Hanson has been intimately connected—the Rochester Philharmonic—but, rather oddly, the conductor on this occasion was Albert Coates. Thereafter Hanson's music attracted the particular attention of Serge Koussevitzky, and, though Hanson's music has been played by all the major symphony orchestras and played often, it is probably Koussevitzky whose enthusiasm for it gave it its most effective impetus.

One hesitates today to use the word "Nordic." There are so many people so eager to attach racial connotations and racial prejudices to everything that one is almost afraid to think, to say, or to be Nordic, Aryan, Slav, or Saxon. For a further reason the popular name of this symphony is unwise in that it has prompted so many people to establish non-existent parallels between it and the works of Sibelius; and, to be sure, there is little ground for this. It is true that Hanson's music sometimes exhibits feeling for the cool and austere harmonies that so often appeal to the northern European, but Howard Hanson is an American by nativity, experience, and temperament and his music basically has nothing whatever in common with the moody, sometimes pretentious, often diffuse, incoherent, and amorphous music of the Finnish master.

The symphony is composed of three movements and a finale: the first, *Andante solenne, Allegro con fuoco;* the second, *Andante teneramente con semplicità;* and the last, *Allegro con fuoco,* leading without pause into the Finale. The form is interesting because, while the first movement is in rather free sonata form, the work as a whole is cyclical in that all the thematic material upon which it is based and out of which it grows is to be found in the first movement, and there is a return to this material in the Finale. The second movement is dedicated to the composer's mother and the third, to his father. The work as a whole, however, is inscribed to the late Felix Lamond, who was the founder of the music department of the American Academy in Rome.

The Boston Symphony Orchestra program notes, always a fruitful source of accurate information, provide an analysis of the symphony in the program for April 5, 1928, as follows:

"The principal theme of the symphony enters immediately, a theme of somberness and austerity, announced by the violoncellos alone:

A horn call interrupts, and the theme is announced once more in a slightly more intense form, interrupted once more by the trumpet. The theme returns in the strings and is developed in intensity and tempo to an allegro. The strife dies away and the second theme is heard, again in the violoncellos:

A development soon leads to the closing theme of the first section, hurled forth by the brass and ending with a foreboding note in the tympani. A pause, and the development section is ushered in by a rush of woodwind. A new theme is sung by the violins:

and the main theme returns in the brass, accompanied by flashes of rhythmic patterns in the strings as they develop a short *fughetta* on the diminution of the theme. The principal theme enters once more, and the intensity of the music grows until it ends with a fierce outburst of all the brass in unison. Silence follows, and the second theme appears very softly in the basses, passes upward through the orchestra, and dies away over the solemn, monotonous beat of the timpani. Two somber chords in the trombones, and the movement ends quietly.

"The second movement begins softly in the strings:

and after a short introduction the principal theme, tender and wistful, is sung by the oboe:

The section ends with a quiet passage in the strings and horns. The second section begins with a short theme given out by the flutes:

A brief climax is reached, and the first theme returns in all the strings in unison to the accompaniment of cascading groups of notes from the second theme in the woodwind and with the solo horn singing through the rich mass of tone. The principal theme is heard once more in the solo horn and the movement ends.

"The third movement begins abruptly with trills in the strings and woodwind, through which breaks the call of the horns and trumpets. The first theme appears in the woodwind,

and the intensity is sustained until the second theme, in the style of an old folk dance, appears in the strings:

The third theme enters abruptly with a crash of percussion and the appearance of two chords which are reiterated again and again, over which the violoncellos sing a plaintive melody:

An oboe and clarinet continue, still to the same insistent accompaniment, and finally every instrument in the orchestra is giving out the same theme, one after another. The storm dies away and the first theme of the movement reappears.

"The finale begins with the principal theme in all the basses, to the accompaniment of a tremolo in the violins. Fragments of the material of the entire symphony pass in review, with constantly increasing intensity, until the slow theme of the third movement is heard once more in the brass to a slowly surging pulsation of the rest of the orchestra. A final outburst of the brass, and the symphony ends."

Symphony No. 2 ("ROMANTIC")

THE "Romantic" Symphony was composed by Dr. Hanson for the fiftieth anniversary of the Boston Symphony Orchestra. It was first performed by that orchestra at the concerts of November 28 and 29, 1930. We are fortunately able to present an analysis of this work which has the complete approval of Dr. Hanson. It follows:

The symphony is in three movements and is scored for two flutes and piccolo, two oboes and English horn, two clarinets, two bassoons, four horns, three trumpets, three trombones and tuba, timpani, percussion, harp, and strings.

FIRST MOVEMENT

The first movement, *adagio-allegro moderato,* begins with an atmospheric introduction in the woodwinds

joined first by the horns, the strings, and finally the brass choir in increasing intensity, and then subsiding. A call in the muted trumpets and horns

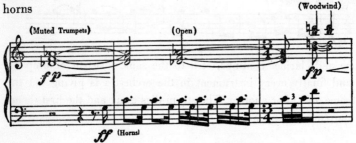

is followed by the announcement of the principal theme, *allegro moderato,*

by four horns with an accompaniment of strings and woodwinds. This vigorous theme is imitated in turn by the trumpets, woodwinds, and strings. An episodic theme

appears quietly in the oboe and later in the solo horn, followed by a transition leading into the subordinate theme.

The quiet subordinate theme, a melody of singular beauty,

serves as the unifying idea of the entire symphony. This theme is in reality two melodies projected simultaneously, theme *a* in the strings and theme *b* in the solo horn. A brief fanfare figure in the muted trumpets

leads directly to the development section. The principal theme now takes on a pastoral character and is presented alternately by the English horn, oboe, horn, and flute, much of the time in lengthened note values.

The development of the principal theme leads to a climax of great intensity. The recapitulation follows quickly and the principal theme returns in its original form, accompanied by the horncall. A vigorous and dynamic development of this material leads to the announcement of the lyrical episodic theme sung by the solo clarinet.

The subordinate theme again appears, rises to a climax, and quickly subsides. The movement concludes quietly with the pianissimo echoing of a haunting theme.

SECOND MOVEMENT

The second movement, *andante con tenerezza,* reveals a mood of nostalgic tenderness. The principal theme

is announced by the woodwinds with a sustained string accompaniment. An interlude in the brass, taken from the introduction of the first movement and interrupted by florid passages in the woodwinds, leads to the subordinate theme.

A transition, again interrupted by a florid woodwind passage, leads to a restatement of the principal theme of the movement. The movement ends quietly in a mood reminiscent of the opening phrase.

THIRD MOVEMENT

The third movement, *allegro con brio,* begins with a vigorous accompaniment figure in strings and woodwinds,

which comes directly from the first movement. The powerful principal theme,

reminiscent of a passage in the first movement, appears in the four horns and is later repeated by the basses. A continuation of the horn theme

follows. The music subsides and the subordinate theme, *molto meno mosso,*

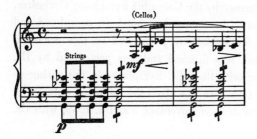

is announced by the violoncellos and then taken up by the English horn, the development of which leads to the middle section, *piu mosso*.

This section begins with an ominous pizzicato accompaniment in the violas, violoncellos, and basses, over which is announced a horncall.

This call is taken up by the trombones and leads into a brilliant fanfare,

first in the trumpets, then in the horns and woodwinds, and then again in the trumpets and woodwinds. The tremendous climax of the fanfare comes with the announcement fortissimo of the principal theme of the first movement by the trumpets, against the fanfare rhythm in woodwinds. The development of this theme leads into a final statement of the subordinate theme of the first movement fortissimo.

A brief coda of this material leads to a final fanfare and the conclusion of the symphony.

Symphony No. 3

DR. HANSON's Third Symphony was written on commission from the Columbia Broadcasting System to commemorate the 300th anniversary of the founding of the first Swedish settlement in America in 1638. At the time of the first performance by the Columbia Symphony Orchestra, February 19, 1937, the fourth movement had not been completed and only three movements of the work were performed on this occasion. Shortly thereafter, the work was finished and was performed by Dr. Hanson as guest conductor with the NBC Symphony in the spring of 1938. The first concert performance was given the following autumn by the Boston Symphony Orchestra, on November 3 and 4, 1939, with Dr.

Hanson conducting. Dr. Koussevitzky was most enthusiastic about the work and conducted it himself on numerous occasions, including the first public performance in New York and elsewhere. The symphony is dedicated to Dr. Koussevitzky.

The Symphony pays tribute to the epic qualities of those pioneers. The first movement, which has the subtitle *andante lamentando-agitato*, is both rugged and turbulent in character, alternating with a religious mysticism. The second movement, *andante tranquillo*, is, as its name implies, for the most part peaceful and brooding in quality. The third movement, *tempo scherzando*, is in the tempo of a fast scherzo, and is vigorous and rhythmic. The fourth movement, marked *largamente e pesante*, begins with the brooding character of the first movement, developing into an extended chorale in antiphonal style, rising to a climax in the full orchestra out of which appears the principal theme of the second movement, the symphony ending in a note of exultation and rejoicing.

FIRST MOVEMENT

The first movement, *andante lamentando*, begins with the introductory theme pianissimo in the low strings, mysterious and brooding,

punctuated by distant horncalls, leading into the announcement of a small portion of the chorale theme *sforzando* in the basses and cellos. This motive

is accompanied shortly by a motive of dynamic intensity in the woodwinds and high strings.

This subsides and leads directly to the principal theme

in the woodwinds and later in the strings. A short development leads to
the subordinate theme of the movement,

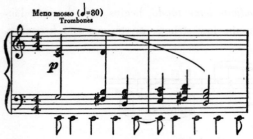

a chorale given out by the trombones and later joined by all the brasses
of the orchestra. This leads directly to the development section, an *agitato* in five-eight meter. In the middle of the development section we
hear a subsidiary theme, a vigorous dance of folklike character.

The development section is then resumed, leading to a short recapitulation of the principal theme fortissimo, followed immediately by the chorale. The movement ends quietly with a chorale theme in muted horns and trumpets.

SECOND MOVEMENT

The second movement, *andante tranquillo,* in extended song form, begins with an intimation of the principal theme in the French horn. This theme, quiet and nostalgic in character, is soon taken up by the entire string section.

The second theme

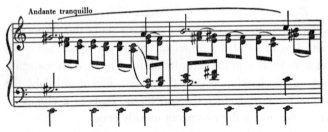

is followed in turn by a recapitulation of the first. This song form is followed by an extended development of both themes, interrupted by a rhythmic figure in the woodwinds of more agitated character. The development of the themes continues, is interrupted again by the woodwind figure, and is followed in turn by the reappearance of the principal theme, subsiding in a short coda of elegiac mood.

THIRD MOVEMENT

The third movement in scherzo form begins with a vigorous rhythmic introductory theme in the solo timpani.

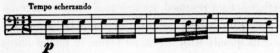

The principal theme of folklike character

appears in the solo oboe. After considerable development the timpani theme reappears, forming a bridge to the trio,

tranquil and lyrical, in the strings. In the working out of this theme it is combined with fragments of the principal theme, the simultaneous development of both leading to the recapitulation of the first theme again in the solo oboe. The development of this theme, accompanied by the reappearance of the introductory timpani theme, leads to a climax of fierce intensity after which the movement quickly ends.

FOURTH MOVEMENT

The fourth movement, *largamente e pesante*, begins with a shrill ejaculation from the entire orchestra

taken from the third motive of the first movement. The introductory
theme of the first movement reappears, followed by the principal theme
pochissimo piu mosso, malinconico.

A brief reminiscence of the chorale theme of the first movement leads
to a vigorous and rhythmic development of the principal theme of this
movement, followed by antiphonal development of the chorale theme by
the three sections of the brass choir. A brief reappearance, *giubilante,*
of the principal theme of the first movement is soon followed by a second antiphonal development of another portion of the chorale theme
over a two-fold bass *ostinato.* This development leads to a towering climax out of which appears the principal theme of the second movement.
The movement ends in a jubilant climax.

Roy Harris

BORN 1898

Nicolas slonimsky, in his quite fascinating article in *The Musical Quarterly* of January, 1947, attached some significance to the fact that Roy Harris, perhaps the most vigorously if not violently American of all American composers, was born on Lincoln's birthday in Lincoln County, Oklahoma, February 12, 1898. Mr. Slonimsky might also have mentioned that George M. Cohan was born on the Fourth of July, and he did mention that Stephen Foster was likewise born on Independence Day; and reminded us too that John Philip Sousa, whose music in a sense is the most thoroughly established of all American music, has a name that ends in the letters USA. Harris himself has written that "The shadow of Abe Lincoln has hovered over my life from childhood." But as a matter of fact, the Lincolnian simplicity, eloquence, and forthrightness that distinguish Harris' work were noted long before the composer himself made any reference to Lincoln's influence upon him.

Harris comes from Scotch and Irish stock. His people arrived in what is now Oklahoma in the days of the Cimarron movement; they staked their claim, cleared their land, and built a house. Later on they moved to California. Young Roy was always interested in music, but his interest in it was somewhat lackadaisical during his formative years, though he did study piano and clarinet and played in the school band. He was twenty-four years old, however, before he finally decided that his reason for being was the creation of music, and this after he had earned his living as a truck driver, as a dairy company employee, and as a milkman—the last profession being responsible for his distressing habit of getting up early in the morning no matter what.

When Harris was twenty-four he went to Los Angeles to study harmony with Arthur Farwell and other details of the musician's trade with Modest Altschuler. His progress was swift, and it was not long before he earned at least a part of his living as a teacher of harmony and as music critic for the *Illustrated Daily News* of Los Angeles. Eventually, because of the success of some of his early works, he was able to get to Paris to study with Nadia Boulanger, becoming one of that brilliant group of young Americans whom this eminent Frenchwoman helped toward realizing their own possibilities. It would be pleasant to relate that from that point onward Roy Harris' music was played more and more widely, more and more successfully. Indeed, this statement may stand without violence to the truth except that it is not the whole truth. Roy Harris has had to fight for almost every one of his performances, and that each was successful did not materially smooth the way for the next one. He has an ingenuous enthusiasm for his own work and a power of salesmanship in promoting it that are utterly unique among American composers; among honest musicians they are utterly harmless and even engaging. Slonimsky remarks, in his *Musical Quarterly* article, that "At the completion of each new work, Harris experiences a state of musical euphoria so spontaneous and so utterly devoid of falsity that it cannot be offensive except to critical prudes. As he worked on his Fifth Symphony (perhaps his finest score, superior to his much more popular Third Symphony) he wrote me on December 12, 1942: 'I have finished two movements of my Fifth Symphony, and it is wonderful beyond my wildest hopes. I am sure that you will be happy about it.' "

Everyone *is* happy about it.

Symphony No. 3

THOSE who are most deeply interested and well informed about Harris' large and growing literature seem to be about equally divided in their opinions concerning his most important contribution. Chamber-music musicians think that he has achieved his greatest expression in chamber music—such as his Piano Quartet, Third String Quartet, or the Viola Quintet; while choral enthusiasts are convinced that his most significant work has been achieved in his choral writing, such as *Song for Occupations*, *Symphony for Voices*, the *Folk Song Symphony*.

But I feel confident that his largest and most enthusiastic audience would unhesitatingly vote his symphonic music most important, and I sympathize with Dr. Serge Koussevitzky in the opinion that: "Harris' Third Symphony is the greatest orchestral work yet written in America."

In years to come we will probably realize that this symphony marks the beginning of a new era of American music; without precedent, yet as bold, simple, direct, and unhesitating as our architecture, our bridges, our roads, our way of speech.

In this work Harris has attempted and solved a most difficult problem in form. Beginning with a bold entrance in the strings, he has succeeded in making an arched span of seventeen minutes' duration. We

all realize that it is infinitely more difficult to write a sustained movement of this length than to write a three-movement work of greater length. I think that this aspect of the Third Symphony is most noteworthy because it is evidence of a new high point of achievement in orchestral resourcefulness. And not only resourcefulness in orchestration, but in all the elements of form: harmony, rhythm, melody, counterpoint. For instance, the long, intense opening for low strings, in

which only organum harmony is used (i.e., fourths, fifths, and octaves), reserve a new harmonic color for the entrance of the violins in
which harmonic thirds and sixths were introduced, while the lower
voices continued on their organum foundation harmony. Again the
complete contrast of the next section when new intensity was achieved
with large sonorities (all the woodwinds) in two-part counterpoint to
the violins, leading to a high climax of only a single voice in the vio-

lins, which prepared the ear for a new kind of intensification. But this
time a soft, very diversified sonority of wide range in the four-part
canonic passage work of the strings; all of which was only background
for the slender, graceful pastoral melodies in the woodwinds. As the

librarian of the Boston Symphony said in wonderment: "I know all
the orchestral literature—but there is something absolutely new—a
sound I've never heard before from the orchestra." And so it is: delicate, fragile, not of man—yet with all the devil-may-care freedom of a
liberated soul. It is doubtful that Harris will ever achieve a greater,

long, gradually growing climax than the growth of this pastoral to its wild, dancing, unleashed madness which leads to dramatic fugue entrance.

Here again a new sonority of the orchestra enters. The work is half over and we have never heard the percussive, *marcato* utterance of a modern symphony orchestra. But when it does come, how welcome it is —with what authority it enters—only to toss about the ribald rhythms with utmost contrapuntal abandon—with an unbridled expulsive force, which could only lead to the long, broad, sonorous weaving of the coda.

The long, tenuous line in the violins which winds its way down through the antiphonal brasses to the final cadence could be cited as one of the highest peaks of achievement in modern form. The whole symphony is a masterpiece in form. Witness *Modern Music*, in the issue of October–November, 1939:

So far, it is safe to say, there is no work to equal it in American music-making. For significance of material, breadth of treatment and depth of meaning; for tragic implication, dramatic intensity, concentration; for moving beauty, glowing sound, it can find no peer in the musical art of America. Here is music of the bleak and barren expanses of western Kansas, of the brooding prairie night, and of the fast darknesses of the American soul, of its despair and its courage, its defeat and its triumph, its struggles and its aspirations. From the great sweep of the opening phrases in the lower strings, through the pastoral middle sections to the importunate plangencies of the dirge and the final climax, there is a sense of inevitable compulsion.

The Third Symphony expounds a new approach to the orchestra. The style is nearer to Beethoven than to the romantic masters, depending on the material itself for interest rather than on the orchestral palette.

Yet one cannot say that the orchestral treatment is without color. On the contrary the color is unique and very clear. The instruments are used in their most telling range. But yet it is not *the* important part of the symphony. It is, one may suppose, a return to the classic attitude in which the medium of expression is taken for granted, to be used as a vehicle of the music, not as an arbitrary end in itself.

This suggests a few comments on Harris' form. He describes his attitude toward form as "autogenetic." He says that a form should grow like a tree grows from its seed; that each work should be a new form— determined by its material. He is extremely concerned about the variation form, as was Beethoven in his later years. But he feels that the variation must be an organic growth of ideas, "*not* just embroidery or species counterpoint exercises on a given *cantus firmus.*" This attitude has led him into a great deal of research work in the study of melodic development. He holds that *literal* sequences are not tenable unless they are only there to constitute a polyphonic background for further development in highlighted voices. This concentration of melodic invention and harmonic texture makes his music difficult to listen to. At first hearing one is apt to get lost—especially those of us who are accustomed to the literal sequential form development of the nineteenth-century masters. Perhaps this explains why Harris' greatest success has been achieved in his recordings. Whole concerts of his recorded music are often given—and record societies invite him to lecture on his music. Harris himself believes that "Records are the American composers' greatest friend."

Symphony No. 5

It is probably incontrovertible that Roy Harris, almost alone among modern composers, has made between one work and its successor a steady progress that nothing has been able to divert. It is not surprising, then, to discover that when Roy Harris presented his Fifth Symphony so respected an authority as Serge Koussevitzky had this to say:

"I think that nobody has expressed with such genius the American life, the vitality, the greatness, the strength of this country." Mr. Harris' contemporaries, who are not always generous to one another, have been constrained to occasionally emotional and always friendly comment upon the Fifth Symphony. Aaron Copland, for example, writes in *Our New Music*: "Harris writes, as a rule, music of a real sweep and breadth, with power and emotional depth such as only a generously built country could produce." David Ewen, in *Twentieth Century Composers*, suggests that "Within a few years he has become, without being guilty of overemphasis, the most important name in contemporary American music." Arthur V. Berger, in the magazine *Listen*, had this to say: "In Harris the typical Western ruggedness, the Whitmanesque optimism which sees to the vast rivers, mountains, plains with their endless resources, and which invokes the American people, free and good and great, which sings their fierce driving power and echoes their passionate hymns of gratitude." L. A. Sloper, writing in the *Christian Science Monitor* on the occasion of the first performance of the Fifth Symphony, pointed out that "promise which was fulfilled for many of us by his Third Symphony and is now confirmed by his Fifth. What distinguishes Mr. Harris as a composer is that he employs technical mastery to give expression to a musical inspiration that is distinctively individual and authentically American."

The first performance of the Fifth Symphony was done during the season of 1942 by the Boston Symphony Orchestra, Dr. Koussevitzky conducting. It happened that during this autumn Russia was locked in her death struggle with the Germans, and Harris, like any and every other patriotic American, was fascinated and profoundly excited by the heroism of the Russians' fight. For that reason he dedicated his symphony "To the heroic and freedom-loving people of our great ally, the Union of Soviet Socialist Republics." A few days before the symphony was performed for the first time he received a radiogram from the Russian Society for Cultural Relations which stated: "Music is a mighty means for communion of people. It helps strengthen ranks of defenders of liberty and democracy. We would like to hear your symphony here." By the time the work was finished and the parts copied, Russia had defeated the Germans at Stalingrad. When, therefore, the

first performance was given Dr. Koussevitzky arranged that it should
be broadcast to Russia by short wave. After the first broadcast Harris
received the following cablegram: "Greetings to Roy Harris from the
composers of USSR! We greet in your person young music of American people. Across seas and oceans we extend you our hand in sincere
fraternal handshake. Long live our victory." *Signed*: Glière, Shostakovich, Prokofieff, Myaskovsky, Khachaturyan, Kabalevsky, Muradeli,
Khrennikov, Biely." Subsequently the work was short-waved not only
to Russia but to our troops abroad no less than eleven different times.

FIRST MOVEMENT

Mr. Harris tells us that the Fifth Symphony is really a Prelude, Chorale, and Double Fugue. The Prelude gets its driving impetus from a
quasi-military rhythm and a thematic fragment not far removed from
an army bugle call:

SECOND MOVEMENT

The second movement is in an extraordinarily contrasting color and
atmosphere. It is roughly divided into three parts, the first sonorous
but dark and somewhat melancholy, with the rather grim voices of
English horn and bassoon projecting the main ideas:

The middle section involves one great soaring line—one superbly rising ellipse one hundred and eighteen measures long. This is the basis of it:

The third section of the movement is what Mr. Harris considers a chorale and to which he refers as "a study in consonant sonorities, both major and minor."

THIRD MOVEMENT

The finale is in fugal form—a device in the use of which Mr. Harris has often demonstrated his superlative skill, logic, and feeling for climaxes of sonorities and emotional significances. It is actually a double fugue.

The double fugue form works out to what we know from both music and literature as an A-B-A form, in which the second part of the trio is in itself a double fugue. The reappearance of the first form of the fugue is a simultaneous working out of both subjects. Of this part of the symphony Mr. Harris writes interestingly as follows:

"All three subjects, as you will see, are twelve-tone subjects. It is my personal belief that one should use the resources of all twelve tones of our musical notation with freedom, but that one should use them in such a way as to achieve tonality. They should be grouped in such a way as to bring out a tonal center, as you will observe these subjects have done. I do not believe that music can afford to set aside the strong architectural harmonic resources of the tonal cadence. Moreover, I believe that tonality is important to freshen the sound of music, aside from its architectural design. Please don't misunderstand me to say that I feel that one should always use the twelve tones of the twelve-tone system. The eleven-tone system attracts me a great deal more, since it preserves the subdominant and the dominant and avoids the *musica diabolos* of the diminished fifth or augmented fourth. This system seems to me a much more logical one and much stronger than the twelve-tone. Moreover it can be very logically arrived at through the combined use of the Ionian and Phrygian diatonic scales, one of which is very bright and one very dark. It gives us tremendously great resources.

"The use of harmony also should freely participate in the use of the whole twelve tones of our notation, as roots for harmony. I am writing a harmony book about this now. This can be done without using chromatic harmony at all, but simply by closely related key relationships around the tonic, subdominant, and dominant.

"Concerning the fugal form of the last movement, it is a large A-B-A form in which "B" is in itself a double fugue with two twelve-tone subjects, both of which are derived from the major-minor third and sixth relationships of the opening motive. The return to subject "A" is a working out in more dramatic terms of all three subjects."

Mr. Harris' comment on the orchestration of this work is of interest. He writes to the author:

"The work was originally scored for woodwinds in four, eight horns, three trumpets in C, two cornets in B flat, tenor and bass tuba, three trombones, with a large percussion section including piano, vibraphone, chimes, etc., and strings. My idea in scoring it this way was to have two different types of brass choirs: the first type, horns, cornets, tubas; the second type, trumpets, trombones, and tubas—the tubas lending themselves to both the sharp-tone brasses and the round-tone brasses. All orchestras should be set up this way, as symphonic bands are, using enough woodwinds to give that velvet tone, when combined with brasses. It worked wonderfully well with the Boston Symphony— a marvelous sound as you, yourself, observed. But it is not practical from a commercial standpoint, because it is too expensive to produce, that is, if you happen to be an American composer."

In a letter to the author dated July 21, 1947, Mr. Harris makes a comment that should properly be included here.

"I realize that the political scene has changed to such an extent that America and Russia are now in very strained relations. I do not feel this in any way alters the situation as it existed at the time the Fifth was written. You may use your own judgment as to using all this material.

"Concerning the Fifth, I gave the following program notes:

" 'I hoped to express the qualities of our people, which our popular dance music, because of its very nature, cannot reveal. Our people are more than pleasure-loving. We also have qualities of heroic strength, determination, will to struggle, faith in our destiny. We are possessed of a fierce, driving power—optimistic, young, rough and ready. And I am convinced that our mechanistic age has not destroyed an appreciation of more tender moods. And it is right that these gentler moods should live on. Otherwise our strength and vitality might degenerate into a ruthless brutality.' "

Franz Josef Haydn

1732–1809

HAYDN, THE FATHER of the symphony, was born at Rohrau, Austria. His father, a mechanic, and his mother, daughter of a cook, were poor in material things, but gifted with a love for music—a rich endowment which they passed on to their son. It was the mother's wish that the boy should study for the Church, but, when finally convinced of his talent, she gave up her ambitions for him, and permitted him to become the pupil of a relative who happened to be a musician.

When the boy was eight years old he became a chorister in the church of St. Stephen, Vienna, and when the weakness of his voice became apparent enough to cause his discharge from this position, he turned to the study of music in other forms. Several years of concentrated work developed his talent, and by the time he was twenty-seven years old he had achieved a conspicuous place in Viennese musical circles. When he won the position of *Musikdirektor* to the Viennese Count Morzin, he felt secure enough to marry. The Count, however, dismissed his orchestra within two years.

More important than his marriage or the position which had made it possible was Haydn's connection with the famous Hungarian noble family of Esterházy. The Esterházys, like so many of the European nobility, were generous and consistent patrons of music. Prince Pál Antal, at the time head of the house, became interested in Haydn and offered him a position as assistant conductor of the orchestra maintained by the family. Haydn accepted, and was emphatically successful. When Prince Miklós succeeded Pál Antal, he made Haydn first conductor, and later practically imprisoned him in the remote and beautiful family estate Esterház, where the composer, far from distraction and care, and cut off from communication with the world, had full opportunity to pour out his ideas in composition, and to satisfy the endless demands of the music-loving prince for new scores.

Prince Miklós died in 1790. His successor, Antal, was no great musical enthusiast, and dismissed most of the musicians who were being maintained at Esterház—among them, Haydn. The composer, however, continued to receive a generous annuity from the estate of Prince Miklós. Now he began to recall the offers he had been forced to decline during the period of his "confinement" at Esterház. By a happy coincidence, J. P. Salomon, of London, one of the concert managers who had, from time to time, asked for his services as composer and conductor, happened to be traveling through Germany when he heard of Prince Miklós' death. Suspecting how matters might be with Haydn, he renewed his offers. Haydn accepted, and the two set forth to London.

His success was immediate and emphatic. He played to none but crowded halls. He was invited everywhere, and honors, including a degree from Oxford University, were heaped upon him. He nevertheless found time to fulfill that part of his contract with Salomon which required him to compose six symphonies for performance in London. He left London, happy, prosperous, and famous, and found at home a measure of acclaim that heretofore had been denied him. A subsequent visit to England resulted in a repetition of his success, and the composition of six more symphonies for Salomon. Among the twelve commissioned by this publisher we find the best of Haydn's symphonies— the "Clock," the "Surprise," the "Oxford," and the "London."

Haydn was summoned back to Austria in 1795 by the then head of the Esterházys, and was received with such honor as he had never before known in his native land. The fact that it came after his success in a foreign country was not lost upon him, and he commented upon it with some bitterness. He was an ardent patriot, however, and had not been home long before he composed the noble hymn *Gott erhalte Franz den Kaiser,* which became the national anthem of Austria, and was in use as such until after the World War. The melody, with variations, also constitutes the slow movement of Haydn's beautiful "Kaiser" Quartet.

Three years after Haydn's final return to the Continent from England, the first performance of his celebrated oratorio, *The Creation,* was given. This was his most ambitious work, and was a magnificent success. The English fondness for this type of music, and the devotion and skill which they bring to bear upon oratorio performances, can be traced in great measure to the works of Haydn in this form.

Haydn was now beginning to feel the weight and the infirmities of many years. Neither his health nor his disposition was improved when he found his beloved Vienna invaded by the French in 1805—and again in 1809. In spite of their attendant slaughter, wars were more politely conducted in those days, and Haydn was treated with great respect by the invaders. Many of the French officers came to call on him, and no doubt to hear some of his music at first hand.

There was a concert and performance of *The Creation* early in 1808. Haydn, physically weak but burning with all his old enthusiasm, was carried into the hall. The performance was a triumph, and the old musician was so excited that his friends thought it best to remove him even before it was finished. From this night he became gradually weaker, and it was evident that his end was near. Haydn himself sensed it, and one day in May, 1809, he summoned his household, asked to be supported at his clavier, and played for the last time the "Emperor's Hymn." Even as he played the French were once more in Vienna.

Five days later the father of the symphony was dead.

It is not without reason that Haydn is called the "father of the symphony." He lived at a time when music in the contrapuntal, polyphonic style, beautifully contrived by both Italian and German composers, had been brought to the ultimate limits of its possibilities by Johann Sebastian Bach. Composers then as now sought individuality and originality in style, and Haydn looked about for some larger form that would give opportunity for exploitation of his truly remarkable fund of musical ideas. The works of Karl Philipp Emanuel Bach, son of Johann, gave Haydn the foundation for his idea. K. P. E. Bach, though his works are of interest chiefly to the musicologist and the historian, is generally credited with having been the first to employ two themes simultaneously in certain formal relationship. This is the basis of the sonata form, which Haydn fully developed, and which in turn is the foundation of the classical symphonic movement. (See note on "The Symphony," page 25).

In the sonata form, two themes of equal importance are treated in several sections, in one of which *duality* of key relationship is maintained; in the second of which *plurality* of key relationship occurs, and in the third of which *unity* of key relationship is effected. Sometimes an introduction precedes the first section, or exposition; then comes the development section; then the recapitulation. Often there is a coda, or tailpiece, to finish off the movement.

Haydn admitted his debt to K. P. E. Bach. It was, however, the wealth of invention and the amazing clarity which marked his works that made Haydn truly great. He brought to bear upon the "bones" of the sonata structure the products of his own fertile imagination, and developed this structure from a stiff and attenuated skeleton to a full-bodied, richly colored, and musically satisfying entity.

That is not to say that the Haydn symphony is to be compared with the romantic or modern. It is too rigidly symmetrical, reserved, stylized, and relatively poor in emotional content. We must, however, consider it against the background of the times, and mark what a bold and constructive departure from the commonplace it represents. The orchestra and its repertoire are today infinitely richer in resources than in Haydn's time, but his music, though it rarely flames and never explodes, still sparkles; though it has little mystery for us, it has magic. He took the best from the world of music as he saw it, and made of it a firm structure upon which the greater men who came after him built so proudly.

Symphony No. 45 in F-sharp minor ("FAREWELL")

MOZART perhaps more than any other composer injected the quality of humor into his music, but in this respect Haydn was not far behind him. Mozart's humor was a good deal more sophisticated and not always as kindly as Haydn's, and Haydn went even farther in a sense: he not only made music serve him in accomplishing a practical joke but made the joke itself serve a very practical purpose. Had there been a musicians' union, very likely this symphony would not have been written.

Haydn was *Kapellmeister* to Prince Nicolaus Esterházy for twenty-eight years. He had a small orchestra at his disposal and with it performed countless of his own works for the delectation of the Prince and his distinguished visitors. Esterházy was so enthusiastic an amateur of music that he sometimes forgot the long hours and busy days which his musicians spent at his castle. Eventually this generated considerable discontent among the members of the orchestra, who at a certain point felt they had been working for much too long a period without a vacation. They took the matter up with the conductor, Haydn himself, and asked him to intercede with the Prince so that they might have at least a brief holiday. Haydn agreed to do so but apparently didn't have the temerity to approach his master directly. Instead, he wrote a symphony which he felt would more discreetly deliver his message. The music followed the conventional form of the symphony, which Haydn himself had devised, until the last movement. Here the music is so contrived that one by one the musicians finish their parts. By arrangement, each musician as he came to the end of his particular part closed his music, blew out the candle on his music stand and departed. At the end of the symphony only two violins are left in the orchestra, playing very softly. The story is told that the Prince was quite captivated with the music as well as amused at Haydn's delicate hint and gave his musicians a special holiday. A few years ago the Boston Symphony played this work on the candlelit stage of Carnegie Hall with all the players attired in costumes of Haydn's period and departing one by one exactly as the score indicates.

The symphony is in every respect one of Haydn's best. Quite apart from the extraordinary ingeniousness with which the last movement is devised, the music reveals Haydn at the peak of his powers and illustrates very clearly and very beguilingly the firm outlines of the symphonic form which the composer had himself evolved.

FIRST MOVEMENT

The structure of this music and its emotional content are so clear, so straightforward, and so forthright that critical comment or explanation is rather unnecessary. The chief thematic material is put forward by the first violins, contrasted colorfully with the small wind choir. Secondary instruments, strings, and second oboe introduce the second basic subject. These two ideas are developed in typical Haydn style with a nicety of detail and a symmetry of contour characteristic of all Haydn's cheerful and ingratiating music.

SECOND MOVEMENT

A sweet tenderness informs this appealing music—a quality of gentle melancholy that so often marks Haydn's slow movements. The violins have the melody, which is treated with masterful simplicity. There are occasional moments of firmness and incisiveness, but for the most part the music is sweetly sorrowful.

THIRD MOVEMENT

Nothing could be more straightforward than this strongly rhythmed minuet, which has touches of rather naïve humor and a general cheery air. It has certain rhythmical irregularities that give it an unusual sparkle.

FOURTH MOVEMENT

The movement begins in a brisk and bustling fashion, but this mood of bouncing vitality is not long sustained. There is a rather surprising and thoroughly charming reference to the theme of the slow movement, and a new and still melancholy melody presently becomes entangled with this reminiscence. After a little while the orchestra begins to diminish, the first oboe and second horn blowing out their candles and going home, the other musicians following one by one until at the end only the conductor (first violin) and his partner are left.

Symphony No. 67 in F major

THIS symphony can well serve as an introduction to the music of Haydn. Its simple, buoyant spirit, the straightforwardness and clarity of its every line, and a certain intimate quality give it a friendly feeling; the transparency through which its structure makes itself immediately discernible also makes the matter of the form of the work quite comprehensible, whether or not one has had the benefit of musical training. There are symphonic works in which Haydn reaches a much higher point of development in form, but this symphony is typical in its revelation of the basic ingredients which the composer used in the development of the symphony. There are works in which the degree of emotional intensity is considerably higher, but for that very reason the artlessness of this one gives it added clarity. The symphony is perhaps more valuable as a study than as absolute music, although every measure is mildly delightful. The light-footed first movement has the closely woven texture of a string quartet; indeed, the other instruments are so inconspicuous, except for certain phrases for the horn near the end, that a quartet of strings could actually give a very passable imitation of a performance of this first movement. The second movement, contrasted both in tempo and in orchestral color with the first, begins rather tentatively, almost diffidently, with quasi-staccato fragments of melody which nevertheless before long coalesce into a rather broad song of the strings. The more extensive use of the winds in this movement gives it a warmer color and a greater expansiveness and solidity than we can find in the preceding movement. At moments, in spite of the heading "Adagio," this section has its playful intervals; it is coy, almost precious, but the prevailing atmosphere is one of serenity, although the ending comes close to flippancy. The third movement, a *menuetto*, is absolutely typical of Haydn and in its downright simplicity, straightforward and almost rigid rhythm, and clear melodic lines needs no comment. Use of a solo violin is unusual and effective. The fourth movement has three well-defined sections, the first and third lively, the middle one much more restrained and with a singing line. Perhaps the profoundest emotional depths of the symphony are reached in this middle section, though in truth there is nothing soul-shaking in it; rather, a tender wistfulness just touched momentarily by a deeper melancholy. All is sunshine at the end.

Symphony No. 73 in D major ("LA CHASSE")

THERE is no occasion for us to feel pity for Haydn or scorn for his employers, the Esterházy family, because of the fact that he wore their livery and was, in fact and in effect, a servant for thirty years. Haydn himself did not feel inferior on this account, and in the order of society in which Haydn lived a musician was at best a high-grade servant. What is more important is that this long service as musician to the Esterházys gave the composer an opportunity such as few have had to concentrate upon his creative work, to experiment, and to dictate musical matters with interference from no one. As he himself once wrote, "There was no one to confuse or torment me, and I was forced to become original." It was, in fact, during this long period that Haydn developed the quartet, evolved the form of the symphony and experimented with orchestral instruments—for all of which we are still greatly in his debt.

This symphony is not, by modern standards, an elaborate work, nor is it one which in any way requires meticulous analysis. It is not even among the most popular of Haydn symphonies, though it is one of the most gracious and pleasant to hear. If it is constructed on a rather small scale, we must not assume that the symphony in D major was necessarily done by a little chamber orchestra at the Esterházys' country place. Indeed, it is likely that this work, one of six known as the "Paris" symphonies, was played for the first time by the orchestra of *The Concerts de la Loge Olympique,* an orchestra comparable in size to any of those we are accustomed to hearing today. Forty violins, twelve cellos, eight basses constitute a rather impressive string section.

Although the symphonies in the "Paris" group have subtitles and have had them since publication, the composer was not responsible. Some French composers invariably added fanciful titles to their works of abstract music, and no doubt it was the French who attached such names as *La Poule* (The Hen), *L'Ours* (The Bear), *La Chasse* (The Hunt), and other familiar names to Haydn's works. Incidentally, it is the last movement of the present work which gives it its name. The work is scored for strings and flutes, oboes, bassoons, and horns in pairs. The omission of clarinets may seem a little strange; in this connection, one may note that Haydn never used the clarinet in his works until his latest years.

The symphony is, as might be expected, in quite formal style. The first movement is in two contrasting sections: a rather solemn but short introduction which proceeds with leisurely dignity until followed by the main body of the movement, a brisk allegro. The second movement, rich in melody, gracious of line, restrained but forward-moving in pace, allows the rich body of strings their full utterance of song. The third movement is the conventional minuet, but usually played perhaps a little more briskly than is common. The fourth movement, with its lively tempo and definitely marked rhythms, bears the title *"La Chasse"* and no other tempo indication whatever. It is not too difficult to deduce from the subtitle that the movement is intended to be played at almost a headlong speed, and so artfully designed is the music that even at a properly abandoned pace the clarity of orchestration and beautifully proportioned form of the movement are never obscured.

Symphony No. 80 in D minor

IT IS not difficult to feel at the very outset of this work that the composer is already much more secure in his medium than we have observed him to be in earlier works. He strides boldly into this hearty, virile music as if he knew before setting pen to paper precisely where each and every note was to lie. This music has a certain manliness, a full-blooded vitality that is typical of the best in Haydn's music. While the orchestra is still essentially a string orchestra, the strings are used with great breadth and boldness. The harmony is so distributed as to achieve greater sonorities than the same type of orchestra has previously given in the symphonies of Haydn. The first movement, at least, is lighthearted and colorful. There are some charming contrasts of woodwind and strings, especially in certain moments where bassoon and violins are opposed.

Mozart could have learned and probably did learn much from the second movement. The fragmentary ornamentation on a lovely singing melody, the daring—for those days—harmony, the essential grace without sacrifice of vigor: all these are qualities for which we have come to admire Mozart and which he unquestionably, in some degree, learned at the feet of Haydn. The *menuetto* is one of unusual energy, and is played considerably faster by some conductors than the characteristic minuet tempo. Whatever the reasons for this, the movement seems to gain in ruggedness by this accelerated tempo, and perhaps that is reason enough. The finale is presto, brisk, elastic, meticulously finished in detail and yet, in spite of its careful workmanship, apparently spontaneous, vital, and friendly. There is some rapid-fire dialogue between strings and woodwinds, especially between the first violins and the two oboes, and a hundred other details that are much better heard than described. Mozart himself, in a movement of the dimensions of this one, never surpassed it, and his debt to Haydn becomes more apparent with each succeeding measure of the finale.

Symphony No. 86 in D major

AT THE time when this symphony was written, circa 1786, musical life in Paris was decidedly active. There were two fashionable musical subscription societies: one, the *Concerts de la Loge Olympique,* the other the *Concerts spirituels.* The *Loge Olympique* considered itself quite smart and sophisticated. Marie Antoinette often attended the concerts with her court, marvelously gowned and blazing with jewels. The orchestra men wore a prescribed uniform ornamented with laces and ruffles, and even swords.

Musical taste in Paris at the time, however, ran more strongly to choral and operatic music rather than to the instrumental. Haydn's symphonies were by no means unknown, but his great success in Paris had been made with his *Stabat Mater,* which had been presented by the *Concerts spirituels.* The competing organization, the *Loge Olympique,* sensing the arrival of a new genius, offered to Haydn a commission for a series of symphonies, and the composer went to work with a will. He produced six short works, of which the present symphony is the fifth and is numbered eighty-six in the revised Breitkopf and Härtel catalog, number ten in the old catalog. An earlier symphony in the same key, to add confusion, is numbered ten in the new Breitkopf and Härtel catalog. The first performance was probably given at a *Concert de la Loge Olympique* in 1789.

The score is a modest and economical one even for Haydn. The late Mr. Lawrence Gilman once commented, with a certain irony, that "this delightful symphony of Haydn's can scarcely be claimed by our high-spirited friends, the modernists, despite their acquisitive passion for the pre-Romantic." How he would have enjoyed reading so many comments on the Shostakovich Ninth Symphony, where indeed that "acquisitive passion" displays itself! Paris itself in 1789 was advanced, sophisticated, and "modern," and perhaps after all Parisians would have joined with the admirers of Shostakovich in regarding Haydn as *avant garde*. Benjamin Franklin had performed his daring exploit with the lightning; the English Channel had been traversed by air, and various other marvels had come to pass; so perhaps it was not too daring of the *Loge Olympique* to give its benediction to the radical modernist Josef Haydn.

FIRST MOVEMENT

The music is remarkably tuneful and generally swift in motion. There is a slow introduction which grows in orchestral power to a very solid fortissimo, whereupon the chief theme of the movement in the first violins moves against a substantial background in chords from the rest of the orchestra. There is a second theme, gracefully melodious and sharply contrasted with the first but not as elaborately treated.

SECOND MOVEMENT

The broad second movement is subtitled capriccio and to scholars is perhaps the most interesting of the four movements. We might be more likely, in modern usage, to refer to this movement as a slow rondo, since there is a frequent return to the basic theme, but each return presents the theme in a different style and feeling, and the form is very free in its almost eccentric modulations and other unusual melodic and harmonic details.

THIRD MOVEMENT

The third movement, or *menuetto*, is in characteristic Haydn style, warm and genial, with perhaps more than the usual contrast between the first section and the middle or trio part.

FOURTH MOVEMENT

The fourth movement, or finale, is a gay and brilliant allegro. The composer indulges his musical sense of humor by suggesting that the second and normally contrasting theme is to be but a repetition of the first; but after a few tentative insinuations this idea is abandoned and a real second theme is presented. This was regarded in the eighteenth century as a quite fetching musical witticism. The movement is in the classical sonata form which Haydn practically invented.

Symphony No. 88 in G major

THE occasion of the composition and first performance of the present work is interesting. Paris in the early eighteenth century, being officially Catholic and officially pious, permitted no performances of its favorite musical diversion—the opera—on the more solemn days of the church calendar. But Paris could not forego music, and so Anne Philidor, of the famous family, made possible the giving of concerts on the holy days. (Anne Danican Philidor, incidentally, was a man in spite of his Christian name.) He founded a society called *Concerts spirituels,* to give concerts at the Salle des Suisses in the Tuileries Palace. It was not long before the spiritual character of these concerts changed into something definitely secular, and their popularity was quickly and emphatically established. Eminent soloists were engaged, and even Mozart, in 1778, composed a symphony for them (D major, K. 297).

The success of *Concerts spirituels* attracted rivalry, and in 1769 the Baron d'Ogny established the *Concerts des Amateurs.* This organization soon became formidable, paying soloists and composers quite generously for their contributions, and developing the largest and best orchestra that had ever been heard in Paris at the time. In numbers it compared quite favorably with the full symphony orchestra of today and boasted forty violins, twelve cellos, eight basses, and a full complement of wind instruments. Gossec was the first conductor. It was doubtless this orchestra that gave the first performance of the symphony noted here, though at the time the *Concerts des Amateurs* had been succeeded by the *Concerts de la Loge Olympique,* which commissioned the work. This organization, for its concerts, borrowed the quarters, the name, and the personnel of a Masonic organization, and it is a curious comment upon the democratization of music and audiences to note that the people who first heard Haydn's work were admitted to the hall only after close examination, as at a lodge meeting, while today the millions hear broadcasts. The audience for the first performance of this work wore, as insignia, a silver lyre on a sky-blue background; the Queen and her ladies were present in *grande toilette;* the musicians wore embroidered coats and played with swords by their sides. But two years later the Bastille fell, the *Concerts de la Loge Olympique* ceased to exist, and a music more democratic if less dignified sounded in the streets of Paris.

* * * * *

Haydn composed two sets of symphonies for Paris. They were commissioned in 1784, while he was living at Esterhaz, and were written between 1784 and 1789. They are in C, G minor, E-flat, B-flat, D, and A. Fanciful titles have with more or less reason been applied to them such as "The Bear" (No. 1); "The Hen" (No. 2); "The Queen of France" (No. 4). The present work is the first of a second series, supposedly of six but of which only five can be definitely identified. It was written in 1787 and can be identified as "Letter V" in the catalog of the London Philharmonic Society, No. 13 in the original Breitkopf & Härtel edition, No. 8 in the Peters edition, No. 29 in that of Sieber, No. 58 in the list of copied Haydn scores in the possession of the Paris Conservatoire, and No. 88 in the Mandyczewski edition of Breitkopf & Härtel.

Haydn had been known and respected in Paris long before the commission that produced these works; in fact, some time before the *Concerts de la Loge Olympique* existed, and while its predecessor, *Concerts spirituels,* was in the full flush of its glory. One of his symphonies was appreciated in Paris as early as 1764, and it is on record that another was performed there with success in 1779. Parisians' love for Haydn's music and for the composer himself did not abate during his lifetime, for we find Grétry writing: * "What lover of music has not been seized with admiration, hearing the beautiful symphonies of Haydn? A hundred times I have set to them the text they seem to demand." (*sic!*) And Alexis de Garaudé, pupil of Cambini, Reicha, and others, singer, composer, professor, and journalist, wrote in his *Tablettes de Polymnie,* that Haydn's symphonies "possessed a wise, elegant, correct plan," and especially remarked about their "clearness, which is

* *Memoires, ou Essais sur la Musique,* 1797.

revealed even in passages that seem to be consecrated exclusively to science." Finally, Haydn's last visitor before his death was a French officer, who sang to him; French officers were among the mourners at his funeral; and French soldiers stood guard about his coffin in the Schottenkirche.

*   *   *   *   *

Among some of our contemporary commentators there is, unhappily, conclusive evidence of one's pleasure in or knowledge of a score only if he knows and can glibly quote, with or without quotation marks, whether it was written at No. 28, Schallplattenplatz, Wien, or at No. 27, Paukenschlagstrasse, Berlin; and the more obscure and desiccated the work, the more intense are the frenzies of the ferrets to uncover its least significant detail, and of the pedants to pronounce upon it their dubious benediction. The classic composers generally, and Mozart, Bach, and Haydn particularly, have suffered from this well-intentioned but, to the music-loving public, crushingly boring procedure.

Happily, in the case of the present work, we need be concerned only with the music itself—not as a score resurrected from some musty library, but as a fragment of a man's life, of his spirit and of his mind. Music is, primarily and finally, something to be heard; it is in its very conception, and in the moment when it first takes wing upon the vibrating ether, a sensuous pleasure. Its first and fundamental result is sensation; cerebration follows. That is why music speaks for itself, and in a language that has no counterpart and no parallel, to those who have the spiritual and physical equipment to respond; others must find their pleasure alone in the drab processes of pedantry.

It is hardly possible to put into words the spirited and virile characteristics of this symphony, for any music which can adequately be described needs not to have been written. A single hearing of the work and the merest outline of its structure and progress should be sufficient for any sympathetic listener to experience its charms.

FIRST MOVEMENT

There is an introduction, adagio, and somewhat tentative in suggestion, in ¾ rhythm; it is composed for the greater part of forthright, short, and strong chords, contrasted with softer passages.

Then, in the body of the movement, the string players (minus basses) join in the main theme, a sprightly one, played at a swift pace.

It is repeated, with more sonority, and now one can hear a vigorous counter-subject in the bass. Worthy of note is the performance of the basses, not only here but wherever employed in the symphony, for they play with a dexterity, a flexibility, and definition of melodic line worthy of their small brothers the violins.

There is passage-playing out of which develops a secondary theme, not far removed in design from the first; and the second principal subject is very much like the first. The little theme in woodwinds—oboes and bassoons—which leads to the end of the movement is also a not-so-distant relative of the first subject. Thus it will be observed that, while the movement does not exhibit any notable degree of melodic invention, it does reveal Haydn's singular facility in development, and his ability to condense into a short, symmetrical, and smoothly modeled form the essence of the charming things he has to say.

SECOND MOVEMENT

The second movement appears now in the key of the dominant, D major, and still in ¾, though naturally at a much different, much slower tempo. It is little more than a song—an earnest one, one charged with emotion and with quietly dramatic force. It is refreshing to observe how these qualities are presented without "overacting," without bombast or sentimentality, without overemphasis or theatricalism. Yet with subtleties of phrase, of accent, of rhythm its full content of emotional significance is exacted from the music.

Cellos and oboe give out a lovely song, with the other strings, as well as horn and bassoon, in accompaniment.

The first violins, after traversing the accompaniment to the thematic melody, detach themselves from the main body of strings and project a decorative figure above the melodic line, and later, with a richer accompaniment, explore the chief melody itself. The flute adds brightness, and later we hear the melody again in a combination of woodwind and lower strings (cellos and oboe). Interesting developments spring from these presentations of the basic melody of the movement and lead to a short concluding section.

THIRD MOVEMENT

If it were not for the absolute equality of the three members of the rhythmic unit here, we would have something closer to a peasant waltz than to a minuet. The conductor must unerringly perceive this quality in the movement and, by subtleties of accent, convey the jovial spirit of the music without for an instant violating the directions laid down by the composer. Yet, in contrast to the downright ¾ rhythm there are

intervals of the most exquisite delicacy, more definitely suggestive of the "polite" minuet which we are most likely to associate with this period of history. Formally, the movement is in the most simplified minuet form.

FOURTH MOVEMENT

Here the dance spirit seems even more powerful than in the preceding movement, which is frankly based on a dance form. Now we have a rondo, apparently based on a country dance tune, filled with sturdy and assertive vigor, and indeed "*allegro con spirito.*" This rondo, as a form, is extensively exploited, as indeed it is in many of Haydn's later symphonies; and this is in contrast to the treatment in the earlier works, wherein the composer seemed to prefer a reversion, in the final movement, to the form of the first. Perhaps the rondo gave him more freedom, as Brenet thinks, for as that penetrating commentator remarks, "In some finales of his last symphonies, he gave freer rein to his fancy and modified with greater independence the form of his first allegros; but his fancy, always prudent and moderate, is more like the clear, precise arguments of a great orator than the headlong inspiration of a poet. Moderation is one of the characteristics of Haydn's genius; moderation in the dimensions, in the sonority, in the melodic shape: the liveliness of his melodic thought never seems extravagant, its melancholy never induces sadness." Moderation, truly present, does not degenerate into flaccidity or monotony when the music is in able hands.

Symphony No. 92 in G major ("THE OXFORD")

ONE of the most charming of the Salomon group of twelve symphonies by Haydn is this one, in G major, which was the musical *pièce de résistance* on the occasion of the conferring of the degree of Doctor of Music upon the composer by the English university. Three concerts were given at Oxford during Haydn's visit, and at the second, Haydn himself conducted this work, since generally known as the "Oxford" Symphony. It exhibits the characteristic grace, vitality, and exquisite finish of all the music in the Salomon group, and perhaps because of its particularly happy spirit and vivacity it is easily one of the favorite Haydn symphonies.

The composer's skill as a conductor was noted with pleasure on this and other occasions. At the time, the art of conducting as we know it was unheard of. Orchestral concerts were directed from the piano, and, from time to time, the conductor played chords from the score before

him, merely to give a degree of security and precision in attack to the
orchestra men. The concertmaster also directed, standing up in his
place and beating time with his bow as a baton, or with his foot, or
perhaps by striking his bow against his music stand. The conventional
baton did not come into use until many years later.

We have a survival of this style of conducting at present, when occasionally a great pianist is also a conductor. Bruno Walter and José
Iturbi frequently conduct and play concertos while seated at the piano.

FIRST MOVEMENT

The symphony begins with an introduction twenty measures in
length, of which all but seven are written for strings alone. Then the
first theme of the main subject occurs. This bold and animated melody

is also assigned to the strings, and is repeated presently by the flute.
The development following involves scales that sweep up and down at
breakneck speed, punctuated by a softly interposed comment of bassoon and oboe.

The contrasting second theme is a more sentimental and gracious
melody, sung by violins. Here the quality of the music suggests the
curving grace of femininity . . . grace and winsomeness in charming
contrast to the virility of the first theme. Stated first by the strings
alone, the theme is repeated with accompanying descending and ascending scales by the flute. In the development of this material woodwinds
and strings superimpose sparkling musical gossip. The second theme,
originally stated by the violin, is now heard in the plaintive voice of
the oboe, and then clear and tranquil in the flute.

SECOND MOVEMENT

There is a gracious dignity and stateliness to the second movement of
the symphony; a formality that suggests panniers, powdered wigs
coiffed high, and satin knee breeches, lace cuffs, and snuffboxes.

The music is in three-part form, with the first and third divisions made up of the same material. The second, for contrast, differs in tonality as well as in subject matter. The strings have the opening theme, a melody of straightforward simplicity. Flute and oboe add

their voices, and the theme is expanded in the measures preceding the second division.

Here the subject in D minor is cast in a more serious mold. The forte chords which introduce it are in direct contrast to the serene termination of the first section. Four notes for bassoon in descending sequence usher in a passage for flute and oboes, whose piquant charm relieves the severity of the strident chords. Strings, in variation, repeat it softly, just before a return of the sinister chords that mark the close of the second division.

Then the piercing voice of the oboe—supported by strings and horns —restates the theme of the first division. Strings continue with it, woodwinds contribute plaintively, and the lovely melody dies softly away.

THIRD MOVEMENT

Like the preceding movement, the menuetto is written in three-part form. The first part is a virile melody presented by full orchestra. The

customary trio is announced by bassoons and horns with pizzicato accompaniment in the strings. The third part of the movement is an exact repetition of the first.

FOURTH MOVEMENT

The lively finale opens with a theme assigned to the strings. Flutes

and horns enter at the sixteenth measure, and the melody is repeated by bassoons and lower strings. Somewhat later the strings announce a second theme, softly; a dainty mincing figure which the flute imitates. In the development, both themes are worked out with fascinating effects, being transferred from the string to the wind section with the finesse of perfect jugglery. One waits, breathless, to hear what more can be achieved with these delightful melodies . . . and suddenly the movement is ended.

Symphony No. 94 in G major (THE "SURPRISE")

THIS delightful and perfect little symphony was one of the group commissioned by the London publisher Salomon. It is number three in the first group bearing the name of the publisher, and was first performed in London on March 23, 1792. Sometimes it is called the symphony *"mit dem Paukenschlag"*—both this title and the appellation "surprise" being assigned to it because of the sudden orchestral crash occurring at the end of a pianissimo passage in the second movement. It has been asserted that Haydn had noticed a number of drowsy people at certain London concerts, and that he inserted the pianissimo string passage, interrupted by the rude *sforzando* in full orchestra, to lull the ladies into a trap of somnolence and then awaken them with a "bang." He is quoted as having gleefully exclaimed, "Here the ladies will shriek!" Perhaps they did in those days, but the bombshell is a squib to modern ears. After all, we have heard Wagner and Stravinsky!

FIRST MOVEMENT

It must always be remembered that the symphonies of Haydn and his contemporaries cannot be regarded in the same light as those of the later classical, and more recent romantic, composers. They are symphonies in miniature, so to speak, and though fascinating in their delicate and perfect workmanship, in their charming melodic line and grace of form, they must not be expected to reveal the large effect, the intense emotional expressiveness, the glamorous color, and wide dynamic range of the more modern symphonies.

The present work is important as well as charming, for in it Haydn reveals a beautiful example of the three-part sonata form which he himself had so highly developed. There is a brief introduction, with a delightfully melodious passage given alternately to a woodwind and horn combination, and to strings. After the fine crescendo and diminuendo there is a distinct atmosphere of anticipation, and here the first movement proper begins.

It opens vivaciously, with the first theme entrusted, appropriately, to the violins, which sing it softly but with sparkle. Its second phrase sounds more vigorously in full orchestra. The theme is "appropriate" to the violins because of its close resemblance to a typical Hungarian gypsy tune. Haydn, whose acquaintance with the wonderful treasury of melody to be found in the folk music of Middle Europe, did not hesitate to draw upon it frequently for thematic material, and the present theme is certainly one of his happiest selections.

The second part of the first theme is considerably exploited and repeated, until the first phrase appears again, in flute and strings. Now the key of D major—the key of the dominant—is emphasized, suggesting that it will be the contrasting tonality in which the second theme of the movement will be proposed. And so it happens. The second theme is not particularly outstanding; you will hear it in the running string passages, but its second phrase will be more conspicuous. This is a vigorously rhythmic and buoyant melody, leading to a transitional passage which precedes the development section of the movement.

The development begins with fragments of the first theme, heard in the strings; some modulations through related keys, and then an announcement of the chief theme in the key of G major—indicating that the development section is finished and the recapitulation about to begin. The development section of this movement is curiously brief and loose in structure, but contains elements that suggest the broader thematic treatment which was later to be a conspicuous feature of symphonies of the romantic school.

In the recapitulation, convention requires that the thematic material be so brought together as to agree in tonality and exhibit *unity* in contrast with preceding *duality* and *plurality* of key relationship. This Haydn neatly accomplishes, and even brings in charming ornamental ideas which have not heretofore appeared in the movement.

SECOND MOVEMENT

In Haydn's time the second movement was a great favorite with his audiences, not alone because it contains the famous "surprise," but because of its intrinsic beauty and charm. It is cast in the form of theme and variations: a movement built up of a single basic theme, manipulated successively in many different derivations of itself. The basic melody is heard in the strings, softly, as the movement begins. It is repeated even more softly, and as it reaches the extreme of pianissimo, we are expected to be startled by the *"Paukenschlag,"* the drumbeat pointing the orchestral crash which gives the symphony its nickname.

In the first variation the melody is given out strongly by second violins and violas, with the first violins presenting a variation of it. The second variation appears in the key of C minor, beginning with sweeping and powerful octaves, alternated with a first-violin passage leading to the key of E-flat major. The third variation is first assigned to the oboe—still in E-flat major—then to violins, and a moment later it appears in a lovely passage for flute and oboe. The fourth version of the theme is announced by full orchestra, fortissimo, contrasted with a softer passage in which the violas have prominence. A fifth variation is projected, but scarcely materializes before the movement softly ends.

THIRD MOVEMENT

The third movement presents another innovation attributed to Haydn —the introduction of a popular dance form as the third symphonic section. Haydn, of course, used the minuet, the dance of polite society in his day. A contemporary composer could use a fox trot with perfect propriety—just as Beethoven incorporated boisterous dancelike movements in his symphonies, just as Tchaikovsky employed the waltz in his.

This minuet is in characteristic style, the first and third parts dainty and playful, the middle part, or trio, somewhat more grave.

FOURTH MOVEMENT

The final movement is a brief rondo, built upon two simple themes, and proceeding at a furious pace through all its short but merry life.

The music must have been particularly exacting for the fiddlers of Haydn's time, for it is demanding enough even today, after all the years of improvement and development in violinistic technique.

Symphony No. 96 in D major ("THE MIRACLE")

CERTAIN European princes of the eighteenth century indulged in the luxury of kept musicians. This had the advantage of making music mint-new, designed exclusively for the entertainment of the patron and virtually inexhaustible in supply. It is true that the composer usually had a status little better than that of a servant in the house, but he had also economic security, time and opportunity to do his work, unlimited rehearsals, and an interested, cultivated, even exacting audience. It is true that some composers of extraordinary talent, like Josef Haydn, who was maintained by the Esterházy family for a generation, acquired such facility that they could turn out their work almost mechanically, in most instances writing to the strict formula which was the norm of excellence. They needed to do little more than rearrange the notes of a used symphony in order to have a new one quite as satisfactory.

The house composer's tenure and therefore his fortunes were completely at the disposal of a patron, and sometimes the patron's whim or demise could bring about very uncomfortable circumstances for the house musicians. This happened to Haydn upon the accession of Paul Anton Esterházy. Nicholas Esterházy, his predecessor, was devoted to music and had improved the facilities for producing it under Haydn's direction, had augmented the orchestra, and increased Haydn's salary. Paul Anton was no such enthusiast. He cut down the orchestra, curtailed the composer's privileges, and in various ways subtracted from Haydn's dignity and such prosperity as he had been enjoying. Haydn prepared to quit. At the critical moment the publisher, Salomon of London, appeared on the scene and persuaded the composer to visit the British capital, where he assured him of both artistic and financial success. These assurances were realized when in 1791 Haydn wrote six symphonies for Salomon, of which the present one is the fourth. London really treated him royally. Poets inscribed odes to him;

painters, no less than three of them, did his portrait; the nobility defer-
entially sought him out and entertained him; and one enthusiast, who
happened to be a manufacturer of hosiery, designed and made for the
composer six pairs of stockings into the fabric of which a pattern composed of the notes of six Haydn melodies was woven. It was during
this visit that Oxford bestowed upon the composer the honorary degree
of Doctor of Music.

Accustomed as we are to the grandiloquence and the magnificence of
symphonic writing of the nineteenth and twentieth centuries, we sometimes wonder how there could have been so much excitement over
music comparatively simple and, except in a mild way, unexciting.
The answer may lie in the fact that audiences of Haydn's time were
concerned more with symmetry and beauty of form, apt and, if possible, surprising turn of phrase, and polished musical etiquette than
with the expression or exhibition of profound emotional storms and
poured-out passions. The neat solution of contrapuntal problems, the
symmetry of a minuet, the dignity of an introduction, and the vigor of
a finale—these were among the qualities that Haydn's audiences looked
for and found, accomplished with egregious success, in his music.

The symphonies of Haydn might be compared to a string of jewels,
all approximately of a size, each with its minor variations of color and
brilliance, each like its fellows in form and symmetry. The differences
among them are, for the most part, chronological and historical rather
than musical. The present work is cut from the same material that
Haydn employed in the others, and there is no occasion for attempting
to find in it any abstruse philosophical meaning, any extreme emotional
suggestion, any notable deviation from the form which Haydn himself
had done so much to develop. In some details, particularly in the use
of two solo violins and again in other woodwind solos, Haydn departed
slightly from convention. The music as a whole reveals a solidity and
earthiness accomplished without heaviness, a sure and inevitable development from its straightforward themes to its rather mild climaxes.
Rhythms and tunes that might have been folk dances—but were not—
appear occasionally, particularly in the third and fourth movements.
There is nothing that requires extended comment or analysis, and little

except the arrangement of notes that distinguishes this symphony from others by the same master hand; and nothing at all to justify the subtitle, "The Miracle."

Symphony No. 97 in C major (SALOMON SET, NO. 1)

FIRST MOVEMENT

THE symphony opens with a short introduction in C major, for strings and woodwinds. The main theme of the movement is ushered in by a fortissimo assertion in full orchestra. This theme is then commented upon by strings and woodwinds in the pleasing variety of tone color which these instruments offer. Woodwinds finally give way to the strings, which state, in unison, a boldly triumphant phrase that directly precedes a second theme. Violins announce this second theme—a lilting phrase timidly introduced and later gaining assurance in a forceful triplet figure. There is a repetition of both themes and their development, leading to the second movement of the symphony.

SECOND MOVEMENT

The slow movement, in 4/4 time, begins in F major. The theme, announced at once by the strings, is a gentle melody, full of happiness and serenity. An emotional surge at the realization of such contentment is expressed by the long violin tone sustained over the ascending crescendo scale in the bass, easily discovered a few moments later. The theme is then heard in a triplet figure in the strings; then there is a milder section in F minor. A return to the major key changes the mood again, and the theme is then presented in delightful variation, mischievously parodying the quiet melody . . . until descending thirds in the various choirs bring the movement to a close.

THIRD MOVEMENT

The minuet, in typical Haydn style, commences with a theme for full orchestra. The trio, or middle section, is a particularly charming one. It is built upon a subject played by first violins, oboe, and bassoon. The opening theme is repeated, and leads to the finale.

FOURTH MOVEMENT

The finale in 2/4 time is in rondo form. It is highly animated, and sparkles with audacity and verve. Here the entire orchestra is involved in friendly chatter; an interchange of queries and answers in the string and wind choirs, such as Haydn delighted to suggest, keeps the music interesting and lively to the close.

Symphony No. 98 in B flat

THIS symphony in B flat is one of the twelve which Haydn wrote for his London visits during which, at each concert, he was expected to produce a new work. All that has been said of other Haydn symphonies could be said of this one, and little more; although it is somewhat curious to find the composer delivering himself, in the second movement, of an adagio which, even among Haydn's dignified slow movements, is remarkable for its gravity and melancholy loveliness. "It might almost be called his 'Requiem for Mozart,'" wrote Sir Donald Tovey in his *Essays in Musical Analysis*. But Haydn follows this movement with a minuet which is full of frivolous gaiety, and indeed the final movement is hardly less lively. Haydn had a certain mischievous wit—witness the "Surprise" and "Farewell" Symphonies. In the finale of this work he stretches out the tempo so that pauses between phrases become longer and longer, by which device he deliberately tempted his audience to break into conversation. Then he surprised them by resuming the music after what seemed like unnaturally long intervals. The composer tired of this fun after awhile and attached a brilliant, headlong coda which rushes quickly to the end.

Symphony No. 99 in E flat

THERE is much to be said in favor of a formula, particularly when it works. We have in our own time numerous instances of artists who have evolved a formula which they could look to for both commercial and artistic success. One might cite the painter Maxfield Parrish, his interesting though sexless figures, his miraculous transparent blues, his masterful drawing, and symmetrical composition; or one might point to Clarence Budington Kelland or to Joseph Hergesheimer or to Branch Cabell for their stereotyped but acceptable characters, their singular style, and their peculiar manipulations of English prose; or in other fields of art one might point to the formulas evolved by the late Stanford White, or even to Corbusier or Frank Lloyd Wright, who just as truly create by a formula as do many other artists.

Haydn evolved a formula that had in it every element of surefire artistic success, and he wrote always with this formula in mind. He poured melody and melodic invention into a mold of his own devising: a mathematically perfect, symmetrically balanced, and proportionally satisfying mold that contained in all their proper relationships every musical element that he chose to use. This formula is so clear, so understandable, so logically designed, and so perfectly finished that there is little point in analyzing in detail symphony after symphony of the dozens that have been left to us. The present symphony is not the most or the least important of Haydn. It is cast in the usual four movements, the first having a slow introduction but being, on the whole, lively and vigorous. The second movement is calm and slow in rhythm. The third is the typical and quite stylized dance form which we know as the minuet; and the final movement is the usual lively and high-spirited allegro.

Of the two different groups of symphonies which Haydn wrote on commission from the London publisher Salomon, the second group was perhaps the better, and, incidentally, this group includes two in the key of E-flat, No. 103 ("Paukenwirbel") and the present work. The symphony we note here was composed while Haydn was home in Vienna between his two London visits and has been catalogued in various ways: as No. 3 in the old catalog of Breitkopf and Härtel, as No. 9 in the more modern catalog of Breitkopf and Härtel, and as No. 10 of the twelve which Haydn wrote for Salomon. It is really something of a connoisseur's item, not likely to be heard often in public performance but, like all of Haydn's symphonies, not only worth hearing but profoundly enjoyable.

Symphony No. 100 in G major ("MILITARY")

IT WAS perhaps ultimately the English rather than the Esterházys who did most for Haydn. Certainly they made him happier and more prosperous than he had ever been. Certainly he produced his best symphonies in England, and, as he himself often said, it was not until he had been to England that he became famous in Germany. The most magnificent and extensive of the Esterházy estates in Hungary has recently been "redistributed" by the Russians after rather thoroughly ransacking it, even fishing out its wonderfully stocked lake, using hand grenades for bait. The estate of Haydn's music could not, however, be more prosperous, even though it has been distributed all over the civilized world; and well did he say, in another connection, that he had been relieved of all anxiety as to the future.

The "Military" Symphony was one of the second group of six for which we have to thank the English impresario and publisher who commissioned them. The manuscript was dated 1794 and the first performance, it would appear, was given at London in the Hanover Square Rooms on May second of that year. The concerts were sold out, and Haydn's success, already established, approached new heights. The gentry, the nobility, and even royalty emulated one another in doing him homage, and he was personally invited by the queen to make England his permanent home. It appears even that he had an affair of the heart, out of which nothing important developed, though the master naïvely said that he would "in all likelihood have married her" if he had been single. London was at his feet, eulogies were written for him, and Oxford University conferred the degree of Doctor of Music upon him.

The second series of London symphonies were even more enthusiastically received than the first, and of these particular attention was bestowed upon the "Military." It seems a very modest little symphony to our ears, accustomed as they are to the mountainous sonorities and endless colors of the modern orchestra. Once having heard "battle music" and similar descriptive efforts of romantic and modern composers, Haydn's symphony, one concludes, must have been dealing with toy soliders. It gets its title probably from the second movement, an allegretto in which trumpets and percussion instruments are used

rather more conspicuously and more extensively than was customary in eighteenth-century music.* There is no occasion for pointing out further detail, and no conspicuous feature to distinguish this from other Haydn symphonies except those just noted. Like all his work in this form, Haydn's "Military" Symphony is notable—not particularly among its fellows, but among the works of other composers—for the grace and symmetry of its form, the geniality and melodious attractiveness of its content, and its peerless craftsmanship. As one biographer and musical commentator † remarks of the London symphonies, including the "Military," they were "suffused with the sense of mellowness and maturity, of long experience and an old age honorably won; too serene for passion, too wise for sadness, too single-hearted for regret, [they] have learned the lesson of life and will question its fate no further."

Symphony No. 101 in D major (THE "CLOCK")

THE number of symphonies written by Haydn exceeds one hundred. It is estimated as high as one hundred and fifty-three, but in a collection of his complete works the number is given as one hundred and four.

When Beethoven could write but nine, Tchaikovsky six, and Brahms four symphonies, it will be easy to conclude that, if Haydn wrote a hundred, the symphony of his time must have been something quite different from that of the romantic and modern composers. It was. It was

* This was called "Turkish" music, perhaps because percussion instruments, widely used in Oriental music, were seldom employed by European composers.

† W. H. Hadow.

infinitely less complicated in scoring, narrower in its dynamic and emotional range, and in every aspect less exacting. It bears the same relationship to a Brahms symphony that a miniature bears to a mural. Consequently, we cannot expect to find here the emotional ferment that agitates the larger and more modern works. The audiences for whom Haydn wrote would have been shocked and displeased, their ears would have protested at, say, the Sixth Symphony of Tchaikovsky. The stylized, the formal, and well-bred, the restrained and polite, the correct and perfect thing, appealed to them.

This is not to intimate that Haydn's music is without charm. Quite the contrary. There is something singularly refreshing and relaxing in the sweet simplicity, the fine direct line, the firm symmetrical contours of this music. The world seems to be turning a degree or so toward graciousness and ease and leisure—enforced or otherwise; perhaps this influence will be felt in music, and such symphonies as this will become even more widely popular.

FIRST MOVEMENT

The movement has an introduction, slow and grave, a foil for the sprightly music that constitutes the main body of this section. A slowly ascending passage for strings and bassoons sounds against woodwind and one section of violins; then, antithetically, violas and cellos in opposite motion give a descending phrase, repeated by flutes. The movement proper begins with a vivacious announcement, by the first violins, of the swiftly ascending scales which constitute the first theme. Later the same instruments are entrusted with the presentation of the second theme, and both are presently involved in elaborate counterpoint, the themes reversed and contrasted and otherwise called forth in contrast to, and support of, each other.

SECOND MOVEMENT

It is this movement which has caused the work to be known as the "Clock" Symphony. The fanciful title is not so farfetched as some. It arises from the firm slow rhythm with which the movement progresses —a rhythm marked by staccato notes of bassoons, violins, cellos, and basses (the strings playing pizzicato), against which first violins play a singularly delicate and simple melody. With occasional robust passages for contrast, the idea presented in the opening section of the movement persists throughout, the respective melody and "ticking clock" parts being assigned to different groups of instruments.

THIRD MOVEMENT

It was a convention which persisted for some time after Haydn that the third movement of a symphony be cast in the form of a minuet. Polite eighteenth-century society knew nothing more abandoned. The present movement is in characteristic form, but somewhat jollier, though not less graceful, than the typical minuet of the period. There is an incident in harmony here which is strange to the music of Haydn but sounds conventional enough to modern ears. It occurs in the trio— the second section of the minuet—and produces a dissonance not at all disagreeable. The eminent critic Mr. Lawrence Gilman held that it was not Haydn's or a copyist's mistake; that it appears in the Haydn manuscript and can be regarded merely as a drone bass.

FOURTH MOVEMENT

It must have been such sprightly and ingenious music as this which captivated the English at the Salomon concerts; indeed, it would fascinate anyone who has ears to hear. The strings have a broad phrase to deliver as the chief subject of the movement, and in a few moments the lightfooted vivacious rhythm asserts itself, sparkling through all sections of the orchestra and eventually involving the ensemble in a brilliant fugue based on the opening subject.

Symphony No. 102 in B flat

THE symphonies of Haydn are informed with a sophisticated musical intelligence, broad and deep; but otherwise are not, as a general rule, profound. The present work often seems an exception—at least in the first and second movements, where we can find assertions as sober as most of Beethoven's and almost as portentous, and melodies as extended and full of sentiment as those of the second movement of the Beethoven Fifth. Yet within the same work one may discover little musical japeries, certain dainty witticisms, mischievous trifles and lighthearted rhythms worthy, and indeed suggestive, of Mozart. The detection of resemblances between one piece of music and another, or between one composer and another, can quickly become a bore; it is indulged in here merely to indicate the extent to which other and later composers were indebted to Haydn.

FIRST MOVEMENT

The opening bars of the introduction are commanding, not so much because of their force but because of their firm dignity and the almost solemn atmosphere that is immediately created. The introduction itself forms a solid point of departure for the brisk vigor of the movement proper, the first theme of which is heard in full orchestra. A companion thematic idea appears suddenly, with nothing tentative or premonitory to indicate its arrival, and the two themes are developed with classical symmetry yet with daring imagination and harmonic ideas that are impressive even to the most sophisticated modern ears.

SECOND MOVEMENT

The somewhat nervous agitation of the preceding movement is here succeeded by an Olympian serenity, expressed in long-phrased melodies of simple, self-contained beauty. The ever-moving accompaniment figure gives forward motion and vitality to the movement.

THIRD MOVEMENT

This is a characteristic minuet movement, a little heavy-handed, perhaps, but with a lift and symmetrical triangular outline of its own. We have come to accept as classic the use of the minuet-form-in-rhythm in the older symphonies; it is entertaining to remember that the employment of the minuet in a piece of serious music was almost as much an innovation about Haydn's time as the introduction of a boogie-woogie movement might be in a contemporary symphony.

FOURTH MOVEMENT

Now Haydn is in a merry mood and reaches deep into his bag of musical tricks to be as entertaining as possible, and to send his audience away with a smile. The light-fingered mischief and musical wit of this movement must have given Mozart something to think about; and for the most part the music here sparkles fully as brilliantly as anything from the hand of that young genius. Fragments of melody are lightly tossed off by strings and woodwind, the bassoon particularly being permitted a moment of well-bred clowning. The withholding of complete thematic statements is amusingly tantalizing; but at the end the theme which generates the light and motion of the whole movement is definitely, if somewhat elaborately, recalled.

Admirers of the Boston Symphony Orchestra may note with interest that this symphony and the Beethoven overture "Consecration of the House" were the most important items on the first program of that orchestra, played on October 22, 1881, under the direction of George Henschel.

Symphony No. 103 in E-flat major ("DRUM ROLL")

THIS happy little work is from the second of two groups of six each which Haydn composed for the London publisher and impresario, Salomon. The symphony is more than one hundred and fifty years old and still is fresh as a bouquet of spring flowers. The scholar may be interested in a few details such as the fact that there is no record of the first performance, though in all probability this occurred in 1794 or 1795, almost certainly in London. Breitkopf and Härtel originally published it as No. 1, the catalog of the London Philharmonic Society indicated it as No. 8, and Breitkopf and Härtel later listed it as No. 103, and it is this designation that is usually applied to it. The symphony is sometimes known as the "Symphonie mit dem Paukenwirbel" —"Symphony with the Drum Roll"—and it is to be distinguished from the Symphony No. 94 in G major, "mit dem Paukenschlag"—"with the Drum Beat"—the latter of which is also known as the "Surprise" Symphony.

There is no necessity to reiterate an analysis of the symphony as Haydn left it to us. The comments in this book having to do with Haydn the musician and with his symphonies in G major (the "Oxford"), in D major (the "Clock"), in G major (the "Surprise"), and in C major (Salomon Set No. 1) expose as much as necessary for the general reader the structural details and perfections which are common to nearly all Haydn's writing in the symphonic form. Neither is there any occasion, nor any opportunity, to associate such music as the present symphony with any story, any picture, or even with any profound emotional attitude. This is music as abstract as music can be, music in which the composer exercises his art within a perfect form and a firm discipline which he himself devised.

FIRST MOVEMENT

As is usual with Haydn, this symphony opens with a grave introduction, in the very first measure of which we hear the roll on the timpani which gives the symphony its popular subtitle. Having subdued his audience and won attention with the somewhat portentous introductory measures, the witty Haydn leads us into a brisk and spirited allegro which constitutes the body of the first movement. The simplicity and clarity of the orchestration, the logic and symmetry of the structure, make any thematic analysis quite superfluous, nor is it necessary to labor the point of Haydn's often-demonstrated wit, exemplified here by the unexpected reappearance of the ominous drum roll in the midst of the gay movement and a reminiscence of material from the introduction. The bright spirit of the allegro, however, dominates and concludes the opening section of the work.

SECOND MOVEMENT

The second movement is sentimental but never for a moment loses the vitality that moves it. It is cast in the form of a theme and variations, all of which are obvious enough. The brisk melody is of singular loveliness, of marked dignity without pompousness, of warm feeling without sentimentality.

THIRD MOVEMENT

If there is anything extraordinary in this movement, a conventional Haydn minuet, it is in the rather exceptional vigor with which it is informed. Here, as in the Haydn symphonies generally, we have the form and rhythm of the minuet, the dance of gentle folk in the Haydn style, but it seems improbable that it could be danced at the tempo usually adopted in a symphonic minuet. The minuet of a symphonic movement is too fast to be practical for dancing, and when played at a tempo that would permit comfortable dancing it sounds slow and heavy-footed. It must be assumed, therefore, that the composer borrowed the form, the rhythm, and the spirit of the minuet but not its pace.

FOURTH MOVEMENT

The final section of the symphony, like the first, is marked *allegro con spirito* and is alive with brisk gaiety. It has been remarked elsewhere in these pages that Haydn was not unacquainted with southern European folk music, and it would appear that in the present symphony and particularly in this movement he remembered fragments of certain folk songs popular in the district where he was born, just as in the opening movement of the "Surprise" Symphony the first theme is suspiciously like a Hungarian gypsy tune. In the present movement, instead of a straightforward presentation of the theme it is, first, in a sense, synthesized, constructed before our eyes and ears with its underlying elements first presented, and then re-presented with the addition of the melodic line which constitutes the most definite contour of the entire movement.

Symphony No. 104 in D major ("LONDON")

THIS joyful, vigorous, and exquisitely modeled music is the last of the one hundred and four authenticated Haydn symphonies and was assigned No. 2 by the London publisher, Salomon, who had commissioned it. It has been differently identified by as many as six other catalog numbers. There is some justification in attaching the title "London" to this work not only because it was commissioned, first performed, and published there, but because the confusion in cataloging makes some special kind of identification necessary. The first performance, with Haydn presiding, was given on May 4, 1795. The composer, who, like most musicians, was not insensitive to the business aspects of his profession, makes it clear in his diary that he was quite well pleased with this evening. "The hall was filled with a picked audience, the whole company was delighted, and so was I. I took in, this evening, four thousand gulden.* One can make as much as this only in England."

The distinguished musicologist Donald F. Tovey, in an essay entitled "Haydn, the Inaccessible," makes a comment that is rather surprising as well as pertinent to the present work:

"Handel and Haydn are, each in a different way, the most unknown of popular classics. What the public hears of Handel represents about one-fiftieth of his works . . . but at all events his complete works are published.

"Haydn is in worse case than any other classic, for not one-tenth of his work is accessible in print at all. . . . No doubt a critical edition of Haydn begun in 1875 would have been as badly begun and as imperfectly carried out as the rest of the series; but the later volumes would have corrected and criticized the earlier, and our knowledge of the most interesting and important chapter in the whole history of music—the early history of the art which Beethoven consummated—would be incomparably clearer than it is at present. Moreover, hundreds of masterpieces would assuredly be brought to light which ought never to have been buried. . . .

"The mutual influence of Haydn and Mozart is one of the best-known wonders of musical history; and the paradox of it is that, while its effect on Mozart was to concentrate his style and strengthen his symmetry, the effect on Haydn was to set him free, so that his large movements became as capricious in their extended course of events as his minuets had always been in the case of their phrases. The orthodox theory of a sonata form . . . will do fairly well for Mozart and Beethoven. . . .

"But with most of the mature works of Haydn, this . . . simply will not do."

One must not expect in any symphony of Haydn, not even in this which is in so many respects the noblest of them all, a music of such cosmic importance and power as Beethoven gave us, nor a music as polished and refined as the symphonies of Mozart. Neither should this

* About $2,000.

music be regarded as a museum piece interesting only to the scholar. True enough, historically this symphony is of notable importance for it marks Haydn's most complete development of the form which he himself had devised. Apart from these things, however, the symphony is intrinsically of musical interest for its definite dramatic power, its passion, its melodic invention, and the inevitable rightness of its orchestration.

FIRST MOVEMENT

One need not be startled when the stately introduction of this symphony in D major begins in D minor. Throughout the movement the thematic material is put forward and answered by contrasting tonal bodies with the responsive phrases almost always in the strings, until in the last measure the oboe contributes its thin, small voice. Here is the musical material upon which the first movement is constructed:

SECOND MOVEMENT

The second movement strikingly reveals Haydn's own growth and development if one compares it with similar movements in the earlier

Haydn music. It sings in a melodic voice of power and passion that somehow seems to free itself from the bounds of conventional structure and to move with a romantic freedom and expressiveness that are rare indeed.

THIRD MOVEMENT

The third movement is a characteristic Haydn minuet, jolly rather than elegant, a trifle heavy-footed perhaps, but engaging nevertheless.

FOURTH MOVEMENT

In the finale Haydn in one more way justifies the subtitle of this symphony, for he built the movement largely on a London street song very popular in 1795. This song was entitled "Red Hot Buns." Its melody, which goes as follows:

presently becomes involved with a second musical idea, likewise melodic in character, and the two are combined and contrasted in an increasingly complicated canonical treatment.

Toy Symphony

FOR many a year Haydn was little known in this country except for this delightful, perfectly fashioned, utterly charming little work. In Germany it is known as the *"Kindersymphonie,"* in France as *"La Faire des enfantes"* or as *"Symphonie Burlesque."* It is related that Haydn in 1788 was amusing himself at a country fair and was quite fascinated by certain musical toys on display there to attract and entertain the children. He bought a collection of them and then wrote this little piece for the purpose of utilizing them. It was played by his orchestra at the Esterházy house. There is no occasion for musical comment on these few minutes of juvenile entertainment except to recommend it for a light moment, and especially for the delight of youngsters. Amateurs get a great deal of fun out of playing it, and sometimes serious musicians do also. The conventional part of the orchestration requires only two violins, one double bass, a piano or harpsichord, and one trumpet. The percussion man, however, will be busy with drums, rattle, triangle, three kinds of bird whistles (quail, cuckoo, and nightingale), and perhaps one or two other handy implements.

Paul Hindemith

————————— BORN 1895 —————————

PAUL HINDEMITH is a Prussian by nativity, by geography, and by accident, but not by temperament. He is full of sunshine and humor and geniality; he has a nature almost Italian in its warmth of spirit though perhaps it is German in its bent toward scholarship, in its impregnable integrity, and its implacable determination.

Hindemith was born in a small town called Hanau near Frankfort am Main. He earned his living by means of music as early as his eleventh year, playing in dance orchestras and motion-picture-theater orchestras. He played the violin in those days but later, like so many violinists of indifferent talent, was attracted to the viola, upon which ungrateful instrument he is a performer of rugged and convincing skill.

It was while playing viola in the Amar Quartet that Hindemith first attracted attention as a composer. This quartet was dedicated to the performance of contemporary and advanced music, and one of its first notable presentations was the performance of the quarter-tone string quartet by Alois Hába, a serenade by Krenek, and other experimental works. Hindemith had already attracted some attention through his opera, strangely entitled *Murder, the Hope of Women,* and it was not long before the Amar Quartet did some of his works and attracted further attention from that section of the public which is interested in controversial music. By 1927 Hindemith had established himself as one of the most influential and interesting men in German music and in this year was appointed professor of composition at the Hochschule für Musik. A few years later he was commissioned by the government of Turkey to reorganize the music of that country in conformity with Occidental ideas, and there he established orchestras, music schools, and standards of interpretation and performance which have been profoundly influential in the development of Western music in the Near East. In 1934 the Nazi Government put Hindemith's music under anathema, and this gesture, together with Hindemith's sympathy with his fellow musicians of non-Aryan heredity, constrained him to leave Germany and settle permanently in America. He has appeared in our country as conductor of his own works and as viola soloist; he has taught extensively and for some time filled a position on the musical faculty of Yale University.

Mathis, der Maler

THERE is a certain fraternity among artists, but the nexus between any two arts, if it exists at all, seems tenuous and fragile. Literary men seldom write with either intelligence or sympathy about music; painters who employ musical subjects often fall into the grossest technical errors and even more often romanticize the subject to a degree that makes the judicious weep; but the musician, who is ordinarily the most sophisticated of artists and the most understanding of and sympathetic with arts other than his own, usually does better than his brethren when he deals with non-musical art works.

Great paintings have often been the catalyst for notable musical reactions. One of Rachmaninoff's most beautiful and apparently most durable works was inspired by a second-rate and sentimental painting by Böchlin called "The Isle of the Dead." One of Moussorgsky's most colorful and most interesting works was based upon an imaginative visit to a gallery of paintings and is perennially popular both in its original form as a piano suite and in the orchestral version devised by Maurice Ravel—"Pictures at an Exhibition." It is unusual to find a contemporary composer turning to such an obvious source for his inspiration, and it is particularly remarkable when so realistic, harsh, and muscular a man as Paul Hindemith looks to a celebrated ecclesiastical painting for the motivation of what well may be his most notable work.

The work which suggested to Hindemith the music of *Mathis, der Maler* is a series of paintings which is the most notable feature of an altarpiece designed for the church of St. Anthony at Isenheim, near Colmar in Alsace-Lorraine. The altarpiece is a masterpiece of Gothic art, and the paintings which are part of it are the work of one Matthias Grünewald, a fifteenth-century artist. Hindemith designed an opera based on incidents portrayed in the paintings, and certain excerpts from the opera have been formed into an orchestral piece which the composer calls a symphony and which we know as *Mathis, der Maler* (Mathias, the Painter). Though the opera from which these excerpts have been drawn and synthesized deals with story and action, Hindemith does not intend in the orchestral version of the music to make what we call "program" music, but, like Debussy in his nocturnes, the composer hopes to evoke emotional and purely subjective responses which might be elicited by contemplation of Grünewald's paintings.

The first performance of *Mathis, der Maler* was given by the Berlin Philharmonic Orchestra, March 12, 1934, Wilhelm Furtwängler conducting. The first American performance was given a few months later by the Philharmonic-Symphony Society of New York. It is rather curious to observe that the opera from which this music is excerpted was not performed until four years later than the orchestral performance— to be exact, at the Zurich Opera, May 28, 1938.

The timelessness of certain ecclesiastical melodies has never been more poignantly illustrated than in this music. This music is modern, it is contemporary, it is even to a certain degree futurist, yet the spirit which informs it is evoked almost entirely by certain church tunes, particularly *"Es sungen drei Engel,"* and *"Lauda Sion."* For an authoritative analysis of the work by one who knows the music and its composer intimately and who has written extensively about both, one may turn to the notes of Heinrich Strobel, for some time music critic of the *Berliner Börsenkurier* and author of a definitive work on Hindemith and his music:

"I. Angelic Concert. (*Ruhig bewegt—Ziemlich lebhafter Halbe.*) The basic key of the symphony is D flat, in the compass of which lie the ancient melodies employed in the first and third movements. In the 'Angelic Concert' the tension between the keys of D flat and G underlies the harmonic construction of the movement. The *cantus firmus,* '*Es sungen drei Engel*' ('Three Angels Sang'), which first is heard at the eighth measure in the trombones, is developed dynamically upward. This is followed by a quick main section. Its first part is based on a theme (flutes and first violins) which may be looked upon as a model of Hindemith's style in melodic development—a melody that is characterized by a wavering between major and minor. A second theme follows in the strings, calmer and more lyrical in character. A third division deals with the two themes in a lightly hovering *fugato* to which, again in the trombones, there is added the 'Angel' subject. The last phrase of the 'Angel' theme leads back to the tender tranquillity that broods over the entire movement, and which evokes the gentle radiance of Grünewald's incomparable picture of the Nativity. A terse coda, fortissimo, forms a joyous conclusion.

"II. Entombment. (*Sehr langsam.*) The two principal subjects of the second movement, the 'Entombment,' are typical of Hindemith's melodic style—the first, in the muted strings and woodwind, with its purely linear structure; the second (in oboe, then flute, with pizzicato accompaniment) with its intervallic structure of fourths and fifths. With what wonderful simplicity do the melodic lines of the woodwind ascend; and how beautiful is the effect of the plaintive call of the clarinet after the brief crescendo and the pause!

"III. The Temptation of Saint Anthony. (*Sehr langsam, frei im Zeitmass-Lebhaft.*) It is in the third movement that the broadest and boldest character is set forth. From the visual tension of Grünewald's painting, an aural tension has been brought about. The power of the music is so marked that one might almost find a poetic interpretation for the movement, although the subjects are developed in a strictly linear manner, and even the most grandiose tonal effects show a cogent musical logic. Hindemith's art of tonal disposition is united to a power of fantasy which surprises even those who know his compositions best. 'The Temptation of the Saint' covers a tremendous musical canvas, from the opening unison of the strings (bearing the quotation, '*Ubi eras, bone Jhesu ubi eras, quare non affuisti ut sanares vulnera mea?*'), up to the chorale in the brass of the closing Hallelujah. The key of D flat is the basis of harmonic development, the symbol of sanctity. The greater the struggle of the contesting forces, the more widely does the music depart from this harmonic foundation. The ascent of the string unisono, which is intensified in an astonishing fashion by the opposing figure in the brass, is a striking example of a crescendo developed in the linear manner. This heroic statement is succeeded by the first onset of the opposing forces (if such an expression can be applied to a process so purely musical), with another subject for the unison strings. A grandiose pas·

sage ends the first division of the movement. There is a long and elaborate development. The battle is already decided when the key of D flat is reached once more with the *fugato*. Clarinets, then the horn, return to the subject of the unisono string introduction; there is heard in the woodwinds the hymn '*Lauda Sion Salvatorem*,' and then, fortissimo in the brass, we are led through the Hallelujah to a resplendent and triumphal conclusion in D-flat major."

Symphony in E flat

THE Minneapolis Symphony Orchestra, Dimitri Mitropoulos conducting, had the privilege of first presenting this work, at a concert on November 21, 1941, in the Northrup Auditorium at the University of Minnesota. New York first heard the work at a concert of the Philharmonic-Symphony Society, again Mr. Mitropoulos conducting, December 25, 1941. Mr. Stokowski, whose admiration for a musical work is not always predicated upon a first performance, also presented this symphony on January 2, 1947, when he conducted the Philharmonic.

We have come to expect of Mr. Hindemith music that is lean and sinewy, at times rather forbidding, at times difficult of acceptance, but always surging with vitality, with stark power, though its moments of tenderness are rare. All of these characteristics are present in this work, but it would seem that there is something less of harshness in the harmony. In spite of the fact that the score has no key signatures, the work is entitled "in E flat," and formal references to this tonality are clear. The music is terse, compact, somewhat abrupt, direct, and candid—all of which are qualities of the composer himself as well as of his work.

FIRST MOVEMENT

A solid and vigorous proclamation of the horns gives out the first theme. This theme is really basic in the movement, for during the greater part of the movement virtually all thematic ideas—and there are many of them—are in one way or another derived from the first. The music is of great sonority, yet additional resources of tone seem always available because of the fluidity and adept calculation of the scoring; and there is a climax of thunderous power. The second section of the movement is of no less solidity than the first, but is considerably gentler and less assertive, with the principal theme in woodwind and brass against a powerfully projected melody in the strings.

SECOND MOVEMENT

In a general way Hindemith follows the accepted structure of the symphony, though there is not a conventional sonata form exhibited. The second movement is based on two principal ideas: the first, at the beginning, entrusted to the voices of English horn, clarinet, and trumpet over a persistent rhythm of the timpani; the second, proposed by the oboe with additional suggestions from the string section. This is developed into a long passage, marked by what Debussy would have called *"sonorité sans dureté."* There is some ingenious writing in canon form later on in the movement.

THIRD MOVEMENT

There is great good humor here. In a broad way the form of the scherzo is used, although its outlines are perhaps far from the classic. They are nevertheless discernible. In the first part of the movement there are two interesting ideas, one the rather timid phrase of the violins, the other a happy song by the English horn and other woodwinds. In the second section, corresponding to a trio, again we encounter two themes, one for the oboe and the other for a combination of English horn and oboe. There is a typical return to the atmosphere and thematic material in new treatment at the end.

FOURTH MOVEMENT

There is no interruption between the third and fourth movements, but there is a marked change in the pace and the mood. The fourth movement is a cycle within itself, introducing a prodigious variety of ideas but achieving unity and coherence through constant reference, direct or indirect, to its basic theme; and it is indeed this theme which eventually becomes the extraordinary sonorous climax of the finale, and of the symphony.

Basil Sergeivich Kalinnikoff

1866-1901

KALINNIKOFF was born in Voina in the government of Orlov, Russia, and spent virtually his entire life within the boundaries of his native land. He was a frail and talented child, but fortunately was in such a situation that both qualities could receive proper attention. He had the best of instruction and his teachers, Ilyinsky and Blaramberg, believed that he was a genius, both because of the swiftness of his progress and, eventually, the substantial and sometimes brilliant quality of his compositions. Long before Kalinnikoff was thirty years old he was appointed a conductor of the Italian Opera at Moscow. After a single season, however, the exertions attendant upon his duties depleted his strength and laid him open to the onslaught of tuberculosis. Forced to abandon conducting, Kalinnikoff established himself in the balmy atmosphere of southern Russia and spent the few remaining years of his life there. It was during this period that those of his works that we know were brought into being. Among these were two symphonies, two intermezzi for orchestra, an orchestral suite, two symphonic sketches, incidental music to Tolstoy's drama *Czar Boris*, a cantata, *St. John Chrysostom*, a piece in ballad form for solo voices, chorus, and orchestra, and various shorter works for piano and for voice. Of these, the only work at all widely known today is the First Symphony.

Symphony No. 1 in G minor

OCCASIONALLY it happens that a moderate talent flares out with a flash of real genius, and this seems to have been the case with Kalinnikoff's First Symphony. This beautiful work is not designed along the lines of the massive Tchaikovsky symphonies, yet in its more modest way it can be considered of value equal to any of them. Like them, it is influenced

by Russian folk music, though it does not appear that there is any literal use of a folk tune.

FIRST MOVEMENT

The first theme is strongly Russian in flavor and has the earthy

charm characteristic of all folk music. It establishes the mood and feeling for the whole first movement which, as it moves through its developments, never lets us forget this pensive little melody. There are other
interesting melodic elements—indeed the symphony is a chain, or perhaps more properly a cycle, of melodies—but even when they are treated
in counterpoint and fugue there is never a moment of obscurity or of
uncertainty or of complexity.

SECOND MOVEMENT

The simplicity and directness and the songlike character of the second movement are set forth and established by a lovely melody that
forms a kind of introduction. The orchestral color darkens, the emotional tenseness becomes somewhat more marked, and the oboe begins
a song of poignant melancholy. Its verses are heard in various instruments and it constitutes the principal thematic material for the whole
movement. A second melody is introduced, and this section of the symphony is devoted to an exquisitely beautiful treatment of the two
themes in counterpoint. The movement attains a perfect symmetry by
the introduction, near the end, of the lyrical subject of the prelude.

THIRD MOVEMENT

In the third movement there is a resurgence of vigor and of brighter
spirits, and this forceful idea is projected immediately.

It is played with staccato assurance, and another subject which presently appears is even more assertive.

This fragment is worth special observation since we will encounter it later on in the finale, somewhat altered in form but definitely recognizable in spite of a rhythmic distortion. The changing moods here are indicated by the substitution of a songlike motif assigned to the oboe, and later a bright and dancelike figure, for the downright utterances that occurred near the beginning. The movement ends, however, in the aggressive humor of the opening.

FOURTH MOVEMENT

The fourth section of the symphony looks backward to the preceding sections for a considerable part of its material. Each movement of the work is symmetrical, exquisitely fashioned and finished; and the fourth recapitulates all three preceding. Of course, the thematic material is treated differently in orchestration, in harmony, and in rhythmic mutations. Of the new material which the composer introduces in this movement, the most important themes are this swift and brilliant one:

and a more lyrical and tender melody:

The references to the first three movements are generally quite literal, but the subject taken from the third movement, already quoted above, undergoes a change in rhythm which alters its motion, though not its contours.

The present interest in all Russian music perhaps accounts for the rather sudden popularity of this genuinely delightful work. It has been played on occasion in Europe since its first performance at Kiev in 1897, and in recent seasons has won what appears to be a permanent place in the repertoire of most first-rate American symphony orchestras.

Ernst Krenek

E RNST KRENEK, one of the most highly individual and prolific of
contemporary composers, was born at Vienna, August 23, 1900,
of Czechoslovakian parents. He lived in Vienna for twenty years and
there was the brilliant pupil of the composer Franz Schreker. He later
established himself in Berlin, in Zurich, and in Weisbaden, where he
was associated in the direction of the opera.

Krenek's most conspicuous achievement, perhaps, was the opera in
jazz, *Jonny Spielt Auf*, first produced at Leipzig in 1927 and in the following season at the Metropolitan Opera House in New York. The
ironic note is sounded frequently in the opera, as indeed it is in most
of Krenek's music, including the Little Symphony written in 1928. In
addition to *Jonny Spielt Auf* and the Little Symphony, Krenek has
written several one-act operas, a comic opera in three acts, a grand
opera in five acts, a ballet, a cantata, and many short works of chamber
music, songs and works for piano, to say nothing of suites, diverti-
menti, a piano concerto, and several *concerti grossi*. His music is, as a
rule, daringly atonal, highly inventive, strikingly individual. To quote
the German critic Leichtentritt, "Krenek is a typical child of his generation, devoid of sentimentality, greedy for fame, fond of sensation,
anarchistic in his aesthetic views, and without the least respect for
tradition."

Little Symphony

ONE must have an appetite for the daring, the "modern," the unconventional and the dissonant to enjoy this music. Even its score is highly
unconventional, calling for two flutes, three clarinets, bass clarinet, two
bassoons, two double bassoons, two trumpets, two trombones, tuba,
harp, two mandolins, guitar, two banjos, Rührtrommell, snare drum,
bass drum, cymbals, timpani, violins, and basses. The first perform-

ance was at Berlin, in November, 1928, Otto Klemperer conducting. The work was played for the first time in America November 6, 1930, by the Philharmonic-Symphony Society of New York under the direction of Erich Kleiber. Perhaps it would be better to give Krenek an opportunity to make his own comment upon the music:*

"The *Little Symphony* makes use throughout of the traditional sonata form. An attempt is made in the first movement to treat A and A flat (major and minor) to some extent as basic tonalities of equal importance. The first theme is in A minor, the second in E major, the closing group in E flat, while in the reprise, A-flat minor and A major enter at the appropriate places. The coda then leads to A-flat major. This principle provides great harmonic variety, and interesting, doubly significant modulations.

"The second movement is in quite simple three-part song form, and the finale is a concise rondo with two—or, if you will, three—subsidiary themes, which unfold in two almost symmetrical parallel parts. The thematic connection is very loose, i.e., the themes are strung together, potpourri fashion, and are bound organically only by the obstinate tango rhythm. This technique offers many opportunities to the composer.

"The last movement, like the closing section of the first, is tinged with the characteristics of the modern dance—though not, however, with any parodistic intention. The 'tango' idea plays in my symphony a role no more or less important than the minuet in the classical symphony. The dance character of the music was suggested by my use in the score of plucked instruments: two banjos, two mandolins, guitar, and harp. These instruments were not employed, however, because of their association with jazz, but because of their appropriateness to the vibrating, rattling, metallic sound which I had conceived for the expression of my music. . . ."

* By permission of the Philharmonic-Symphony Society of New York.

Franz Liszt

1811-1886

O NE OF THE MOST spectacular and eccentric geniuses in the history
of music, Franz Liszt may be remembered longer because of what
he did for the music of others than by his own creations. His family
was an obscure one, in the service of the famous Hungarian noble family, the Esterházys. His father was sufficiently interested and capable in
music to give the child piano lessons, with such success that at the age
of nine years Franz made his debut—and a successful one—as a concert pianist. This attracted the attention of certain wealthy patrons of
music, who subscribed to a fund which guaranteed some years of further study for the boy. The result of this was that when Liszt was only
eleven years old, he gave a concert in Vienna which won the hearty
approval of everyone who heard it—including Ludwig van Beethoven.

Liszt was now regarded as an important musician, in spite of his
childish years; but he was not a completely developed one. He was not
permitted to enter the Paris Conservatoire, where he sought further
training, but he found teachers elsewhere who helped him greatly. He
began a series of concert tours which took him virtually all over the
Continent, and to England, and which established him without question
as the greatest pianist of his day. His admirers were virtually idolatrous; and one of them, the Countess d'Agoult, whom Liszt met in
Paris, became his mistress and bore him three children. Even in father-
ing these extralegal progeny Liszt did a service to music and to a composer whose music he was to espouse with enthusiasm; for one of them,
Cosima, became the wife of Richard Wagner, and his helper and ferocious protagonist to the end of her days.

In 1849 Liszt settled at Weimar, and became director of the court
theater there. He abandoned the career of a virtuoso to accept this position, and did so in order that he might be in a position to forward the
works of other composers. This act, though it may not have been done

without an eye to his own limitations and advantages, was nevertheless not without elements of a fantastic generosity—a quality which always had distinguished the man. From one point of view it fits neatly into the pattern of his life and character. Though a pianist whose gifts have never been duplicated, Liszt was always at his best in works by other composers, and had a singular adeptness in comprehending their meanings, and exemplifying them with more accuracy and expressiveness than the composers themselves. He was indifferent or, at the most, tolerant when musicians played *his* music badly, but would fly into terrible rages if they played imperfectly, say, a Beethoven sonata. Richard Wagner, perhaps in compensation for holding his tongue in his cheek as far as Liszt's own music was concerned, praised Liszt as an executant, and, in effect, asserted that here Liszt was really a composer; that he did not *reproduce*, but *produced*, the music of other composers.

In his later years Liszt, after having had a merry time of it in his youth, and always a brilliant and worldly life, turned with strange devotion to the more ascetic type of Catholicism. While in Rome he became a member of the Franciscan brotherhood, and was invested with the minor orders—porter, reader, exorcist, and acolyte. He was tonsured, and wore clerical garb, in which he is often pictured, the center of interest in a brilliant salon.

After attending a performance of *Tristan und Isolde* at Bayreuth, July 4, 1886, Liszt was stricken with his final illness. He died a few weeks later.

The composer left behind him an astonishing amount of work, vocal, instrumental, and literary. Much of his music is bombastic and vacuous; some of the piano transcriptions are exceedingly brilliant and vulgar; but there are treasures among his works, nevertheless. The arrangements of some of Bach's organ works are superb; and the Hungarian Rhapsodies, while not profound as a rule, are wonderful display pieces. Liszt invented the "symphonic poem"—music of symphonic dimensions but free in style, and usually in one movement—and though others have made better use of the form, Liszt will be remembered for having devised it.

A Faust Symphony in Three Character Pictures
(AFTER GOETHE)

LISZT was one of many artists who were attracted to the strange story of Faust, especially as related in Goethe's dramatic poem. His musical version is not strictly a symphony, but a symphonic poem in three movements. Liszt himself conducted the first performance of the work at Weimar, September 15, 1857. It is dedicated to Hector Berlioz.

FIRST MOVEMENT
Faust

The composer attempts to apply the quality of universality to the suffering, the dissatisfaction, the jaded impotence and weariness of Faust; and would use Goethe's protagonist as a lay figure bearing the burdens of all humanity. Lower strings, muted, and presently touched with piercing woodwinds, suggest the disheartened and gloomy mood of the hero. Once this melancholy atmosphere is established, there is a quickening and a brightening in the music, and a transitional passage, in which emphatic phrases are proposed and answered in strings and woodwind, leads to the main portion of the movement.

Now the music takes on a totally different character. Faust dallies with the dreadful notion of selling his soul. At one moment, he is filled with terror and repulsion; again, as the possible joys of recovered youth are suggested, he rages with longing, with ambition, with desire. He doubts, he hesitates, he falls; and a quiet passage, strings against woodwind, suggests the workings of the magic. Now life is infused into the scene, as Faust, his veins expanded with new, warm, rich blood, looks about him for a world—and a woman—to conquer. An aggressive utterance of the trumpet suggests the burning glance with which he contemplates his surroundings and his future. The remainder of the movement is filled with ceaseless activity, climax after climax, yet at the end there is a suggestion of the sense of satiety and depletion which was noticed in the introduction.

SECOND MOVEMENT
Marguerite

Oboe, against an arpeggiolike figure in the solo viola, suggests the sweet maid Marguerite; but in that keen and pensive and somewhat passionate voice of the oboe there are suggestions of unnamed longings and a certain restlessness. These are satisfied with the entrance of another theme in woodwind, supposedly indicative of the dawn of love. There is a passage of intense beauty, wherein the strings sing of passion not only awakened but returned and realized; and an amorous conversation of cellos and violins. Near the end of the movement we are reminded of Faust's resolution by a reference to the trumpet's bold cry in the first movement.

THIRD MOVEMENT
Mephistopheles

One of Liszt's directions for interpreting this movement is *"ironico"*; and the character of the musical content lends itself admirably to ironic treatment. Here the motives of the preceding movements are horribly distorted and burlesqued. Mephistopheles sneers and jeers at the recollection of Faust's grandiose plans and resolutions; he mocks the thought of an innocent virgin. Sometimes he roars in paroxysms of laughter; he poisonously snickers, through the medium of sharply plucked strings, at melancholy Faust. And as the movement proceeds toward its close, the Devil rocks from side to side in Gargantuan scornful mirth. He is restrained toward the end, and a chorus of men's voices sings philosophical reflections upon the vanity of life.

Gustav Mahler

G USTAV MAHLER was born at Kalischt, in Bohemia, to parents who were poor in this world's goods, but not unacquainted with more permanent and desirable treasures in the form of books and music. The boy soon showed signs of interest in both. When he was six years old he preferred playing the piano to games, and, when he was eight, gave piano lessons to a seven-year-old pupil. Music so fascinated him, and so clearly revealed itself as the dominating passion of his young life, that his father finally took the boy to a famous teacher at Vienna and asked if Gustav had sufficient talent to justify the expense of a musical education. The answer was definitely in the affirmative.

Mahler entered the Vienna Conservatory at the age of fifteen. At the end of the very first year he won a prize for piano-playing, and another for composition. Later he distinguished himself further at the piano, and there is evidence that he could have had a virtuoso career with that instrument had he so chosen. During and after his period at the Conservatory, Mahler supported himself by teaching piano; but not long after leaving the school, he obtained the first of a series of positions as conductor in various minor musical centers. Eventually he became assistant to Anton Seidl, later to Arthur Nikisch; and finally chief conductor at Budapest. He was established as an important musical figure in Europe, and so it was natural that when the post of conductor of the Vienna Opera became vacant, Mahler was chosen. Later he directed the Vienna Philharmonic Society.

In 1907, Mahler was engaged by Conried to conduct at the Metropolitan Opera in New York, and during the season of 1908–09 he was appointed to direct the Philharmonic Society. A terrific schedule of concerts was undertaken, and the health of the composer, never robust, gave way under the strain. He had conducted two seasons with the Philharmonic, but was unable to finish the third. He returned to Europe, vainly sought to restore his health, and finally went home to Vienna, to die.

To estimate the works or the importance of Mahler within the limitations of this book is not possible. For an adequate biography one may turn to that very sympathetic one written by Gabriel Engel, and published (1932) by The Bruckner Society of America. Mahler's music, when performed in America, has created unprecedented sensation, and success; yet it is played all too infrequently. When Leopold Stokowski gave nine successive performances of the "Symphony of a Thousand" in Philadelphia and New York, it made, to quote the conductor, "an impression on the public unlike anything else I have ever experienced . . . so deeply moved the public that the greater part of the listeners were in tears at the end of the performance."

In spite of public receptivity, conductors as a rule have neglected Mahler's works until comparatively recent years; and we must half sadly, half hopefully join in his own frequent and confident declaration: *"Meine Zeit wird noch kommen"*—"My time will yet come." There are indications that his "time" is imminent.

Symphony No. 1 in D major

COMPOSERS often have the same attitude toward their work as has the painter who recoils in hurt and horror when he hears of his picture, "Beautiful—but what does it represent?" Perhaps the composer has better reason to be affronted by similar remarks, for unless he is frankly writing program music he is trying, through an immaterial medium, to represent something immaterial and subjective; whereas it is not wholly unreasonable to suppose that the painter, using tangible materials, visible forms, designs and colors, must have had some visible and material inspiration for them.

Mahler often expressed a horror of program music, yet entitled some of his works with names which definitely suggested stories or at least something of the material world; in some instances he actually wrote a kind of program for his work. He confessed, too, the influence of nature upon him and suggested that "the world may give me . . . the title 'The Singer of Nature,' for, since childhood, nature has meant everything to me." He even wrote a kind of program for the first performance of the music we are considering here, and again for the Second or "Resurrection" Symphony. In spite of this he could write that "It [the program for the Second Symphony] only gives a superficial indication, all that any program can do for a musical work, let alone this one, which is so much all of a piece that it can no more be explained than the world itself.—I'm quite sure that if God were asked to draw up a program of the world He had created He could never do it. —At best it would say as little about the nature of God and life as my analysis says about my C minor Symphony. In fact, as all religious doctrines do, it leads directly to misunderstanding, to a flattening and coarsening, and in the long run to such distortion that the work, and still more its creator, is utterly unrecognizable." In the face of such a statement it is somewhat presumptuous to offer any extended analysis of this or any other work of Mahler; perhaps an unqualified acceptance of his dictum would invalidate the very existence of this book. In the face of Mahler's own inconsistency, however, we may at least take the risk of quoting the program that he himself wrote for the first performance of this music at a Philharmonic concert in Budapest, November 20, 1889. On this occasion it was entitled "Symphonic Poem in Two Parts." Mahler himself conducted. Some years later the work was performed at Weimar, again under the composer's direction, and it was programmed as the "Titan" Symphony. In addition, Mahler permitted to be printed in the program the following descriptions of the five sections of the work:

"From the Days of Youth
  "I. Spring and no end. The Introduction portrays the awakening of nature in the early morning.
  "II. Flower Chapter. [This Andante was omitted from subsequent performances.]
  "III. Under Full Sail.
"Commedia umana
  "IV. The hunter's funeral procession; a dead march in the manner of Callot. [Jaques Callot was a French engraver who died in 1635.] The following is to serve as explanation if it is necessary: The composer found the exterior incitement to this musical work in the burlesque pictures of the hunter's funeral pro-

cession in the old fairy-tale book well known to all the children of South Germany. The beasts of the wood escort the coffin of the dead forester to the grave—hares carry the banneret, while a band of Bohemian musicians leads the procession in farcical attitudes, accompanied by cats, toads, crows, and others making music, and by stags, roes, foxes, and other four-legged and feathered animals. This movement, conceived as the expression of a now ironically joyous, now mysteriously brooding, spirit, is followed by 'Dall' inferno' (*Allegro furioso*) as the sudden outbreak of a deeply wounded heart.

"V. *Dall' inferno al Paradiso.*"

When the symphony was published in 1897 Mahler had eliminated all descriptive notes and titles, but with the above as a guide one can make reasonable deductions and inferences as to the composer's meaning, and analysis becomes interesting or useful only to the scholar and the musicologist.

Symphony No. 2 in C minor
[*For Orchestra, Chorus, Soli Soprano and Contralto*]

THIS gigantic work was written in 1895. Performances in America have been exceedingly few, primarily because of the extensive orchestral resources required by the score, and also because of the indifference to the music of Mahler which existed for many years, among both conductors and audiences here and abroad. The decline of ultramodern music during the past few seasons has had a counter-effect in the development of public taste for music of the post-Wagnerian period, during which Mahler and Bruckner produced their greatest works.

The symphony required an enormous orchestra, chorus, soli soprano and contralto, pipe organ, and church bells. A recording of one of the few performances ever given, when all the requirements of the score were available, is in existence.

FIRST MOVEMENT
Allegro maestoso

The music is full of powerful contrasts. The solemn atmosphere which surrounds the music early in the first movement is often interrupted by high drama and heroic song; the suspension of vitality that sometimes seems to be indicated is frequently contrasted with musical utterances suggesting the most vigorous action. Intermingled with these come frequent melodies of the most ingratiating and buoyant character. Strings and brass are used for contrasts of both timbre and emotional significance, but the resolute song that forms the basis for the movement is finally dominant.

SECOND MOVEMENT
Andante moderato

Those who have too eagerly accepted the dictum that Mahler is dull and heavy should turn to the elastic rhythms and charming melody of this movement for a demonstration of the falsity of the accusation. Here a little folk song is carried forward, of a quaint and moving rhythm. Ultimately there is a leisurely development suggesting a fugue and a climax of impressive power in brass and strings, but the movement ends in an atmosphere of quiet courage and complacence.

THIRD MOVEMENT
With quietly flowing movement

The movement has some of the stark and detached quality which in recent seasons we have come to associate with much of the symphonic work of Sibelius. Normally this movement would be the scherzo of the symphony, but that term cannot be applied to it with any degree of accuracy. Though there are flashes of humor and mischievousness and often quite frisky rhythms, the mood of the movement is not exactly playful. Its atmosphere is at moments quite pastoral and the composer makes use of what are unmistakably old folk songs and dances.

FOURTH MOVEMENT
Primal Light (Contralto solo. Very solemn but simply; like a chorale.)

The fourth movement of the symphony is inspired by verses taken from a collection of Germany poetry, *Knaben Wunderhorn*. This verse is sung by a contralto voice accompanied by the orchestra. The orchestra, in fact, projects its own wordless interpretation of the verses in contrast and complement to the verses sung by the contralto. They are as follows:

Thou red, red rose!
Ah, man lies in bitter throes.
Yea, man lies in greatest woe—
Far rather I would to heaven go.
I entered upon a broad highway.
Then came an angel bright and wanted to stay me.
Ah no, I would not let him stay me!
Ah no, I would not let him stay me!
I am from God, I will go back to God!
The merciful God, the merciful God, a candle will be sending,
To light my way into a blessed life unending.

FIFTH MOVEMENT
Finale: *"The Great Summons"*

The inspiration of the fifth movement is also a poem, entitled *The Resurrection,* written by the German poet Klopstock, with the orchestra supplying a rich and variously colored background. The poem is delivered in the form of solos for contralto and soprano with chorus in the background. The climax is one of the most splendid in all music. Here chorus, orchestra, and organ join in a fervent outpouring, above which rises the clangor of great bells. At the end the music reaches a degree of sonority almost unmatched in symphonic music.

Symphony No. 5 in C minor
[*In Three Parts*]

I.   1. Dead March—with measured step—like a funeral train
        Suddenly faster, passionately, wildly
     2. With stormy emotion. With utmost vehemence
II. 3. Scherzo. With force, but not too fast
III. 4. *Adagietto,* very slow
     5. Rondo finale: allegro

IT IS entirely possible that we are doing Mahler no service in commenting in print upon his work. No one more actively hated program notes and musical commentary and, for that matter, program music. It is curiously ironical, therefore, that so much should have been written about his music, so many of his works given fanciful titles, not to mention the fact that he himself resorted to words as the carriers of his musical ideas. Of his ten complete symphonies, five have been given more or less authentic subtitles. The First is known as the "Titan"; the Second, as the "Resurrection"; the Third, as the "Summer Morning's Dream" or even "Programme" Symphony; the Fifth, as "The Giant"; and the Eighth, as the "Symphony of the Thousand."

It is curious that with his antipathy respecting program music he could have said, as he did: "When I conceive a great musical picture, I always arrive at the point where I must employ the 'word' as the bearer of my musical idea. My experience with the last movement of my second symphony was such that I ransacked the literature of the world, up to the Bible, to find the expository word." Likewise, he went to a collection of Chinese poems published under the title *The Chinese Flute* for the inspiration and text of his *"Das Lied von der Erde"*; and to the hymn *"Veni, Creator Spiritus"* for the essence of his Eighth Symphony; and possibly to Jean Paul Richter's romance *The Titan* for the inspiration of his First Symphony. Yet he expressed an abhorrence of program books, argument and analysis of any and every kind. Thus, when the present work was performed for the first time at Cologne, October 18, 1904, with the composer conducting, there were no program notes. Incidentally, there was considerable applause and some hissing. When the work was performed a few months later by the Berlin Philharmonic, again there were no program notes. Later there was a performance in Munich which Mahler himself conducted, and after the concert he was invited to supper with some of his admirers. During the post-concert conversation someone mentioned program notes. Ludwig Schiedermair recalls * what then happened: "Then was it as though lightning flashed in a joyous, sunny landscape. Mahler's eyes were more brilliant than ever, his forehead wrinkled, he sprang in excitement from the table and exclaimed in passionate tones: 'Away with program books, which breed false ideas! The audience should be left to its own thoughts over the work that is performing: it should not be forced to read during the performance; it should not be prejudiced in any manner. If a composer by his music forces on his hearers the sensations which streamed through his mind, then he reaches his goal.

* Gustav Mahler: *Eine biographischkiritische Würdigung.*

The speech of tones has then approached the language of words, but it is far more capable of expression and declaration.' And Mahler raised his glass and emptied it with *'Pereat den Programmen!'* "

A really thorough analysis of this symphony or of any other Mahler symphony might fill half of this book. Such an analysis was printed serially in 1904 in a famous musical magazine, and it occupied twenty-three large octavo pages. For anyone who feels that technical analysis is desirable and necessary, this remarkable piece is probably still in print and is published by the Peters Edition.

The Fifth Symphony was begun in 1901 and finished in the spring of 1903 while Mahler was living in his villa on Lake Wörther. This was a productive period for him; it resulted in the publication of many songs, shorter works, and particularly the grim but beautiful *"Kindertotenlieder."*

On hearing and reflecting upon this work, it is entirely possible to be in agreement with the late Philip Hale, who, with his almost infallible instinct, likened it to the great statue that stood before Nebuchadnezzar in a dream. "And the form thereof was terrible. The image's head was of fine gold, his breast and his arms of silver, his belly and his thighs of brass, his legs of iron, his feet part of iron and part of clay." Mr. Hale meant to indicate that the symphony is a gigantic mixture of good, even great, music, and music the banality of which is but meagerly covered by the application of musical device, with the confused colors of orchestration. The idol had feet of clay indeed, for in spite of technical skill of the highest order the symphony has long stretches marred by the most serious fault any music can have—boredom. The second section of the work, however, need not answer to such a charge. It is perhaps more abandoned and less self-conscious than anything Mahler has written in symphonic form. The scherzo is not the gayest or the best of Mahler's music, but it is certainly entertaining, if at moments somewhat heavy-handed.

The first part of section three, *adagietto,* seems the most sincere and the most profound in feeling—the most sincere and genuine in spite of the fact that one may perceive traces—and more than traces—of Wagnerian influence; just as in the finale, the Beethoven of the Ninth Symphony frowns momentarily. Here let us respect the composer's advice, "The audience should be left to its own thoughts over the work that is performing."

Symphony No. 9

A CONDUCTOR is often like a bachelor obstetrician who, after supervising many an accouchement, becomes possessed of an intolerable longing to father a child of his own. The doctor no doubt has all the normal instincts of a man, but under the social law his bachelorhood prohibits him from exercising them, while under the natural law his inhibitions keep him a bachelor. Yet the will to create, to beget, to immortalize himself, is strong. It must often be so with a conductor, especially with a great conductor whose talents make, for him, every great score an open book; and there must come a time when he wearies of the obstetrics of other men's brain children and longs to present his own to the world. It is unfortunate that this should be so because as a rule such a situation is brought about by a kind of artistic envy and a sense of inferiority arising from a misconception of the conductor's own creative opportunity; and neither of these supply adequate motivation for a great art work. The conductor qua conductor is as truly a creative artist as the composer, and occasionally his contribution to the realization of a composer's work is more important than the author's. Sometimes the conductor does not appreciate this, or if he does, is not satisfied. He feels that he, too, experiences soul-storms and private drama that can be expressed only in music, and when he attempts to express them, seldom realizes that he is drawing on his experience as a conductor and his acquaintance with the work of other men, and more or less innocently, as though he had been cuckolded, presenting their perverted offspring as his own.

Mahler's talents as a conductor were distinguished. As a student of the problems presented by great symphonic music, he felt that there were within himself problems of equal interest, problems that were even cosmic in their implications and importance. Their importance, as it turned out, was apparent chiefly to himself. The consensus of music lovers, notwithstanding the Mahlerites and the Brucknerites, seems to be that Mahler's music is often lacking in that quality of universality which is essential to any great art work. An astute commentator, Henry Boys, has remarked that Mahler felt "a fervent desire to communicate"; but what he had to communicate was not precisely of world-shaking importance. It cannot be said, or at least it cannot be substantiated, that his message was so abstruse that earthbound souls—such as the present commentator—cannot understand it; for Mahler had at his command a technique of composition that could clarify any idea, if the idea were there to be clarified. The average devotee of the symphony finds in Mahler's music a curious combination of purpose and vagueness; an attempt at simplicity that often achieves banality and boredom; an insistence, repetitiousness, discursiveness, and prolixity that in this decade are difficult to dissociate from some of the harangues of the late Corporal Hitler. Yet philosophically he was far removed from Hitler. He was a man, as Mr. Boys remarks, "of great complexity"; a man of great breadth—but often, like some of our great American rivers, a mile in breadth and an inch in depth. Yet the very volume of Mahler's music, as with the volume of our rivers, encloses within itself a superlative power, and more than a power, a potentiality of incalculable dimensions.

FIRST MOVEMENT

Mahler is reported to have asserted that all music since Beethoven has been program music. In a sense, as has been intimated elsewhere in these pages, all music is program music; but the term in the sense in which we generally understand it certainly cannot be applied to the Ninth Symphony of Mahler, though elsewhere in his music, indeed in four out of his nine symphonies, he found it expedient to use poetry to make his music intelligible. Certainly the opening of this movement is abstract enough, even mysterious; it continues with periodic melodic suggestions from the second, the first, and again the second violins until a powerful and significant declaration is poured forth from the trumpets.

This undergoes various mutations and is subjected to many a violent dynamic contrast. Its extended treatment in combination with other

thematic material would constitute a complete movement in a symphony of ordinary length, but Mahler has many a thematic idea to
present before he is finished with this movement. There are at least
eight themes of importance in the movement, all of which are thoroughly and lengthily adumbrated. Of all these motives, the most important, perhaps, are the one quoted above and this one:

which is heard near the beginning of the movement and is exploited
rather more thoroughly toward the latter portion of this part of the
symphony.

SECOND MOVEMENT

The exaggerated simplicity which Mahler sometimes attempted to
bring to his music and which only too often ended in vagueness and
obfuscation is rather well exemplified in this movement. The music is
based on an Austrian peasant dance—a kind of heavy-footed waltz
with a decided accent on the first beat of the three-beat measure. In
this instance, however, Mahler also superimposes upon this rugged
rhythm and simple melodic material a kind of perverse and distorted
unhappiness which this particular dance type was never intended to
convey. This must be the "tragic undertone" which Bruno Walter finds
in this music. The familiar Mahler device of sudden dynamic contrasts
is freely employed.

The first theme is rhythmically typical of all the thematic material
employed in this movement. Violas and bassoons give it a tentative start
and the clarinets presently introduce the melody, as follows:

The movement ends with a return to this thematic idea and extends itself to infinity in a diaphanous pianissimo.

THIRD MOVEMENT

This section of the symphony is called a *rondo burleske* and has a feeling of rakish gaiety decidedly unusual in the music of this composer, who took himself so seriously. The first part of the movement is based on this jolly theme proposed by the violins:

It is hardly necessary to have musicological commentary on this part of the music. While it is rather highly elaborated, the structure is basically simple and the tunes are easily identified, even when, toward the end of the movement, the thematic material is treated now in a mocking, now in a sentimental way. This treatment no doubt suggested the subtitle of the movement, *rondo burleske*. There is a very exciting concluding passage.

FOURTH MOVEMENT

There is no occasion for extended analysis of this movement. It is music to be listened to, rich in invention, often songlike in its contours, superbly handled in its dynamics and its dynamic contrast, and even occasionally suggestive of certain music that was to come into being long after Mahler's voice was stilled. The resources of the orchestra are very thoroughly exploited—from the solitary elegance of the solo violin to wonderfully orchestrated crescendi which develop climaxes of power such as are seldom heard in the concert hall. Not long before the end there is a mountainous orchestral peak. From this point onward the music thins out and the instruments are subtracted one by one from the ensemble, until only the violins pianissimo are whispering in their highest register. There is a concluding section recalling the first theme of the movement, played nostalgically and reminiscently by the strings, muted.

Das Lied von der Erde (SONG OF THE EARTH)

[Symphony for Tenor, Contralto, and Orchestra]

THIS deeply reflective and philosophically beautiful work was first performed in America by the Philadelphia Orchestra, under Leopold Stokowski, December 15, 1916, following its presentation under Bruno Walter in Munich five years previously. Notwithstanding the inclusion of the solo voices, it is in every respect a symphony; and one built along imposing lines. There are six movements, each based on one of a group of Chinese poems. The verses are philosophical, but not necessarily gloomy, although the final one has the immemorial bittersweetness of farewell. Indeed, the music is regarded by admirers and students of Mahler as his artistic leave-taking.

The solo voices sing alternately. They are not woven into the music in Wagnerian style, but stand forth against an exceedingly rich orchestral background, serving as an accompaniment, but absolutely symphonic in scope. No description of the music is adequate without the words of the poems, which, unfortunately, cannot be reproduced here. The titles of the poems, which will give clues to the significance of the movement with which they coincide, are as follows:

1. *The Drinking Song of Earthly Woe*
2. *Autumnal Solitude*
3. *Of Youth*
4. *Of Beauty*
5. *Intoxication of Spring*
6. *Awaiting a Friend; the Farewell of a Friend*

The verses date from the eighth century, and are from the poems of Li Tai Po (1, 3, 4, and 5), Tschang-Tsi (2), Mong-Kao-Jen (6a) and Wang-Wei (6b). They were translated into German by Hans Bethge, and modified by Mahler to suit his purposes; an English version was made for the Philadelphia Orchestra program by Dr. Phillip Goepp.

Harl McDonald

OR HARL MCDONALD music has been an art, a science, and a business. At this time or that, one aspect will have the ascendancy, but
music has always dominated his life. He was born on a cattle ranch in
the Rockies above Boulder, Colorado. Since his was a musical family,
he had a healthy admixture of outdoors and of music in his upbringing.

Early lessons on piano, violin, and French horn led to professional
engagements. Work with a number of Los Angeles church choirs
helped finance further education. Study in Europe was made possible
by prizes awarded for a "Suite for Orchestra" and a ballet.

In 1927 he was appointed lecturer in composition at the University
of Pennsylvania and since then he has made Philadelphia his home.
From 1930 to 1933 under a grant of the Rockefeller Foundation he
collaborated in research dealing with the measurement of instrumental
and vocal tone, new scale divisions and the resultant harmonies. In
1933 he became Director of the Music Department of the University of
Pennsylvania, where in addition to administrative duties he taught
numerous courses and directed various undergraduate musical organizations. He gained wide renown as a choral conductor at this time.

In 1934 he was named to the Board of Directors of The Philadelphia
Orchestra Association. This allowed him an insight into the executive
and financial problems of the organization and gave him an opportunity also to work in close collaboration with the conductors. He was
appointed manager of the orchestra in June, 1939, continuing his
activities as composer, conductor and professor at the same time.

During the past few years Mr. McDonald's compositions have been
performed by many American and European orchestras. In addition to
many works for piano, voice, violin and chorus, the list includes
Festival of the Workers (1933–34); Symphony No. 1, "The Santa Fe
Trail" (1934); "Rhumba" Symphony, "Reflections on an Era of Tur-

moil" (1935); Symphony No. 3, "Choral" (1936); *Three Poems for Orchestra on Traditional Aramaic and Hebraic Themes* (1936); Concerto for Two Pianos and Orchestra (1937); Symphony No. 4 (1938); and *Lament for the Stolen,* for chorus of women's voices and large orchestra (1939), and a tone-poem "Bataan" (1942).

In spite of this catalogue, Mr. McDonald's interests have not always been exclusively musical. A little patch of silver in his skull is a memento of a youthful ambition as a rodeo performer. A nose slightly out of plumb is a reminder of the fact that he once proudly raised his arm as amateur champion lightweight of the Southwest. He found out, however, that the sport was injurious to his hands and regretfully hung up his gloves.

Symphony No. 1 ("THE SANTA FE TRAIL")

"THE Santa Fe Trail" is a program symphony in three movements.

"When I was a small boy in the Southwest, I heard many of the old men describe their experiences in the early days when they came to the new country. Coming, as many of them did, from the orderly and restricted life of New England, this first plunge into a brutal, uncaring existence was a terrifying experience. From small communities in which the welfare of every individual was a matter of concern to all, they marched forward to a world in which their lives were held by a precariously small margin, and death was frequently attended only by buzzards and coyotes. With few words and long periods of silence, they painted pictures so vivid that they must remain clear in my mind as long as I live. My purpose in this work is to re-create in tone something of the spirit and experiences of these pioneers.

FIRST MOVEMENT
The Explorers

"Across the face of the great plain of infinite sweep moves a group of tiny figures. Surveyed from a distance, one would hardly be conscious that they move at all, so slight is their progress from day to day. A cloud of dust hangs over them, partly concealing their advance, making breathing an agony, and red-rimming their eyes. By night they

shiver under insufficient blankets, and by day their lips and faces are
blistered by the sun and alkali dust. It seems to many of the group that
they have always been a part of this dust cloud moving westward, and
occasionally they speculate on their chances of ever escaping it.

"An exclamation focuses every unbelieving eye upon the dim outline
of distant mountains, and weeks of weary plodding are forgotten in the
new impatience to reach the Spanish settlements. The excitement is
climaxed when they reach the crest of the first range, and gaze in
ecstasy at the panorama which is unfolded before them. Behind them
the desert sleeps on, undisturbed.

"This movement opens *molto andante* (the desert), and leads to an

allegro risoluto (the mountains), becoming again *molto andante*.

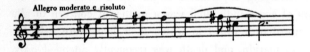

SECOND MOVEMENT
The Spanish Settlements

"This movement (an *allegro scherzando*, with a trio, *molto moderato*,
of Hispanic-Jota patterns) reflected the spirit of the life in the Spanish
settlements, where the explorers come upon a kind of life which is
beyond their comprehension. At first these cold men of the North and
East are dimly aware of the gaiety and indolence of the Hispanic life,
but soon it becomes the pulse of their existence.

THIRD MOVEMENT
The Wagon Trails of the Pioneers

"This third movement, *allegro moderato e vigorosamente*, is built on several subjects, and represents the many influences—Hispanic,

Allegro moderato e vigorosamente ($\flat$=110)

Nordic, and American Indian—that combined to build the spirit and substance of the Southwest. In this movement I have carried to com-pletion the principal subject of the first movement, and while there is a considerable interplay of thematic material in the three movements, I have given more thought to the sequence of emotional states than to any purely technical devices of structure."

Symphony No. 2 ("RHUMBA")

IN 1935, at the time of the first performances of his second symphony, Mr. McDonald wrote the following explanatory notes:

"It is no claim to distinction in the congregation of creative artists to say that one of my major interests is in the field of social and eco-nomic problems. Naturally, our troubled times have led to more and more speculation and discussion along these lines, and several years ago I began to think of a large-scale composition which would be based on my reactions to and reflection on the current turbulent scene.

"About a year ago, I chanced to spend some time in Pittsburgh, where I was greatly excited by the wonderful work being done in the Carnegie Institute of Technology and the Mellon Research Laboratories. It seemed that at last mankind had been liberated by the scientist, and that we no longer need to fear the bitter decree, 'by the sweat of thy brow shalt thou eat bread.' In the midst of this scene of effortless pro-duction and new methods of creating an age of plenty for humanity, I came face to face with bread lines, hunger, labor strife, and the final intervention of the Federal government. Out of all these contradictory experiences I began to write, not of my social philosophy, but of my experiences. Tumult, accomplishment and frustration, industry and stagnation, were all a part of the scheme, and I felt and hoped that I was getting something of the pulse of my own day. At about the time that I was sketching the third movement and had completely immersed myself in the spirit of our hectic, dynamic gaiety, there came very disturbing news of the Fascists and Nazis, adding unbelievably to the complications surrounding our precarious state of civilization.

"This fixed in my mind the character of the fourth movement, and the score was finished shortly after.

"This symphony is in no sense a program composition, and the title, 'Rhumba' Symphony, has to do only with the fact that I have used rhumba rhythms in the third movement.

"My reflections on our turbulent age are entirely personal, and I make no effort to paint graphically, nor do I wish to create the scene of my experiences in the minds of listeners.

"Some people will find bitterness in parts of this music, and I hope in other parts they will find ecstasy and elevation. The realization that great multitudes are living in want while we debate the problem of overproduction; that the ambition and spiritual development of thousands of young people is aborted every year because the greatest industrial nations of history can't use their man power—all this must lend a flavor of bitterness to any thoughts of our times.

"With all this tumult of accomplishment and frustration, I am always conscious of the fact that I am living in an age that has an almost insatiable appetite for gaiety and entertainment. In this part of my score I have used a rhumba, for the two reasons that I like rhumba rhythms and also because they seem to be a part of the pulse of our times.

"The modern orchestra affords innumerable colors in which one might picture the martial hosts that are springing up all over the earth. The swashbuckling blackshirts, brownshirts, and their ilk occupy an alarmingly important position on our stage, but I cannot feel the rhythms of marching soldiery without sensing their avowed purpose of bringing death. I have suggested all this in the fourth movement.

"There is considerable interplay of thematic material, except in the third movement. There are no devices of form or structure for the sake of adherence to the traditional, yet the first and last movements are noticeably in sonata form, with a few individual excursions."

Felix Mendelssohn-Bartholdy

1809-1847

FELIX (the happy one) was a well-chosen name for Mendelssohn, for fortune smiled on him, and bestowed on the boy her choicest gifts—a diadem of genius for his curly head, inherited wealth from his father, a winning charm of manner, and a graceful upright physique.

The Mendelssohn family, though of Jewish origin, eventually became Christian, one branch being received into the Roman Catholic faith, the other, including Felix, accepting Protestant Christianity. The primary reasons for this were political and social, rather than religious. Some of the Mendelssohns added the name "Bartholdy" to their branch to distinguish it from other branches.

From boyhood Mendelssohn won laurels as a pianist, first appearing on the concert stage at the age of nine. He and his sister were devoted, and practiced at the same piano, their delightful mother sitting near by with her knitting. Felix also counted landscape painting, Greek, and composition among his studies, in all of which he was remarkably bright.

At twelve he began to compose, and a year later he met Weber. At once admiration, which he never lost, was born in the heart of the lad for that romantic composer. Although the influence of those for whom he had great respect affected him—he loved Handel, Bach, and Beethoven deeply—he never "copied" anyone, and his music has a style and character very definitely his own.

His pen flowed with melody, giving to the world a perennial springtime of music. He "discovered" Shakespeare in the German editions when he was but a boy, and admired the English poet so much that he wrote the charming music inspired by *A Midsummer Night's Dream*, the Overture to which was completed when Felix was but seventeen years old. Later, Mendelssohn lived in England, and was enormously popular there.

He was particularly fortunate in friends, numbering among them Schumann, Chopin, Spontini, and Moscheles. He himself was the favorite of kings and emperors, who vied with each other to do him honor. Loving life, loving beauty, loving people, this magnetic personality drew everyone to him. He lived, wedded, and died happily; and he left happy music behind him.

The character, the personality of the composer are invariably revealed, somewhere or other, in his music. Not always does he speak, deliberately, from the depths of his soul, and yet he often reveals, unwittingly, depths of which he himself is scarcely conscious. He says more than he intends to say. There are moments in the music of Beethoven, for example, when the tragedy that haunted his life stalks boldly across the page. Again, there are times when the grim humor of that strange man rises above his melancholies, and he laughs gruffly at his own misery. Yet he could write his gayest music—and he *could* be gay—while in the depths of unhappiness, just as the struggling poet, starving and sweltering in a city garret in midsummer, might sing his daintiest song of Christmas lights and Christmas snows.

But Mendelssohn very consistently revealed his *real* self—the cheerful, successful, contented, happy man that he was; and there is nothing in his music to indicate that his gaiety is constrained. The delicacy and sprightliness that were integrated with his character shine forth in his music; his love of the refined, the aristocratic, the cultured, is faithfully reflected in his work.

Symphony No. 3 in A minor ("SCOTCH" SYMPHONY)

SCOTTISH music and Scottish history inspired this symphony, though we will happily find in it no sound of bagpipes or battle. Mendelssohn had visited Scotland in 1829; and heard the pipers skirling their wild music, and had visited the very room at Holyrood where Mary had lived, and stood on the spot where an Italian musician, once a favorite of the queen, had been murdered. "I believe I have found," wrote the composer, "the beginning of my Scotch symphony." It was not so Scotch, however, that it could not be misinterpreted, for it is related that when Robert Schumann heard it, and was told that it was Mendelssohn's "Italian" Symphony, he declared it so charmingly represented Italy as to compensate one for never having been there!

The symphony was performed for the first time at Berlin, March 3, 1842, under Mendelssohn's direction.

FIRST MOVEMENT

The movement has a grave introduction; portions of its thematic material are supposed to have been written down by Mendelssohn on the second day of his visit to Scotland. There is a "motto" theme, heard at the beginning, and recurring at periods through the work, which is probably the musical idea that so promptly impressed the composer.

The movement proper is in somewhat more vigorous, but not less romantic, style than the introduction. There are typically Mendelssohnian melodies, gently melancholy, and a return to the somberness of the introduction.

SECOND MOVEMENT

The second, rather than the third, is the scherzo movement of this symphony. A transitional passage for horn and woodwind precedes the establishment of the graceful rhythm—one which, however, seldom becomes boisterous. One might have expected Scottish dancing here, but though the spirit of the music is light and gay, there is none of the robust vigor associated with, say, a Highland "fling."

THIRD MOVEMENT

The third movement may have been suggested by Mendelssohn's reflections at Holyrood Castle. It has gravity, even majesty, with a reflective and somewhat melancholy note that could be a remembrance of the tragic events that came to pass in that gloomy keep. But the music could as well suggest the wild hills and solemn forests of Scotland, or the overbearing sadness of plains and lonely moors.

FOURTH MOVEMENT

If anywhere this symphony is, in a musical sense, definitely Scotch, it is in the final movement. Here the wild Highlander, claymore in hand, sweeps down from his rugged hills joyously to do battle; but we are spared a too literal description of the fight. Here, too, is the impetuous, the vigorous dance of the North, and a retailing in suggestive musical terms of the glorious deeds of Scotland's heroes. There is a contrasting section, somewhat more restrained, yet even more suggestive of Scottish music.

Symphony No. 4 in A major ("ITALIAN" SYMPHONY)

MORE than one hundred years ago, Felix Mendelssohn, after a leisurely and roundabout journey from his beloved England through Germany and Austria and Switzerland, arrived at Rome for a sojourn of several months. The moment of his visit was most fortunately timed. He witnessed and was fascinated by all the great popular festivals, with their colorfulness, their mad abandon, their wild dances and often charming songs; and what impressed him even more as an artist and musician were the gorgeous rites accompanying the coronation of Pope Gregory XVI, at which Mendelssohn was a spectator.

The sights and sounds of Italy, the soft beauties of the Alban hills, the grandeur of Rome, and the ever-near spectacle of the sea—which always fascinated him—all left their mark upon the music Mendelssohn composed during his Roman visit. It is interesting to note, and perhaps reveals musical and personal characteristics of the man, that he was definitely, almost indignantly, unsympathetic toward the liturgical music of the Catholic Church, as performed during the ceremonies at St. Peter's and elsewhere. Considering the often lush sentimentality of Mendelssohn's own music, it is not remarkable that he could not appreciate the austere and passionless beauty of the Gregorian chant. He did not, by any means, lack spirituality; but to him an emotion could not be detached from the warmth and naturalness of human relations, and a music designed to celebrate a deity of such powers and magnificence as are attributed to the Christian God must needs, in Mendelssohn's notion, be itself splendid and adorned and rich with Oriental sumptuousness.

The present symphony appears to have been composed, in large measure, during Mendelssohn's stay in Rome. Certainly it has a definitely Italian flavor; it is colored by the impressions of sights and sounds which so delighted the composer in that sunny land. Mendelssohn himself never heard it, as it was among the great mass of manuscript left behind at his death, nine years after he had written it.

The symphonies of Mendelssohn have passed through a curious cycle in public estimation. Mendelssohn enjoyed an enormous prestige among his contemporaries, and almost anything he wrote was warmly received. The symphonies attained the peak of their popularity in America perhaps during the "gay" '90's, and the first twenty years of this century. Then for some years they were played with relative infrequency, and only during the past several seasons have they begun to win back toward the place they once occupied. The taste of the concert public seems to incline toward more robust fare, in these times; yet there is a suave charm in Mendelssohn's music which will not be denied. As long as there are people who love beautiful melody and finished musical craftsmanship, Mendelssohn will have an audience; and while more and more people turn to the symphony orchestra for their musical entertainment, the symphonies of Mendelssohn, peculiarly attractive to the unjaded musical appetite, will have their devoted admirers.

FIRST MOVEMENT

The spontaneous flow of melody—rarely a deep flow but always clear and shining—that characterized most of Mendelssohn's works is exhibited almost in the first measure. Violins are entrusted with the principal theme, woodwind and horns supplying a richly colored accompaniment. An interlude, in which the introductory motive of the movement is heard again in woodwind against a crisply staccato counterfigure in the strings, precedes the more powerfully scored representation of the chief musical idea.

Mendelssohn was a romantic, both in the literal and musicological meanings of the word. He was not thereby prohibited from the sacred ground of classicism, however. Furthermore, a man with his love of fine workmanship could not always forego the intricacies of the classical style. Hence it is not so surprising to find in this vigorous and free and beautifully fashioned movement, as part of its development, an ingenious *fugato* in the strings. It occurs approximately four minutes after the beginning of the movement, and leads to a general interweaving of previous thematic material, which persists to the close of the movement.

SECOND MOVEMENT

There is something songlike in almost everything that Mendelssohn has left us. Melody—song—came to him almost as easily as to Schubert. Someday a great pianist will really understand and cultivate Mendelssohn's *Songs Without Words*—and he will have a popular success of impressive proportions. The present movement is a song so lovely and so simple and so moving that, as someone has aptly said, it would, if written apart from the symphony and appropriately titled, have rivaled in popularity the famous *Spring Song*. Let us hope so.

Particular interest attaches to the brief introductory figure, not because, as Sir George Grove remarked, it is "like the cry of a muezzin from his minaret," but because, apart from its intrinsic appeal, it appears frequently and importantly at intervals throughout the movement. The introductory figure is heard in woodwind (flute, oboe, bassoon) and the upper strings. It is succeeded by the chief theme of the movement, which you will hear in the mellifluous combination of oboe, bassoon, and viola, to an accompaniment by low strings and woodwind.

Some of the more fanciful commentators upon Mendelssohn's music have referred to this movement as "The Pilgrim's March." This idea was doubtless begotten by the fact that the music was written while the composer was in Rome, and undoubtedly under the influence of what he saw and heard there. Probably he observed many a pontifical procession and penitential march, but in this case, as in most others where an imaginative title is attached to a musical work, there is no reason to suppose Mendelssohn had any picturesque idea in mind.

THIRD MOVEMENT

Musical scholars have not always agreed with Mendelssohn's brother-in-law, who stated that this movement was originally a part of an earlier unpublished work. Such matters are not of particular interest here; what does interest us, however, is the sprightly and vigorous

music, logically placed and developed in this symphony, which we find
in this delightful scherzo. Melodically and rhythmically, it is one of
the pleasantest things in symphonic form which Mendelssohn has left
us. Violins have a graceful and lively tune; bassoons and horns, contrasted both in timbre and in melodic figure with violins and flutes,
give us the highly effective trio, and a combination of strings against
bassoons, brass, and timpani supplies interesting color and rhythm.

FOURTH MOVEMENT

If we are told that the slow movement of this symphony represents
a procession of penitents, we are equally at liberty to believe that the
present section represents the same devout people after having received
the absolving sacrament. Here is a typical Italian peasant dance,
directly based on the saltarello—a rather rowdy and certainly vigorous
performance, done by men and women in pairs, in which arms and legs
are used as violently, if not as elegantly, as possible. The dancers circle
about, approaching and retreating, with the woman manipulating her
apron, now in inviting gestures, again as if to repel her suitor. Meanwhile rapid and exhausting steps, with hops and skips, soon have the
dancers breathless. It is a dance of quite vigorous and abandoned character, but definitely not lascivious or lewd.

Mendelssohn, having been in and about Rome during the festival
periods, must have seen the saltarello many times, and he did indeed
capture here the bounding vitality and spirit of it. The peculiar rhythm
of the dance is introduced at the second measure of this movement, in a
figure for woodwind and strings. Five bars later the chief subject of
the movement—a series of thirds in the flutes—is heard. Later a third
musical idea, exposed in a dialogue between the two sections of violins,
is introduced. Here there is an impressive climax of animation and
brilliance, succeeded by an even more frenetic outburst when, after
the violins introduce a new theme, the music adopts the mad rhythm of
the tarantella. (This is a wildly exciting and vigorous dance, supposed
anciently to drive from the body the poison of the tarantula's bite.
When the dancer was exhausted, he was either dead or cured.) Both
dance rhythms are now employed with brilliant effect, the original
impulse of the saltarello becoming dominant at the end.

Symphony No. 5 in D minor ("REFORMATION")

ONE might suppose that, having been numbered the fifth in the sequence of Mendelssohn symphonies, the "Reformation" Symphony was the last to come from the composer's hand. This is not the case, however, for though when it was published twenty-one years after the composer's death it was catalogued as No. 5, it dates from 1830, thus antedating the "Scotch" Symphony No. 3 and the "Italian" Symphony No. 4. During his visit to Rome, Mendelssohn had not been favorably impressed by the music of the Church that he heard there, but it is quite possible that it was during this interval he conceived the idea of a symphony or some musical work that would celebrate the three hundredth anniversary of the promulgation in 1530 of the Augsberg Convention, the manifesto of the Lutheran Church. Mendelssohn was an enthusiastic Protestant and he had planned this symphony for the occasion under the title "Symphony for the Festival of the Reformation of the Church." It was to be played at a festival projected in Germany, but because of political and other reasons the festival did not come about and the symphony, therefore, was not played on the occasion for which it was designed. As a matter of fact, it was not played at all for about two years after it was finished, and then the first performance did not take place in Lutheranism's German home but actually had merely a few rehearsals in the more or less Catholic city of Paris. The first public performance did take place in Germany on the fifteenth of November, 1832, at Berlin, with Mendelssohn himself conducting the symphony and appearing as soloist in several piano works. The symphony, in spite of Mendelssohn's very high regard for it, was not an overpowering success at its first performance and has not since that occasion established a degree of popularity comparable with that enjoyed by the "Italian" and "Scotch" symphonies or certain other works of this composer. The reasons for this are not difficult to define, nor is it impossible to agree with the Paris verdict, which was that the work was too studious, too involved, and too lacking in ingratiating melody to be a successful work. It can be proven from the score that the work is sometimes turgid and dull, that it is self-conscious and academic, and that it suffers from most of the faults that so often appear in an art work designed for a specific occasion. The "Reformation" Symphony is not often performed, and, opportunities for hearing it being so few, the existing recorded versions are of at least musicological interest.

FIRST MOVEMENT

This is not program music, and the only connection that can be established between it and the occasion for which it was designed lies in the two specimens of liturgical music which Mendelssohn uses. The first is the Amen from the Saxon liturgy, which one remembers was used also by Richard Wagner.* This appears at various intervals dur-

ing the first movement. The second liturgical idea borrowed by Mendelssohn has a somewhat closer but by no means intimate connection with Luther and the church he established: the majestic chorale *"Eine feste Burg ist unser Gott,"* the text of which is sometimes attributed to Luther and the music to Johann Walther.

The first movement has a ponderous introduction, with organlike harmonies delivered from the most sonorous brasses against the celestial calm of the Dresden Amen in strings played very softly. The middle section of the movement is vigorous and involved almost to the point of confusion, but the clashing musical ideas are eventually resolved by a reintroduction of the Amen, which ushers in the concluding section.

SECOND MOVEMENT

The second movement of the symphony is really Mendelssohn at his best. His scherzos, beginning as far back as the overture to *A Mid-*

* In the Prelude to *Parsifal.*

summer Night's Dream, which he wrote when he was seventeen years old, are among the most charming and wonderful in music, and the present one is typical.

THIRD MOVEMENT

The third movement is much slower, establishing, through the dark tonality of G minor, the rather somber and introspective atmosphere of the beginning of the work. Perhaps Mendelssohn meant us to ponder for awhile the central thought of his music, which, indeed, is the central thought of Lutheranism particularly, and Christianity in general —a thought that is presently expressed as we proceed without interruption to the fourth movement in a straightforward proclamation of the chorale, "A Mighty Fortress Is Our God." Consideration of this idea encourages the development of a much brighter atmosphere, and the music grows in intensity, sonority, and exaltation to the end, where occurs, shouted forth with all the orchestra's power, a final assertion of *"Eine feste Burg."*

Darius Milhaud

BORN 1892

D ARIUS MILHAUD, one of the most distinguished of contemporary composers, was born in Provence, September 4, 1892. He was exposed to the usual academic exercises of a French boy and eventually matriculated at the Conservatoire, where both Widor and d'Indy were among his instructors. He was an ambitious young man and had his eye on the Prix de Rome, but the incidence of the first World War prevented his competing when he was ready for this notable award. Within the Conservatoire, however, he did in fact capture most of the available prizes. During the later months of the first World War and the succeeding years circumstances were not propitious for aspiring composers, and Milhaud joined the French diplomatic service. He was an attaché at the French Legation at Rio de Janeiro, Brazil, for two years, and during this period he met another distinguished Frenchman, Paul Claudel, poet and diplomat,* with whom he was later to work in collaboration. When Milhaud returned to Paris in 1919 he became identified with the group of French composers known as *"Les Six"* ("The Six"), who made manifesto against what they considered the tiresome romanticism of Franck and the nebulous impressionism of Debussy.

Milhaud soon became known both in Europe and America and visited our country in 1922, presenting himself as pianist and as conductor, and playing much of his own music. He is at present on the faculty of Mills College, Oakland, California.

Symphony No. 1

MILHAUD'S works are extraordinarily numerous. He has written for almost every musical form—operas, ballets, incidental music for plays, motion picture music, string quartets, and sonatas for a variety of

* Later Ambassador to the U. S. A.

instruments, suites, several concertos, five symphonies for small orchestra, five études for piano and orchestra, and almost innumerable other works. The most notably successful of Milhaud's works, perhaps, are the ballets *Le Boeuf sur le toit, Saudades do Brazil, La Création du monde, Suite provençale,* and the present symphony. This work, which is entitled simply "Symphony," was composed in honor of the fiftieth anniversary of the Chicago Symphony Orchestra and dedicated, as a note in the score indicates, to the orchestra. Milhaud has told the author of the excellent Chicago Orchestra program notes that when World War II began he was unable to do creative work for a very considerable period, so disheartened, discouraged, and unhappy was he, but the idea of writing a symphony for the Chicago Symphony Orchestra gave him courage to resume his work. The music was written at Aix-en-Provence, which happens also to be the birthplace of Milhaud, during November and December, 1939, and was finished on the nineteenth day of the latter month. It was performed during the following season. The scoring is conventional except for the percussion section, which is rather elaborate, including triangle, bass drum, cymbals, tambourine, gong, side drum, tenor drum, and tambour provençale.

FIRST MOVEMENT

The first movement is tranquil, as indeed a pastorale should be. The mood of serenity is established by a solo flute, accompanied by the first violins pizzicato in this engaging melody:

The violins themselves respond with a melody of their own a little later on, a melody which lies in perhaps the loveliest register of the instrument.

Upon the basis of these melodic ideas the composer develops a rather elaborate movement which, while it seldom loses its atmosphere of

tranquillity, does forget for long moments its pastoral quality. The movement is given a beautifully rounded form, emphasized by the recollection, near the end and in the shining voice of the clarinet, of the first subject quoted above.

SECOND MOVEMENT

Mr. Milhaud describes this section of his work as "rather dramatic and robust with a *fugato* in the middle." His description is precise except that it neglects to mention a feeling of well-being, a splendid euphoria that animates and invigorates this entire section of the symphony. The *fugato* which the composer mentioned is rather remotely based on the first important subject of the movement. This subject

appears first in the clarinets, but in the *fugato* treatment its derivative is presented by the second violins. The *fugato* is for the most part in the strings, violins, cellos, and basses playing with the idea in a right merry way. The playfulness tends to disappear as the sonorities develop, and the close of the movement, though based on this jolly fugue, is mightily impressive.

THIRD MOVEMENT

There is a certain honest piety in the atmosphere of the music here—not the mockery of the cynical Frenchman but the simple, tender, and intimate kind of piety one may encounter among the French peasants. This feeling dictates the nature of one of two subjects on which the movement is built—an utterance very like a chorale. We hear this in almost organlike sonorities in the woodwind and horns contrasted with a second subject clear and singing for the strings alone. There are various apparently unrelated fragments of melody which give the composer opportunity to explore the orchestra's resources of tonal color. At the end of the movement the quasi-ecclesiastical is re-established by a re-presentation, very sonorous, of the chorale subject.

FOURTH MOVEMENT

If one recalls the *Suite provençale* of Milhaud, and indeed other works, it is difficult to escape the conclusion that the songs and dances of Provence had something to do with this music. Here we return to the country, but the atmosphere is festive rather than pastoral as it was in the opening movement. Certainly this theme,

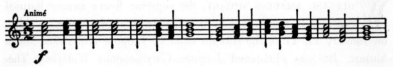

articulated by the brass, and above it, the violins, indicates that something pleasant and jolly is going to happen. Not long afterward a dance, which certainly must have had its origin among the people of Provence and very effectively scored for high and low woodwinds, gives new animation to the scene.

The two ideas noted are, at length, both used extensively and eventually contrasted in counterpoint. There is a new access of orchestral power and rhythmic vitality toward the end of the movement.

Wolfgang Amadeus Mozart

W OLFGANG AMADEUS MOZART, the supreme figure among natural geniuses in music, was born at Salzburg, in the Bavarian Alps, on January 27, 1756, the seventh child of Leopold and Anna Maria Mozart. He was christened Joannes Chrysostomus Wolfgang Theophilus, to which at confirmation was added the name Sigismundus. Most of his works were signed, simply, W. A. Mozart.

Mozart discovered the family clavichord when he was only three years old, and he began to pick out harmonies on this instrument, an ancestor of the piano. A year later his father, a professional musician, began to give the child lessons. He soon began to "compose little pieces," some of which remain in existence. In 1762, with his elder sister Maria Anna, familiarly "Nannerl," he was taken by the father to Munich and Vienna. At the Austrian court, Wolfgang climbed into the lap of the Empress, and he and Nannerl, who was then in her eleventh year, were accepted as playmates by the young princes and princesses. At Vienna he was said to have learned, without instruction, not only the organ but the far more difficult violin. The following year the family went to Paris, where Wolfgang's first compositions appeared—four sonatas for piano and violin. In 1764, they went to England, remaining more than a year. It was at this time that his father said of him that his "high and mighty Wolfgang" knew everything in his eighth year that could be required of a man of forty. On the return to Salzburg, Mozart continued composition and study. In 1767 he composed his first oratorio. Again in Vienna, the following year, he wrote his first opera, *La Finta semplice,* which now and again is revived and staged.

In 1769 an Italian tour was arranged. In Rome he achieved one of the great feats of musical history. This was in Holy Week, when he went to hear the Sistine Chapel choir sing Allegri's Miserere, which it was forbidden to copy and circulate under pain of excommunication. On going home, he wrote down the entire work from memory, correcting only a few passages at a second hearing. This came to the ears of the Pope, who sent for Mozart, not to excommunicate the youth, but to give praise to his extraordinary genius. Not long afterward he was made a Knight of the Papal Court.

By the time he was eighteen years old, Mozart had to his credit something like twenty-three sonatas, eighty-one brief symphonic works, nine Masses, three oratorios, five organ sonatas, and miscellaneous works beyond record.

In 1768 he had been appointed concertmeister to the Archbishop of Salzburg, but his patron died in 1772 and gave way to a successor who cared nothing for Mozart's genius. Moreover, the income was small, and he resigned in 1777, resuming the post after his mother's death in 1778.

The young man, while in Mannheim, had fallen in love with Aloysia von Weber, who seems for a time to have returned his affection. He married, however, Aloysia's sister Constance, in 1782, establishing family ties with another great composer, Carl Maria von Weber, who was a nephew of Fridolin Weber, the girls' father. With his wife Mozart now settled in Vienna. The two met with poverty, but it was during their life together that the three great operas, *Don Giovanni, The Magic Flute,* and *The Marriage of Figaro,* were given to the world. All were artistically successful, and it seems that one of them, at least, was a source of profit; but Mozart, like many men absorbed with the ambitions and the problems of achievement and not possession, remained poor. Then, too, there was parsimony in musical and court circles.

Just before completing *The Magic Flute,* Mozart was commissioned to compose a Requiem for Count Franz von Walsegg, who shabbily intended to have it performed as his own work. But constant labor, pecuniary failure, family troubles, illness had brought Mozart close to the end of his physical resources. After the success of *The Magic Flute,* composed upon a plot derived from Freemasonry, his health, never good, broke down. He began to feel that his days were numbered, and he worked unremittingly upon the Requiem, sensing that it was to be his own.

The very day before his death, he asked that the finished score be brought in to him. He distributed the soprano, tenor, and bass parts among those around the bedside, reserving the contralto for himself. The music was sung, but at the end of the *Lachrymosa* he no longer could contain himself. He knew the eyes of death were upon him, and under their gaze, the spirit of Mozart broke. The next day was his last. After hours of agony and delirium, there came unconsciousness. Toward midnight he revived for the last time; he sat erect, and his eyes filled with light. Then he sank upon the pillow and turned his face to the wall.

He was buried, in a storm of wind and rain, in an unmarked grave in the paupers' cemetery of St. Marx, in Vienna. His widow, seeking the spot a few days later, could not find it, for the keeper of the cemetery himself had taken no note of it. Sixty-eight years afterward, the city of Vienna built his monument. It was not necessary then, for his music, gentle, innocent, childlike for the most part like his character, was written in something more durable than stone.

Symphony No. 25 in G minor

THE musical importance of Mozart's Symphony No. 25 in G minor is less than its historical significance. It is impossible to describe any music of Mozart as uninteresting, insignificant, or unimportant, but the musical value of his work naturally grew as his genius grew, and the importance of the present G minor symphony is to the great G minor symphony very much like the importance of a boy to a man. If the boy is father to the man, then this little work is worthy of special note.

Although Mozart had, not long before the creation of this work, the opportunity of hearing some of the Haydn symphonies, it is difficult to prove that Haydn's work influenced him to any appreciable degree. As a matter of fact, in this very work he began a turning away from the strict formalism which Haydn so thoroughly established; and he began to exhibit a more romantic, though disciplined, feeling toward his own life and work which gave his music a warmth and profundity not always evident in his earlier works. That is not to say that Mozart in any degree abandoned the structural forms of which at so early an age he had become completely a master, but he adapted them to his own purposes, expanded the sonority, color, and expressiveness of the orchestra and dared to be himself.

The music is alive with nervous vitality and dynamism. It is interesting to note that it is cast in the tonality of G minor, one which Mozart rarely used, and then only for some of his most passionate and profound utterances, as, for example, the favorite G minor symphony, the string quartet in the same key, and certain other works of comparable caliber. This symphony is notable also in that it requires four horns instead of the conventional pair, adding a distinct element of sonority and warmth not common in Mozart's music.

All four movements are brief, concise, forceful, and to a discernible degree excited and even febrile. The first movement is in quite strict sonata form, clear and bright and requiring no exhaustive analysis. The second is the conventional andante, rounded, symmetrical, and lovely in its melodic elements, and to some listeners reminiscent of Bach in his more emotional moments. The third movement, *menuetto*, is not particularly distinguished among Mozart's movements in this form, though, being a work of Mozart, it is distinguished indeed with respect to other composers. The brisk and concise fourth movement is a bold, spirited, virile allegro with a forthright theme assigned to the unison strings, contrasted with a second theme in the relative major (B flat).

Symphony No. 26 in E flat

OF COURSE, while we refer to this little work as a symphony, it would more properly be called sinfonia, *ritornello*, or overture, since it bears little resemblance, except germinally, to the fullblown symphony we know, or even to some of the later symphonies of Mozart. It is a symphony in embryo as contrasted with, let us say, a work of such heroic proportions as Mozart's own "Jupiter," the gigantic Ninth of Beethoven, or any of the incomparable symphonies of Brahms.

This rarely played little work, in spite of its brevity, includes three well-defined movements, integrated by connective tissue. They are obvious enough without analysis. Vestigial remains of the *concerto grosso,* in which orchestral choirs are contrasted, can be observed in the first movement. The second section is tender, and, in the best sense, sentimental. The third sparkles with spring rain and spring sunshine. The rounded and polished whole is a tiny but precious gem in the treasury of Mozart's thousand works.

Symphony No. 28 in C major

THE scholars tell us that in this engaging little symphony Mozart synthesized two influences which had been brought to bear upon him in the months preceding the composition of the C major. He had lately been in Italy for a year or more, and it was during this sojourn that he accomplished the fantastic feat of memory in writing out, after a single hearing, the celebrated Miserere of Allegri. During this time, too, he made the acquaintance of Martini, the master of counterpoint, and was exposed daily to the strongest Italian musical influences. On his return to Salzburg and later to Vienna, Mozart became acquainted with some of the latest music of Haydn. He was almost ferociously enthusiastic about this music, and it is indeed true that in subsequent works of the young genius the influence of Haydn is distinctly marked. At the same time the broad melodic lines of the Italian school, sometimes highly elaborated but always in a functional way, worked their way into his music; nevertheless, the structural solidity of the Germans gave his music a new degree of coherence, firmness, and symmetry.

The present symphony dates from about 1773. Apart from the influences just mentioned, which are quite evident in this symphony, the work is primarily of historical interest. The strict sonata form is more clearly defined here, thematic development is longer, more exhaustive than in earlier Mozart symphonies, and various technical devices originated by Haydn are employed with perhaps more skill and effect than their originator accomplished.

Though it is obvious that in this symphony Mozart felt the first impact of both Italian and German influences, though quite probably his first enthusiastic acceptance of these influences constrained him to submit to them to a rather marked degree, there is nevertheless about this music an aura of that perfumed aristocracy, that faultless refinement of taste, that conscious elegance which we associate always with the music of Mozart, and which were uniquely his.

Symphony No. 29 in A major

THIS symphony is the work of an eighteen-year-old boy—but a boy who in those few years had in his musical development lived a lifetime, who had in a sense achieved what required a lifetime in the case of certain other masters. Nevertheless, and despite the composer's sophistication, it is not impossible to find in this music much of the exuberance and lightheartedness one would expect from a boy of eighteen with the world, or least his world, at his feet. No cosmic events, no deadly passions, no unrequited loves or personal tragedies are celebrated here. This symphony is a succession of songs—finished, polished, and ornamented, to be sure, and with the most sophisticated skill—but essentially simple, songlike ideas nevertheless. There is no occasion for analysis unless for the benefit of the scholar, to whom the score itself would be more informative than anything that could be written here. To those who like music for its own sake and because it makes them feel a certain euphoria, or because it pleases their senses, or because it distracts them from the workaday world, analytical comment on such music as this is quite superfluous. In passing, one might note, however, the extreme economy of orchestral resource which Mozart characteristically employs here. For, aside from normal string orchestra, he requires only a pair of oboes and a pair of horns. It may with profit be recalled that "a work of art, of perfect mechanism and delicate shading may be produced from the simplest materials."

Symphony No. 31 in D ("PARIS")

IT CANNOT be effectively argued that this is the most important, the most interesting, or the most popular of Mozart's symphonies, but like everything from the hand of its composer it has its special, singular virtues and points of interest. In 1778 Mozart was twenty-two years old—an age at which most young geniuses, in common with ordinary young people, are likely to be a source of tormenting anxiety to their parents—the more so when their parents, as the parents of young geniuses so often will be, are absorbed in exploiting them. Mozart was shipped off to Paris in March of this year, largely because his father was afraid that Wolfgang was contemplating marriage or worse, the object of his affections being Aloysia Weber, sister of the girl he eventually married. Paris at the time was absorbed in a variety of musical matters, and it seems unlikely that Mozart's arrival was regarded as an event of great importance; nevertheless, it was not long before the director of the principal musical establishment of the French capital invited the young man to compose some music for the *Concerts spirituels*. The result of this invitation was the present, the "Paris," symphony.

Mozart in a letter seemed not at all overconfident with respect to the public's reception of the work. He wrote: "If it will please the public I can't tell, and to tell the truth I don't care, for if it doesn't who is it that is not pleased? The few intelligent Frenchmen are sure to like it and the idiots—well, it is no great misfortune if it doesn't please *them*; however, I am hoping that the *asses* will find something in it to like for I have not forgotten the *premier coup d'archet*, which is their criterion. The brutes make such a fuss about it and what the deuce is it?"

In fact, the performance was distinctly successful although the conductor thought that the andante was too long and too involved. Mozart thereupon wrote a new slow movement and eventually a third, and it is the third version which we commonly hear in performances of the "Paris" symphony today.

Mozart was much distressed because of the unsatisfactory rehearsal of his work, but perhaps there was a special divine blessing upon it since it was performed by the *Concerts spirituels* on the Feast of Corpus Christi, and the public loved it.

FIRST MOVEMENT

Like so many works of art especially commissioned for an occasion, this symphony is not so much distinguished for inner compulsion and conviction as for external brilliance and technical skill. Again, Mozart at this time was luxuriating in the facility and constant readiness of his own powers and perhaps was not at all unwilling to demonstrate them. He was more than willing to modify his own taste and judgment to accommodate those of the Parisian public; as Wagner and others did after him, he was willing to bow to criticism though he did not concede its validity. Such feelings do not as a rule motivate the noblest works of art, yet it was not possible for Mozart to write anything inferior or cheap or totally lacking in the elegance of style and perfection of workmanship that were peculiarly his own.

The movement is marked *allegro assai* and begins with the *coup d'archet* which Mozart ridiculed but which, to please his audience, he adopted. This is nothing but an orchestral tutti, the virtue of which is its absolute perfection of ensemble. The movement is swift, gay, and brilliant, but thoroughly conventional in structure. It is interesting to note that in this symphony, that is to say in the first and third movements, Mozart employs the clarinet for the first time in his symphonic work.

SECOND MOVEMENT

The second movement is one of Mozart's less obvious andantes and, more than either of its companion movements, is informed with a sweet sincerity and genuine feeling that seem quite spontaneous and unstudied; though in truth the effect is brought about by artistic skill of the highest order. There are two melodious themes, one involving at first strings and then the woodwinds, and the other, the first violins alone.

THIRD MOVEMENT

It was the third movement of this symphony that really made the work a success at Paris. It is rather a typical Mozart allegro, in which an astonishing variety of effect is achieved with relatively modest orchestral resources; in which typically light-footed Mozart rhythms, supported by characteristically Mozart vigor, keep the music alive and moving through every measure.

Symphony No. 33 in B flat

TCHAIKOVSKY daringly used a waltz as a movement in one of his symphonies, and something very near to a waltz in another; Harl McDonald used a rhumba as the scherzo of his Second Symphony; and for exactly the same reasons and with quite the same justification, the classic composers used the minuet as a symphonic movement. It was a popular dance form accepted by polite society. It gave rhythmic contrast, lightened somber moods and essentially is graceful and dignified. In the symphonies of Mozart and Haydn we always expect a third-movement minuet. The present symphony is a partial exception. The minuet movement in symphonies was not liked in Salzburg. Apparently Mozart was conscious of this, for in the first performance of the work, which came about in Salzburg in 1779, Mozart omitted the minuet but in a later performance, very likely at Vienna, the *menuetto* was inserted in the manuscript.

The symphony is remarkable for this and for other reasons. In it appears the basic idea of the fugue in the fourth movement of the "Jupiter" Symphony, a theme of which Mozart must have been enamored, for he used it not only in the "Jupiter" but in the Credo of his Mass in F, in the Sanctus of the Mass in C major and in the first movement of the sonata for piano and violin in E flat.

The symphony is typically Mozartian and of such extraordinary clarity and artful simplicity that no structural analysis is necessary. The interpolated *menuetto* is of especial vigor for the most part, though in the middle section, or trio, it relaxes the insistent and dynamic rhythm long enough for a quite lovely and gentle melody. The fourth movement presents the greatest variety of ideas and is the most highly elaborate; yet elaborations never becloud its transparence, nor is form, perfect as it is, allowed to interfere with expression.

Symphony No. 34 in C major

WHAT has been said of the Symphony No. 29 applies with equal force to the present work, and, in addition, one need only point out (if indeed the music itself doesn't make the point clear) that this symphony is somewhat less frivolous than the A major, and at moments it is even rather solemn. Here again we find the economy of material—indeed a more stringent economy, since the work is for strings only except for a single bassoon, and this merely doubles and reinforces the bass. In one more detail this work differs from most other symphonic compositions of Mozart; it has three movements instead of four, the conventional minuet being omitted. In truth Mozart did plan a *menuetto* for this symphony, but never completed it.

Symphony No. 35 in D major ("HAFFNER")
[K. 385]

MOZART had the unfortunate talent of being able to compose quickly and easily, and at will. This faculty exposed him to the demands of courts and musical dilettanti, and he, on his part, pressed as he often was for funds, was seldom able to refuse. The result was that in spite of his expressed determination to do nothing slipshod, he wrote some music that was considerably less valuable than his best.

This symphony was written to order, and in the short space of two weeks; this at a time, too, when Mozart was quite busy with other matters. Nevertheless, it cannot be dismissed as one of the composer's many occasional pieces, for it ranks, both in musical merit and in popularity, with any of his symphonies except the great "Jupiter." During the early months of 1782, Mozart was much preoccupied with work on the opera *The Elopement from the Harem,* and incidentally with efforts to win his father's consent to his marriage with Constance Weber. Beset by work and worry, he was not overjoyed to receive a letter from his father, informing him that a well-to-do merchant of Salzburg named Haffner desired to commission music for a festive occasion, and was interested in having Mozart write it. Partly because he needed the money, and perhaps partly to install himself in the good graces of his father, the composer grudgingly undertook the work.

As originally planned, the music was to take the form of a suite, including two minuets, an andante, a march, and a finale. Such was the pressure of work, however, that Mozart was unable to complete the composition as planned, and later revised it to bring it closer to the conventional symphonic form. He omitted the march and one of the minuets, and enriched the orchestration by the addition of flutes and clarinets. As the Symphony in D major, then, he left us one of the most charming of his works.

FIRST MOVEMENT

There was certainly no occasion for profundity in the composition of this symphony, nor shall we find it here. All is brilliance and gaiety as the movement opens, with the theme, a vigorous and buoyant one, put forth by the whole orchestra. There are moments of hesitation, perhaps of doubt, and the vigorous subject returns with accessory scales and impetuous strong chords. Ingenious development, in which the principal subject is seldom difficult to locate, brings us eventually to a brief reflective period, not sad, but for a moment withdrawn from the first outbursts of joyousness. The chief subject returns, and is treated with various ingenious contrapuntal devices, and exchanged, in canon form, between bass and treble. Fluttering yet brilliant trills, rushing scales, and emphatic chordal pronouncements are used in sustaining the jolly mood to the end of the movement.

SECOND MOVEMENT

The slow movement is always tender, sometimes impassioned, but, excepting a brief moment for the sake of contrast, never solemn. Its chief interest is the opening melody, assigned to the violins, and full of warm and vibrant feeling. Now the violins are taken to their upper ranges, and the theme becomes one of airy grace and loveliness. After a repetition of this part of the movement, there occurs an interlude of almost ecclesiastical solemnity, but without ecclesiastical gloom. The prevailing note of warmth and ease and complacence is resumed with the return of the opening section, which, in somewhat modified form, and with its melodic line somewhat changed, brings us to the close of the movement.

THIRD MOVEMENT

What would be the scherzo in a modern symphony is, of course, a minuet in a work by Mozart. No dance form, except the polonaise, is so fitted to the expression of stately and dignified festivity. The familiar three-beat rhythm of the minuet is very definitely marked, and the melody written over it has the softly lustrous brilliance of candlelight. The trio, or middle portion of the minuet, brings about a touch of intimacy and tenderness, as if some bewigged and powdered dandy paused a moment in the dance to "whisper sweet nothings" in his lady's ear— and then the opening section is repeated with brilliance.

FOURTH MOVEMENT

All the lighthearted vigor and suggestion of merriment which Mozart could in so unique a fashion command is applied to the finale of this charming work. There are but two musical ideas of importance—yet the composer weaves of them a glittering and exquisitely designed web of sound, highly elaborated, yet delicate. The first subject is intoned quite softly by the strings; it is repeated with a slight alteration, and the humor of the movement is at once established. The second subject is somewhat more restrained on its first presentation, but grows in vigor and in wit as it is developed. Incidentally, the movement is marked presto (very fast), and Mozart wrote to his father that it should be played as rapidly as possible. A first-class symphony orchestra of today can make a very brilliant and glowing effect in this movement and, at the same time, can preserve the essential clarity and cleanness of detail so vital to the good performance of Mozart's music.

Symphony No. 36 in C major ("LINZ")

COUNTLESS are the tales of Mozart's facility and celerity in his creative work. Perhaps many of these stories are apocryphal, but in the instance of the present symphony we have evidence from the composer himself of the incredible swiftness with which this work was brought into being. On October 31, 1783, Mozart wrote to his father, "When we arrived at the gates of Linz, a servant was standing there to conduct us to the old Count Thun's where we are still living. I really cannot tell you how they overwhelm us with kindness in this house. On Thursday, November 4th, I am going to give a concert in the theatre and as I have not a single Symphony by me, I am writing away over head and ears at a new one, which must be ready by then. I now end because I positively must get on with my work." Three days later this symphony was completed. It was dedicated to Count Thun and was performed as scheduled on November 4, 1783. We know how hastily it was composed and under what pressing difficulties. Yet, though it is not the most original of Mozart's symphonies, it must be included among his best.

FIRST MOVEMENT

Aside from its mature and confident character, it is notable in several other details, particularly in the fact that it is the first of Mozart's symphonies in which an introduction appears. This is brief but impressive, with a certain serene majesty and philosophical complacence not always evident in the music of this master. Even when the atmosphere changes from one of contemplation to one of forthright cheerfulness there is still a remarkable dignity and poise.

SECOND MOVEMENT

The second movement, *poco adagio*, is not so much a contrast with the mood of the first as an intensification of it. This is one of the most solemn and introspective movements in all Mozart's symphonies. At times there is evident a growing incandescence in the music, a warm and passionate eloquence, a candid admission of melancholy by no means frequent in Mozart's symphonies.

THIRD MOVEMENT

The third movement is in the conventional minuet form but stands apart from the conventional in that in rhythm and tempo it is much more suitable for dancing than the usual minuet movement. In the middle section there is a particularly delightful melody heard in oboe and first violin, and later on some interesting play between members of the woodwind family.

FOURTH MOVEMENT

The fourth movement perhaps reveals the full stature of Mozart at his best. Swift, vital, and witty, it moves from thought to thought and theme to theme with the agility, logic, and symmetry of musical contour that only Mozart has ever achieved. There is a brief contrasting section where thoughtfulness replaces wit, but the predominating spirit returns after a little while, especially in a passage which has been compared in its quality to Wagner's music describing his character Beckmesser. The movement ends, however, in a spirit of unadulterated gaiety.

Symphony No. 38 in D major ("PRAGUE")
[K. 504]

THIS engaging little symphony dates from 1786; it was composed during December of that year and performed at Prague early in 1787— probably on January 19—for the first time, and under the direction of the composer. In that month Mozart conducted two concerts, and this work was played at one of them. One of his biographers, Franz Niemtschek, of Prague, wrote "the symphonies which he [Mozart] chose for the occasion are true masterpieces of instrumental composition, full of surprising transitions. They have a swift and fiery bearing, so that they at once tune the soul to the expectation of something superior. This is especially true of the great Symphony in D major, which is still a favorite of the Prague public, although it has been heard here nearly a hundred times."

Mozart had a good time during his visit at Prague, both because of the warmth of the public toward his music, and the gay parties that had been arranged for him. Prague knew his music; his opera *The Marriage of Figaro* had been presented there during the preceding season with prodigious success. People went about the streets whistling the tunes of the opera, as they were to do again less than a year later, when they became acquainted with *Don Giovanni.*

As has been noted, the performance of the present work brought forth the warmest enthusiasm. At the conclusion of the symphony, the audience would not let Mozart depart until he appeared and improvised at the piano for their delectation; and when he played an impromptu set of variations on the aria *"Non più andrai,"* his audience was completely at his feet.

One of Mozart's letters to his friend Gottfried von Jacquin gives an interesting sidelight on his enjoyment of Prague and his success there, as well as an indication of his sly humor. On the very evening of his arrival at Prague, he attended a ball, perhaps given in his honor—the "Breitfeld Ball, where the flower of the Prague beauties assemble. You ought to have been there, my dear friend; I think I see you running, or rather limping, after all those pretty creatures, married and single. I neither danced nor flirted with any of them—the former because I was too tired, and the latter from my natural bashfulness. I saw, however, with the greatest pleasure, all these people flying about with such great delight to the music of my *Figaro* transformed into quadrilles and waltzes; for here nothing is talked of but *Figaro,* nothing played but *Figaro,* nothing whistled or sung but *Figaro,* no opera so crowded as *Figaro,* nothing but *Figaro*—very flattering to me, certainly."

It is at once obvious, upon hearing the music, that it was designed for and can adequately be played by a quite small orchestra. Indeed, most music contemporary with this was so designed. Probably any version used today employs a fuller orchestra than Mozart had at his disposal when he first conducted the work; for at that time the orchestra of the Prague Opera House, also used as a concert orchestra, was meager, with a string section numbering only six violins, two violas, and two basses. Small orchestras were not the invariable rule, however, even in Mozart's time, and on great occasions bands of as many as two hundred players were assembled! And the orchestra of the Loge Olympique, in Paris, was comparable in size to any of our symphony orchestras of today. The symphony is scored for pairs of oboes, flutes, bassoons, horns, trumpets, timpani, and the usual strings.

FIRST MOVEMENT
Introduction, *Adagio, Allegro*

One of the remarkable things about this symphony is that it *has* an introduction of appreciable length—uncommon in Mozart and in his contemporaries. This section of the work makes no pretense to form; it is free, almost rambling in style, but by no means weak or purposeless. The strong chords in unison at the beginning suggest portentous matters, and the wandering figures given to the strings, as well as the pause, piano, on the harmonically unsatisfying dominant, indicate a somewhat tentative attitude.

Then the movement proper—a typically Mozartian movement, informed with vigor and with bright spirit—gets fairly under way. It may be stressing the obvious, nevertheless it is impossible to avoid mention of the anticipations of other works that lie implicit—and sometimes almost explicit—in this movement. Suggestions of both *Don Giovanni*, and of certain melodic details of *Die Zauberflöte*, are inescapable. The movement is formal, the themes straightforward, their development thorough and rather unusually lengthy.

SECOND MOVEMENT
Andante

Now the music moves to the key of the dominant (G major), and develops a vernal freshness and measured calm at contrast with the somewhat nervous activity of the preceding movement. Yet it has pace and grace, and even at the slower tempo one feels the coursing of its lifeblood and the vitality that is in it. The movement is in sonata form, but its adherence to that mold is not intruded upon one's attention. The texture of the music, too, undergoes a change, and gains in suavity what it loses in brilliance and rhythmic impulse by the omission of timpani and trumpet, which are *tacet*.

THIRD MOVEMENT

A Mozart symphony without a minuet movement is almost a curiosity, but here is one. We are wont to assume that all, or nearly all, symphonies of this period employed the minuet in one movement—the surviving member of the suite form that preceded the symphony. As a matter of fact, in Mozart's own time there were protests from the musical intelligentsia—evidently as irritating a breed then as now—against the employment of the minuet; it was not sufficiently serious, it was vulgar, it was gay, it disturbed the line and mood of the music. The lighter touch is always incomprehensible to, and therefore resented by, the humorless dolt; music must, regardless of its nature, always be played "with a straight face"!

The movement is full of animation and zest; and beneath its sparkle and glow and apparent joyous freedom there are, nevertheless, the elements of strict form. It is rich in contrast and color, and notable for the marked extremes of dynamics as well as shrewd juxtapositions of orchestral color which Mozart introduces. Eric Blom, commenting on the symphony as a whole, remarks, "The wonder of the symphony is, however, that in spite of the variety of the visions it may suggest to the hearer, it is a perfect whole. Every structural part and every thematic feature is exquisitely proportioned. No separate incident is allowed to engage attention independently of the scheme in which it is assigned its function, even where it is as incredibly beautiful as the second subject of the first movement, which is surreptitiously introduced by a passage that is apparently merely transitional, or as engagingly sprightly as the second subject of the finale with its bubbling bassoon accompaniment."

Symphony No. 39 in E-flat major

THIS, one of Mozart's best-loved symphonic works, is one of the last three of the forty-one he wrote between the age of eight and the day of his death. These three last symphonies are unquestionably his most completely developed works, and of the three this is the gayest and least important. It has neither the heroic quality, the exquisitely controlled vigor, the almost epic grandeur of the "Jupiter," nor has it the utter perfection, the spirituality, or the emotional impact of the incomparable G minor. It has less in common with its companions and more in common with its predecessors than any of the group of three final symphonies. It is not less interesting on that account.

An artist's life, and particularly the life of an artist in the eighteenth century, has little to do with his material circumstances. That is probably less true of a twentieth-century artist than it was of, let us say, Mozart, for he could write this exuberantly gay music under the most uncomfortable, discouraging, and irritating circumstances. When this music was written, the composer, who had been the darling of princes and the pet of luxurious courts, was dead broke. He had to apply to a friend—and this was no new thing with him—for "loans." To the second application he appended this rather pathetic footnote: "If you do not assist me in this emergency I shall lose both my honor and my credit, the only two things I am anxious to preserve." Well might he be "anxious" with respect to both of these qualities, for upon reading his letters one discovers that they were both often in serious jeopardy. He might have been more accurate had he written "eager" instead of "anxious."

Apart from these circumstances, the present symphony is not essentially different from many of its predecessors, except that its virtues are present perhaps in a more highly developed state. The orchestra required is somewhat more elaborate than Mozart ordinarily used, especially in that it is a little sturdier in the wind section. The structure and melodic charm of the music are not of the kind that require pedantic comment. The usual conventional forms, including a third-movement *menuetto* of unusual grace and charm, are present and are infused with

a brightness and lightheartedness characteristic of Mozart at his best, as well as touched with fleeting shadows of melancholy that are likewise discernible in Mozart at his gayest.

Symphony No. 40 in G minor

THE Mozart cult can be as boring and as obnoxious as the Gilbert and Sullivan cult (from which it is not in essence very far removed) or the cult of Buchmanism, vegetarianism, parlor-pinkishness, or musicology. The very preciousness of so much of Mozart's music seems to beget a singularly repulsive preciosity among his worshippers, and to such of these as can tolerate anything so vulgarly overblown, so distended and so lush as a symphony, the G minor Symphony is the apotheosis of their hero. Of course, to a great number of Mozart-maniacs, a full-dimensional symphony, even when so nicely scaled and delicately constructed as this one, is brash and opulent and, worst of all, too readily apprehended by the innocent and the uninitiated; and the real Mozart devotee turns with disdain from such music to the austere beauties of the string quartet. Those of us who belong to the not inconsiderable section of the music-loving populace that is relatively normal love this symphony, nevertheless, for its grace and charm and artful simplicity, for its finish and its proportions, for its polished perfection; indeed, for exactly what it is—a device for giving a pleasure that is in no way mysterious, may be profound, and even important; that derives from intimate contact with a mind and heart that were sophisticated, sensitive, fastidious—but always human.

Some iconoclast once remarked that "Mozart's whole musical language is . . . the language of comic opera." There is a certain validity in this statement, although in his comic opera Mozart often touches peaks of high drama and depths of tragedy, and in his noblest work, the Symphony in C major (K. 551) (called the "Jupiter"), he accomplishes the quality of sublimity. It must be remembered, however, that this fantastic genius tossed out creative work, even symphonies, with no more effort than an expert accountant gives to preparing your income tax return; that many of his works were exactly as neat, as perfect, and occasionally as mechanical as that same income tax return; and that sometimes, by a happy concatenation of circumstances and a coincidence of time, talent, and material, some of these hurriedly contrived works attained a degree of formal perfection and a degree of emotional appeal that are unique. The Symphony No. 40 in G minor is one of these. It is distinctly possible that a fact no more romantic than economic pressure brought about the creation of this jewel among symphonies, as it brought about, within the same period of six weeks, the Symphony in E flat (K. 543) and the "Jupiter," as well as half a dozen other works of more or less importance.

FIRST MOVEMENT

The clarity, the symmetry, and the logic of this music make analysis rather superfluous, and the emotional atmosphere is so definitely, though not overemphatically, established that exhaustive comment along that line is likewise unnecessary. It does seem a little absurd, however, to attach to this music too profound or abstruse emotional significance, for it certainly possesses no such thing. The first movement is at the outset full of nervous agitation, but it is difficult to find in it anything dark or melancholy. Indeed, it is so straightforward that one may almost anticipate each phrase that is to come, and the fact that

the movement begins in the key of G minor—a rather dull and somber tonality—does not justify the conclusion that here Mozart is being publicly unhappy. The truth is that the second subject of the symphony

is in the much brighter key of B-flat major and is full of healthy vigor and assertiveness. The second principal theme of the symphony is likewise in the key of B flat and while, because of the instrumentation employed, it has a certain shadowed color, the underlying rhythm is so vital that there is no time or space for sadness.

Overemphasis on the precision of Mozart's musical ideas can and often does completely distort, devitalize, and freeze the suppleness and grace of this music. One may often hear it presented as a stylized, rigid, granitic monument carved from the score with implacable drive and determination; or as a musical mummy handled with tender care and squeamish caution. The truth is that the music plays itself and needs only to be sounded to be given its value and to follow the course that its designer indicated, to accomplish its purpose. It wants not to be driven with a baton of steel, or forced into rigid postures which certainly Mozart could not have imagined; nor should it be treated with the drooling affection, the sweetness, like a combination of *schlagobers* and frangipane, which some contemporary middle-European conductors are wont to give it. It sings by itself.

SECOND MOVEMENT

In the second movement there is a period of relief from the agitation of the first. There is a space of serenity, a waiting, a preparation for the more vigorous and eventually the more excited music that we are to hear in the third and fourth movements. In spite of its serenity, nevertheless, the music probes profounder depths than are usually explored in Mozart's music. While there is no occasion for speculating upon what obscure motives might have moved this music, it is obvious that here is a serious, if not melancholy, interlude: an interlude that is thoughtful and introspective, though it weeps no tears.

THIRD MOVEMENT

The third movement is in the classical minuet form, but exhibits a good deal more vigor, and an almost rugged quality that certainly was not a common ingredient of symphony movements in this style during the time of Mozart.

FOURTH MOVEMENT

There is a new influx of life and power and restless energy in the final movement, yet there is no violation of the proprieties; the movement is cast in strict form and based on two melodic ideas that combine grace and vitality. The first one is the more energetic:

The second has an inherent grace and lightness to which the woodwinds lend their shining colors:

The development of both of these is accomplished with sweetness and certainty and brevity which is the soul of wit, and constitutes the essence of the fourth movement.

Symphony No. 41 in C major ("JUPITER" SYMPHONY)
[K. 551]

THE "Jupiter" Symphony of Mozart represents one of the greatest feats in the history of music. The forty-first of Mozart's symphonies, it was written, with two others, within a period of six weeks; to be exact, between June 26 and August 10, 1788. This fact alone would establish Mozart's as one of the great musical intellects of the world; add to it the circumstance that the composer was under spiritual and physical stress at the time, and we have an almost miraculous feat of composition. With his wife ill, and with no apparent source of income, with creditors harassing him, Mozart, driven to desperation, summoned every ounce of physical and mental energy and produced in this short period not only three symphonies but the greatest of all his symphonies. It was also his last.

How the name "Jupiter" came to be attached to this work, or by whom it was first applied, is not clear. In order to appreciate it, the C major Symphony must not be compared with the Fifth or the Ninth of Beethoven, but with the earlier symphonies of Mozart himself, or perhaps with those of Haydn. Thus compared, the majesty, the dignity, the loftiness of thought and seriousness of purpose, together with the relatively magnificent scope of the work, immediately demonstrate the appropriateness of the somewhat cryptic title. It frequently happens that the works of a composer are given names by popular fancy or sentiment. It happens much less frequently that these names are justified either by the composer's intent or the material of the composition itself. In this case, however, it is generally conceded that the fanciful name which tradition has assigned to Mozart's last symphony is deserved and fitting, and for its use we have the authority of no less a personage than Mendelssohn.

It should be remembered that Mozart himself was hardly sensible of the real and full poetic power of the symphonic form. The symphony in his hands did not reach its highest development, and, wide as is the gulf between his early symphonies and the "Jupiter," the latter was written when the symphony was still in the formative state. There is nevertheless an unconscious, rugged strength in it; a frank and concise statement of ideas, a coherency, a proportion and balance, and, as far as those qualities mentioned are concerned, a work very unlikely ever to be surpassed.

The symphony consists of four movements, the first, *allegro vivace;* the second, *andante cantabile;* the third, *menuetto,* and then the finale,

molto allegro. It is more heavily orchestrated than was usual in Mozart's symphonies; in fact, it approaches the modern symphonic work
in the deft arrangement among the instruments of items of musical interest, and in the contrasts and the power achieved by the composer
with the instruments at his command.

FIRST MOVEMENT

Preparation for the final climax of the "Jupiter" Symphony begins
with the first note of the first movement. Through three entire movements that preparation is carried on and worked out completely, and
so it is not unnatural that we feel the atmosphere of suspense gathering
more and more heavily as the music takes its course; nor is it strange
that the first three movements seem like an immense prelude to the last.
In this one characteristic the "Jupiter" is distinguished among all Mozart's symphonies, and here makes its closest approach to the modern
symphony as well as its greatest departure from the composer's earlier
works in the same form.

Since the first three movements, as we have noted, are in a loose sense
but a prelude to the last, it follows that the profoundest depths will not
be plumbed here as the symphony begins. But broad phrases for the
full orchestra ring out in the opening sentence; phrases with a distinctly upward, cheerful inflection. Half-melancholy, half-merry utterances in the upper strings respond; a bold brief passage in which the
orchestra speaks with all emphasis, and we come upon exquisite counterpoint, with woodwind and the lower strings in duet. You will look

vainly here for sustained melody; it is not in the composer's scheme of
things at the moment. Rather he passes before one's attention a succession of episodes which are treated almost as separate entities. Far from
being meaningless, however, they are indices of the plane of the entire
symphony, and they grow in significance as they are repeated.

The redistribution of items of musical interest among the instruments of the orchestra is the commanding feature of the second portion of the first movement. The principal themes, almost fragmentary as they are, have already been given out; no new thematic material appears.

The significance—and the aptness—of the popular name of the symphony not infrequently is questioned at various places throughout the work. There is, it is true, little reason for naming the symphony after Jupiter Tonans—the Thunderer; the work is much too finished and refined. Nor has it the flashing brilliance that would evoke the patronymic of Jupiter Fulminator, the god of Lightning. If we need find a definite contact between the symphony and the supreme among the gods, it must lie in yet another title of the ancient Roman deity—Jupiter Invictus, Jove the Unconquerable. The spirit of the work is one of invincible optimism—a vague and perhaps unreasoning cheeriness that in intensity of expression varies between joyous fanfares and frivolous titillation of the musical scale. The present moment in the work is largely of the latter character, and might indeed justify a question of the appropriateness of the title did we not remember that even Jove had his lighter moments.

The movement does not long continue on the rollicking note, however. There is some presentation of previous themes with colors enriched either by the addition of other instruments to the voices which originally announced the thematic material, or by giving out previously heard ideas in new voices. The flute and bassoon sometimes double the melody of the upper strings an octave above and below; horns and the heavier strings are more conspicuously used. One familiar with the spurious Twelfth Mass will find expressions here strongly suggestive of certain of the more florid and grandiose passages in the Gloria of that rather gaudy work.

SECOND MOVEMENT

For the moment, Mozart has done with the bravura style. After the first movement, his audience is quite under his control; its attention has been seized with no uncertain hand, its anticipation aroused and quickened. All available resources have been brought into play upon the thematic material already put forth, and any further exploitation of it would lose the ground already gained in the mind of the listener. But the composer is not yet ready to present the great climax of the symphony. It is necessary then not only to abandon the bravura mood for a time, but also to produce a new thought, presented in a new way. In this necessity, the style of the second movement originates.

One cannot but feel the solidifying of the elements of the symphony as the second movement proceeds. There is stricter adherence to the lovely melody—the principal theme of the movement—given out at the beginning by strings *con sordino* (muted). A massive chord, delivered

forte by the whole orchestra, answers each opening phrase of this flowing utterance, and now begins a more coherent, more knowledgeable, a fuller and richer musical treatment of the composer's thought. The melody in the strings is fortified by the woodwind, with a pulsing accompaniment by the remainder of the orchestra.

There is more of pure sentiment in the second movement of the "Jupiter" Symphony than in any other portion of the work. Here is the most candid emotional expression and the closest approximation of the style of the modern symphony. Particularly in the present section of the movement, we sense that the composer has searched the secret places of his heart and brought forth utterances of poignant eloquence. The cold formality and reserve of the first movement have melted under the warm suasion of the lovely melody, and the melody itself—you have already heard it as the theme of this movement—has agitated the deeper springs of feeling, so that, quite unexpectedly in Mozart, the movement is thrown into a veritable emotional ferment. There are intimations of joy and of tears, of aloof contemplation and swift activity, and of remembrance. But, recalling the devotion to form and structure that was the earmark of the symphony in the time of Haydn and Mozart, you will not expect the large impassioned utterance of Beethoven, the soul-searching pathos of Schubert, or Tchaikovsky's gorgeous trappings of woe. There is always the restraint which is perhaps even more forceful than utter abandon. The movement is like a Horatian ode in the moderation and invariable graciousness of its suggestion of the deeper feelings. Yes, and there is also the spice of a Falernian cup in the occasional light figures that come to belie certain hints of melancholy.

THIRD MOVEMENT

Powdered wigs and silver buckles. Mincing step and curtsy low. Candles glinting from a thousand prisms. Lavender and old lace. And the quaint courtliness of a day that is forever gone. Such is the picture suggested in the third movement of the symphony—a picture that Mozart must have frequently seen in the original, and one which often was animated by music from his pen. Vienna was dancing-mad in the latter part of the eighteenth century, and not only Mozart but Haydn and, later, Beethoven wrote music for its frequent masquerades and other parties. Some of this music has contributed to the fame of its composer, but never won the respect of those for whom it was written; a pleasure-craving public looks with nothing more than contemptuous toleration on those who provide it with amusement.

Strings give out the simple subject of the movement at the very beginning, with an orchestral tutti on the answering cadence, emphasized

always by the timpani. Woodwind and strings vary the theme somewhat, and there are fragments of charming counterpoint in which two simple melodies become artfully entangled. There is little elaboration of the thematic material, but the delightful rhythm, the grace and delicacy of the entire movement sustain interest to the very last note.

The playful character of the *menuetto* arouses the suspicion that we are being prepared for a return to serious things. Throughout the three-movement "prelude" the composer has led us farther and farther away from his real intent. He has aroused us with the promises of the first movement; lulled into calmness the agitation of the first with the suavity of the second, and awakened the dreams of the second with the elastically springing rhythm of the third. How could the alertness produced by the third movement be justified and satisfied, how could the *promising* character of all three movements be fulfilled, except by a noble conclusion?

FOURTH MOVEMENT

In the fourth movement of the "Jupiter" Symphony we come upon one of the transcendent things in all music, and certainly the zenith of Mozart's writings. Seizing upon what is perhaps the most formal and constricted of musical structures—the fugue—he has made of it "the vehicle for a flow of fiery eloquence, and has spread abroad glory and beauty without stint." A simple theme, a rigid form, yet warmed and lighted with the white incandescence of Mozart's genius in a truly inspired moment. No one, however, unfamiliar with the technicalities of the art, can be insensible to the magnificence of this movement as it grows from the first timid utterance of the violin into an elaborate fabric of beautiful sounds, glowing with the richest orchestral colors, intricately woven of many voices, yet clear, logical, final in the perfection of its pattern.

The four-note phrase of the first violins—the first notes heard as the movement begins—is derived from an old church tune of indefinite age and origin. It has been used by Mozart in several of his more important works, and indeed by other composers as well. It appears in the Credo of Mozart's Mass in F major, in the Sanctus of his Mass in C major, and in one of his symphonies. Bach, Mendelssohn, and Handel have used it in its original or in a derived form, and in spite of its ecclesiastical origin it can be traced to so profane a work as *Tristan und Isolde,* though, we are told, "its appearance there in the passionate disguise which Wagner's imagination gave it was no doubt fortuitous."

This single phrase is the basis for the entire movement. Its first pronouncement leads to some bars of introductory matter, bold, authoritative, and large in style. A few moments of this, and the great five-voice fugue begins, with first violins, second violins, violas, cellos, and basses in turn weaving their separate colors into the intricate pattern. Each voice entering cuts off the last note of its predecessor, and presently we are in the very midst of one of the world's masterpieces of polyphony. The rhythm is swift and always moving; the orchestra speaks in its noblest and most emphatic accents; now, at last, Jove thunders.

The music here is ever in a state of flux, and it is not easy to separate out from the glowing mass the components that give it being. We sense rather than see the constant growth and development; imagination and senses are held enthralled, and only by a distinct effort of the pure intellect are we able to discern the elements that make up the complex and yet homogeneous structure of this music. We do note the strengthening of the melodic factors by the addition of woodwind to the strings; the wonderful entangled scales—a kind of *chevaux de frise* with which the composer surrounds the more solid portions of the movement. Wood and brass now have a larger share of the great fugue, and underneath their sonorities ring always the emphatic timpani. Power and vigor increase steadily as the movement proceeds, and still Mozart has reserved the most wonderful achievement of all for the end, where all the principal melodic and rhythmic elements of the movement are combined in a perfectly harmonized unit.

Much of Mozart's writings, it must be conceded, were no more than *pièces d'occasion;* many were "pretty," more were ingenious, all were charming. But the spirit of the times was not one likely to encourage the writing of music calculated to give expression to the deeper pulses of human life and thought. Particularly was this true in Vienna, then the world center of musical life, where the public was intoxicated with the elaborate pleasures of the court, and where Mozart's patrons, when they commanded his services at all, did not ask for opera, cantata, or symphony, but for dances. Therefore, his production of the present work was the more remarkable. Mozart put aside the exigencies of time and circumstance, and, we imagine, wrote a symphony after his own heart. There has been nothing, and there are no indications that there will be anything, in music to surpass it in its special virtues. In it, the inner Mozart spoke. He wrote not for the age, but for the ages.

Serge Prokofieff

PROKOFIEFF, with a group of other and somewhat younger composers, is of the musical hierarchy of the Soviet Republics today.
The ultraconservative would have us believe that music, or any other
art that will not or cannot contribute something to the Soviet political
scheme, is lightly regarded, if regarded at all, by the powers that be in
Russia. The radical, on the other hand, holds that this is as it should be,
and that the social and political experiment now in process under the
Soviets is of such magnitude, of such importance to humanity, that
every human activity should in some manner be devoted to it. Between
these extreme views lies what is perhaps the truth—that valid music,
like any valid art, does and should reflect contemporary life, but need
not and generally should not be polemic.

The more recent music of Prokofieff falls upon this middle ground.
Rarely has he fallen to the mischievous delusions of extreme musical
radicalism; he has demonstrated the soundest kind of composition,
even to writing a charming symphony in the classical manner; and his
major works, including some of the most modern ones, are highly interesting and effective.

Prokofieff was born in the Ekaterinoslav district of Russia on April
23, 1891. He was something of a child prodigy. At six he composed a
march, a waltz, and a rondo, and three years later exhibited the beginnings of a tendency which has since materialized into some of his best
music—the preference for composition accompanying stories of his
own invention. Before he was ten years old he had written a three-act
opera to his own story entitled *The Giant*, and at twelve years he completed another opera based on Pushkin's *Feast During the Plague*. A
boy with such talent could hardly have existed without further development and he had the benefit of working under such masters as Glière,
Rimsky-Korsakov, Liadov, and Tcherepnin.

Prokofieff left Russia in 1918, coming to America by way of Japan, and then established a home in Paris. In 1934 he returned to Russia and has, with the exception of a few brief intervals, lived there since.

There is a mischievous quality apparent in almost all of Prokofieff's music, though it is not always obvious. Even his "Classical" Symphony was not without elements of mockery. His Opus 17, entitled *Sarcasms for Piano*, is frankly what its title implies. In the suite *Lieutenant Kije*, Opus 60, and *Peter and the Wolf*, Opus 67, his humor is more pointed but less obvious, wittier and better humored than some of his earlier mockeries, yet one may easily read into these later works political satires not without an element of bitterness.

Prokofieff had been engaged for many appearances in America as pianist during the season 1939–40, but the difficulties of the war intervened.

"Classical" Symphony

THIS little symphony, aside from its charming melodic content and polished formal perfection, is interesting chiefly because of the composer's purpose in writing it. Bearing in mind that Prokofieff is one of the most radical, as well as one of the most intelligent, of modern composers, it is illuminating to discover that "the composer's idea in writing this work was to catch the spirit of Mozart and to put down that which, if he were living now, Mozart might put into his scores."

What Mozart might put into his scores now is anybody's guess; but there can be little doubt that Prokofieff has recalled that blithe spirit in the delightful music he has written here. The melodies, the structure, the dance movement (a gavotte rather than the classical minuet)—all could have been written by Mozart, except for curious surprising echoes in the harmony, occasionally; and turns of phrase that reveal somewhat more of sophistication than we find in any of the old master's symphonies, except the "Jupiter."

The symphony is in four short movements.

Symphony No. 5

IN THE year 1946 and in other years, music, and every other form of art developed in the Union of Soviet Socialist Republics, was stultified,

eviscerated, and vitiated by Soviet political considerations. It is difficult for a non-Communist or a non-fellow traveler to discover how a
concourse of sweet sounds can be political, but our more advanced
Marxists seem to have sharper perception, and more than one composer, including both Prokofieff and Shostakovich, has been damned
because his music was reactionary, diversionist, bourgeois, or otherwise offensive to Russia's assorted dictators.

The Fifth Symphony of Prokofieff seems to have escaped this stigma.
There are musicians who feel that it too might as well have been suppressed, but on the other hand there are musicians, such as *Serge Koussevitsky* and *Artur Rodzinski* and *Serge Prokofieff*, who feel quite differently about it, and one of the three—the composer himself—asserts
that it is important likewise in the fact that "it is a symphony about the
spirit of man." On reflection, one may reasonably conclude that perhaps it is.

Prolific Prokofieff, according to report, has devised literally hundreds of compositions, most of which—one may assume, wisely—have
been discarded. It is of particular interest, nevertheless, that Prokofieff
has written in all forms and of all his writings has chosen to regard a
hundred different works as worthy of his name, the present work being
the one hundredth. The composer remarked in an interview with the
Moscow correspondent of the *New York Times* early in 1945 that he
had worked on this symphony for several years. This is no doubt true
insofar as the assembling of material is concerned, and yet to cast this
work into its form required only a month, and another month to or-
chestrate it. The symphony was written during the summer of 1944 and
was played for the first time on January 13, 1945, in Moscow, with the
composer conducting. Its first American performance was given by the
Boston Symphony Orchestra in November, 1945, and in the spring of
1946 the work was presented by Artur Rodzinski and the Philharmonic-
Symphony Society of New York.

To one who knows Prokofieff chiefly through a *Peter and the Wolf,*
a "Classical" Symphony, or a piano concerto, the Fifth Symphony does
not seem characteristic. On the whole it has much of the acrid quality
that one associates with the music of the later Shostakovich, and with
this many of the orchestral clichés by which the contemporary Russian
composer warns his audience that he is about to be whimsical. The or-

chestration frequently is brilliant at the top, muddy at the bottom, and empty in between. The vitality of the music lies not in thematic invention, which is only moderately apparent; nor in perfection of form, which is only approximate; nor in either daft or deft orchestration, either of which sometimes brings a certain degree of attention; but rather in an ingenious series of rhythmic patterns sometimes clear, sometimes involved, sometimes straightforward, sometimes contrasted one with another, and always interesting.

FIRST MOVEMENT

The first movement reveals two thematic elements in differing rhythms, and these are exposed and developed in fairly conventional form though sometimes unconventional harmony. There are evanescent flashes of the "Classical" Symphony's delightful lightness, but the texture of the movement is certainly more substantial, if somewhat coarser in weave, than that of the earlier masterpiece.

SECOND MOVEMENT

The second of the four movements is a brisk allegro, perhaps properly to be called a scherzo. Here more than any place in the symphony one may come upon the stigmata that identify the Prokofieff we have known. The humor of this movement is perhaps slightly on the heavy-handed side, but nevertheless it has the bounce and vitality and satirical quality that so often give to Prokofieff's music its most engaging charm. The woodwinds are deftly employed and the movement as a whole has a rounded, cyclic construction that achieves a gratifying symmetry.

THIRD MOVEMENT

The third movement is as near to being sentimental as a contemporary Russian composer seems willing to go. There is a quite lovely melody, first in the woodwinds, then in the strings; and in one register or another, as well as in occasionally distorted form, this melody influences the whole movement, much as a ground bass would direct the progress of a *ciaconna*. There is a contrasting section in somewhat gayer mood, but the movement closes, nevertheless, in an introspective atmosphere.

FOURTH MOVEMENT

The fourth movement is quite jolly, with a vigorous theme presented by the lower strings contrasted with a second idea proposed in the contrasting tone color of the solo flute. With this material the composer contrives a quite exciting finale, conventional enough in form and development though at moments startling in harmonic ideas. To gain its climactic effect this movement must be played at a pace which is almost impossible, mechanically, for some of the instruments of the orchestra; yet the movement has been heard played with a frenetic excitement that is pleasantly painful and, before it ends, pleasantly almost intolerable.

Sergei Vassilievitch Rachmaninoff

--------------- 1873-1943 ---------------

MORE OFTEN than not, material circumstances discourage the development of musical talent, but in the case of Rachmaninoff, they indirectly brought about the discovery of his genius. He was born on April 1 of a wealthy family, at his mother's estate in the province of Novgorod. The first nine years of his life were spent in the seclusion of this remote and very "Russian" part of Russia; the boy lived as the typical youngster of his class, without, perhaps, a great degree of development, but quietly and happily. He had shown considerable interest in and talent for music, but no great attention was paid to this side of his personality until a change in family fortunes made it impossible to send him to the aristocratic school his parents had chosen. Since some formal schooling and some preparation for life were imperatively necessary, Rachmaninoff was sent to the Conservatory of St. Petersburg, in the hope that his musical talents might prove to be of such caliber as would enable him to provide for himself by their exercise.

At the Conservatory he was a distinguished student, but no prodigy. It was apparent that his musical foundations were broad and firm, and work at St. Petersburg further solidified them. It was not until he had transferred to the Moscow Conservatory and, on the completion of his studies there in 1892, had won a gold medal for his opera *Aleko* that he gained serious attention. At Moscow Rachmaninoff studied with his relative Siloti, a pupil of Liszt; and with Taneiev and Arensky, both distinguished composers. At Moscow he came under the influence of the great Tchaikovsky also, for the latter was at the time active in the affairs of the Conservatory. Doubtless this accounts, in a measure, for the melancholy that often pervades Rachmaninoff's music, for he had reverent admiration for Tchaikovsky and, though never imitative, was unquestionably influenced by the older master.

Succeeding years brought him positions of honor and responsibility, and gave him as well considerable time to devote to composition and conducting. During the season of 1909–10, Rachmaninoff paid his first visit to America. When the tour was first proposed, he was hesitant, expressing the belief that he was not known to America, and that therefore a concert tour could not be a success. He was persuaded, however, and found that America knew him not intimately but well, through one of his smaller compositions—the famous C-sharp minor Prelude for piano. The American tour was but the first of many successful ones. Rachmaninoff made his home here following the First World War, and was so completely adopted that he has come to be regarded almost as an American institution.

Though a contemporary, Rachmaninoff was by no means a modernist in the musical sense. Highly individualistic, his music is nevertheless marked by the conservatism inherited from his teachers and impressed by the composers he most admired. Furthermore, there was in the man as there is in his music a rugged honesty, a deep and serious sincerity, which would almost certainly inhibit him from seeking after the often false gods of sensational modernism. His place as a pianist is among the greatest, and as either pianist or conductor, he brought to bear upon music a technique so highly developed that it cannot be forgotten, and a rare and grave musicianship always refreshing and always satisfying.

Symphony No. 2 in E minor

RACHMANINOFF in an interview once very gracefully dismissed the idea that he is a pupil of Tchaikovsky, though proudly admitting that he had received help and suggestion from that great master. The Tchaikovsky influence is very definitely felt in this symphony, but, though the music is for the most part grave, and at times even melancholy, its seriousness, passing through the purifying alembic of Rachmaninoff's own personality and genius, is freed of any trace of morbidity, of excess, of despair.

This symphony dates from 1908, during which season it was performed for the first time at Moscow, Rachmaninoff conducting. Also
during this year the composition was awarded the coveted Glinka prize
—the second time Rachmaninoff achieved this distinction, the first
being on the occasion of the publication of his Second Piano Concerto.
The E minor Symphony was played for the first time in America at a
concert of the Philadelphia Orchestra, November 26, 1909; Rachmaninoff was the conductor. The symphony, which is very long, is usually
played with cuts, which have been authorized by the composer.

FIRST MOVEMENT

One cannot but reflect, in hearing the shadowy and somber opening
of the introduction, how incredibly beautiful and subtle a language is
music! Its implications, its suggestions, its forecasting of its own progress, its power to bring into being the germ of an idea and to indicate,
all in a little moment, the direction of its development—all are singular
beauties of this wordless yet so comprehensible language. This music,
hard upon the intensely somber and reflective first measures, when the
violins enter above the declining lower strings, implants a thought
which at the moment seems an inconsiderable fragment of the web of
tone that is being woven before us, yet later, in developed form, is to be
recalled with piercing and significant emphasis as the first theme of the
movement. The whole introduction is a closely woven network of melody, and of harmonies rich and dark; so that when the voice of the *cor
anglais* appears, it stands forth in clear and solitary loveliness, and
with an intensity in its passionate brief song that is like the final distillation of all that has gone before.

With a few measures establishing a new rhythm, the curving melody
of the main theme traces its way in the violins—and we remember the
darker and more solemn intimations of this song in the introduction. It
is vital and moving and bright now; and it gives such impetus to the
orchestra that a brief climax of vigor and assertiveness is developed.
There is a pause, a suggestive phrase of clarinets, and then comes the
second theme—a simple figure of three notes, yet, in its particular orchestral color and the setting against which it makes itself heard, it is
one of the most poignantly eloquent expressions of loneliness one can

find in music. Soft woodwinds give it voice, and strings suggest a comforting answer.

It is easy to perceive in the two melodic ideas, which now become the basis of the symphony, the healthy and contemplative quality of Rachmaninoff's melancholy. Here, certainly, is none of the facile tearfulness of Tchaikovsky, nor yet a storming and inconsolable grief; rather, a gentle regretfulness that is not without a sanguine note. In succeeding passages the latent power and virility of the music assert themselves: then there is a recession of the orchestral powers through a long and, ultimately, a delicate diminuendo, which continues until but one voice —a solo violin—remains. This recalls the first theme, and inaugurates a period of development in which all apparent possibilities of the subject are alluringly explored. The little second theme, colored more brightly still, in its brief utterance conveying a feeling of intolerable sadness, returns momentarily. The movement is not to close in this spirit, however. A potent rhythm in the typical plastic and vital Rachmaninoff style is introduced in the concluding measures, and the music ceases after a final aggressive rush.

SECOND MOVEMENT

The second movement constitutes what might be called the scherzo of the symphony. Brilliant strings establish a swift rhythm in two short measures, and the horns pour out a wild sweet tune, to which the violins are presently attracted. There is another and even lovelier cantabile for the sweeping strings, and sudden secretive passages in which a return to the urgent rhythm of the beginning is suggested.

Perhaps it was the composer's rare and delightful sense of humor that prevented his graver moments from becoming too solemn, and invested his humorous ideas, paradoxically, with a saturnine suggestion. At any rate, given the tonality and the instrumentation of this movement, one could imagine the beginnings of a tragic utterance; Rachmaninoff preferred a tragicomedy. The occasional moments of pompousness are, with brusque good spirits, thrust aside; the insistent rhythm of the opening returns again and again, and eventually involves the whole orchestra in its humor. Nor does the faintly ominous suggestion of the brass, in the closing measures, overcome the spirit of wry-faced badinage.

THIRD MOVEMENT

In the tangled web of melody devised by Rachmaninoff for the third movement, there is an atmosphere strangely compounded of both peace and longing. In the first song of the strings one can feel it, and yet more strongly in the lovely solo of the clarinet. The whole tangle of melodies that twine themselves into this lovely fabric are, notwithstanding their involutions with one another, always clear and individual; as if the composer had deliberately chosen to utter the same sentiment in half a dozen ways simultaneously. Near the end, we are recalled again to the cryptic significance of the first movement's theme.

FOURTH MOVEMENT

Almost belligerently, the music leaps out from the orchestra, in a theme of boundless vigor and elastic rhythm, coursing freely and powerfully. For a time it is completely in control; then, its powers spent, the orchestra pauses upon a long-held note of the horn, *con sordino*. The basses, plucked, descend step by step into their lowest range; then begins a grotesque little march that once more infuses vitality and mobile rhythm into the orchestra, and the bold opening subject returns.

The strings sing a more romantic melody, which establishes the mood of the section of the movement based on the second theme. There is a long diminuendo, with harmonies almost visibly suspended, finally resolving in a tenuous pianissimo. There are sudden silences and sudden attacks; remembrances (flute) of the first theme in the first movement; suggestions of the quaint march of the previous section, and finally a conclusion of noble power and brilliance.

Symphony No. 3 in A minor

RACHMANINOFF's Symphony No. 3 in A minor, Opus 44, is not the first of his works to be designated as Symphony No. 3. As far back as 1913 there existed a work for chorus, solo voices, and orchestra entitled "The Bells," and when it was performed by Leopold Stokowski and the Philadelphia Orchestra in 1920 it was described as the composer's third symphony. Opus 44, one of the last important works composed by Rachmaninoff, was begun early in 1935 while Rachmaninoff was in America, and it was completed during the late summer of 1936, which Rachmaninoff spent at his vacation home in Switzerland. This work, like several others by the composer, was first performed in America by the Philadelphia Orchestra, and in the case of the Third Symphony the composer himself conducted. The recorded performance likewise was done under the direction of Mr. Rachmaninoff.

Rachmaninoff's preoccupation with melancholy was as intense and as complete and as habitual as Tchaikovsky's, but with this difference: it never was morbid, never seemed self-pitying, never devitalized, nor despairing. It was through a process that we probably would now call psychoanalysis that his will to create music and his confidence in his ability to do so were fully re-established after a period of uncertainty.

FIRST MOVEMENT

The characteristic melancholy of this music is of the solemnly introspective kind so often encountered in Rachmaninoff. It is not necessarily grief-inspired or grief-inspiring. It is, rather, a thoughtful attitude apparently induced by serious consideration of life in the whole rather than by reflection upon life's more tragic aspects. The mood is established in the introduction, but then the innate vitality and wholesomeness which always seem to come to the rescue in Rachmaninoff's music succeed. The music is contemporary but not "modern." One seldom finds unconventional harmony or daring devices in Rachmaninoff's composition. In its melodic invention, as well as in other directions, it is original, to be sure, but never startlingly unique. Rachmaninoff followed well-trodden paths and never depended upon innovation, much less novelty, to attract or hold attention to his music. The thematic material of the present movement, beautifully melodious as it is, proceeds to its logical development with a warmth of orchestral color, a firmness and definiteness of structure almost always characteristic of Rachmaninoff's works.

SECOND MOVEMENT

The composer expended his loveliest melodies in the second movement of this symphony and an inescapably beautiful one appears as the movement opens. It is assigned to the horn; and there are others of sig-

nificance given to solo flute and solo violin. The middle section might almost constitute a third movement or scherzo, since the change of rhythm and tempo bring the music from its opening adagio to an *allegro vivace*, and as the rhythm and tempo change, so does the mood of the music, graduating from the reflective atmosphere of the beginning to a rather jolly and very vigorous spirit exhibited mostly in the string choirs of the orchestra. Toward the end, however, the contemplative character of the opening bars returns once more.

THIRD MOVEMENT

Rachmaninoff rarely imposed upon himself or his music the restraint demanded by the stricter musical forms, but in the present movement he inserts a fugue, and a very thoroughly developed one too. The thematic material for this fugue is implicit in the vigorous motif that appears shortly after the impetuous opening bars. This subject is suc-

ceeded by a gentler songlike one during which the allegro is succeeded by an andante; but when the fugue begins the quick and energetic allegro returns and carries it along. Contrast in color, both in feeling and in employment of orchestral instruments, continues throughout the movement, with the end, of course, cast into a massive mold, swift and burning with energy.

Nikolai Rimsky-Korsakov

1844-1908

RIMSKY-KORSAKOV was born in a little Russian town called Tikhvin. Of aristocratic family, he never faced the physical hardships and difficulties that have beset so many of the great musicians and composers. The development of his musical talents was handicapped, however, by the very fact of his fortunate birth. While the education of which he was assured by the standing of his family included an elementary instruction in music, this had presently to be abandoned in favor of one of the very few professions regarded as suitable to a young man of his birth—that of a naval officer.

He had shown such marked ability in his primary musical studies that even while a student in the Naval College, and later as an officer on a three-year cruise, he was able, under great difficulties, to pursue his studies. His first symphony was composed during this long voyage, and was sent in sections to Balakirev, another Russian composer of note, for correction.

After his period of service in the Russian navy, Rimsky-Korsakov soon became one of that important group of Russian composers who form the so-called neo-Russian school. Among them were César Cui, Balakirev, Borodin, and Mussorgsky, all of whom were playing conspicuous parts in the development of Russian music as we know it today.

Following his First Symphony came two compositions which attracted to Rimsky-Korsakov the attention of the whole Russian musical world. These were the symphonic poem *Sadko* and *The Maid of Pskov,* an opera. Now the composer retired from his duties in the navy, and accepted a position as professor in the St. Petersburg Conservatory. He held a succession of musical positions, and as a teacher was conspicuously successful, developing as his pupils such noted musicians as Liadov, Ippolitov-Ivanov, Sacchetti, Gretchaninov, and Glazunov.

Rimsky-Korsakov had already become successful as a composer when he began to entertain serious doubts as to the thoroughness and utility of his own musical education—which had been largely accomplished through self-teaching. Accordingly, he set about acquiring the most thorough knowledge of the classical requirements of the composer, and by this noble gesture of self-discipline called forth the admiration of all his musical friends, including the great Tchaikovsky, who paid him an exceptionally warm tribute.

The music of this composer is, generally speaking, strongly marked with national characteristics. What is perhaps even more remarkable is the fact that it is sometimes deeply tinged with the wondrous colors of the East—the East which, though we infrequently realize it, lies close, in spirit as well as in location, to Russia. Yet Rimsky-Korsakov could compose, also, in so definite an Iberian strain as we note in the *Spanish Caprice*. In the field of opera the Russian master achieved conspicuous success, chiefly with *Sadko*, *Snegurouchka*, and *Le Coq d'Or*.

Symphony No. 2 ("ANTAR")

THERE are those of us, particularly among professional musicians and especially among composers, who profess a certain contempt for what has come to be called "program" music—that is, music which purports to delineate a picture or tell a story. The truth is that the quality of no music is affected by its association with the material world. If music is grateful to the senses, satisfying to the intelligence, and ably performed, it matters little whether or not we are asked to associate it with a story. In a certain sense all music is program music, for it is not music at all if it fails to communicate to us its creator's emotional and intellectual processes, and these in effect are the story of his life. In this sense all art works are autobiographical and all music programmatic.

Rimsky-Korsakov's Second Symphony was suggested by a story of a possible historical character, Antar, by the Russian author Sennkowsky. The historicity of this story is open to question, but according to legend the hero was a poet turned misanthrope who lived in seclusion among the ruins of Palmyra in the vast solitude of the desert Sham. Disappointed by the ingratitude of his fellow human beings who so often requited with evil the good that he sought to do them, Antar had abandoned human associations forever; he spent long days in bitter reflection upon his unhappiness, and one day his meditations were disturbed by the sudden appearance of a gazelle of notable grace and beauty. As he was about to set off in pursuit of the lovely creature, he was distracted by a strange sibilance in the air above him. A shadow fell across his course. He looked up and saw, darting through the air in pursuit of the gazelle, a monstrous bird. Antar abandoned his pursuit of the gazelle, drove off the bird, and of course by that time the gazelle had disappeared. Wearied with his labors, Antar fell into a deep slumber.

He dreamed that he had been translated to a magnificent castle shining with gold and jewels, filled with unimaginable luxury, and staffed with hordes of slaves eagerly waiting to do his bidding. He discovered that the castle was the home of the queen of Palmyra, the fairy Gul-Nazar, and that the gazelle which he had saved from the talons of the great bird was a materialization of the fairy herself. Because Antar had come between the bird and the fairy-gazelle, she offered him the fulfillment of three wishes, the three most desirable pleasures of life. He accepted the offer, and named as the most desirable of enjoyments the Delights of Vengeance, the Delights of Power, and the Delights of Love. Apparently not all of Antar's cynicism had been exorcised by the fairy's magic, for even after she had granted him these favors he asked a fourth—that she should take his life if the last of the aforementioned delights should pall upon him. She agreed.

The fairy, being both available and amenable, became the object of Antar's newly felt love. After a long period of happiness she observed in her lover occasional periods of absent-mindedness; suspecting the reason, she recalled her promise. With mingled sadness and desire she took him once more in her arms, and the fierceness of her passion flowed through Antar and dissolved his heart. He died with his lips upon hers.

With so specific and detailed a program it is not difficult to submit one's imagination to the spell of this music, and to associate various incidents in it with details of the story. Rimsky-Korsakov's Second

Symphony dates from 1868, and was given its world *première* at a concert of the Imperial Musical Society at St. Petersburg during the following year.

FIRST MOVEMENT

The first movement suggests the vastness and warmth and loneliness of the desert and the melancholy grandeur of the ruins of Palmyra. There is a lovely melody, quite Oriental in character, floating over rich harmonies in the wind and an accompaniment of still more Oriental character in the violins. This theme is associated with the gazelle; a little later the violins suggest vibrations of dark wings as the great bird stoops to his prey. Later, the percussion suggests the brief conflict which drives off the bird, and its fierce departing cry is echoed in the violins. At a further point in the movement the theme which we have associated with the gazelle, and another, related theme which may reasonably be assumed to represent the fairy, are associated. The grandeur of the fairy's castle is suggested by musical tapestry of glorious richness and color into which the themes of the castle, the fairy, and Antar himself are intricately woven. Near the end of the movement we hear the motif which suggests the hero himself as after his dream he finds himself alone among the ruins.

SECOND MOVEMENT

The second, the third, and fourth movements are devoted largely to musical suggestions of Antar's enjoyment in the fulfillment of his three wishes. The Delights of Vengeance are suggested in the present movement, and truly enough there are overtones and undertones of ominous quality. Not long after the beginning there is a mighty crash as the hero discharges his resentment toward the evils of the world, and a climax of feverish brilliance is built up as the movement proceeds.

THIRD MOVEMENT

In the third movement Antar is portrayed as employing the Delights of Power generally rather than specifically toward vengeance, as in the preceding movement. There is a military suggestion, not unnaturally, and echoes of the sounds of marching men. The power of peace may be implied in a somewhat more tranquil melody, which is extensively developed and comes to a climax, wherein Antar is reminded of the source of his power by the introduction of the motifs suggesting both the fairy and himself.

FOURTH MOVEMENT

The English horn and the oboe, both of which resemble certain primitive woodwind instruments of the Orient, are used with significance in this movement, which sets forth the Delights of Love. The music is full of sweet languors, interrupted occasionally by more passionate comment from various sections of the orchestra. It requires no extensive exercise of the imagination to feel the suggestive power of these yearning melodies. It is to be remembered, though, that Antar foresaw that even the delights of love can grow wearisome. His beloved, too, remembers her promise, and at the first sign of indifference brings about the release of his soul—this happy moment being symbolized by a glittering glissando from the harp.

Albert Roussel

1869-1937

ALBERT ROUSSEL was born at Turcoing, April 5, 1869. He was orphaned when a little boy, and was reared by his grandfather, mayor of his native town. Throughout his youth and his school years, Roussel exhibited marked interest in and talent for music; but he was educated as a naval officer, and eventually accepted a commission in the French navy. His vocation gave him time for what was, in his youth, little more than a hobby; and his travels brought him to strange and distant scenes, whose life and color eventually made themselves felt in his music.

Curiously enough, it was a brother of the opera singer, the late Emma Calvé, who was responsible for bringing Roussel to the attention of Colonne. The attitude of this distinguished musician, and later, of others, convinced Roussel that he should make music his lifework, and he resigned his commission to become a student under Gigout and d'Indy.

It has been said of Roussel that he possessed every desirable characteristic of a great composer excepting the power of invention; which perhaps is a somewhat euphemistic manner of saying that he was uninspired. This is too harsh a dictum; and while unquestionably certain of his contemporaries were more gifted in this respect, the sane quality of his music, its freshness, its shrewd adaptation of new and growing ideas, its meticulous craftsmanship, its color and poetry—these are qualities decidedly worthy of consideration, and their possessor must be and is worthy of a hearing. The fact is Roussel has had a generous hearing, in America and elsewhere; and while the circle of his audience has not progressed very far beyond the more or less esoteric groups, it is still a growing circle. Roussel was perhaps the last of that group of French composers who brought French music to an exceedingly high

degree of development, and his departure was a lamentable event in
the eyes of those who knew him and his work.

Symphony No. 3 in G minor

A FRENCH contemporary has characterized Roussel's music as having
"a thousand refinements without affectation," and perhaps this is as
terse and complete a description as anyone could ask. The G minor
symphony can be contained almost completely within this definition,
though its acceptance in the repertoire of American orchestras is predicated more directly upon the circumstances of its composition than
upon any great charm which it has for American audiences. Dr. Serge
Koussevitzky invited Roussel to take part in the fiftieth anniversary of
the Boston Symphony Orchestra in 1930. The composer accepted the
invitation and appeared in person, armed with this music, which he had
completed only a few months before. The first performance was given
by the Boston Symphony Orchestra, Dr. Koussevitzky conducting, at
Boston on October 23, 1930.

Roussel remembers in this symphony a device closely related to
French clarity and coherence of thought, the device which notable
Frenchmen before himself had applied to the symphony with resounding success: the circular form, which locks the symphonic movements
in a symmetrical and logical pattern. In three of the four movements of
this symphony a theme composed of only five notes supplies the basic

material. The first movement is full of sonority and vigor, from which
both sonority and vigor are little by little abstracted until, in one of its

manifestations, the dominating theme is given out by a flute alone with a diaphanous string accompaniment. A conventional sonata development follows and the climax is built, still on the five-note fragment which is the essence of the symphony.

The second movement reverses this whole process so far as treatment is concerned, but the five-note theme is still the motivating power. Where a church mode was used in the first movement, now the classic fugue is employed to expose some of the possibilities of the vitalizing idea of the symphony. There are four voices in this ingenious and perfectly worked-out fugal treatment: first the flutes, then oboes and clarinets, then English horn and violas, and finally a combination of bass clarinet, bassoon, and cellos. The third movement brings about a new atmosphere. Instead of fugues and Phrygian modes we have a lively, sonorous, but never heavy-footed waltz. In this movement the five-note motto of the symphony does not explicitly appear, but in the finale it is the climax of the entire work.

Charles Camille Saint-Saëns

1835-1921

C HARLES CAMILLE SAINT-SAËNS was born in Paris, October 9, 1835. When scarcely more than an infant, he exhibited a love of music and a certain aptness for it. His mother and her great-aunt were quick to perceive this, and saw to it that he was given the beginnings of a thorough musical education. They were careful, however, not to force his talent, but his attainments as a child were nevertheless astonishing. His First Symphony was performed when he was but eighteen years old. A few years later he was capably filling the post of organist at the Church of the Madeleine. For a term he was professor of piano at a conservatory, and during his tenure had as pupils such famous musicians as Fauré, Gigout, and Messager.

His activities were many and varied; he appeared in public as pianist, organist, and conductor; he soon became famous as one of the leading spirits in French music. He wrote a book of poems, essays on musical subjects, several short plays, and papers on scientific subjects, as well as music in almost every form. He visited the United States on two different occasions, the second being the Panama-Pacific Exposition, to which he was a representative of France.

As a composer, Saint-Saëns is distinguished by the formal and technical finish of his work, and his extraordinary talent for orchestration. He is seldom profound, but he is never obscure; and the occasional lack of depth in his music is more than compensated by its grace and frequently acute, though kindly, sense of humor. Romain Rolland, the sympathetic biographer of so many great musicians, says of Saint-Saëns, "He is tormented by no passions, and nothing perturbs the lucidity of his mind. He brings into the midst of our present restlessness something of the sweetness and clarity of past periods, something that seems like fragments of a vanished world."

Symphony No. 2 in A minor

THE collation of any artist's work usually involves problems of historicity which, to anyone but the historian and the scholar, may be completely a bore. Nevertheless, for the record, it should be noted that this work, which is programmed, on those rare occasions when it is programmed, as the Second Symphony of Saint-Saëns, is in chronological order his fourth. In the order of composition the second symphony of Saint-Saëns was a work in the key of F major, written in 1856 and publicly performed a year later by the *Societé des Jeunes Artistes*. The composer evidently was dissatisfied with it, for he suppressed further performances and destroyed the score. Following this *débâcle* Saint-Saëns wrote another symphony, and it was performed by the same organization in 1860. With that fastidiousness which characterized him, Saint-Saëns discarded this work also and it has never been played again so far as recorded musical history can reveal.

Saint-Saëns actually composed five symphonies, the present one being chronologically the fourth, but with the actual second and third symphonies discarded we have here the symphony in A minor, regarded by the composer and by the public as the Second Symphony. This work was composed in 1859, first performed in Paris March 25, 1860, and published in 1878. Comment on it is included in this book not because it is a work of major importance or even that it is major with respect to Saint-Saëns' minor works, for he has left us better things, but primarily because of a certain historical value and a place which it has in the pattern of the development of symphonic music in France during the nineteenth century. Opportunities to hear the work are few, for it has not achieved a degree of popularity that induces present-day conductors to program it. It certainly is not lacking in charm, but its charms are not such as to generate a compulsion to hear it. It is sweet and lovely music which, in these days of sensational goings-on in the orchestral sphere, seems too gentle, too lacking in aggressiveness, too modest, too well-bred for existence in this noisy world.

* * * * *

Surely this is a salon piece, correct, expressive within the limits of politeness, technically sound, and somehow quite satisfying. There is a leisurely introduction, and the chief part of the movement is cast in a mold in which restrained vigor and technical perfection are exhibited convincingly. The second movement centers around a charming and rather innocent little melody diffidently suggested by muted violins and, a little later, an English horn solo. This is a kind of *romanza*, contemplative rather than melancholy and arriving eventually, after pleasant peregrinations, at a conclusion that could have been forecast from the second bar. The most assertive part of the music comes in the third movement, which is animated by an urgent rhythm that never gets out of hand. Indeed, it is restrained long enough for certain oratorical episodes which one writer of some imagination has found reminiscent of Beethoven. Perhaps the most entertaining part of the symphony is the last movement, wherein an Italian dance form—the *saltarello*—is used to vivify the composer's ideas. The *saltarello* is a rough and leaping and very swiftly paced dance once popular in the hill towns of Italy. It has its purposes here, and serves to give impulse to melodic material which otherwise might have seemed banal.

Symphony No. 3 in C minor

THE habitual concert-goer is more intimately acquainted with Camille Saint-Saëns through such works as *The Carnival of the Animals*, the *Danse Macabre* and certain concerted works, than through his Third Symphony, which is not often performed; yet the scholars consider this symphony his most important orchestral composition. The work was written for the London Philharmonic Society and was first performed by that group May 19, 1886 under the direction of the composer himself. During the following season, on February 19, 1887, Theodore Thomas conducted the Third Symphony with the Philharmonic Society of New York. It is rather curious that though the work was written for the London Orchestra, the published score indicates that it is dedicated to Franz Liszt. This seems a little odd because Liszt had died some time before the first performance of this music.

Saint-Saëns was one of the several French composers who seriously attempted in his music to exploit the improvement and invention that had come into being with respect to orchestral instruments, and here he uses an extraordinarily full and colorful orchestra: three flutes, two oboes, English horn, two clarinets, one bass clarinet, two bassoons, one contrabassoon, four horns, three trumpets, three trombones, tuba, pipe organ, piano, triangle, cymbals, bass drum, and the usual complement of strings. It is possible that the infrequency of performance may arise from the fact that some of these instruments are not always available, and not all concert halls can boast a pipe organ, which instrument has a rather important part in the symphony.

FIRST MOVEMENT

The symphony is cast into two formal movements, though each is subdivided so that the net effect is actually that of four rather short movements. In the first there are two strongly contrasting sections preceded by a short adagio introduction, based on this idea:

The introduction presents a rather melancholy episode involving chiefly the woodwinds, which are entrusted with two short themes and accompanied by strings pizzicato. Following the introduction, the first main section of the movement begins *allegro moderato*. It is informed with a certain nervousness and even melancholy—an atmosphere suggested by the melodic episodes developed by the woodwinds, particularly clarinet, bassoon, and English horn; but, as is the way with Saint-Saëns, there is a clarifying and pacifying atmosphere soon to come, and when the two main themes of the movement are simultaneously involved there is a purging of inquietude and distress, a pacific interlude which brings us to the second main section of the first movement. Here the organ is first conspicuous, supporting an interesting theme given out by the strings. The balance of the movement is developed along these lines.

SECOND MOVEMENT

One could hardly suggest that this symphony abjectly follows the cyclic curve so magnificently employed by César Franck and other nineteenth-century French composers; rather, it perhaps anticipates the full development of this device, and we may note it here shortly after the beginning of the second movement where a very significant reference to the first theme of the first movement occurs. In the course of this section there are various references to basic material previously introduced, and though these are often disguised in rhythm and harmonization, they are reasonably easy to identify. The *allegro moderato* with which the second movement begins grows into a swiftly coursing

presto; there are alternations between these tempi until, not far from the end, the presto is interrupted by a somewhat somber idea. This, with certain reminiscences of other moods, is maintained until we come imperceptibly into the second section of the movement. Here again the organ prominently appears, as does the piano, which in this instance requires two players. There is some development of the noble theme exposed near the beginning of this part of the movement. Rather brief fugal treatment leads to a songlike passage entrusted to the woodwind. In the brilliant concluding measures, or coda, the opening theme in a new version appears in the strings. It is extended to magnificent dimensions, and the climax is powerful and profoundly moving.

Franz Schubert

1797-1828

ENTANGLED by circumstance, betrayed by fate, Franz Schubert lived and died with no more consciousness of his true greatness than had his contemporaries. Some few there were who dimly saw his worth and rendered him the meed of praise, yet among most men of his time, and indeed among many who came after him, his was the proud if unhappy privilege of speaking in a language they could not understand.

And with a final ironical gesture, fate again has pursued him even beyond the grave. To his work many a modern composer of popular music has gone for inspiration and sometimes for material, with rewards in money that poor Schubert, dogged by poverty, could scarcely have conceived.

Old Michael Holzer, the local choirmaster, who instructed and adored the boy Schubert, outlived him. Yet, departing life at the age of thirty-one, the composer left a treasury of music rarely excelled by any composer either in quantity or quality. The number of his matchless songs reached the hundreds, and in larger musical forms he worked with a fluency and facility seldom equaled before or since his time. His music is a faithful reflection of the warm, genial, lovable, guileless nature that was his, and it is no wonder that its peculiarly direct and intimate appeal touches instantly all who hear it.

Inadequately taught in several important branches of the art of composition, Schubert left his mark upon practically every established musical form. That his was a rare genius, a congenital gift of song far richer than many great composers possessed, cannot be denied. Cultivated, as it was, in a more or less haphazard fashion, it flowed into some of the loveliest music ever heard by mortal ears. What might have been, had not the world permitted him to starve, is indicated in the breath-taking beauty of his later works. Ranking though he does with the greatest musicians of all time, he nevertheless was taken off long before his powers had achieved their full maturity.

Sir George Grove says of him: "The spectacle of so insatiable a desire to produce has never before been seen; of a genius thrown naked into the world and compelled to explore for himself all the paths and channels in order to discover by exhaustion which was the best—and then to die."

This starved immortal left an estate of less than ten dollars. His loved Viennese have erected over his grave (a step from Beethoven's) a tablet with the inscription:

Music Has Here Entombed a Rich Treasure
But Much Fairer Hopes
Franz Schubert Lies Here

Symphony No. 4 in C minor ("TRAGIC")

THIS symphony dates from 1816, Schubert's nineteenth, and a year which saw the creation of more than one hundred different works, and following a year during which Schubert had written one hundred and eighty-nine compositions including so incontestable a masterpiece as the *Erlkönig*. But Schubert's musical immaturity was far behind him at the age of nineteen, and indeed it can be asserted that the full flower of his most mature genius revealed itself here in this symphony.

As usual, Schubert was at this time in financial difficulties and very eager to gain the appointment as teacher in the Government School at Laibach, which carried with it a munificent salary of approximately $100 annually. In his application for the job, Schubert wrote of himself in the third person, saying, "In every branch of composition he has acquired such knowledge and ability in the playing of the organ, violin, and in singing, that according to the enclosed certificate he is declared to be the most capable among all the petitioners for this position." (P.S.—He did not get the job.)

There are few moments in the Fourth Symphony which could establish any justification for its subtitle, "Tragic," which Schubert himself appended to the last page of the score. We can only surmise that the music was written at a time when his circumstances were more painfully reduced than usual and when perhaps the neglect of the symphony rather than the music itself was tragic. We owe the revival of this music in this country largely to the superb performances of it by Mr.

John Barbirolli and the Philharmonic-Symphony Society of New York. Happily too, we need not wait upon the exigencies of a conductor's program making for repetitions of the work, for Mr. Barbirolli has wisely put his performance on record.

FIRST MOVEMENT

The introductory section, adagio, is serious but hardly tragic in character. It is based on a subject which, after the introductory tonic chord in C minor, is given to the violins, then to the cellos, and finally disintegrated among woodwind and strings. The principal subject of the movement, which runs as follows:

is informed with a nervous vigor—a quality which, however, never eliminates the curiously plaintive suggestion that is almost always noticeable in Schubert's music.

Without attempting a scholarly analysis of the movement, which presents many unconventional points for discussion, one must point out a striking example of Schubert's unique facilities in effecting changes of key. The simplest modulation and the one conventionally required by the sonata form would be to the dominant minor or relative major—in this case either to G minor or to E-flat major. The second subject appears instead in the key of A flat, which so far as formality is concerned, has no immediate relationship to the key of the movement.

FIRST SUBJECT

SECOND SUBJECT

SECOND MOVEMENT

The second movement is one of those incomparable streams of melody that Schubert alone of all the great composers could generate. If ever a man's essential personal qualities were reflected in his music, certainly Schubert's were, and it is pleasant to believe that this movement, with its gentleness and its sweetness, its soft complaint and its moments of passion, brings us in contact with the spirit of this strange, lonely, weak, lovable, and incomparably gifted man.

The principal theme is one of those almost vocal and articulate melodies that go to a heart as directly as they came from one. It is not without interest, however, to note the curious resemblance between this theme

and the Impromptu in A-flat major, Opus 142, No. 2, which in its opening bars has practically the identical subject, and the feeling of which runs quite parallel to that of this movement. It is of further notice to observe that the four Impromptus which constitute Opus 142 were originally intended to form a sonata, of which the Impromptu in question would have been the second movement, just as it is the second movement of this symphony. The piano pieces were published in 1838, and the symphony was written twenty-two years before. Could it be that Schubert, faced with some material crisis or the importunities of a publisher, searched in his orchestral works for material easily adapted for piano?

THIRD MOVEMENT

There are many instances in this symphony where not only the later Schubert but composers of a later day and as far removed from Schubert as Richard Wagner are foreshadowed. The curious chromatic line of the melodic elements in the minuet, and particularly in its first section, is neither characteristic of Schubert's day nor of the modified dance form in which this movement appears. Nor is the syncopated rhythm any more typical. By the displacement of the rhythmic emphasis normal to the minuet, Schubert has almost created a new dance rhythm here and one to which only sluggish blood will not respond. The chief melodic element of the movement runs as follows:

FOURTH MOVEMENT

The fourth movement is somewhat discursive with a plethora of melodies too bright, too long, and too generous for close organization into any strict form. Here again the forward-looking Schubert may be discerned, particularly in the daring (for his period) treatment of the brass, notably the horns, which at moments sound in their fullness and agility and significance almost Wagnerian.

Symphony No. 5 in B flat

COMPLETE candor must permit the statement that the Fifth Symphony of Schubert is considerably more interesting historically than musically. That it has a very engaging kind of charm, that it has melodic facility and fluidity, no one will deny, but it would be reckless to assert that it has anything to equal the nervous intensity of the Fourth, the tenderness and pathos of the Eighth, or the incomparable loveliness of the great C major. It has, however, flashes of the Schubert that was to be, and as an index of his musical development it is not without significance. Further, this symphony seems to have grown in a very charming and natural way. It would appear that it came into being because the

little group of musicians which originally gathered at the house of Schubert's father to play quartets expanded into a small orchestra, and was able to undertake works of larger demands.

In the case of Schubert's symphonies there has been, from a catalog point of view, considerable confusion, and indeed this is true of the works of many composers. In the present instance, however, we do know that the work was begun in September of 1816 and finished on October 3 of the same year. We know this is so because the manuscript of the work exists, and Schubert's own signature at the beginning and end attests its authenticity and its historic position. The symphony was first played by Schubert and his group of friends, but was not done in public until 1873, when a performance was given at the Crystal Palace in London under the direction of August Manns. About ten years later the first American performance was presented by the Boston Symphony Orchestra under the direction of Georg Henschel.

FIRST MOVEMENT

This is the Schubert who had more adoration for and confidence in the music of Mozart and Haydn than in his own. Stylistically the music is much more closely related to the music of those composers than to the Schubert of the "Unfinished" and the C major (No. 7). There are moments, though, when we can see and hear the shape of things to come, as, for example, in the second theme of the first movement, unmistakably Schubertian, which goes like this:

The treatment is as formal as Schubert knew how to make it.

SECOND MOVEMENT

The second movement is charming, if conventional, beginning with a melody for the strings alone played *andante con moto.*

The composer fortifies the sonority by adding other instruments and in rather simple fashion devises a graceful and appealing movement with no astounding features whatever.

THIRD MOVEMENT

The *menuetto* is perhaps the most pronounced genuflection toward Mozart in all of Schubert's music. It is strictly conventional in form and is based on the basic and determined idea which, completely simplified, looks and sounds like this:

FOURTH MOVEMENT

In the fourth movement there is less of Mozart and more of Haydn. This music is smiling and genial, somewhat less conventional than the preceding movements and managing to achieve formality of structure without permitting the architectural bones to show through too clearly.

Symphony No. 6 in C major

THOSE who constitute the lunatic fringe of the musical world, the parasites and the camp followers of music, the little men who batten upon the largesse of the recording companies and acquire collections of records at the expense merely of the labor involved in writing ill-considered, ill-tempered, and ill-informed reviews, are inclined to regard the symphonic music of Franz Schubert rather lightly. The B minor, more popularly called "Unfinished" Symphony, is rather shrugged off as something for a "Pops" concert or as the inspiration for a musical comedy; the symphony in C major is patronized as the ultimate creation of a man deficient in technique but at moments quite inspired. In truth there is little derivative in the Fourth, Fifth, Sixth, Seventh, or Eighth Symphonies of Schubert, and any one of them is in every respect the equal of any even-numbered symphony of Beethoven. One might go further and say that the Fourth, Seventh, and Eighth

Symphonies of Schubert are the equal of any symphony of Beethoven and superior to most of them. The Sixth Symphony excited the admiration of so great a scholar and composer as Dvořák, who recalled playing the Sixth Symphony, as well as the Fifth, many times with his students' orchestra at the National Conservatory, and Dvořák remarked that even the students shared his pleasure and recognized the beauty of this music. We consider here the Sixth Symphony of Schubert, which, though by no means a widely popular work, has been making its appearance more and more frequently on symphony programs during the last few years. The erratic but gifted Sir Thomas Beecham has contributed something to the fecundation of this work by a very interesting performance played and recorded with the London Philharmonic Orchestra.

Schubert's symphonies are either defiant of scholarly analysis or in no need of it, but when one listens to them the need is never apparent. Schubert above all composers made his music sing. His musical thought was always songlike; his musical technique was, perhaps because of this, somewhat deficient in matters of conventional harmony and counterpoint. Yet in its own natural way Schubert's harmonic ideas were lovelier and more original than those of most composers since his time. The unexpected, delightful, and by no means illogical modulations that characterize all of his work, and particularly his orchestral music, are an endless wonder; yet they came about almost spontaneously, and Schubert himself was dissatisfied with them because they did not conform with convention. Let us thank him that they did not.

In the Fourth Symphony Schubert seems to have been moved by a young man's restlessness, impatience, nervous and not always firmly directed strength. In the great C major Symphony he was vouchsafed glimpses of something beyond the world and yet something that surrounded the heart of humanity. In the Sixth Symphony, however, he is still working toward the realization of himself. He is neither completely free of earlier faults and influence, nor has he achieved the certainty and cosmic power that informed his last two orchestral works. The symphony, nevertheless, is fairly pure and quite characteristic Schubert. As in most of his symphonies, there is a slow introduction, followed presently by the swift allegro of the main movement itself. There are fragmentary melodies, particularly one which is used with thematic importance, and which Schubert apparently borrowed from himself later when he composed the music to *Rosamunde*. The second movement, andante, like the first, is fairly conventional in style except for the appearance of some of those extraordinary changes of tonality so characteristic of Schubert and, as he handles them, so completely inimitable. The swift-running third movement is, if properly performed, light and airy and possessed of a rather pensive gaiety. Here Schubert makes no reference to the heavy-footed German dances that might have inspired, rhythmically, part of the first movement; this music is swift and delicate and dainty, with its feet never on the ground, always in the air.

In the fourth movement Schubert exhibits an assertiveness and vigor rather unusual in his music, although foreshadowed in certain parts of the Fourth Symphony. He uses the wind instruments with exceptional boldness. The fourth movement, and with it the symphony, ends in an atmosphere of good spirits and aggressive vitality.

Symphony No. 7 in C major

HERE is the symphony that is generally looked upon as Schubert's greatest. It is interesting to discover, therefore, that at some of its first performances the musicians of the orchestra regarded it with such contempt as to influence their playing of it! In fact, on one occasion, when Mendelssohn, enthusiastic as he was in bringing the work to the attention of the public, wished to conduct it at a concert in England, the project had to be abandoned because of the attitude of the orchestra players.

The symphony was completed early in Schubert's last year of life, 1828, but like the "Unfinished" B minor, was never heard by the composer. Robert Schumann was responsible for bringing it to light from the vast mass of manuscripts in the hands of Ferdinand, brother of the composer, and eleven years after Schubert's death it was performed in Leipzig under the baton of Felix Mendelssohn. It was this great musician's enthusiasm, aroused by the work itself and the warm recep-

tion given it in Germany, which led to his attempt to perform it in England.

This symphony, it should be noted, is often referred to as Schubert's Tenth. It was, in fact, his last, and the tenth in chronological order, but was marked No. 7 in the catalogs of Breitkopf & Härtel, Schubert's publishers; since then it has been more generally known, in Europe at least, as the Seventh.

FIRST MOVEMENT

The present symphony, more than any other, perhaps, reveals something of the Schubert that might have been. Somewhere he had found new sources of power. The wondrous flow of lovely melody had never abated, but fortifying this, and supporting it with a compelling vigor and virility, lighting it with a superb grandeur, vitalizing it with new and mighty forces were the beginnings of full maturity in his art. In the Seventh Symphony Schubert is not always the employer of a sweet persuasiveness, the plaintive sufferer, the gently melancholy poet. These elements exist in the symphony, to be sure; it is difficult to find a page from Schubert's hand where they are not present. But now Schubert evoked from some hitherto undiscovered reservoir an influx of driving power, irresistible force, majestic and dominating and compelling utterance that even his most appealing works had not known.

The strange, the prophetic and portentous utterance proclaimed by the horns in the opening measures of the symphony is one of the unforgettable things in music. Here in this single phrase are intimations of grandeur and of glory, of agonies and triumphs, and of limitless solemn joys, projected with all the eloquence and insight and mystical understanding of "Thanatopsis." The solemn pronouncement grows in boldness and is answered more gently in the voices of woodwind. Trombones presently take up the bolder part of this dialogue in a figure derived directly from the opening sentence of the horns. Now the strings, in an agitated figure, climb upward from the broad melodic foundation laid down by horns and trombones; a swift crescendo develops and after perhaps four minutes of music we hear the bold and brilliant theme that ushers in the movement proper.

This theme, divided between strings and woodwind, takes the form
of a vigorous dialogue, the three-bar phrase of the strings answered by
two bars in the woodwind. Now it is expanded into a mighty paean,
joyous and triumphant, vital and vigorous to a degree suggestive of
Beethoven in his most assertively jovial moments. The second theme

follows closely and, in spite of its milder character, is by no means
of secondary importance in the movement, as its rhythm provides the
motive power for many measures of this part of the symphony. It is
assigned to the oboes and bassoons which, together with other members
of the woodwind family, Schubert uses with singular felicity.

Now begins the development section of the movement, extensive,
exhaustive as only the melodic facility and ingenuity of Schubert could
have made it. Yet there is never a suggestion of straining for effect,
never the artificial device of the pedant, but always the inevitable logic
and coherence and intelligible speech of the truly great composer.

Even when the two principal themes, as different as they are, become
welded together and developed simultaneously, the clearness of the
melodic line is never clouded. Meanwhile there is a steady growth in
emotional intensity and dynamic effect, suggestive reminiscences, in the
woodwind, of the important second theme, violent bursts of tone punctuating the steady advance toward a climax, and at the end, a movement
toward and finally an explicit statement of the powerful theme that
opened the introduction.

SECOND MOVEMENT

A few measures of introduction, intimating what is to come, precede the main theme of the movement, in which Schubert once more employs the woodwind—the oboe now, accompanied by strings, in a pensive but vital and moving little theme that in its persistent rhythm belies the faint melancholy of its melody. A continuation of the theme in the

clarinet's reedy voice and the parallel major key of A . . . a few violent interjections of a new phrase in full orchestra . . . another of those unexpected and delightful modulations of Schubert, and we come upon the second theme of the movement. It sings in the passionate voices of the strings, and songlike it is in every smooth phrase. This theme, too, is developed and extended. There is a period of hesitation, of tentative suggestions of the first and chief theme, and we enter upon the further development of the thematic material given out in the first part of the movement.

It is worthy of reflection that, contrary to his habit, Schubert revised more carefully than usual the score of this great symphony. Gifted with facility in creating melody as was no man before or since his time, and lacking certain technical elements considered necessary to the composer, it was not unnatural that he should sometimes have failed of clarity and conciseness. Even his friends, who were by no means hypercritical, remonstrated with him on this score. The gentle Schubert, amenable as always to their persuasion, studied with pathetic earnestness the much-revised and, as a rule, starkly simple scores of his adored Beethoven . . . and finally, impatient, gave up and despaired of ever following a method so painstaking and laborious.

Perhaps, nevertheless, he had some inkling of the greatness and immortality of the present work, for he corrected and revised it most carefully. The results are obvious and perhaps particularly so in this movement. Intricately entangled melodies remain exquisitely clear, nor can the charge of what sometimes seems unnecessary and almost absent-minded repetition be leveled at Schubert with respect to this symphony. One follows the smooth and clear line of melody like a guiding hand.

A melody of almost agonizing loveliness sings in the expressive voice of the cello, immediately following a powerful utterance by full orchestra and a pregnant pause. And presently the oboe, in its pensive penetrating tone, joins in a countertheme. This marks the end of a new thematic material, and, as the classic Greek dramatists would have it, here is the peripeteia of the movement. Just as Schubert had led us to this point through the unfolding of new musical ideas and their development, so we are led to the emotional and dynamic climax of the movement by a review of those ideas and their logical (musical) consequences.

THIRD MOVEMENT

Forthright vigor and energy worthy of Beethoven, and a certain *quasi*-playfulness more delicate and light than we might find even in the writings of that monumental figure, mark the scherzo of the Seventh Symphony. The lively if rugged figure bowed so emphatically upon the strings is instantly contrasted with the delicate voices of the woodwinds,

further attenuated by the violins, and presently contrasted in its later developments with a countertheme proceeding from the cello section.

Here are the elements upon which Schubert rears the structure of the first half of the movement, exploiting their possibilities to the limit, yet never losing, in the development of the musical figures, the energy of the rhythm or the clearness of the theme.

The trio, or second part of the movement, opens in somewhat chastened mood, but still with a vital and moving rhythm underlying the woodwind subject which forms its important theme. Strings in arpeggios accompany the woodwind. Presently the music sounds vaguely familiar, and almost before we realize it the original vigorous, dancelike theme of the first section of the movement, in somewhat altered form, has returned. And upon great chords springing from this powerful subject the movement ends abruptly.

FOURTH MOVEMENT

Here is a finale worthy of comparison with that of Beethoven's gigantic "Choral" Symphony. Indeed, in a sense this movement is superior to the closing chapter of the Beethoven Ninth, since it expressed adequately what Schubert wished to express, and did so without reference to resources foreign to the medium in which he was working. In the qualities of grandeur and clarity and pure musical delight, in its magnificent virility and invincible vigor, it is in no way inferior to Beethoven's "last word in symphonic music."

But comparison should not be the basis for judging it. One's own mind and senses, after all, constitute the final criterion for the evaluation of any artwork, and Schubert will not suffer if that standard, and none other, be applied to this or any of his music.

The triplet figure which appears in the opening measures has a curious part in much of the movement. It was the extraordinary use of this device that aroused the uncomprehending contempt of the musicians who made it impossible for Mendelssohn to conduct the symphony in England, though why the simple, if unusual, figure should arouse their ire is not quite clear. Extensively used though it is, the triplet figure is not the chief theme of the movement. That appears later, with scarcely a hesitant moment between it and the introduction, but with the triplet rhythm still distinctly in evidence. And never during

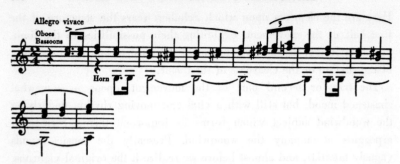

the subsequent working out of the chief theme is the vigorous figure absent from the music. In fact, even when a third theme, ushered in by four notes upon the horn, appears in a prominent position in the scheme of the movement, the interrogative triplet still can be perceived.

There is extensive thematic development, a return to the four notes of the horn, which in turn give impetus to gigantic forces engaged in the superb elaboration of the horn motive itself. And as always in Schubert, the movement rarely if ever digresses from a path leading straight to its climax, and though at times it seems, from the over-powering splendor of the music, that that climax has been reached, new and dazzling heights of magnificence are achieved. Pelion is piled upon Ossa—and there is not a moment's release from the thrall of this music until the last mighty chords die into silence.

Symphony No. 8 in B minor ("UNFINISHED")

THE "Unfinished" Symphony dates from 1822, in the latter part of which year it was begun by Schubert. It was destined never to be completed, and to lie, ignored or forgotten, until 1865. From that year, when, long after the death of the composer, it was first performed, it has never ceased to enthrall every listener. Few symphonies in the concert repertoire now approach it in the universality of its appeal; no other, perhaps, has the singular directness of contact with the inner-most places of the human soul invariably achieved by this exquisitely beautiful music.

To call it the "Unfinished" Symphony is, in a sense, to apply a very misleading name to it. It is, as a symphony in conventional form, incomplete; for there are but two movements instead of the usual four. In this sense only is it "unfinished." But in a larger sense, it is utterly perfect in finish. It leaves nothing unsaid. It explores the most mysterious regions of the human soul and heart. In language of inexpressible beauty it communicates from composer to hearer an intensity of passionate emotion, a degree of spiritual exaltation, a completely satisfying and wholly expressive message. Music can go no farther; Schubert himself, having said in these two movements all that even he, with his almost inexhaustible flow of melodious expression, could say, gave over the task of writing two more sections. And when you have heard the "Unfinished" several times, you will not wonder that even genius could add nothing to it.

Schubert never heard this symphony. His work on it was not, however, interrupted by death, for he lived several years after having laid it aside, convinced, perhaps (in spite of his sketches for a third movement), that there was nothing to add to it. It is amazing to realize that all the vast wealth of new and distinctly original tonal colors, melodies, and style in the "Unfinished" was conceived wholly in the imagination of the composer; his external senses never experienced them! Consider, then, their perfection, their beauty, their completely satisfying expressiveness, their utter rightness and finality—and you can never think of this deathless music as "unfinished."

FIRST MOVEMENT

Melody sings through the symphony from the very first note. The opening phrase is a somber legend in the vibrant voices of the cellos and basses, and high above the shimmering tones of the lighter strings that respond to the first prophetic utterance, a second song, piercing sweet, flows onward in the pensive notes of the oboe, with the more

robust voice of the clarinet heard underneath. You will not have to *listen* for these lovely streams of melody; they come forth, urged by the insistent rhythm beneath them, to surround you and envelop you in a gentle tide of glowing tone.

On the repetition of the woodwind melody, another figure, stronger, more solid, as if it were a substance compounded of the ethereal melodies that have gone before, appears. It is well to mark these chords, for later in the movement they are to become, temporarily, of first importance. Now they give an intimation of a thought that is to be developed more fully as a contrast with the chief theme of the movement—yet that is still withheld from us—the antithesis appearing before the thesis!

Suddenly the horn and bassoon speak as one voice; one note that lingers, changing color as it fades into a short phrase that ushers in again the iridescent accompaniment of the violins. Now comes what is technically known as the "second theme" of the movement. Yet this, the lovely, languishing song of the cellos is certainly the most well-remembered theme in the entire symphony; certainly one of the most beautiful melodies ever written by mortal hand; certainly a living, moving, vital song that lingers ever in the echoing chambers of the soul, once it has penetrated there.

Now the movement is launched; now we behold the marvelous succession of melodies, and the infinitely varied versions of them that flow in a smooth and uninterrupted stream from Schubert's inspired hand. But there are passionate outbursts, too, and intense dramatic utterances, sometimes taking force from their very faintness, sometimes from their vehemence, as they are shouted forth in the orchestra's fullest and most powerful voice. There are moments of spiritual sadness and exquisite pain, but they are balanced by utterances of such tremulous ecstasy as to obliterate, in a phrase, what memories of haunting melancholy appear, as they always do appear, in Schubert's music.

There is gentleness—a gentle persistence—in the constant recurrence of the chief song of the movement; a reiteration that will not be denied, a "pious stubbornness" that will not, cannot, be thrust aside except in the mighty chords, given in full orchestra, that close the movement.

SECOND MOVEMENT

The essentially lyric quality of Schubert's genius is exemplified most beautifully in the first movement of the symphony. We have heard there a succession of exquisite melodies, contrasted strikingly with dramatic episode as well as with derived forms of the melodies themselves. Here in the second movement, the essential beauty and contrast is achieved more particularly by another characteristic of Schubert's inspired musicianship—namely, modulations; modulations mysterious, unexpected, unconventional, and always superlatively beautiful. Modulation is, in simple terms, a radical change in musical effect, caused by a change of tonality, or "key." To select the key to which the modulation is to be made, then to make it by logical musical processes, requires skill of no mean order. The simplest and most obvious and easiest modulation is from the key of the tonic, which is the note "do," to the key of the dominant, which is the note "sol," for example, from the key of C to the key of G. Recall, for the moment, the first few measures of *The Star-Spangled Banner*. Suppose it to be written in the key of C. The notes to which you sing "O say can you see, by the dawn's . . ." are in the key of C, but on the next phrase, "early light," there is a perfectly simple and natural modulation to the dominant key, G, ending on the major chord of the dominant.

The most difficult modulations are those from the tonic key to one lying close to it in the scale; for example, from C to D flat. It is impossible to illustrate the difficulties of such a mutation without involving a highly technical discussion; it is sufficient to say that Schubert makes such difficult modulations so deftly, so naturally, that one is scarcely conscious of the means by which the entire character and significance of the music are so suddenly and so subtly altered.

But do not dwell on the technical skill and perfection in this second movement. Abandon yourself to beauty, and this music will surge about you and hold you suspended in an imponderable substance of such beauty as snatches away the breath, and arrests momentarily the incessant pulsings of life. To give to it all one's soul is to enjoy from it in return a term of such exquisite spiritual joy and solace and deep satisfaction as words cannot express. Give yourself, then, to this music, and it will give to you something above and beyond yourself; some brief fleeting sight of that unquenchable flame by virtue of which man thinks himself immortal.

The mood of the symphony is changed as the second movement begins. The bass strings intone a descending passage in pizzicato, portentous like the footsteps of an advancing fate. This melancholy figure persists, and then gives way to a pensive dialogue in the woodwind, the violins singing softly in the background. Later the heavy footfalls of destiny draw closer and closer, stronger and more positive; the gentle plaint uttered by flutes and violins and clarinets appears again and

again—yet we begin to feel in the music a certain attitude of resignation, of acquiescence, that is typically Schubertian. Toward the close of the movement the final version of the early woodwind melody appears, mightily augmented, and again comes that ominous progression of bass notes, like the restless pacing of some giant creature, underlying all, and shadowing the bright orchestral colors that tint every measure of the symphony.

There follows what Schumann names as the best discourse upon music—*silence*.

Robert Schumann

T HOSE WHO HOLD that environment and heredity are the two deter-
minants of human characteristics would be at some pains to account
for the musical genius of Robert Schumann. He was born in the year
1810 in the small provincial town of Zwickau, in Saxony. His father
was a bookseller, his mother the daughter of a surgeon. Neither had
musical ability to transmit to Robert, and while the father recognized
and encouraged the talent of the boy when it appeared, the mother,
widowed when her son, at the age of seventeen, had to choose a career,
was able to exert so much influence upon him that he matriculated at
the University of Leipzig as a student of law, instead of devoting himself to music, as he wished to do.

The Schumanns were middle-class people in fairly comfortable circumstances. It is pleasant to relate that the composer never experienced
the woes of poverty that made the lives of so many great artists tales
of heartbreaking misery. Robert Schumann was sent to school with the
other little boys of the town and, though a very quiet child, was in every
respect, except his precocious aptitude for music, a normal lad of his
years.

Schumann began to compose at the age of seven years; he soon was
busy with musical young friends organizing informal chamber-music
concerts, for which he wrote most of the music himself. He appeared in
public, too, as a pianist. His formal musical education, however, was
interrupted for a period of many years. In fact, his interest in music
seems to have been less keen during his adolescent years, perhaps
because of the pressure of his duties as a scholar in the Academy at
Zwickau. But if music suffered during these years and the later period
spent at the University of Leipzig, there was some compensation in
Schumann's avidity for books and literature, for which his father's
bookstore furnished a plentiful supply of the best material. This period

had without a doubt a tremendous influence on Schumann's later activities as a music critic, and even made itself felt in his music. The presence of strong literary and musical tastes in his personality resulted in a strange but happy union of those two natural enemies, the musician and the critic of music, in this single and singular nature.

Schumann's law-student days were of inactivity, unless dreaming and gloomy introspection may be called activity. They may, if we agree with Rossetti:

> *Unto the man of yearning thought*
> *And aspiration, to do nought*
> *Is in itself almost an act,—*
> *Being chasm-fire and cataract*
> *Of the soul's utter depths unsealed.*

Gentle and retiring, he could not partake of the boisterous student life with any degree of pleasure; dissatisfied with his position, he found refuge in the writings of poets whose philosophies coincided too nicely with his own.

In 1829 Schumann left Leipzig for the University of Heidelberg. He and another music-loving student were wont to gather at the house of a professor in the university, and it was here that Schumann first met Wieck, the father of the girl who was to be his wife and the most devoted and accomplished interpreter of his works for the pianoforte. About this time eight works for the piano, a quartet, and a number of songs came from Schumann's pen.

After three years of study of the law, Schumann, finding quite intolerable the prospect of still more years within university walls, decided to abandon all else for music. His mother, after much persuasion, agreed to permit him to do so if the consent of his former instructor, Wieck, could be obtained. This worthy man advised the youth—Schumann was but twenty years old—that if, after serious self-examination, he felt that music was truly his métier, there was nothing to do but devote himself to it wholeheartedly. This Schumann did.

After leaving Heidelberg, he resumed his study of the piano with Wieck, but unfortunately after a year's work was forced to give up his playing. Eager to attain a perfect technique in the shortest time, he had devised a mechanical arrangement which he expected would aid him in developing digital dexterity. By means of this device one of the fingers was held back while the others practiced exercises. The result of using it was that the tendons of the right hand were strained and for some time the member was powerless. Eventually Schumann recovered the use of the hand, but his ambition to become a great concert pianist was made forever impossible. The happier effect of this unfortunate occurrence was that Schumann was practically forced to rely entirely upon his ability as a composer if he was to continue a musical career.

It was during this period of his life Schumann became interested in Clara Wieck, then a child of only thirteen years, but already giving evidence of pronounced talent as a pianist. The composer in his writings betrays even at this early time feelings which he did not himself recognize until some years later; Clara Wieck was one day to be Clara Schumann, and the composer's devoted partner in the task of presenting his work to the world.

At this time, although Weber, Beethoven, and Schubert had been dead but a few years, and Mendelssohn's star was high in its orbit, music was not in its happiest state. The compositions of the day were trivial, or superficially brilliant, or hopelessly mediocre, yet the public taste tolerated them; they were received with complacence. Such a condition of affairs was irritating to Schumann and certain friends, who, not confident of their ability to effect a reformation through their own musical productions, decided on a journal of criticism as the best means of gaining their end—the purification and elevation of musical composition. So, in 1834, the *New Journal of Music* made its appearance, and for ten years thereafter, under the editorial guidance and with the energetic participation of Schumann, the *Journal* carried on its mission, with notable results.

In 1840 the marriage of Robert Alexander Schumann and Clara Wieck was celebrated at a little church near Leipzig. This event marked a sudden and radical change in the life of the composer. He devoted himself to composition, withdrew more and more from the world, his affections and his interests centering in his wife and in the beloved children who were the delight of his later days. Clara Schumann dedicated herself to the noble task of standing between her sensitive, retiring, and sometimes irritable husband and the world without; of interpreting to the world the works of his hand and heart and intelligence. Never did her devotion falter; never did she grow weary of her task, and the deep joy of his married life must have had a profound effect upon Schumann's artistic career.

Schumann's compositions were evolved with ease and frequency now for a number of years. The composer seemed to have opened up new springs of thought and imagination, and a wealth of musical ideas flowed from him in full volume and with startling rapidity. The mental strain of producing in such voluminous quantity soon began to tell on him. He had never been robust, and now signs of breakdown gradually appeared. A change of scene was found necessary, and the Schumanns moved from Leipzig to Dresden. Several important works, notably the C major Symphony, were produced, and Schumann's health improved to such a degree that during the year 1849 alone he wrote thirty compositions. His manner of living became less circumscribed; he did some teaching, occupied a chair in the Conservatory of Leipzig, and later held the position of *Kapellmeister* at Düsseldorf, where he was very happy and active for a time.

It was not long before the nervous troubles that had beset him at intervals throughout his life reappeared, manifesting themselves among other ways in a marked desire for seclusion, and certain eccentricities of conduct in public. Schumann was himself conscious of his infirmity, which indeed closely bordered on insanity; and he expressed the wish that he be placed in an asylum. One day in February, 1854, he left his home, quietly and unobserved, and threw himself from a bridge into the Rhine. Some boatmen rescued him, and he was carried home. A period of perfect mental clearness followed this unhappy incident, and the composer finished the variations which had been begun just before his attempted suicide. But the end was not far off. The last two years were spent in a private asylum near Bonn, where, as Sir George Grove writes, "gradually the pinions of his soul drooped and fell," and in the arms of his loved wife he died on July 29, 1856. He was buried at Bonn, where a monument was erected over his grave in 1880.

Symphony No. 1 in B-flat major ("SPRING" SYMPHONY)

THE title, "Spring" Symphony, so often attached to this music, has more justification than the usual fanciful names that somehow become associated with musical works. Schumann wrote the symphony in the springtime of his life, during that marvelously productive period immediately following his marriage. He wrote to a friend that it was inspired, in part, by "that vernal longing which influences men until they grow aged, an emotion which surprises them every year." On another occasion he declared that, in the conception of the idea for the symphony, he had been influenced by a poem, of Adolph Böttger, upon a vernal theme. Finally, Schumann himself temporarily entitled the work "Spring" Symphony, and added subtitles of appropriate character. These facts must not, however, lead us into assuming that this is a "program" symphony, for the composer finally abandoned the titles, and wrote, "I do not wish to portray, to paint, but I believe firmly that the period at which the symphony was created influenced its form and character, and shaped it as it is."

The symphony was first performed, under the direction of Mendelssohn, on March 31, 1841, at Leipzig. It was an immediate, almost a sensational, success. The first American performance was given at Boston, by the Musical Fund Society, on January 15, 1853.

FIRST MOVEMENT

Schumann, the critic, was responsible for the most apt of musical epigrams: "The best discourse upon music is silence." He must have meant that one should not, in clinical fashion, dissect music to discover its meaning. Surely he was not wrong in this. The ultimate end of music is the creation of beauty. A symphony, a flower, a sculpture is not beautiful with its anatomy laid bare. It is not detail of form and structure that normally stimulates our imagination and emotion, but the effect of the whole, wrought directly upon the heart through the senses. It matters little, except to the musicologist, that this movement is in sonata form, that it is preceded by a short introduction, out of which grows the principal theme; or that the subsidiary theme is given to woodwinds (clarinet and bassoon).

What does matter is this: here a sensitive, intelligent, and articulate man communicates to us the joys and longings and mysteries of a manhood realized and fulfilled; and he communicates through the one most sure and most expressive, direct, implicit medium . . . music. The

Cloud Spirit, "dark and pregnant with storms," of which the poet Bött-ger sang, appears but briefly upon the bright horizon outlined here, and it is by no means difficult to observe Schumann's instructions to "read between the lines, how everywhere it begins to grow green, and how a butterfly takes wing."

The mysterious, pale light of springtime illumines many a passage in the movement, and many are briefly darkened by swift-flying clouds, laden not with savage storms but with sweet rains. There are indeed touches of sadness, the sadness and nameless pain that must accompany birth and growth; but the music is always exalted, always filled with vitality, and there are climaxes of magnificent impetuousness. The movement is graceful and symmetrical as a young tree—and, at the final climax, touched with a glitter like the early morning sun upon quivering, dew-wet leaves.

If the details interest you:

The second theme begins in a strange key, but ends in the conventional tone of the dominant. Woodwinds presently fortify it, and the strings, richly figured, add contrasting color and movement. Development and exposition bring constant transformation of both first and second themes, with wonderful play of light and shade and interesting transfers of the thematic material from one section of the orchestra to another. The tempo relaxes from the vigorous allegro from time to time, but ultimately returns to it toward the close of the coda. Here the brass projects brilliant missiles of tone, and a series of bold chords, edged with the hard glitter of the triangle, ends the movement.

SECOND MOVEMENT

Youth is not ended by union with the perfect mate, nor is maturity thereby accomplished. The "long, long thoughts" of a boy must return now and again to the young man, to make his new burdens momentarily heavy, to make him wistful for boyhood joys. Perhaps it is in this mood that the second movement reveals itself. The single basic theme is a melody for the violins, poignantly sweet and nostalgic, sung against the subdued voices of the other strings. Now the cello's passionate tones repeat it; now the bittersweet tones of the oboe combine with the suave utterance of the horn in the same pensive utterance, while wandering strings trace around it an intricate figuration. Presently it dies away, and trombones give forth a more determined thought, repeated by the strings, and leading to the

THIRD MOVEMENT

The last melodic idea of the second movement becomes the inspiration of the third. It is as if the man suddenly asserted himself, putting away the things of youth with a bold assertion of vigor and purpose. The theme is delivered with great boldness.

It is interesting, historically, to note here the combination of the old-fashioned minuet-style third movement, *à la* Haydn, with certain elements of the Beethoven scherzo. The first part of this section is rather stylized and formal, the short divisions repeating and returning in quite the classical manner. By comparison, the latter section of the movement is light and free and playful. It moves with great rapidity; instead of the stately one-two-three of the minuet we find a busy agitation, crisp staccato scales, a romantic interlude, and finally, almost as if Beethoven had written it, a whimsical and mischievous return of the scherzo spirit that chases romance and formality off into the distance.

FOURTH MOVEMENT

"Yet ah! that Spring should vanish with the rose,
—That Youth's sweet-scented manuscript should close."

Schumann felt that the last movement is "the farewell of spring." Such a farewell is wistful and sad, as the passing of youth must always be. Yet spring's frivolities are soon forgotten, unregretted, in the blazing noonday of summer. The earth grows big with life, as life grows great with living; the year's full stature, like that of man, is a thing for proud rejoicing, not for tears.

The music here suggests both the passing of the springtime and lusty joy and thanksgiving for summer's coming. Bold chords in full orchestra inaugurate a term of jubilation, involving a brisk tune tossed back and forth between first and second violins, a jaunty air for bassoons and oboes, and swift syncopated scales for the nimble strings. At moments there is a kind of hasty piety in the air, and again, a sweetly sad utterance of woodwinds that sigh briefly for departed youth and vernal joys. Schumann's "farewell of spring," if the closing measures of the movement may be taken as an indication of its temper, is also a warm, a buoyant, and exalted welcoming to summer.

Symphony No. 2 in C major

IF THE period at which it was composed influenced the character of the First Symphony of Schumann, the converse is true in the case of the Second. The composer himself has written down the fact that while he worked on this music, he was suffering greatly from physical disorders, and indeed, he says that he deliberately occupied himself with the ex- acting labors of composition that he might be distracted from his pain.

Surely there is no reflection of the invalid's petulance or weakness in this deep and sturdy music. Apart from the slow movement, there is perhaps a degree less of the feeling of romance which we associate so often with Schumann's music; but there is power and muscularity; there is vigor and assertiveness; there is, on the whole, such aptness and such pointed expression that the music, regardless of the circumstances surrounding its creation, ranks with any that Schumann wrote.

The symphony as played today is not in the form that was presented, at a concert in Leipzig under the baton of Felix Mendelssohn, Novem- ber 5, 1846. Schumann was not satisfied with the work, and extensively revised it, particularly as regards orchestration; and it was not played in its present form until some years after the performance of the origi- nal version.

FIRST MOVEMENT

There is a firmness and unity in the texture of the whole work, which arises in part from the fact that Schumann sought to integrate the four movements by thematic and structural relationship and continuity. Some persistent thought or image must have been deep in his mind, for the opening theme of the introduction to the first movement can be dis- cerned as a vital element in each of the movements; and it has within it the germ from which springs the chief motive of the first movement.

Schumann himself reported, not long before the completion of this work, that he continually imagined the sound of trumpets in the key of

C. We cannot conjecture what that strange signal meant, but as the introduction begins, we hear the "trumpets in C" themselves, sounding with other brasses, sounding with serious voices a noble proclamation. A more sentimental, a gentler utterance is the answer of the woodwinds, and it is wise to note both these ideas, for we shall encounter them again as the music progresses. The introduction leads swiftly to the main body of the movement, and quickly two themes are presented for development. The first is assertive and dynamic and strong; the second, touched with a certain gentleness. Since Schumann declared that the first movement reflects the struggle between his aching body and his active mind, perhaps it is not unreasonable to regard these two themes, and their development in contrast, as indicative of the composer's pain and his battle with it.

A long-held note in the basses (to be technical, a "pedal point") leads to a return of the principal theme of the movement, and, in the concluding section, once again the trumpets are sounded in C as at the beginning, but with a new and curious force and directness.

SECOND MOVEMENT

The gaiety of Schumann is rarely reckless, and never abandoned; but in this delightful and rhythmically fascinating movement he makes one of his closest approaches to a complete outpouring of playful happiness. Yet even here there is a remembrance of conflict and of opposing ideas, expressed both by contrary rhythms and by opposing melodic lines. Again, there are two sections, differing in character much as the two themes of the first movement, in the trio, or middle part of the scherzo. Yet, toward the close, the ringing assertion of horns and trumpets again reminds us of the underlying and unifying thought of the symphony.

THIRD MOVEMENT

Here is the Schumann that we know and love best—the dreamer, the romanticist, the lover. If this lovely music does not speak of passionate devotion, of sentiment exposed in the inmost recesses of the heart, then no music ever has so spoken. And, though the music is touched with melancholy, it is never *too* sweet, never *too* sad; but simply expressive and beautiful. Here is a glowing web, woven of melodies. The first comes in the tremulous and eager voices of the strings; the oboe penetrates with its peculiarly pointed tone, and presently comes the bassoon, whose sad utterance at this point paradoxically gave Schumann much pleasure. The upper string voices continue in accompaniment, and another melody moves through the basses.

A second theme is entrusted to strings and trumpet and horn, and, after its close, the loving melody that disengaged itself from the orchestra at the beginning returns to haunt us again.

FOURTH MOVEMENT

We should not always think of Schumann as gentle and romantic— as almost a sentimentalist, restrained by artistic politeness and convention. The fact is, he often is exactly so; but there are times, and this movement is one of them, when his music certainly lacks nothing of vigor, of virility and aggressiveness. The cycle of fashion and of public taste has but lately returned his symphonies, with any degree of frequency, to the concert hall. In certain respects—in his decorum and restraint and poise, in grace and suavity—he resembles (musically if not chronologically) the "gay '90's," yet as a profound and intelligent artist he undertook, and sometimes betrayed, wrestlings with the spirit which provoke stirring music. Perhaps we were not in the mood for Schumann a few years ago; and perhaps the more recent and more difficult days have made us turn more strongly toward his music, and welcome it because it can lay hold of and move us, without frenzies and without hysteria.

A swift scale passage, which is to be used now and again during the movement, brings us quickly to the bold emphatic utterance of the principal subject. The lower strings, viola and cello, together with clarinet and bassoon, present another thematic idea in the idiom of the slow movement. The scale passage that introduced the movement is again employed as a kind of connective tissue between the two chief subjects, and the first subject is heard again, and for the last time in the movement. There is a climax of great power and enthusiasm, succeeded by the "still small voice" of the oboe in a new musical thought, which the late Lawrence Gilman, eminent critic of the *New York Herald Tribune*, traced back to a string quartet composed by Schumann some years previous to the completion of the present work. The oboe's theme is the concluding thought of the movement but Schumann will not have done with it until it is broadened and expanded into a magnificently triumphant utterance, bringing to us, finally, the noble pronouncement of the brass which is the keynote of this symphony.

Symphony No. 3 in E-flat major ("RHENISH" SYMPHONY)

IF THE historians do not err, Schumann, like many composers, was a poor conductor; and this fact, combined with the thin and often inept orchestration of the Third Symphony, would doubtless account for the fact that the work was unenthusiastically received (except by the loyal Clara Schumann) when it was first presented, Robert Schumann conducting, at Düsseldorf, February 6, 1851. Its popularity on concert programs today is not to be accounted for by any increase in powers of discernment on the part of modern audiences, but by the fact that the work has been reorchestrated; almost, in places, rewritten, by intelligent and sympathetic musicians. *They* perceived the latent beauty of the work, and have done their best to discover it to us. By far the most successful version of the symphony is that arranged by Frederick Stock, conductor of the Chicago Symphony Orchestra; and it is this version which we usually hear in public performances.

The name "Rhenish" is implicitly authorized by the composer, who said that he wished to convey through it some of the spiritual atmosphere of the Rhineland, and who, it is recorded, was inspired in the writing of the fourth movement after witnessing the installation of a cardinal in the cathedral of Cologne.

FIRST MOVEMENT

The rhythmic figure in ¾ time which underlies the first statement of the opening theme (full orchestra, at the beginning of the movement) is essentially the vitalizing principle of this section of the work, and can be felt almost always through the elaborations of the thematic material. After the first bold proclamation, the lower strings take to themselves the melodic line of the opening subject, while above them the violins weave a melody of their own. The nobility and vigor in which the movement began is somewhat modified presently, with the introduction of a new subject, reflective and sad, by clarinet and oboe, with responses by strings and woodwind. With these two ideas in mind, the composer builds before our eyes and ears a beautifully articulated structure, full of contrast yet almost perfectly balanced, inclining slightly but happily in the direction of the proud and powerful motive with which the music began. Yet at the very moment when it would seem this noble expression is to dominate and triumph, there are fascinating anticipations and suspensions and delays, until with all their jubilant sonority the horns put forth a brilliant version, conclusively establishing the brighter spirits in a position to conquer. The concluding passages rise to a climax of tremendous power.

SECOND MOVEMENT

The second movement approaches the form and character of the conventional scherzo more closely than any other section of the symphony. Aside from its lightness and engaging rhythms it has several features of musical interest. It employs, as its basic theme, a version of an old German drinking song; in the modern orchestration by Mr. Stock, we hear at least two instruments which were not in the original score—*cor anglais* and triangle. The *Rheinweinlied* is sung by cellos and violas, and is answered by a gay tune in counterpoint.

The middle section of the movement modifies the prevailing jollity somewhat. It begins with the theme in *cor anglais* (in the original score, clarinet). The first part of the scherzo is repeated, but in much more colorful instrumental apparel, accented with fiery sparks from the triangle and the tinkling of the tambourine.

THIRD MOVEMENT

Schumann is definitely himself in this movement—quiet, romantic, full of tenderness and restrained passion. Yet the Stock version of the symphony takes as great liberties with this movement as with any of the five, not only in orchestration but in certain alterations of the melodic line. Mr. Stock's version certainly improves the music as regards fullness of tone.

A melody of notable smoothness and lovely contour opens the movement, in woodwind voices, clarinet predominating. The *cor anglais* is employed in the modern orchestration to present, with strings, the second theme—another flowing melody. Upon these two little songs Schumann develops a sentimental interlude of appealing tenderness.

FOURTH MOVEMENT

This music has often been called "the cathedral scene"; and not without some justification, for Schumann originally labeled it, "In the character of an accompaniment to a solemn ceremony." The rites attendant upon the elevation of a cardinal, which took place in the magnificent cathedral at Cologne, and which Schumann witnessed, impressed him deeply and inspired this sonorous and dignified music.

Trombones and horns announce the organlike motive; it becomes the firm basis upon which the composer erects an edifice of tone, as elaborated, lofty, and dignified as a Gothic arch. Powerful utterances of trombones are faintly echoed in woodwind and strings. The movement is intimately connected, thematically and otherwise, with the

FIFTH MOVEMENT

into which the music passes without pause. This section may represent the festivals of the people in honor of the installation of their exalted ecclesiastic. It is swift and joyous and brilliant. In the original version there are suggestions of folk music of the Rhineland, which Mr. Stock has somewhat emphasized in his rearrangement; there are also references to the preceding movement and its ecclesiastical motive. A climax of great brilliance and majesty is developed, the movement ending in a festive mood.

Symphony No. 4 in D minor

IN THE version in which it is usually presented today, this is the last as well as the greatest of Schumann's symphonies. Chronologically, it is the second of his works in this form. Schumann himself was dissatisfied with it, especially on the ground that the orchestration lacked sonority and color, and for this reason, he withdrew it after its first performance in 1841. Ten years later he reorchestrated it, and it was played, under the composer's direction, at Düsseldorf, March 3, 1853. Meanwhile he had completed the two works now known as the Second and Third ("Rhenish") Symphonies, and the one which we are considering now was published as his Fourth.

The Fourth is the least "polite" and most passionate utterance of Schumann in the symphonic form. By no means lacking in those romantic and melodious qualities which have endeared his music to generations of audiences, the Fourth often exhibits a vehemence, an intensity, and power for which we look in vain to the other symphonies. It is not spectacular, but it is strong and sane and sweet. It is not an ideal vehicle for the virtuoso conductor, but for one who possesses insight and sincerity, it is eminently satisfying.

FIRST MOVEMENT

By the device of thematic relationship, the composer sought to achieve in this music a coherence and unity more intimate than usual in the conventional symphony of four movements. It is intended that the movements shall be played without pause; indeed, Schumann himself, in the title to the work, mentioned that it is "in one movement." Various editions nevertheless divide the work into three, four, and even five sections, using the composer's subtitles: introduction, allegro, romanze, scherzo, and finale. Since the introduction and allegro are logically indivisible they shall be considered here as one movement.

The somberness and restraint of the introduction are expressed through the important first theme, which is heard at once in the strings against a coldly perfect octave. Almost from the first note there is a

continuous accession of power and emphasis, growing to passionate utterance as all the strings are involved, searching the upper and lower registers for tones sufficiently expressive for their message. A quickened pace, and still more exigent evocations of the orchestra's powers, bring about a brief but tense moment of anticipation, and the movement proper—the allegro—begins.

The basic idea of the movement is expressed through a theme given at once to the violins—a flashing figure that darts swiftly about amidst the emphatic chords of the full orchestra; chords which seem to give it impetus, and from which it rebounds continually with undiminished force and with clearer accent. There is no formal treatment of the thematic material, nor is there any other subject in the movement, so conspicuously placed or developed, as to entitle it to the importance of a conventional second theme. The first subject alone seems to contain within itself possibilities of development and variation which are quite satisfying, and to the free exploitation of these possibilities the movement is devoted. The driving rhythm rests, now and again, on strong octaves delivered forte by wind instruments; then, after a moment's pause, it is again in fierce and restless motion. There is, presently, a brief lyric passage, against which the nervous fluctuations of the first subject are presented—but it is merely an episode, quickly overcome by the impetuous leapings and swift rhythms of the original theme and its developments.

SECOND MOVEMENT
Romanze

The grave sentiment, the romantic melancholy so often disclosed in Schumann's music, are beautifully evident in the second movement. There is a sad little melody, sung by oboe and cello, against a string accompaniment, pizzicato. Here are both resignation and complaint,

and, as if to nullify both, there appears, suddenly and surprisingly, the more passionate theme of the introduction; richly harmonized, and put forward in the string choir's warmest tones. A solo violin presently wanders with feminine grace through a curved and descending figure of more cheerful emotional content; but the plaintive song of the oboe and cello return at the end.

THIRD MOVEMENT
Scherzo

The scherzo is the only movement of this symphony which is in conventional form. Its spirit, however, is not precisely as playful as the title scherzo would imply. Though the rhythm is strong and lively, the gaiety seems calculated and forced. But neither is there morbidity or cynicism. The downright and forceful accents maintained by timpani seem to keep the music moving away from reflectiveness, or seriousness, or cryptic meanings. The trio, the contrasting section of the movement, brings a definitely cheerful spirit to the music, and a bright touch of lyric grace in contrast to the heavy humor of the first part. After the formal re-presentation of the main portion of the movement, there is a long passage of declining power, which leads without pause into the

FOURTH MOVEMENT
Finale

The final movement recalls the fact that Schumann first conceived this music as a kind of fantasia, unified and coherent. The extensive use in the concluding section of the work of themes and material from the first movement is significant. Here they are transformed and even glorified; the former restraints are joyously cast aside, and we have in this movement a powerful, a virile, and optimistic expression. In rhythm and in dynamics, Schumann here exacts a great measure of the orchestra's resources, and accomplishes a revelation of his own powers quite unique in his symphonic music.

After the diminuendo in which the previous movement ended, there are surprising recollections, in the violins, of the main theme of the first movement. The brass, too, projects powerfully a phrase derived from the opening section of the symphony, and it is upon this phrase that the present movement is largely founded. There is a quickening of the tempo, a stubbornly held chord in full orchestra, and the main section of the movement begins with further reference to the first part of the symphony and the introduction of new thematic ideas, partly in strings, partly in woodwind. These are magnificently developed in a broad and free style; strong and often syncopated rhythms urge always onward; fierce outbursts of the full orchestra punctuate long and eloquent and vehement musical sentences. The concluding passages have a vitality and abandon that leave no question of the joy and exaltation that brought forth this music.

Dmitri Shostakovich

BORN 1906

At first glance it might seem curious that two different surveys of Russian music made a few years ago omitted mention of Dmitri Shostakovich—yet within the past few years several of his works have been played by leading American orchestras, and almost overnight he has been recognized as one of the most important, if not the most important, of composers living within the Soviet Union.

Shostakovich was born at St. Petersburg (Leningrad) and now lives there. He studied under Glazunov at the Conservatory, Leningrad, and some of his earlier scores distinctly show the influence of his teacher. Doubtless in the belief that art should, in a proletarian state, mirror the life of the proletariat, some of his symphonies attempt to be political in purpose and flavor, but it is significant that neither of these has been successful outside of Russia. He has written in many forms, and has had performed a satiric opera, several ballets, incidental music for the drama, and music for the sound film. There is also some chamber music, and we know of many smaller pieces for the piano.

Shostakovich aroused vigorous comment both in Russia and the United States with his second opera, *Lady Macbeth of the District of Mzensk.* The official newspaper, *Pravda,* ran an article against it, and for a while it seemed as if government displeasure would fall upon the composer. At the New York production, on February 5, 1935, many members of the audience were shocked by the unblushing realism of the orchestral noises that accompanied the love scene.

Symphony No. 1

The composition bears the simple title, "Symphony for Orchestra, Opus 10." The score requires a large modern orchestra, including a piano. There are no polemics in this music, so far as a capitalist can discover—in which respect the music differs from the composer's "May" and "October" Symphonies.

FIRST MOVEMENT

Highly original as this music is, there are definite traces of the later romantic composers—particularly of Strauss and Wagner—discernible in it. The second division of the theme of the introduction, sounded in the dry tones of the bassoon, is not very unlike a theme from Strauss' *Heldenleben*, and is similarly treated; it forms a starting point for the development section of the movement.

This is a singularly lucid yet compact score. Its harmony, while quite definitely modern, is not shocking, and long before the symphony is played through it ceases to sound harmonically unusual. While strict form is certainly not observed in the movement, the texture of the music is firm, the direction of its movement always logical, its contours satisfying.

The main thought of the movement is proposed, after some measures of introduction, in a melody given to the clarinet, with the string section supplying a forthright and vigorous rhythm. In spite of the vitality of the music, there is a certain cold detachment, a surgical exactness about it which, while highly interesting, is not, in the present movement at least, exciting emotionally.

A few measures in which the strings, pizzicato, inaugurate a change of mood, precede the introduction of a theme somewhat more sentimental, and heard variously from woodwinds and horn. Periods of agitation and vehemence alternate with gentler expressions, and the movement concludes with recollections of its opening theme.

SECOND MOVEMENT

There is a wry, sardonic humor in the second, the scherzo movement of the symphony. Gaiety is at a premium in Russia these days; everyone is so busy. Here the orchestra seems very busy, too, and almost quarrelsome in the struggle for possession of the theme, a swift descending scale passage, given out by piano after a short introduction by woodwind and string bass. There are wonderful pianissimo effects, and a charming, rather naïve little theme first sounding in flutes, clarinets,

and then oboe, and finally made into a climax of great force by blaring
brasses. There is a further climax, and a period of great agitation; then
fortissimo chords punctuate the end of this mood.

THIRD MOVEMENT

The tearful voice of the oboe projects a sad strain, over an accompaniment of tremulous strings, as the central thought of this movement.
Again, a solo cello phrases the melancholy thought, giving to it a touch
of warmth and sentiment such as has occurred but rarely in the symphony up to this point. There is an interlude of brooding, expressed
through strings and brass, and a second theme for oboe. This, instead
of subsiding under the pervading gloom, is developed into a powerful
utterance of the brass, bold and sinister. The opening ideas of the movement return, and then, with a crescendo roll of the military drum the
music passes directly into the

FOURTH MOVEMENT

Here is the most interesting movement in the symphony—chiefly because of the waywardness of its moods, the almost freakish variations
of color and tempo, and the skillful, often unusual use of the orchestral
instruments. A curious and effective quality of tone is produced by the
violins, playing *sul ponticello* (near the bridge) in strange harmonies;
a solo for timpani, with abrupt yet delicately shaded variations from
forte to piano, and a gigantic climax, involving the enormous orchestra
with all its powers and its swiftest pace, are striking features of the
movement.

Symphony No. 5

Shostakovich "has torn off the masks and exposed the false and lying
methods of the composers of bourgeois society."—A. Ostretsov, in
Pravda.

"Every composition should be considered formalistic * in which the
composer fundamentally does not have as his aim the presenting of new
social meanings, but focuses his interest only on inventing new combi-

* "Formalism" was the sin of which Shostakovich was specifically accused, after
the triumphantly successful performances of his opera *Lady Macbeth of the District of Mzensk.*

nations of sounds that have not been done before. Formalism is the sacrifice of the ideological and emotional content of a musical composition
to the search for new tricks in the realm of musical elements—rhythm,
timbre, harmonic combinations, etc."—President Cheliapov of the Moscow Composers' Union.

"There can be no music without ideology. The old composers,
whether they knew it or not, were upholding a political theory. Most of
them of course were bolstering the rule of the upper classes. . . . We,
as revolutionists, have a different conception of music. . . . Even the
symphonic form, which appears more than any other to be divorced
from literary elements, can be said to have a bearing on politics. . . .
Music is no longer an end in itself, but a vital weapon in the struggle.
Because of this, Soviet music will probably develop along different lines
from any the world has ever known."—Dmitri Shostakovich; Interview
in *The New York Times.*

"It is in this service that Soviet composers are engaged, and, as such,
belong completely, body and soul, to that one vast organization, of
which music is only a part, that serves the proletariat. The Soviet composer enjoys privileges and an esteem in the Soviet Union far greater
than artists in any other society, but his bondage and his duties to the
interests of the Soviet Union are airtight. As a citizen of the Soviet
Union, he belongs to the proletariat, and his life and work must serve,
in whatever form they express themselves, the people of the Union."—
Victor I. Seroff, in *Dmitri Shostakovich, The Life and Background
of a Soviet Composer.* *

"I am a Soviet composer, and I see our epoch as something heroic,
spirited and joyous."—Dmitri Shostakovich.

.   .   .   .   .

BEFORE discussing the five latest symphonies of Shostakovich, consideration of the quotations above might be helpful. There is scarcely a
phrase in these sentences with which this writer can agree. This kind of
comment, nevertheless, is regarded as having induced Shostakovich, in
full career, to recant his beliefs, recast his style, remold his ideas, and
drastically change the intellectual and emotional content of his music.
It did no such thing.

Let us look at these statements for a moment. As for the first one:
how tragic that the grim mask has been torn from the face of Beethoven, the genial one from the face of Bach, the spiritual one from the
face of Franck, the knowing one from the face of Brahms, and the mas-

* 1943: Alfred A. Knopf, New York.

culine one from the face of Tchaikovsky. Bach, who loved God, Beethoven, who served man, Franck, who talked with angels, and Brahms, who talked to himself, are exposed by a youth who talks with Stalin. How tragic and how wonderful that a little man in his twenties, by the small weapon of his pert, brisk, and facile talent, could unmask these "false and lying composers of bourgeois society"!

.   .   .   .   .

The First Symphony of Shostakovich revealed to the world a young composer of notable gifts: a man of originality and daring, a certain flippant wit and the always irresistible exuberance of youth. The author of this book feels a certain satisfaction in the fact that he encouraged the first performance, brought about and collaborated in the first recording of this work by Leopold Stokowski and the Philadelphia Orchestra, and arranged for a presentation, simultaneously, of the recording to the Russian consul in New York and to the composer himself, on the very day when the U.S.S.R. was recognized by the United States Government, under the leadership of the late Franklin D. Roosevelt. The promise which this work seemed to give so definitely was not fulfilled in succeeding works. An opera based on Gogol's *The Nose*, produced at Leningrad January 13, 1930, proved to be of no great import, and the Second and Third Symphonies had indifferent success. It was not until Shostakovich's second opera, *Lady Macbeth of the District of Mzensk*, that a crisis in his career came about. Though the work was highly successful inside and outside of Russia, it was the occasion for the sudden and apparently unprovoked resentment of the government authorities. True enough, it could be condemned for its loathsome vulgarity, its delineation of all that is vile and bestial in human nature; but it was not on these grounds that the Soviet authorities objected. It is said that Stalin himself inspired the comments in the newspaper *Pravda,* which included such remarks as these: "From the first minute, the listener is shocked by deliberate dissonance, by a confused stream of sounds. Snatches of melody, the beginnings of a musical phrase, are drowned, emerge again, and disappear in a grinding and squealing roar. To follow this music is most difficult; to remember it, impossible. . . . All this is coarse, primitive and vulgar. The music quacks, grunts, and growls, and suffocates itself, in order to express the amatory scenes as naturalistically as possible, and love is smeared all over the opera in the most vulgar manner. The merchant's double bed occupies the central position of the stage. . . . Lady Macbeth is having great success with bourgeois audiences abroad. [Its greatest successes were in Russia.] Is it not because the opera is absolutely unpolitical and confusing that they praise it? Is it not explained by the fact that it tickles the perverted tastes of the bourgeoisie with its fidgety, screaming, neurotic music?"

Of course, Shostakovich was writing to a libretto, and apparently the fault was fundamentally in the text rather than in the music. That, however, did not spare him, and he suddenly found himself metamorphosed from the white-haired boy of Russian music to the role of a musical outcast. The results of the official discipline applied to him were evident at once. He rather forgot the Second and Third Symphonies. His Fourth, which already was in preparation, was hastily withdrawn, and Shostakovich retired to commune with himself and perhaps with the local commissar about what he should do next. He did permit to be produced a ballet called *The Limpid Stream* which had an exceedingly cold reception, but when, by November 21, 1937, his recantation was adjudged complete, his Fifth Symphony won a prodigious triumph. Shostakovich, with this music, for some inexplicable reason, was restored to the good graces of the Kremlin.

The Fifth Symphony was composed to celebrate the second decade of the Soviet Republic. After the first performance in Leningrad, the symphony was performed for the first time in America at a broadcast concert of the NBC Orchestra from New York, April 9, 1938, the conductor being Artur Rodzinski. The first public performance was given at a concert of the Illinois Symphony Orchestra, November 16, 1938, Izler Solomon conducting. If with this symphony Shostakovich rehabilitated himself with his political masters, the fact was totally ignored in America; though here the symphony was received with extraordinary warmth.

What had happened to Shostakovich? Had his political deviation been corrected? Had he learned how to say what the Kremlin wanted said?

The Soviet functionaries evidently were convinced that he had, but no unprejudiced musician could possibly agree with them. The difference between the Fifth Symphony and the First or Second or Third is a difference in degree, not in kind; it is a development, not a divagation. It could have been prognosticated many years previously, on the assumption that the composer *would* develop, *would* improve, *would* mature, *would* create something worthy of his talents. In style, the Fifth Symphony is not essentially different from any other symphony of Shostakovich. It even employs the clichés common to his other works, and there are many of them. In the Fifth, as in the First, Second, Third, Sixth, Seventh, Eighth, and Ninth, a combination, let us say, of bass tuba and piccolo in a jumpy little tune is still regarded as irresistibly witty; the same trivialities, the same bombast, the same mockeries, the same cold, mechanical, self-conscious tricks with which previous works have familiarized us and with which subsequent works have nauseated some of us, are found in the Fifth Symphony, the difference being merely that they are a little more slick, a little more developed, and a little more convincing. There is the same buffoonery, too—a tragic kind of buffoonery. Perhaps Shostakovich is more subtle than we have believed.

FIRST MOVEMENT

The first movement begins with what the late Lawrence Gilman called an "intervallic" theme, proposed in sections by high and low strings antiphonally. A second subject, broadly lyrical, grows out of this. The movement is amplified in emotional intensity and quickens in pace as it progresses; the melodious secondary theme becomes more importunate, more commanding, and, finally, dominating in the brass. The deliberate tempo of the beginning is restored after awhile, and the rather well rounded-out movement, recalling in the most urgent voices of the strings some of the material of the opening, ends in a rather restrained mood.

SECOND MOVEMENT

There is good-humored music here, in what might be regarded as a rather typical scherzo; but its treatment is a little closer to that of a German waltz than to any other style we know. Its tunes are straightforward, earthy, and brief.

THIRD MOVEMENT

There is a certain resemblance between the thematic material of the third movement and that of the first, though this resemblance may not be evident at the beginning. The melodic element here grows out of tentative utterances of the strings, but when it is full-fledged establishes quite definitely its relation to the opening theme of the movement. This entire section of the work depends very heavily upon the string choirs, and with the growing power of the strings, and the agitated figure that they delineate when the woodwinds enter, there is a distinct accretion of emotional tensity to the end.

FOURTH MOVEMENT

Both the rondo form in which this movement is cast and the fact that the composer refers now and again with remarkable appositeness to certain thematic material of preceding movements give this section of the work a formality and clarity not always too evident in the music of Shostakovich. Here the composer calls upon the orchestra's fullest resources of energy and sonority; and his demands upon them are expressed with increasing exigence to the very end.

Symphony No. 6

By THE Fifth Symphony, Shostakovich somehow rehabilitated himself, and the wildly acclaimed performances of it made him again the national musical hero of the Soviets. He lost no time in emphasizing and capitalizing on this situation. He had been, through his own unaided effort, snatched from the jaws of death, artistically speaking; though the Fifth Symphony had revealed nothing that could not have been anticipated as logical development of his long-evident talents, it had been received as a confession of faith and an *apologia pro vita sua*.

The Sixth Symphony of Shostakovich was intended, one may surmise, as the second half of a "one-two" punch. As such it failed, and for two reasons. It was first presented, in Russia, at the insufferably long two-months Festival of Soviet Music at Moscow, on December 3, 1939. By that time the authorities had been convinced of the composer's orthodoxy, the public excitement over the exorcism of his bourgeois devils had died, and the music-loving people were more interested in certain other new works—Prokofieff's magnificent cantata *Alexander Nevsky,* Shaporin's *On the Field of Kulikov,* and Koval's *Emelian Pugatchov.*

The second reason for the indifferent reception of this work was, and is, the fact that it is in many respects the Fifth Symphony diluted and warmed over. Soviet audiences were slow to accept the work, but the ever hospitable concert public of America received the Sixth Symphony with cordial, though rather well-controlled, enthusiasm. The first performance of the Sixth, outside of Russia, was given by the Philadelphia Orchestra, under the direction of Leopold Stokowski, November 29, 1940. There were subsequent performances by the Boston and Pittsburgh orchestras, Koussevitzky and Reiner conducting.

The instrumentation required is for the most part conventional, though the inclusion of and rather extensive use of such instruments as triangle, tambourine, tam-tam, xylophone, and celesta adds an unusual sparkle.

FIRST MOVEMENT

The structural differences between this symphony and its predecessor are both obvious and in effect superficial. The number, arrangement, and character of the movements are different; the inclusion of melodies reminiscent of certain tunes that everyone knows is either a mockery or a bid for popularity—probably the former; but in its essential nature and color this work is not, actually, far removed from the Fifth.

The first movement reveals, instead of the conventional allegro, a broad largo, quite solemn, quite long (it is longer than the combined second and third movements), and quite effective, as Shostakovich's slow movements almost always are. The section begins with a quite emotional theme in the woodwind and strings, first in the lower registers and moving eventually, with an intensity of expressiveness, into the higher levels of the first violins. Then strings, alone at first, suggest a new and equally gracious melody which is expanded to a commanding degree of power. There is expansion of these ideas—particularly the second—in which woodwind voices (particularly English horn and flute) are conspicuous over a mysterious background of trilling string tone. Here the familiar device of Shostakovich, in which he violently, sometimes even humorously, contrasts not only tone but pitch, comes into play—with the high-voiced winds poised against the strings' lowest tones.

SECOND MOVEMENT

The second movement, with its rapid rhythms, might properly be regarded as the scherzo of the symphony. The serious mood of the first is quite forgotten, and the music, driven by a powerful and insistent three-beat rhythm, moves through its swift and fantastic course toward a climax of tremendous sonority. There are some entertaining diversions in the woodwinds, solo, the clarinet having a particularly notable passage in which its assertive high register is effectively employed.

THIRD MOVEMENT

The finale is even swifter than the preceding allegro, and, as Paul Affelder observes, the basic theme is inescapably reminiscent of the theatrical finale of Rossini's *William Tell* overture. This is not the only suggestion of familiar music discernible here; the second theme recalls the last movement of the Mozart G minor symphony, and then a fragment of the "Anvil Chorus" in Verdi's *Il Trovatore*. With a change of rhythm comes still another suggestion of a familiar and not so respectable tune, the Mexican folk song "Blue Skies" (*"Cielito Lindo"*). The introduction of these melodies can hardly be accidental, and one is at liberty to conclude for himself whether they are insinuated here that they might be mocked by the receptive Russian public, or recognized and therefore liked by the friendly Americans.

The climax of the movement actually begins in one of the smallest voices of the orchestra—a solo violin—and rises to a compelling degree of sonority, moved by what Leopold Stokowski asserts are Russian folk dances (though the rhythm is almost purely a march). The conclusion is very loud.

Symphony No. 7

THE Seventh Symphony of Shostakovich was promoted, particularly in America, by the most extraordinary program of propaganda that has ever been conceived for a piece of music in modern times. The reasons for this were several: the war was on; Russia was our ally; and anything that we could do to mollify her exigent demands was to be done. Furthermore, it was known, and had been known for some time, that Shostakovich, the darling of Russian music, had been working on a new symphony; and American conductors, or at least conductors earning their bread in America, vied with each other for the—at that time —problematical privilege of presenting Shostakovich's newest work to the American public.

The preliminary rehearsals for this work were run through by the orchestra of the Bolshoi Theater of Moscow, but were held at Kuibyshev, and the first performance was given in the Hall of Columns of the Palace of Rest and Culture in Kuibyshev on March 1, 1942. The sad state of musical facilities in Russia is indicated by the fact that, we are told, forty rehearsals were given to prepare this work. A fourth-rate American orchestra, with a conductor capable of reading, could have done a good performance with less than one-tenth as much preparation. The first American performance was the radio concert of the NBC Orchestra on July 19, 1942, under the direction of Arturo Toscanini (with three rehearsals) ; the first performance open to the general public was given a few days later by the Boston Symphony Orchestra under the direction of Serge Koussevitzky at the Berkshire Music Center, Tanglewood, Lenox, Massachusetts. This concert was a benefit for the Russians, as was a second one on the program of which the symphony appeared, conducted by Frederick Stock with the Chicago Symphony Orchestra, at Ravinia Park, Illinois, August 22, 1942.

Shostakovich himself said in a radio broadcast that "The symphony is devoted to the events of 1941—war. [Notwithstanding the fact that most of it had been written before Russia had felt the war.] This does not mean, of course, that it gives a naturalistic imitation of the war, but nevertheless it is an interpretation of the war. My Seventh Symphony is devoted to the ordinary Soviet citizens who have become heroes of this patriotic war. That is its fundamental theme."

Certain thematic suggestions may be of use in following this extraordinary music:

FIRST MOVEMENT

In the first movement there is a broad and basic theme sounded so-
norously in the strings:

The movement has, a little later, a second theme also in the strings but
with a portentous bass figure in the accompaniment:

These materials are cannily exploited, and the first intimation of war
and the rumor of war comes with suggestions from the snare drum and
then with a marching figure plucked from the strings with the violins
playing *col legno* (with the wooden back of the bow):

The emotional climax of the movement is reached after a change in
tempo to a very slow rhythm with a mournful threnody evoked from
the bassoon:

SECOND MOVEMENT

The second movement is lively almost to the point of being a scherzo,
and its vigorous forward movement is initiated by the second violins:

There are certain subsidiary themes, notably a rather mournful but not sluggish theme given to the oboe, but the essential substance of the movement is more properly contained in a melody assigned to the E-flat clarinet in its highest and shrillest register—a quality of tone which, on reviewing other works of Shostakovich, appears to be a favorite sound in his ears:

There is a tailpiece attached to this movement which is of no great thematic interest but from the point of view of orchestration is unusually attractive. It employs thematic material with which we are already familiar but the instrumentation involves bass clarinet with a curious, rapidly repeated figure by the two flutes and a bass flute. The movement ends quietly.

THIRD MOVEMENT

Knowing as we do Mr. Shostakovich's devotion to the state and the state's contempt for anything smacking of religion, "the opiate of the people," it is rather surprising, and would be touching if we did not sense a note of mockery, to find the third movement beginning with what amounts to a hymn. This sounds in the woodwind, horns, and harps; having made his genuflection, Shostakovich looks about him with a cynical eye and decides upon this brisk principal theme of the movement, projected by the first violins:

There is another important germinal idea in this movement, and it generates a series of entirely new and different thoughts. It sounds forth *marcato* in the horns, and goes like this:

At the end, though, as if leaving the church, Shostakovich bows once more toward the altar with the pious theme that opened the movement.

FOURTH MOVEMENT

The fourth movement, an allegro, begins on a pedal point * on G in the cellos, basses, and timpani. What appears to be the basic theme of the movement, but actually is not, is intimated tentatively by the violins, playing almost entirely on or below the D string, pianissimo.

There are other themes, of more or less importance, but none has so much to do with the tremendous energy of this movement as has this one, again in the violins:

Subsequent to this, the horns have an absolutely new idea to pour forth in their brilliant tones, but this idea is episodic, as far as structure is concerned, although eventually it is developed into a heroic proclamation in which the entire orchestra is involved. A building up of sonorities here leads us through a number of tonalities to the original white, bold, natural, open key of C major. The first theme of the opening movement sounds boldly in the brazen voices of three trombones in

* A fixed note around which varying harmonies circulate without violence to the harmonic scheme.

unison, and the work comes to a close on a gigantic outpouring of the elements of a major chord in C major.

Symphony No. 8

SHOSTAKOVICH says that he had intended his Seventh, Eighth, and Ninth Symphonies to constitute a kind of trilogy celebrating Russian activities during the war. There is no reference to lend-lease, so far as a bourgeois mind can detect, but there are many intended references to Russian valor, which we all applaud, Russian fortitude, which we can easily match, and Russian victory, which in no small measure we shared. The Eighth Symphony, constituting the middle part of this ex post facto trilogy, is, one feels, the least interesting of the three. Apparently it is intended to represent the period of crisis and post-crisis during which the Germans came so close to victory, and then were driven back. Yet, of course, it is impossible to manufacture or even to imagine a precise program for the Eighth Symphony. The words of the composer himself, delivered to Gregori Schneerson of the *Moscow News*, would probably be more indicative of the meaning of this work than anything else that might be said here: "I can describe the philosophical concept of my new symphony very briefly: Life is beautiful. All that is dark and ignominious will disappear; all that is beautiful will triumph."

FIRST MOVEMENT

The symphony is in five movements, the first being a long and slow section. The military note is almost entirely lacking. The marches and countermarches of victor and vanquished are not strongly suggested here, although in truth there are march rhythms, but they are so slow as to be almost funereal, and the melodic contours suggest the elegiac rather than the triumphant mood. Antiphonal phrases exchanged between strings and woodwinds are notably conspicuous near the beginning, and there are winged melodies soaring high in the strings above a low and persistent bass. Out of these innocent materials the composer works up a climax of unpleasant stridency and great force. The rather pastoral solo for English horn, which presently succeeds, is a relief and a joy to hear.

SECOND MOVEMENT

Again we hear a marchlike rhythm proceeding with constant accretions of orchestral force and accent, striding along like a dress parade.
Curiously, there is an unpredictable change of rhythm from common
time to ⅜, whereupon the music takes on a much lighter character and
leaps about underneath solo passages for piccolo, E-flat clarinet, and
other woodwinds. These disappear into silence before the fortissimo
chord which closes the movement.

THIRD MOVEMENT

And still the suggestion of marching men, but vague and ghostly.
The whole viola section joins in a rather heavy-handed march, and the
feeling of this spreads to the upper strings and later to the brass. Both
sonorities and tempi broaden to build a climax of impressive power.
There is no interruption between this movement and the

FOURTH MOVEMENT

There is, however, a marked change in tempo. One may observe a
vague reference to the beginning of the symphony, played quietly with
the strings *con sordino*. One commentator regards the movement as a
passacaglia, but if one is very familiar with this form, and very con-
scientious about it, it might be a little difficult to establish that this
movement fits into the strict pattern. There is, however, a kind of theme
and variation treatment here, the theme being based upon the second
subject of the first movement. The mood is rather subjective, rather
contemplative, and rather serene, and the texture of the music, for all
its dissonance, is delicate and agreeably colored.

FIFTH MOVEMENT

The fifth movement follows the fourth without pause. Here the composer uses a number of the orchestral prima donnas in a succession of
solos, with the accompaniment strongly rhythmic but yet not obtrusive,
and often in the strings pizzicato. Some of the instrumental solos are
gathered together eventually to form a loose kind of fugue, in which
we hear most conspicuously violins, flutes, cellos, oboes, and certain

other instruments. In a kind of stretto there comes an almost unbearable increase of tension, arriving at its climax in a brazen assertion of a phrase abstracted from the first movement. At this point the quasi-pastoral atmosphere has been completely dissipated, but it is restored eventually during a long and charming solo for bass clarinet. Solo instruments again become prominent, particularly cello, bassoon, and violin; and an atmosphere of peace and serenity is established toward the end. The movement ends quietly.

Symphony No. 9

The Ninth Symphony of Shostakovich purports to be the third of a symphonic trilogy celebrating the Russian war tragedy, war effort, and victory. All the friends of Shostakovich and all his admirers—who number millions—looked forward to the Ninth Symphony and expected a supreme paean of triumph. The war had been won; the nation looked toward Shostakovich for the final word that would immortalize the Russian victory. When the Ninth Symphony finally was produced, all were surprised, and many were disappointed.

One day in 1945 Shostakovich sat down before a number of newspaper correspondents in the studio of Vladimir Vlasov to play a piano reduction of his new Ninth Symphony. Among those present were Robert Magidoff, Russian correspondent of *The New York Times*; Gregori Schneerson, correspondent of the *Moscow News* (New York Edition); D. Rabinovitch, native correspondent of the *Moscow News*; Daniel Zhitomirsky, and perhaps one or two others. All expected a thundering proclamation of victory. After the hearing none would admit disappointment, but all expressed astonishment, for, according to Magidoff, "It is the simplest piece the mature Shostakovich has ever written and also the gayest, most youthful, and most melodious. . . . Its spirit is probably best revealed in the concluding movement. Good-natured and gay, it rises in tempo until it ends in a burst of irrepressible merriment. When Shostakovich had finished playing, he rubbed his hands with satisfaction and said, completely without self-consciousness, 'It is a merry little piece. Musicians will love to play it and critics will delight in blasting it.'"

It is possible to say that Shostakovich overestimated the reaction of his music from both musicians and critics. For orchestra musicians, it is a workaday piece—not difficult, not exciting, though by no means uninteresting. As for the critics, they apparently do not regard the music as important enough for "blasting." Its techniques are not materially different from anything back as far as Shostakovich's First Symphony; in its spirit, it is merry to be sure, but in relation to its subject, utterly trivial. It is a curious fact that most of those who heard Mr. Shostakovich play his piano reduction were startled at a concert by the Leningrad Philharmonic Orchestra on November 3, 1945, when the full orchestral score was played, because of the utterly different character which the music had in its proper form. This orchestral performance was given under the direction of Eugene Mravinsky. The first performance in America was at the opening concert of the Berkshire Music Festival at Tanglewood, Lenox, Massachusetts, by the Boston Symphony Orchestra, July 25, 1946, Serge Koussevitzky conducting. The orchestration is conventional.

*   *   *   *   *

For a technical analysis of the music, we can do no better than turn to the notes of Daniel Zhitomirsky, friend and associate of the composer, who actually watched this music in the process of gestation, and whose remarks were printed in the program of the Boston Symphony Orchestra on the occasion of the performance there. They are here reproduced, by permission.

"The Ninth opens with an Allegro of Haydn-like simplicity with a fair share of slyness and subtle irony. Shostakovich revives in its very essence that spirit of unrestrained and bubbling mirth which lived in classical Allegros up to Rossini's overtures. The peculiar 'classicism' of this music is ultra-modern. The first theme—as if often the case with early classics—glides effortlessly and imperceptibly not so much as an individual melody but rather as a kind of animated motion. Elements of buffoonery appear in the subordinate theme. A naïve and simple formula of accompaniment dashes in; a pert but not ungraceful song appears against this background. The headlong fascination of movement grows unintermittently in the elaboration. The composer cleverly handles various shades of the comedy aspect. One of these, embodied in a new variation of the familiar subordinate theme, is particularly expressive.

"The second movement (Moderato) reveals the world of bright and romantic lyricism. The main theme is songful and is of romance-like nature (remotely reminding one of Katherine's romance from *Lady Macbeth of Mzensk*), and at the same time refined and whimsical in its outline. The texture of this piece is of captivating lucidity; it is a fine, almost incorporeal 'pattern on glass' as if radiating peculiar chaste beauty.

"The third movement is a precipitous scherzo (Presto). Its music rushes past one like a gust of wind with piercingly whistling upflights and downsweeps. The theme of the scherzo, or rather the pattern of its first bars, is the embryo out of which uninterrupted movement grows and develops. The theme of the middle section of the scherzo, with its stressed theatrical pathos verging between serious agitation and irony, is poignantly relieved and expressive.

"The fourth movement (Largo) was conceived as a contrasting intermezzo between the scherzo and the finale. It consists almost entirely of a large bassoon solo of an improvisational character against the background of sustained chords. This is moment of deep concentratedness. It is important not only by itself but as a certain lyrico-philosophical commentary to the whole work, stressing the precious human sources of all this light and unrestrained flow of music.

"The finale (Allegretto) in its spirit is akin to the first movement but it has more of buffoonery than of spontaneous gaiety. There is in the main theme of the finale both the classical naïveté and extravaganza of variety-stage dance. The development of the finale overflows with vigor and abounds in brilliant comedy touches; a short Coda brings this merry theatrical 'run' to top speed."

Jean Sibelius

S IBELIUS, the son of a medical officer in military service, was born at
  Tavastehus, Finland, December 8, 1865; he now lives at Järven-
pää. He was left an orphan at an early age, and was educated by his
grandparents, who intended for him a classical training with the ultimate aim of the boy's becoming a lawyer. Even as a child, however,
Sibelius determined to become a musician, and though he obediently
went to school and later to the University of Helsingfors, from which
he was graduated, he began, immediately he was his own master, to
study the violin. But from boyhood he had, informally but intensely,
studied music, and was in some degree prepared for the strenuous work
which he now began.

In 1889 Sibelius left Finland for Berlin, to study composition; two
years later, he went to Vienna, where he was a pupil of Karl Goldmark.
He remembers that the first performance of any of his works was given
at Helsingfors, in 1887; it was a series of variations for string quartet.

The composer soon developed a highly individual style, founded, it
is true, upon the music of the classical masters, yet so informed with
Sibelius' own unique spirit and character as to seem very far removed
from the compositions of the nineteenth century. His is a music which,
fortunately, cannot be at once assimilated; yet even regarded superficially, it has a strange charm which deepens to fascination the more
the music is heard. Sibelius' music has been the dubious beneficiary of
a powerful propaganda, both in America and England. This has
brought about more frequent playing of his works, but has also aroused
the skepticism of a considerable section of the discriminating public—
a skepticism, let it be added hastily, which is only in rare instances justified. He has suffered, too, from quasi-authoritative interpretations by
completely unskilled and inferior conductors, both in Europe and
America—a circumstance which contributes little to the impression his

enthusiastic but misguided propagandists seek to create for his music.

Sibelius has visited America. In 1914 he came to the United States to conduct several of his works at a music festival at Litchfield, Conn.; he visited Boston and several other centers of musical interest. It was during this visit that Yale University conferred upon the composer the degree doctor of music; several of his works were played during the commencement program.

The Finnish master now lives in a small village, not distant, yet by its character infinitely remote from the capital city of Helsingfors, Finland. He prefers seclusion and simplicity, yet is gracious and hospitable to those who find the difficult way to his threshold. He has written seven symphonies, as well as numerous other works; and it is reported that he is at work upon an eighth symphony.

Symphony No. 1 in E minor

THE First Symphony of Sibelius was written in 1899, when the composer was to a certain extent under the influence of Tchaikovsky; and this influence, at brief intervals, is quite marked in this work. Sibelius is one of the most distinctly individual and original of composers, but as a young man, naturally he was conscious of the heritage left by the preceding great masters. The later symphonies depart almost entirely from any "influence"; the first—and it is not said in disparagement— is the most derivative and least individual of the seven that Sibelius has so far written. It is not less interesting for that reason; on the contrary, as the last great symphony of its type, it has a very special interest.

The first performance of this music was at a concert devoted to Finnish music, given in Berlin, under Robert Kajanus, July 18, 1900. The first performance in America was by the orchestra which, more than any other, has devoted itself to the works of the Finnish master: the Boston Symphony Orchestra—January 5, 1907.

FIRST MOVEMENT

The symphony opens with an introduction in which the clarinet sings a wandering melody of singular appeal—a lonely voice moving in solitary loveliness over the ominous rumblings of drums. The song of the clarinet is like a thesis for the symphony; abandoned presently, it nevertheless reappears later with new significance and importance.

The chief subject of the movement proper is suggested by the strings —violins first, with derivations of the theme presented by cellos and violas. The contrasting and subordinate thematic material is divided rather definitely between strings and wind, but there is always a close relationship between the items assigned to either group. Once we have observed the principal and the subordinate thematic matter, there is a short period of development, ending in a climax of great intensity, with full orchestra thrusting out savagely in great masses of tone, and a terrific thundering of timpani. The second chief theme, closely following this outburst, is sung by the flute against a transparent screen woven of the tones of violin, viola, and harp.

The development and conclusion of the movement are broad and free, and are built mainly upon a titanic struggle for dominance, carried on between the various thematic elements that have been introduced. There are references, both rhythmic and melodic, to the principal themes, and even a suggestion, in the incontinent cries of the woodwind, of the melody of the introduction. Rhythmically, the movement from this point onward is for the most part developed out of the second of the two principal subjects, but the subject itself, imminent from time to time, is never permitted another explicit statement of itself and is abandoned with finality when the brass so mightily asserts itself near the end.

SECOND MOVEMENT

The second movement is filled with a nostalgic loveliness. There is nothing here of Tchaikovsky's passionate yearnings, nor even of the more reticent and perhaps deeper *Sehnsucht* of a Brahms slow movement; but we feel a gentle and pathetic desire for some remembered and intangible joy, as of a dream that, on awakening, seems both ephemeral and real.

Violins and cellos sing of this sweet and pathetic desire; then the earnest voices of bassoons and other woodwinds emphasize it with a new melody. The music broods upon these subjects for a while, and presently a third theme, now in horns accompanied by harp, intrudes. But it is a remembrance of the first theme that brings about the most vigorous development of the movement.

THIRD MOVEMENT

The basis of the entire movement is the almost brutally violent figure given out by three timpani at the beginning. With all its power, this figure somehow suggests a heavy-handed humor; the humor, perhaps, of the northern peasant, whose sense of the absurd is his chief stimulus to mirth. The second theme, though contrastingly lighter, is clearly influenced by the rhythm of the first, and only in the trio, which is much more restrained and gentle, do we escape from the fierce assertive gesture that lies in the first thunderous utterance of the timpani. At the end, there is a swift accelerando, a growth in power, and the great drums, with the whole orchestra, thunder once again and for the last time.

FOURTH MOVEMENT

The finale is like a series of three mountainous waves, rising to terrifying heights of power, subsiding to simple, if not precisely placid, fluxes of orchestral tone. The opening subject is developed clearly from the song of the clarinet in the introduction to the first movement; but its character has undergone a marked change. Where it once sang of loneliness and contemplation, it now assumes a dark and tragic significance. As if it had provoked them, suggestions of the imminent chief theme of this movement are heard deep in the strings; the theme itself appears, against ominous beatings of drums, in the woodwind. With this impetus, the first great wave of the movement takes form, and rushes out from the orchestra in powerful and resistless surgings, moving toward a mighty crashing climax.

The second theme is in marked contrast with the first. It appears, presently, in the violins and, a little later, is compared with the original theme. Now the second great wave form of the movement gathers itself for another climax. It is not long in developing, and at its peak demands almost the ultimate of the orchestral resources. A presentation of the second theme in clarinet is the interrupting idea which begets the formation of the third, and final, wave of tone which sweeps the orchestra like a storm.

Symphony No. 2 in D major

IN THE Second Symphony, Sibelius makes a definite break with the influences and derivations that can be marked in the First; he establishes himself here as a composer of distinct individuality, with a style and idiom uniquely his own. Here also we can observe the two most characteristic features of Sibelius' music—its strongly national character and the amazing economy and effectiveness of its orchestration. This is the real Sibelius, terse, powerful, and convincing; devoid of the factitious and the unnecessary, naked and pulsating and enormously vital.

This may be, as some commentators assert, Sibelius' "pastoral" symphony, but it is scarcely more descriptive of his native land than others of his musical works. The spirit of Finnish folk music is always strong in Sibelius; images and atmosphere of fiord and crag and gray unfriendly seas, of sparsely covered meadows and acrid salt marshes, are always evoked by it. In this particular work, however, we can feel something more powerful; something of the aroused patriotism of *Finlandia*, as well as the laconic finality exhibited so wonderfully in the Fourth Symphony.

FIRST MOVEMENT

The uncanny certainty with which the composer selects the one most effective voice through which his melodies shall be projected is beautifully revealed throughout this music. It has been said that Sibelius conceives a melody and its instrumental expression simultaneously; that he is incapable of dissociating melody and instrument. If so, he has developed this valuable faculty to the point of papal infallibility, for when a melody sings out from the orchestra of Sibelius, we somehow feel that *that* is the one inevitable voice through which the given melody could be proclaimed.

The first movement is filled with the subdued light of a Finnish land-scape. At once the foundation of the movement is laid—a markedly rhythmic figure in the strings which is at once an intimation of a musical thought presently to be expressed and a dominating idea in the symphony. The first theme itself is given out, briefly, by oboes and clarinets; the accompaniment of the throbbing strings continues. Both ideas are developed freely and at some length, but the orchestration remains superbly simple. An atmosphere of severity rather than of gloom, of a harsh relentless vitality asserting itself with quiet strength rather than with bombastic proclamations, colors the whole movement. New thematic material, presented by woodwind in octaves, above the pulsing figure heard from the first in strings, reveals the picture in another aspect and in new colors, but does not alter its outlines. At the end the mesmerizing throbbing of the strings, having wrought its charm and created its mood, sounds less assertively.

SECOND MOVEMENT

The stubborn and sometimes gloomy patriotism of his fellow countrymen seems to be the moving spirit of this strange music. In it are outlined grim forebodings, and the realization of them; sturdy opposition, tragic defeats, and a kind of wild and suppressed nobility. The timpani, pregnant with thunders, give out threatening rumblings; then the low strings, pizzicato, sketch the melodic line of the movement. The weirdest voice in the orchestra—that of the bassoon—sings sadly of sorrows and tears and terrors, and there is menace in the dull roar of the great drums that sound below. Such an atmosphere rarely endures for long in the music of Sibelius; presently it is dissipated in a stormy climax that evokes the orchestra's fullest powers.

The folk-song influence is distinctly felt in the presentation of the second principal theme. It must be remembered here, as always in the music of Sibelius, that the composer does not borrow his melodies from the folk music of Finland; but so intensely feels and loves the native music that his own melodies quite naturally adopt its characteristic outlines.

The strings, divided, present the poignant melody, and at the same time accompany themselves; later added color is given by woodwinds.

The palette is reversed, after a few moments, with the theme in the woodwind and accompaniment by strings. There is a distinct lightening of the gloom that has heretofore pervaded the movement, and with each succeeding climactic wave the feeling of strength and assertiveness and hope grows stronger. Though there are frequent disjointed remembrances of thematic fragments scattered throughout the movement, its unity and power and vitality are maintained, even though its dynamics are, temporarily, held in restraint. The final climax is of crushing power and vehemence.

THIRD MOVEMENT

If there were a program for this symphony, the third movement would undoubtedly be regarded as the "call to arms," the "awakening of national pride and spirit," the taking up of a struggle against oppression. The movement springs into agitated life with the very first note. The violins have a lightfooted figure, which not only establishes the mood of the scherzo, but also supplies a rhythmic basis against which other thematic elements are projected. A curious combination of glitter and shadow—flute and bassoon—utters the second chief subject, still animated and nervous like the first.

The trio, or middle section of the scherzo, is in marked contrast to the first. Here the piercing tones of the oboe are arranged in a simple and appealing melody, its thinness and sharpness relieved by the warm and softly sonorous accompaniment of bassoon and horn. The strings are momentarily invoked, but during its brief moments this part of the movement maintains a calm and pastoral atmosphere. The elastic rhythms of the opening section return, and after a final reference to the quiet melody of the trio, a long crescendo begins, and leads with ever-developing power directly into the

FOURTH MOVEMENT

Here the blazing and imperious proclamations of this music sound a mighty song of triumph. This is the Sibelius of *Finlandia;* this is boldness and spaciousness and powerful uncomplicated assertiveness. The main theme is brief, strong, and simple. The strings, down to and

including cellos, pronounce it with vigor. Woodwinds present a second, and strongly rhythmical, idea, and the two are developed in a series of

climaxes piled upon one another like mountains. Yet there is here, as in most of Sibelius' moments of excitement or grandeur, something of godlike passionless detachment; as if some remote being handled mighty intractable forces with unerring firm hands, and, inexorable and unperturbed, molded them to his will. It is curious that this music, that can be so moving and so mighty, can at the same moment be so cold. It has the beat and the breath of life, but its life stream moves deliberately, inevitably, fatefully, and never passionately. That the music of this composer rarely has in it the quality we call sensuousness is one of the many apparent contradictions we find in it, for though it seems to omit this quality, it is the very character of the sounds Sibelius makes the orchestra produce that most fascinates our ears and most powerfully calls forth our response to this music.

Symphony No. 3 in C major

THE Third Symphony of Sibelius dates from 1907, during which year it was completed and first performed at Helsingfors, Finland. The first performance in our country was given by the Russian Symphony Society, Modeste Altschuler conducting, at New York, January 16, 1908. It is interesting to remark that the Philadelphia, one of our great symphony orchestras which has been friendly indeed to music of Sibelius, waited until December 11, 1936, to perform the work, Eugene Ormandy conducting. Subsequent performances have been by no means frequent, and to a certain degree this is an indication both of the popularity of the work—or lack of it—and of its standing among the symphonies of Sibelius.

While it is not, to American audiences, the most acceptable of the Finnish master's symphonic works, it is notable for several reasons. In it the composer exhibits an economy of both means and material that had not been noticeable in his two preceding symphonies. Again, here he seems to have suspended the sometimes incontinent, episodic, and occasionally almost incoherent manner that can be observed in the first two symphonies. Here his orchestra is smaller, the symphony as a whole is shorter, and even the movements individually are shorter than those of earlier works. Here the brass, instead of stridently dominating, is sternly restrained for the most part and thereby gains in force when it is brought to the fore. Here the composer very obviously relies most heavily on the string choirs, with a resultant lightness which not only more aptly fits the humor of the symphony, but is a relief from the ponderous, ominous, portentous, or merely shouting brasses of the earlier works.

The Third Symphony—if one is accustomed to the occasional turgidity of the First and Second—is by comparison remarkably clear and relatively simple. The form of the first movement approaches that of the classical sonata and its outlines are never obscured by extraneous or make-weight material. The treatment of the very moving second movement is too simple to require anything in the way of description, since it gains effect by a mere series of alterations in harmony on a single simple theme. Only in the last movement is there complexity resembling that of earlier Sibelius works; and even here the structure is more symmetrical, more solid, and more comprehensible. What is perhaps most important of all in the character of this ingratiating work has been pointed out very aptly by the London critic, Cecil Gray, in his revealing and almost affectionate book on Sibelius. "In feeling and atmosphere, too, the Third Symphony provides a striking contrast with its two forerunners. The somber, restless tone of the first, the strenuous and impassioned character of the second, give way to a mood of unclouded serenity and sunny gaiety, particularly exemplified in the delightful middle movement, which is perhaps the most attractive and original of the three."

Symphony No. 4 in A minor

THE Fourth Symphony of Sibelius is incomparably his finest. Here is music as compact, as ungracious, as refractory and fantastic as a rock carven by the beating of timeless oceans. Indeed, it *is* music of stony caverns and of dark northern seas. Sibelius, the confessed devotee of nature, here casts his deep and austerely loving glance across the bare landscapes of his native land, and, perhaps unconsciously, paints them in their strong dark color and rugged outline. Only a pale and chill sunlight shines here; only in strange piercing harmonies, like the distant cries of wild sea birds, does brilliance come to this music. Yet it is not gloomy. It is thoughtful and strong and gaunt, as a man grows who lives a long life in the winters of rugged Finland; its melancholy is contemplative and contained, rather than doleful and abandoned. It is like a play, a story without a heroine, for it has no trace of sensuousness or passionate yearning; yet, far from being sexless, it is music that is definitely masculine.

The assertion that the music of Sibelius contains no padding is, like most dogmatic assertions, untrue. The rocky and rough-hewn structures which he has erected frequently contain, in their interstices, some very plastic and adhesive material, sometimes made of fine particles of the basic structure, sometimes of foreign matter. But it would be difficult to find any such in this stark and rawboned symphony. Through its lean and firm and compact flesh one sees the very skeleton, yet it is strangely complete and highly finished music.

FIRST MOVEMENT

The power, achieved by rare economy of means, that Sibelius exhibits in this movement is almost terrifying—almost like the elemental strivings of the brute forces of nature. The savage bowing of the low strings on their monotonous and limited phrase is as pitiless as the grinding of great stones in some subterranean cavern; the solo cello that presently suggests a theme is not the romantic voice we know, but a grimly regretful one without passion and almost without emphasis. There is no brilliance, but only wildness and keenness even when the upper strings, bowed with ever-growing force, begin an advance toward a discordant and unresolved climax. Brasses vehemently thrust out threatening lances of tone, bright and deadly; again strings shriek like wild winter winds. From a few phrases the composer builds a brief but mighty movement, free in form, yet tremendously restrained and laconic and stern. He dwells upon his thought until it is clear, in the simplest and strongest terms; he proceeds, with merciless logic, to the next. There is no lingering upon a lovely phrase—though there are phrases of strange harsh beauty; there is no sweeping and brilliant and persuasive peroration; only a swift dissolution of the music into pale harmonies immaterial and distant as Northern mists.

SECOND MOVEMENT

Perhaps the uncommunicative Finn has humor like this—terse and rough and wry. The man who wrests his living from nature's grudging hands has little time for laughter. But here *is* laughter, harsh and unaccustomed, bold and sardonic. The peasant's cruelly acute sense of the ridiculous is almost his only stimulus to mirth, and here, perhaps, is an illustration of it. The curious cry of the oboe is almost pathetic, and it is roughly elbowed aside by rude interjections of the strings. In contrast comes an almost waltzlike passage, definitely reminiscent of Tchaikovsky. Contrabassoon and, later, after a swift descent of strings, an almost painfully vehement protestation from the brass banish temporarily the mood of labored humor and recall the fierce brazen interruptions of the first movement. Woodwinds in a graceful descending figure achieve gaiety once more, but that sullen remembrance of the preceding movement has vitiated the spirit of this one, and it dies, abruptly and unexpectedly, in a feeble flicker of tone.

THIRD MOVEMENT

In this truly beautiful and affecting movement Sibelius makes the closest approach to sustained melody that can be found in the symphony. Flute informs us of a lovely theme, of pastoral simplicity, clarinet continues it; both are supported by soft harmonies in the strings. A solemn chorus of brass warms and weights the orchestra's tone, and, later, a bassoon suggests a more serious thought. It is the cello, however, which holds forth upon the basic theme, against a tremulous string accompaniment. And the elements of this theme, as well as of others, are strangely dissipated through the movement, though often there are brief passages of very moving melody. The string orchestra, for a space, has almost complete possession of the composer's thought, rising to a climax that is all but passionate, and then resigning once more in favor of flute and clarinet, which present their respective phrases much as at the beginning.

The strange insolvent harmony of Sibelius is, paradoxically, occasionally resolved here into even such usual things as chords built upon tonic and dominant. Yet at the end, where the unsatisfying harmony gradually attenuates to a unison C sharp in muted horns and violas, against which a succession of thematic fragments are thrown by woodwind and strings, there is no relaxation of the rigors of this music. It closes in a kind of hypnotized weariness, wan and without color, given life and motion only by the ominous and inconclusive notes plucked from the basses.

FOURTH MOVEMENT

It is curious that Sibelius can convey an effect of richness and color and fantasy, entirely without any feeling of warmth. He accomplishes this notably in the fourth movement, with a hard brilliance of orchestration, and with imaginative resourcefulness not easily surpassed in symphonic music. It is with difficulty that one defines the mood of the music, or its significance, if it has any particular significance, for it encompasses every emotional state except sentimentality.

There is merriment, and grotesquerie, and arresting, forbidding passages of ominous portent. There are bright jinglings in the icy tone of the glockenspiel; wild bells and powerful ring out, further on; an oddly syncopated figure in the strings suggests awkward dancing; eventually the trumpet, beginning pianissimo and gradually forcing out a flaming tongue of tone, recalls the ominous brazen utterance of the first movement. But the harmonies are dry and hard and unrelenting, even to the end.

Symphony No. 5 in E-flat major

THE Fifth Symphony of Sibelius is certainly the most popular of his works in this form; and very possibly the greatest. There is evidence to indicate that the composer himself regarded it as one of his most important works, for upon it he lavished his labor, and revised, altered, corrected, and rewrote it with a passionate determination to make it say, finally, what he wished it to say. That he has accomplished this may possibly be established by the public's present estimate of the work.

This music was written during the distressful period of the First World War—mostly during 1915. Between the Fourth (1911) and the Fifth, Sibelius had been concerned with "program" music to a considerable extent (*The Dryad, Scènes historiques, The Bard, Les Océanides*) and had considered the writing of a ballet to be called *King Fjalar*—an idea which he ultimately rejected. It is clear from his conversation and correspondence, at this time, that he wanted to write purely symphonic music again, and that ideas for it were taking form in his head. The necessity for income, and the importunings of publishers, alike pressed upon him and alike were distasteful. He wrote, "I cannot become a prolific writer. It would mean killing all my reputation and my art. I have made my name in the world by straightforward means. I must go on in the same way. Perhaps I am too much of a hypochondriac. But to waste on a few *pas* a motif that would be excellently suited to symphonic composition!"

Sibelius has always been reluctant to discuss his own work, though voluble enough about other music and other musicians. It is evident, however, that he made for himself a definite decision to devote all his life and energies to the composition of the music he felt nascent within him, and to turn from the immediate and profitable demands to the necessities of sincere self-expression. He adopted a mode of living in which solitude played a vital part; he withdrew from the turmoil of warring Europe and immersed himself in the flood of his own inspiration that now seemed to release itself. He wrote in his diary (1915) about "this life that I love so infinitely, a feeling that must stamp everything I compose." And again, in September, 1915: "In a deep dell again. But I begin already dimly to see the mountain that I shall certainly ascend. . . . God opens His door for a moment and His orchestra plays the Fifth Symphony."

The first mundane performance of the work was given at Helsingfors,

under the direction of the late Robert Kajanus, on December 8, 1915—
the birthday of the composer. It is evident that the version heard on
this occasion differed materially from what we now know as the Fifth.
Less than a year after the first performance, Sibelius decided upon a
revision, and rewrote the symphony in a greatly condensed form. This
new edition of the work was performed on December 14, 1916, at
Helsingfors, the composer conducting. He was still unsatisfied with the
music, and planned further revision. In early 1918 he was busily engaged upon this, and it can safely be said that the final version of the
work represents a really radical rewriting. Sibelius himself, in a letter
dated May 20, 1918, comments upon it. He writes: "The Fifth Symphony in a new form, practically composed anew, I work at daily. The
first movement is entirely new, the second movement is reminiscent of
the old, the third movement reminiscent of the end of the first movement of the old. The fourth movement the old motifs, but stronger in
revision. The whole, if I may say so, a vital climax to the end. Triumphal."

The final revision of the Fifth Symphony was completed late in 1919,
and performed, at Helsingfors, with Sibelius conducting, on November
24. The first performance in America was given by the Philadelphia
Orchestra, Mr. Stokowski conducting, October 21, 1921. The Boston
Symphony programmed the work during the same season, and played
it on April 7, 1922.

Some reference must be made to the divisions of the symphony into
movements. Cecil Gray, whose admiration of Sibelius is idolatrous and
whose knowledge is encyclopedic, regards the *tempo molto moderato*
and the *allegro moderato, ma poco a poco stretto* as one movement (the
first) ; and he justifies this by two pertinent facts—the recurrence of
thematic material, and the fact that in the score Sibelius did not number
the movements. Of course the letter quoted above clearly establishes the
fact that Sibelius regarded the work as in four movements. The point
is of little moment certainly—except to the type of mind that attaches
more importance to such details than to the nature and effect of the
music itself. The symphony is scored for a quite conventional orchestra
—woodwinds in pairs, three trumpets, three trombones, four horns,
timpani, and strings.

FIRST MOVEMENT
Molto moderato

Seekers after occult meanings, revelations of personal griefs and joys, and similar matters would be hard put to it to find in this music any reflections of the troubled world in which Sibelius lived when it was written. The truth is that, while his music it utterly individual, it is not personal; it is cosmic and universal, as any great art work must be. The storms that sometimes sweep across his pages are never the secret and morbid paroxysms that gripped a Tchaikovsky, nor even the earthy passions that Wagner sometimes sang. Rather they are born of earth and sky and water; of solitudes and reflections; of a consciousness of the littleness of man and the magnificence of nature. This is not to imply that, at least in his symphonies, Sibelius is describing anything of the material world; quite the contrary. This work happened to come into existence not long after the composer had been concerned with certain descriptive works; and when questioned about it, he replied with both diffidence and asperity, "I do not wish to give a reasoned exposition of the essence of symphony. I have expressed my opinion in my works. I should like, however, to emphasize a point that I consider essential: the directly symphonic is the compelling vein that goes through the whole. This in contrast to the depicting."

In his sturdy assertion that his music speaks for itself, and the implication that any music which needs to be, or can be, explained needs not to have been written, Sibelius comes nearest to justifying Ernest Newman's daring but penetrating dictum associating Sibelius and Wagner in the same company. "The truest analogue to him [Sibelius]," writes Newman, "is to be found in a rather unsuspected quarter. Sibelius has never been influenced by Wagner, or, indeed, been particularly attracted to him. Nevertheless he is, in a way, of the company of Wagner—not in virtue of the contents of his music, for no two mental worlds could well be [more] different, but in virtue of the artistic type of which, at bottom, they both conform. . . . With Wagner, music was not music unless it was the expression of something—not necessarily the expression of a poetic or pictorial concept, but still *expression;* that is to say, the musician must come to his job full of something that on the one hand cannot be said in any other way but that of music, while on the other hand it must say itself according to the inexorable laws of its own inner being, making its own form as it goes along, not keeping anxiously before it, all the time, a derived formula to which, at all costs, it must for propriety's sake conform." Certainly this statement is as true of Sibelius as it is of Wagner; certainly no one has been more indifferent to form for the sake of form than Sibelius; no one has done more violence to accepted forms, and with such irrefragable logic; no one has made music which so infallibly created and justified its own inevitable forms.

While Sibelius himself has testified that in the revisions of this symphony it became considerably condensed, one cannot find the extraordinary compactness, density, and tension that mark the unique Fourth. The thematic basis of the first movement is simple—first, the horn melody heard at the beginning, developed in wind instruments and timpani; second, a brief clear utterance, of quite contrasting character, in the woodwind. Strings are used with extraordinary, though subdued effect, particularly where used in harmonics of ghostly quality; they are brought forward very little in the first part of the movement.

There is a melancholy figure given to the bassoons—and at this the mood of the music reaches its not very profound nadir—and the second subject is extensively developed. Always there is remarkable integration of thematic material—especially remarkable in Sibelius, who is often discursive and episodic; and the unified, the almost cyclic character of the movement is emphasized by occasional references to the principal subject, especially in its presentation, triumphantly, at the end of the *allegro moderato*.

The second section of the movement, because of the dancelike rhythm and much-quickened pace, is regarded by many as a true scherzo, and by some, including Sibelius, as a movement in itself; though there is no break between it and the preceding section. The mood becomes lighter; the texture of the music less weighty; the sentences contracted and more crisply uttered, and there is new thematic material. A solo trumpet in rather brisk 3/4 emphasizes the more vigorous rhythm in contrast to the previously prevailing 12/8, with a figure which is brilliantly developed toward the conclusion, where once more the orchestra shouts bravely out the triumphal version of the opening theme.

SECOND MOVEMENT
Andante mosso, quasi allegretto

This is a rather placid movement, devoted for the most part to the exposition of a simple theme and a set of variations. The theme appears after a series of introductory chords given out by the winds, and a few tentative pizzicati from the lower strings. It comes first in the flutes— a simple, charming melody in thirds, now ascending, now descending, always shifting in outline but always borne by the same rhythmic impulse. The entire movement is devoted to the exploitation of this theme in variations that pose no problem for anyone, though the dissonant seconds that appear occasionally are a little surprising in view of the generally sweet and tranquil character of the movement.

THIRD MOVEMENT
Allegro molto

There are frequently moments in the music of Sibelius when one hears almost inevitably the beat and whir of wings invisible, and this strange and characteristic effect almost always presages something magnificently portentous. We have it here. The strings create it and, by gradually drawing in the woodwind, intensify it; the inevitable burst comes then in the horns, with a vigorous presentation of a strong passage in thirds, in sustained, forte half-notes. This theme is the very heartbeat of the movement; and in fact, as noted by Cecil Gray, it has animated foregoing portions of the symphony as well as this one— notably in an accompaniment figure in the slow movement. There is a subsidiary, but important, thematic role assigned to woodwind and cellos, against horns and the upper strings; and there are unexpected mutations to other tonalities. That which occurs just before the coda, to G-flat major, is rather startling in method and effective in achieving the required *misterioso* atmosphere; and it leads to the magnificent proclamation at the end which, as Lawrence Gilman has written, "is the crown of the work, and is in many ways the most nobly imagined and nobly eloquent page that Sibelius has given us."

Symphony No. 6 in D minor

IT IS significant that when the terrifying news of the Russian attack upon Finland in the Second World War startled the radio listeners of the United States, the first thought in a million minds was for the safety of Sibelius. Few composers have in their own time commanded the attention, the reverence, and the affection with which the world has paid tribute to the great Finnish master. There are those, and their numbers are not inconsiderable, who hold that Sibelius is vastly over-rated as a composer, but there seem to be none who would temper the world's estimate of him as a man, or the affection in which the musical world holds him. That the specter, if not the spectacle, of war should approach him, a man so sensitive and so full of love for his fellow men, seems a ghastly crime of our so-called civilization.

It is fortunate that there exists on records a performance of the Sixth Symphony of Sibelius, and one which some day may be regarded as a priceless historical document. The performance is as authentic as we could expect, for it is done by Sibelius' own countrymen with an enthusiasm and possibly with a penetration hardly to be found else-where.

FIRST MOVEMENT
Allegro molto moderato

There are a number of curious features in this symphony which set it apart from all others of Sibelius. Though loosely integrated, as most of his symphonies are, there is a unity of spirit and a similarity of thematic material running through all four movements that are really remarkable. Again, rather paradoxically, while the music represents Sibelius in his most mature period, it has passages that could quite logically have been written by a Wagner or a Debussy. This is particu-larly noticeable in the opening phrases; and while they are in no sense imitative, it is rather difficult to listen and not recall the wonderful music that accompanies young Siegfried's miraculous contacts with the speaking birds. The harmonies are clear and open as those of Debussy, the spirit is mystical and full of melodious charm, but the hand is that of Sibelius nevertheless. As the opening phrases grow in intensity, and especially upon the dissonant entry of basses, we finally make up our minds that though Sibelius certainly knew the music of Wagner and Debussy, no one but himself could have written this particular passage.

The mystery and cold dark beauty of the northland make themselves felt in this music, as almost invariably they do in the music of this composer. One cannot divorce the idea of great sea birds planing among dark rocks and narrow fiords. A remembrance of that incomparable tone poem *The Swan of Tuonela* comes again and again, and it is not difficult to hear the fluttering of wings and the wild harsh cries in the figures which the composer assigns to strings and woodwind.

Thematically the movement is loosely articulated, but its rhapsodic spirit is consistent and continuous until toward the end, when the low brasses, with some violence in tone, give somber pronouncements and quite the rushing evolutions of imaginary birds and half-imagined spirits. The use of chromatic and diatonic scales is characteristic, and some interesting harmonic clashes are developed. The movement as a whole, however, is quietly rhapsodic rather than formal, and we find in it no release of those mighty powers which Sibelius alone of moderns can summon from the orchestra.

SECOND MOVEMENT
Allegro moderato

But for some change the rhythm of the second movement might almost be a continuation of the first. The strange dissonant cries of the woodwinds and the quiet conflict of rhythms as well as of tones suggest a more intense emotional atmosphere, however. The occasional passing of unrelated tonalities produces an atmosphere of restlessness, of struggle, almost of bewilderment, and the acidulous comment of the oboe is a protesting voice rising sharply from a soul that seems to be in turmoil and confusion.

THIRD MOVEMENT
Poco vivace

The third movement is probably the shortest of Sibelius' symphonic movements. The composer has often asserted that he does not use in his music the folk song of Finland. Granting the accuracy of this, it is

nevertheless true that the spirit of Finnish folk song is often present in
his music, and occasionally even authentic details of folk music are
noticeable. The constantly reiterated notes which we observe in this
and other movements of the symphony represent a common characteristic of Finnish folk song, and the use of 5/4 rhythm is very frequent
in Sibelius' and almost invariable in Finnish folk music. As this brief
movement develops we feel the unleashing of orchestral forces and the
composer begins to call with more insistence for the orchestra's mightiest utterances.

FOURTH MOVEMENT
Allegro molto

The fourth movement is marked by a much brighter melodic line
than the composer has heretofore employed in the symphony. The
beautiful thematic strain introduced at the beginning is very possibly
of folk-song origin, or if it is not, certainly it is modeled very precisely
along the lines of many native Finnish melodies. Later we observe a
marvelous effect of distance and mystery, accomplished by deft orchestration involving woodwind and horns. Still later an organ point in the
brasses against a long descending figure provides a source of interesting harmonics and dissonances. The movement is almost like a succession of songs, but as so often happens in the music of Sibelius, it is
distinctly episodic, and accomplishes unity of mood not only within
itself but with the other movements of the work without having to labor
for structural or formal unity. The music fades and dies on a long-held
minor chord in the strings, bringing the symphony to a close.

Symphony No. 7

THE symphonies of Sibelius are uniquely defiant of conventional analysis. This happens because, as in the case of the Seventh, there is no
conventional form; or rather perhaps because the form is a unique and
plastic one devised by Sibelius himself and not belonging properly in
any category. Again, analysis becomes difficult and even superfluous
under the influence of the dark and mystical moods which Sibelius
evokes in this and other symphonies; yet the music is by no means

shapeless; it speaks the common language of humanity in such terms that anyone who will can understand and needs only to listen.

Though there are no such divisions as we could call movements in this work—rather, it is in one movement—there are nevertheless sections which to some extent do correspond with the conventional divisions. There are many extended episodes, and in a sense the symphony has neither one movement nor four, but many movements. The work was composed prior to 1925 and Sibelius himself had planned to conduct its first performance at a music festival in England. Illness prevented his doing this. The first American performance of the work was given by the Philadelphia Orchestra with Mr. Stokowski conducting, April 3, 1926.

Though the symphony is rather definitely in C major, the opening bars are in A minor; but the relative key is achieved in the mighty climax that forms the end of the work. The economy of instrumental means which Sibelius employs is worthy of note. The woodwinds are in pairs; there are three trumpets, three trombones, timpani and strings, no bass clarinet, no English horn, no tuba, and no percussion whatever except the timpani.

The muted thunder of the timpani sounds mysteriously at the beginning, and a scale passage ascends through the strings and establishes itself as the most important single thematic idea in the whole work, though it is often disguised, inverted, or dissected. It is without much development until at least two-thirds of the way through the symphony. Now comes a whole series of contrasting themes—a songlike idea in C major, first put forward by the lower strings, then by the violins. A solemn utterance of the trombone solo has special significance. The music moves at an ever-faster pace until we come upon a section which in its swiftness and emotional character might correspond to a typical scherzo movement. Indeed, Mr. Lawrence Gilman was here reminded of the mood of the scherzo in Beethoven's "Eroica."

A new melody with the character of a simple folk song and a further idea suggested by the woodwinds presently succeed the rapid section. It is interesting to note that while Sibelius' melodies often have the character of folk songs or folk dances and certainly do suggest the native music of Finland, the composer himself has stated unequivocally that never anywhere in his music has he used a melody that was not entirely his own. Certainly he had little occasion to do so, for melody flows in a continuous stream through most of his works, and his power of melodic invention seems boundless.

Presently we feel a certain acceleration once again, and as the pace approaches presto, the strings, divided in eight parts, give forth pianissimo a mysterious and agitated figure with the violas and cellos outlining the swift figure against the persistent pedal G of the violins, basses, and timpani. A piling up of orchestral masses accomplishes a deceleration of the tempo, and as it becomes adagio brazen voices pour forth in a heroic fortissimo their mightiest utterance. There are swift changes of dynamics, modulations between A minor and C major, and a final climax in a massive projection in full orchestra of the tonic chord in C major.

Richard Strauss

BORN 1864

ONE OF THE most extraordinary musical personages of today is Richard Strauss. Born in 1864; informed with the classical musical traditions of Haydn, Mozart, Bach, and Beethoven; regarding, at twenty-one years of age, such composers of the *fin de siècle* as Chopin, Schumann, and Brahms as not quite conservative, Strauss stands today, though full of years and prolific of accomplishments, one of the most modern, most radical of composers.

Daring, insistence upon individuality of expression, radicalism—call it what you will—is supposed to be the prerogative of the young. Strauss outdoes the younger generation of composers in daring—but with this difference; there is a rationale in his music that places it in a class quite apart from the often meaningless, deliberately strident, and ugly manifestations of the musical impulses of certain modern composers. Strauss is, indeed, modern—but his music is never freakish, never novel for the sake of novelty, never daring for the sake of self-advertisement.

Strauss was born not into the family of Johann Strauss, the "Waltz King"—to whom he bears no relationship—but the son of Franz Strauss, leading horn-player of the Munich Opera Orchestra, who recognized and fostered the musical talent of his child. The boy's training was rigidly classical, and his precocious gifts fed upon the works of the musical giants exclusively. Not until he was a young man of twenty-one did he become familiar with the more recent of the great composers.

When but a child he wrote his first composition. He was only twenty when Theodore Thomas, beloved founder and conductor of the Chicago Symphony Orchestra, played a symphony of Strauss' at a concert in New York. One year later the composer attained to a position of eminence in the music world, by succeeding to the conductorship previously held by von Bülow.

The career of Strauss presently took a curious turn. Acclaimed, twenty years ago or more, as unquestionably the most modern as well as the most gifted of living composers, he had the musical world at his feet. His concerts were crowded to the doors; enthusiasm was tremendous. A few years later, the same Strauss found almost more musical enemies than friends. Critics attacked him savagely; his new ideas, definite and reasonable as they seem now in contrast to the nebulous fancies and impossible theories of some musical poetasters, were scorned, or discounted, contradicted, and angrily denied. The audiences that had practically worshiped him had almost disappeared. He had become a "radical."

Today, though Strauss, like every man of eminence, has his antagonistic critics, he is accepted as one of the greatest living composers, if not the greatest. Though the processes of time have not yet caused his so-called radicalism to seem conservative, the essential soundness and sanity, and the strange and compelling beauty of his music, are strikingly in contrast with both classical and ultramodern music. He has developed and perfected the tone poem, the possibilities of which Liszt first perceived. He has elaborated the leitmotiv, or musical phrase attached to a definite person, place, thing, or situation. He has projected a new conception of counterpoint, in which simultaneous melodies are considered separately as melodies, without regarding their mutual harmony or dissonance.

His music is alive with vigor and vitality . . . full of conflict, as indeed it must be to express the subjects which Strauss sets forth to illustrate. It is music of immense vigor and vitality. It is music of glowing color—for Strauss is a master among masters of the art of orchestration.

And—what will be of interest to the great bulk of music lovers to whom music is a stimulant of imaginative pictures—Strauss above all present-day composers depicts in tone the phenomena of the material world. To call his music merely "programmatic" is to slander it. For he seldom descends to mere imitation of familiar sounds or stereotyped musical idioms for the suggestion of "falling waters" or "galloping horses," or similar picturesque incidents of ordinary "program music." With Strauss, a fanfare of brass may mean not merely a call to arms, but the causes of an empire's downfall; a fluttering of strings may signify not a springtime zephyr, but a storm within the soul. Though it may revolve about material beings and objects, the music of Strauss is nevertheless powerfully subjective and symbolic.

Alpine Symphony

THERE is a question whether or not, if a composer himself had not supplied a number of subtitles and a kind of program for his music, it would have, in the minds of any listener, the meaning which he designed. Music intended to signify a storm might likewise signify "anger" or "confusion" or "battle." Music intended to suggest the ascent of a mountain might possibly mean to the listener the act of walking upstairs. Yet, once given the program, it is not too difficult to associate music with the ideas of the composer, and in this way the music mentioned here is of considerable eloquence and of the highest technical skill. Strauss is one of the most conspicuous masters of orchestration music has ever known, and while it is often possible to find grounds for a quarrel with his esthetic ideas, his realization of them is almost invariably eloquent, convincing, and accomplished with matchless technical perfection.

The present work was performed for the first time at Berlin by the Dresden Royal Orchestra, Strauss himself conducting, on October 28, 1915. In contemporary accounts there appears to have been some feeling of relief. The composer had for the most part renounced what were called "cacophonic effects," though in fact none of the Strauss works which had been heard up to that time now impress us as particularly noisy or dissonant.

The sequence of scenes which Strauss attempts to depict in this music are given as follows and are easily identified: "Night—Sunrise—The Ascent—Entrance into the Forest—Wandering Beside the Brook—At the Waterfall—Apparition—In Flowery Meadows—On the Alm (Mountain Pasture)—Lost in the Thicket and Brush—On the Glacier—Moments of Danger—On the Summit—Vision—Elegy—Calm Before the Storm—The Thunderstorm—The Descent—Sunset—Night." The symphony is in one movement and the episodes follow one after another without pause. The orchestra is extraordinarily large, requiring the usual instruments but nearly twice the number of winds: four each of woodwind, eight horns, four trumpets, four trombones, bass tuba, pipe organ, baritone oboe, wind machine, and a thunder machine. In addition, there is an off-stage band of horns, trumpets, and trombones. The music is highly descriptive, ingenious, and for the most part of very little emotional significance. The Elegy has a certain eloquence, and the following storm picture, which begins with a descending figure in the trumpets which is exactly the reverse of the ascending figure previously heard, is one of the noisiest musical storms ever written.

The somewhat episodic character of the music and the fact that it is played through without division into movements have suggested to some scholars that the work should not be called a symphony at all. It can, however, be divided into conventional symphonic movements. The sections comprising Night and Sunrise could constitute a conventional slow introduction. The first movement proper might include the Ascent; it would not be unreasonable to regard as a scherzo the sections including the Mountain Pasture and Flowery Meadows. The fourth movement might begin with the scene on the Summit and conclude with the vigorous music of the Storm and Descent.

Sinfonia domestica

MANY students of the music of Richard Strauss regard the *Sinfonia domestica* as his greatest work—at least in the sense that it exhibits his unique talents and sometimes strange style of composition more thoroughly than any of his other works in the larger forms. Other critics regard the work lightly and even scornfully, and some have not been able to reconcile the employment of talents like those of Strauss and a great symphony orchestra and the sacred symphony form to depict the trivia of family life. When the work was first performed under the direction of the composer at Carnegie Hall, New York, on March 21, 1904, the attitude of the critics was quite diversified.

The *New York Sun*, in its headlines, was inclined to treat the event facetiously. Some of the headlines were as follows:

"THE SYMPHONY DOMESTICA—HOME SWEET HOME AS WRITTEN BY RICHARD STRAUSS—PAPA AND MOMMA AND

BABY CELEBRATED IN A HUGE CONGLOMERATION OF OR-
CHESTRAL MUSIC."

Two days after the concert, the *Musical Courier* printed a comment
which, although it may have been taken seriously at the time, can
now be regarded only as ironical:

"Monday evening, 21 March, 1904, Carnegie Hall was the scene of a
musical event so important that, by comparison, everything else pales
in significance that has been done here in music, since the first production of the Wagner 'Nibelungen' Operas. On Monday evening, 21
March—the date will play a role in history—a vast auditorium full of
enthusiastic men and women heard the first public performance on any
concert stage of Richard Strauss' latest and greatest work of orchestra,
his *Sinfonia domestica*. The conductor was Richard Strauss and the
players were the Wetzler Symphony Orchestra."

Ernest Newman, certainly one of the most penetrating and profound
of present-day critics, has a wholesome respect and regard for this
remarkable work. He has written as follows:

"The work made a sensation at the time," he wrote, "partly because
the simplicity of the subject—papa, momma and baby—brought the
program, at any rate, within the scope of the intelligence of the
average man. People who were puzzled almost to the point of insanity
by *Zarathustra* and its *Übermenschen,* and its *Genesende,* and all the
rest of that queer fauna, could recognize at once when the baby was
squealing in its bath or the lullaby was being sung over it; and they
had a kindly fellow-feeling for the terrible musician who now seemed
to be even such a one as themselves."

Notwithstanding the association of the music with the commonplace
events that take place in the typical home every day, Strauss refused,
before the first performance, to permit the music to be accepted as
program music. "This time," said Strauss, "I wish my music to be
listened to purely as music." Yet a year later he contradicted himself,
as he has done more than once before and since. An official program for
the symphony was published prior to its first performance in London,
and here were described the domestic details which the music was intended to represent. As has happened so often, once a story or program
of any kind is attached to a piece of music, it becomes thereafter in-

separable, and since these domestic details have some official sanction, we are perfectly justified in accepting them as being musically described in the symphony.

Introduction and Scherzo

There are three principal themes assigned respectively to the husband, the wife, and the child. The theme of the husband is divided into three sections, marked respectively *gemächlich* (easygoing), *träumerish* (dreamy), and *feurig* (fiery), and which, taken together, offer a characterization of the father.

The wife's theme is the second theme of the composition, divided into two sections marked *sehr lebhaft* (very lively) and *gefühlvoll* (with feeling):

The child's theme is the third and is described by Strauss as being of "almost Haydnesque simplicity."

It is played on the *oboe d'amore,* an all but obsolete instrument, and its revival in the *Sinfonia domestica* is worth notice. It is built a minor third lower than the ordinary oboe, with a hollow globular bell in place of the customary conical one. The tone compared with that of the ordinary oboe is more veiled, and perhaps, rather more pathetic in character. It is met with considerably in Bach, a famous example of its use occurring in the *Christmas Oratorio.*

Following the entrance of the child theme, there is a passage which has been interpreted as describing the child taking a bath. Toward the end of the introduction, we have one of the most frequently commented upon examples of the extremeness of Strauss' programmaticism. The child's bath is interrupted by the arrival of relatives, who discuss the important question of whom does the child resemble. In the muted trumpets and clarinets the figure is accompanied on the score by the

written notation: "Aunts: 'Just like his papa.'" Whereupon, an answering figure, given to trombone, horns, and oboes, is noted: "Uncles: 'Just like his momma.'"

In the "official" program the scherzo is described as dealing with *Elternglück* (joy of the parents) and *kindliche Spiele* (child playing). The child theme occupies considerable attention in this movement. In the lullaby scene, where the child is being put to sleep, we stumble upon an interesting musical coincidence. Quite by accident, no doubt, the music is identical for a few measures with the very famous "First Venetian Gondola Song" from the first book of Mendelssohn's *Songs Without Words.*

Sinfonia Domestica

Mendelssohn

Adagio

The programmatic divisions of the adagio movement are given as *Schaffen und Schauen* (doing and thinking), *Liebescene* (love scene), and *Träume und Sorgen* (dreams and worries).

The family is asleep and their gradual awakening is depicted by a subtle restlessness which creeps into the music. The rhythmic variants of the previous themes are developed with remarkable ingenuity. The movement is an excellent example of the rich palette which Strauss uses for his orchestral coloration and also of his tremendous ability for polyphonic elaboration. The glockenspiel sounding seven times at the close of the movement indicates that it is 7:00 A.M.

Finale

"In this way," runs the program, "we reach the final fugue. The principal subject of this is also a new version of the child theme. Its subtitle is *lustiger Streit* (Merry Argument), *fröhlicher Beschluss* (Happy Ending), the subject of the dispute between the father and mother being the future of the son. The fugue (the chief subject of which is another variant of the child theme) is carried on wth unflagging spirit and humor and great variety of orchestration."

Igor Stravinsky

BORN 1882

S TRAVINSKY, one of the most interesting of contemporary composers, was born at Oranienbaum, near St. Petersburg, Russia, June 17, 1882. His father was an opera singer at the Imperial Opera House and naturally hoped for talent in his little son. He found it; and saw to it that it was thoroughly developed. He built better than he knew, for later, when the father wished Igor to adopt the law as a career, he found that the young man had become so enamored of music that he would not abandon it. Although he entered the University at St. Petersburg for legal studies, love of music eventually tempted him away, and when in 1902 he met Rimsky-Korsakov he made the final decision. Rimsky accepted Stravinsky as a pupil, and from that time onward his development was swift and sensational.

Stravinsky lost little time in producing a number of works of great interest, but nowadays not considered among his most important compositions. In 1910 came *The Firebird*, which though it showed definitely the musical background and the influences which had had their effect on the composer, nevertheless also revealed flashes of the Stravinsky who was to startle and even to captivate, for a time, the whole musical world. *Petrouchka*, dating from the following year, established Stravinsky as a highly individual and even revolutionary composer. Two years later came *Le Sacre du printemps*, and this astonishing work not only fortified Stravinsky as one of the most ingenious and original of composers, but touched off a conflagration of discussion of his music that has not ceased to the present day. The three works mentioned are unquestionably the greatest from the hand of Stravinsky. In them he not only developed but exhausted the particular line which he was following. Realizing this, he has shown new methods in subsequent works, such as *Les Noces* (1923), *Oedipus Rex* (1926), and *Apollon Musagètes* (1928). *The Symphony of Psalms* represents still another

469

departure. In these works Stravinsky has almost entirely abandoned his earlier style, and has adopted an attitude of great reserve and, at times, almost ascetic simplicity. None of these later compositions has had anything approaching the success of the earlier three.

In his California home Stravinsky has continued composing, not always greatly, during recent seasons, but if he were never to write music again, it seems reasonable to believe that his position among the first of the twentieth-century composers would be absolutely and permanently established.

Symphony of Psalms

THE *Symphony of Psalms*, strictly speaking, is more cantata than symphony and is included in this book only by virtue of a rather broad interpretation of the word "symphony." It is a work for orchestra and chorus, in which the choral parts actually are the most important; yet the orchestral parts are of such interest that it seems some mention of the work, however brief, should be made here. In the opinion of more than one critic of standing the *Symphony of Psalms* is Stravinsky's magnum opus, and there are those who will assert that it is the most important musical work to come into being within the past several years. It was written in 1930, dedicated "to the Glory of God" and to the Boston Symphony Orchestra; it was written for the golden anniversary of that organization. The first American performance was given at Boston, by the Boston Symphony Orchestra under Serge Koussevitsky's direction, December 19, 1930. This, however, was not a world *première*. The first performance anywhere took place in Brussels six days prior to the Boston celebration.

*   *   *   *   *

To those who know the music of Stravinsky only through *Petrouchka*, *The Firebird*, and the *Rite of Spring*, the *Symphony of Psalms* will seem strange, austere, stark, bare-boned, and ascetic. It is apparent in much of Stravinsky's later music that he has been striving for his effects with remarkable economy of means, with a tendency away from a preponderance of string tone and toward a preponderance of wind instruments, particularly brass. In this music his passion for austerity is indulged, not inappropriately, to a very remarkable degree.

There are no violins, no violas. The cellos and basses remain in the orchestra but the burden of the music is in the main assumed by the woodwinds and brass. Here too the instrumentation is unusual, for there are five flutes rather than the conventional two, four oboes, four B-flat trumpets and one little trumpet in D, and two pianos, as well as a harp.

There is a gaunt simplicity in this music which, in spite of the contemporary quality of its technical treatment, establishes a religious atmosphere of medieval naturalness, directness, and reality. The curious character of the orchestration achieves a pellucid clarity even in the complicated fugal development of the second section. The composer's meaning stands forth clearly, unmistakably, and with the reverence and devotion that the beautiful text suggests. The devotee of liturgical music might find much to quarrel with in this remarkable score; those who find their most complete religious expression in simple hymn tunes doubtless look upon this music as painfully exotic, sophisticated, and self-conscious; but those who concede, as one should, the sincerity and passionate religious feeling of the composer, will doubtless find in this music a profoundly expressive religious utterance worthy to crown the career of the very great artist who conceived and executed it.

The Latin text used in the performance, with a free English translation, follows.

Psalmus XXXVIII, Verses 13 and 14

"Exaudi orationem meam, Domine, et depreciationem meam: auribus percipe lacrymas meas.

"Ne sileas, quoniam advena ego sum apud te, et peregrinus, sicut omnes patres mei. Remitte mihi, ut refrigerer priusquam abeam, et amplius non ero.

Psalm XXXIX (King James Version)

"Hear my prayer, O Lord, and give ear unto my cry;
    Hold not Thy peace at my tears:
For I am a stranger with Thee,
    And a sojourner, as all my fathers were.
O spare me, that I may recover strength,
    Before I go hence, and be no more.

II
Psalmus XXXIX, Verses 1, 2, 3, and 4

"Expectans expectavi Dominum, et intendit mihi.

Et exaudivit preces meas; et eduxit me de lacu miseriae, et de luto faecis.

Et statuit supra petram pedes meos; et direxit gressus meos.

Et immisit in os meum canticum novum, carmen Deo nostro.

Videbunt multi et timebunt: et sperabunt in Domino.

Psalm XL (King James Version)

"I waited patiently for the Lord;
And He inclined unto me, and heard my cry.
He brought me up also out of an horrible pit, out of the miry clay,
And set my feet upon a rock, and established my goings.
And He hath put a new song in my mouth, even praise unto our God:
Many shall see it, and fear,
And shall trust in the Lord.

III
Psalmus CL

"(Alleluia)

Laudate Dominum in sanctis ejus: Laudate eum in firmamento virtutis ejus.

Laudate eum in virtutibus ejus: laudate eum secundum multitudinem magnitudinis ejus.

Laudate eum in sono tubae: laudate eum in psalterio et cithara.

Laudate eum in tympano et choro: laudate eum in chordis et organo.

Laudate eum in cymbalis bene sonantibus: laudate eum in cymbalis jubilationis: omnis spiritus laudet Dominum.

Psalm CL (King James Version)

"(Alleluia)
Praise ye the Lord.
    Praise God in His sanctuary:
    Praise Him in the firmament of His power.

Praise Him for His mighty acts:
Praise Him according to His excellent greatness.
Praise Him with the sound of the trumpet:
Praise Him with the psaltery and harp.
Praise Him with the timbrel and dance:
Praise Him with stringed instruments and organs.
Praise Him upon the loud cymbals:
Praise Him upon the high sounding cymbals.
Let every thing that hath breath praise the Lord.
Praise ye the Lord."

Symphony in C major

IT IS a far cry from *Le Sacre du Printemps* to the Symphony in C major of Stravinsky. *Le Sacre, Petrouchka,* and *The Firebird* seem to enclose a definite and never again to be approached period in Stravinsky's life, and his later works have explored in many directions; indeed, in all directions except backward. There is another and more subtle difference, too, between the early and the present Stravinsky, perhaps exemplified most clearly in the *Symphony of Psalms,* which is sincerely intended as a devotional cantata, and the dedication of the work we discuss here, which is as follows: "This symphony, composed to the glory of God, is dedicated to the Chicago Symphony Orchestra on the occasion of the Fiftieth Anniversary of its existence." Thoughts about God appear with increasing frequency in Stravinsky's latest works, and the attitude of worship toward the Christian deity is fantastically at variance with the exuberant enthusiasm with which the composer treated the pagan rites in an earlier work. The C major symphony was completed by Mr. Stravinsky at his home in Beverly Hills, California, August 19, 1940, and performed for the first time during the following season of the Chicago Symphony Orchestra at its fifth concert.

FIRST MOVEMENT

It has been remarked that Stravinsky has made musical investigations in every direction except backward. Perhaps this statement should be amended, for while in various works Stravinsky has originated his own forms or even on occasion discarded everything resembling formality, here we find him achieving a cold, clear logic and instantly discernible unity and inevitability of sequence and of growth, of theme developing out of theme; in short, a movement as careful, precise, and convincing in its architecture as any that Mozart left us. Another interesting aspect of Stravinsky's later work, and particularly of this symphony, is the economy of means by which he accomplishes his end. There is no resemblance whatever between the huge and complicated scores of *Petrouchka* or *Le Sacre* and this lean, muscular, "traineddown" music. If this results in a certain bleakness, that is precisely, one must conclude, what the composer intended.

Here is the essence of the first movement:

This is the essential idea for the whole movement. There are other themes, in truth, but this is the musical thought that gives the movement its essential richness, power, and variety, for it is to this subject that the composer returns again and again, explicitly and implicitly, in whole and in part. There is, in fact, an ancillary idea in which the sharpness of the oboe and the hoarseness of the bassoon are contrasted with strings. There are magnificent and ingenious developments of both of these matters, and with almost imperceptible and yet, on reflection, a calculated and irrefragable logic, we are led back to the first theme. The composer thereby achieves symmetry and balance and, in the painter's sense, a "composition" completely satisfying.

SECOND MOVEMENT

This ingratiating music is quite free in style, yet never, in all the variety of voices that appear, loses its clarity, coherence, and serenity. It is like a series of arias: sometimes pensive, sometimes touched with melancholy, sometimes exalted and lordly. A tender colloquy between oboe and violins begins the movement. Lower strings suggest an accompaniment and farther on the woodwinds add their most melting tones. The tenderness of this movement reveals another side of Stravinsky's musical nature—all too seldom revealed in his most recent works.

THIRD MOVEMENT

Rhythms of the dance motivate the exuberant gaiety of the third movement. It is in three sections—a minuet, passepied, and fugue. The first two sections are rather complicated rhythmically and suggest some of the devilishly difficult yet fascinating irregular pulses of *Le Sacre*. The fugue is not a conventional one, particularly with respect to the fact that, as one will notice in the subject here,

the bars are of varying length and have varying rhythms. Yet the proportions of the whole are so precise, so correct, so logical, and so satisfying mathematically that one is scarcely conscious of irregularities. Fortifying one's satisfaction with the architecture of this movement are fragments of material recalled from the opening sections of the movement. To follow the development of the fugue one should observe the principal instrumental voices employed in it, which are: first, trombone, then horn, third, the basses, then woodwind and brass.

FOURTH MOVEMENT

The fourth movement begins rather deceptively with broad chords played adagio by the bassoon and woodwinds. A few moments of this rather portentous exordium, and the orchestra enters upon the allegro, with the middle strings having important material all to themselves, contrasted with the rest of the orchestra as a body. There is some recollection of the opening chords, some fugal and highly ornamented treatment of basic thematic material, and once again the bold, strong, long-held chords of the opening reappear, now with even more sonority and emphasis. Upon the most powerful projection of these, the symphony ends gloriously.

Symphony in Three Movements

STRAVINSKY'S *Symphony in Three Movements* had its world *première* at a concert of the Philharmonic-Symphony Society of New York on January 24, 1946, with the composer conducting. The symphony is dedicated to the Philharmonic "as an homage and appreciation of my twenty years' association with that eminent musical institution."

The symphony is one of the most recondite of Stravinsky's works. It is unique not only among contemporary works for symphony orchestra but striking even among Stravinsky's own works. Its resemblance to any other is very faint; it departs far from convention, from tradition, from formality. It proceeds by a kind of agglutinative development, by means of a sequence of themes which continually attract to themselves additional particles until they are built up into great masses, organized and integrated, at least to a degree, by common rhythmical impulses. If symphonic writing can be regarded as a kind of analysis in that thematic material is dissected and explored in all its essential possibilities, this work might credibly be regarded as a synthesis, for instead of taking thematic material apart the composer actually draws together into a concrete mass any number of thematic atoms. The thematic material is expanded by agglutination; by additions from without, as it were, instead of by the inflation of atoms from within itself.

Mr. Stravinsky's own comment on this work may be an intimation of the emotional background which brought about its creation. He writes in the program of the Philharmonic-Symphony Society of New York, "This Symphony has no program, nor is it a specific expression of any given occasion; it would be futile to seek these in my work. But during the process of creation in this our arduous time of sharp and shifting events, of despair and hope, of continual torments, of tension and, at last, cessation and relief, it may be that all those repercussions have left traces in this Symphony. It is not I to judge."

A descriptive analysis of such music as this, partly because of the composer's disclaimer of a program but also because of the nature of the music itself, is not only difficult, it is virtually impossible. Repeated hearings as well as the closest study of this score are necessary to comprehend fully the meanings of this music and its curious, unconventional, yet convincing structure. A friend of Stravinsky, Ingolf Dahl, conceding the difficulty of analyzing a musical synthesis so closely integrated as to become a new musical element, nevertheless proceeds to give us, in the program of the Philharmonic-Symphony Society, some acute observations and indications of the nature of the music. We quote them: *

"The musical world, which has hardly taken cognizance of the fact that in Stravinsky's Symphony in C (1940) it was given a masterful example of classical symphonic procedure, already will have to take notice that with his new Symphony (1945) Stravinsky has moved on to the exact opposite of traditional symphonic form. In this new work there is no sonata form to be expounded, there is no 'development' of closely defined themes, which would be stated, restated, interlocked, combined and metamorphosed, as symphonic themes are wont to be. Here, on the contrary, we have another example of that additive construction, for the invention of which Stravinsky is justly famous and which has proved so influential on the younger composer. It is a formal principle which conceives of music as the succession of clearly outlined blocks, or planes, which are unified and related through the continuity of a steadily and logically evolving organic force. This, of course, is the exact opposite of classic and romantic symphonic thought, just as the comparable additive principle of romanesque architecture is differentiated from the interlacing connectivity of the gothic or baroque.

"Harmonically, too, the new Symphony speaks a language which its composer has not spoken for a long time. His immediately preceding diatonicism is widened immensely, and an integral part is played by many of the intervals which gave the period from 'Sacre' to the 'Symphonies pour instruments à vent' its character. It cannot be coincidental that simultaneously with the composition of the new work Stravinsky undertook a revision and reorchestration of parts of the 'Sacre' and 'Petrouchka.' It is as if in today's Symphony he overlooked from his vantage point the rich landscape of his achievements and molded his wider view into a new synthesis.

"The tenor of this synthesis is one of great seriousness. There is no place for irony, wit, or that kind of playfulness which brightened even

* By permission of the Philharmonic-Symphony Society of New York.

so serious a piece as the Symphony in C. But now it is not the *kothurnus* of Greek tragedy on which the composer stands, as in 'Oedipus Rex' or 'Duo Concertante,' but the soil of the world of 1945. One day it will be universally recognized that the white house in the Hollywood hills, in which this Symphony was written and which was regarded by some as an ivory tower, was just as close to the core of a world at war as the place where Picasso painted 'Guernica.'

"This simile is naturally not accidental. Again the styles of these two masters appear as parallels: the construction in large asymmetrical planes separated by distinct contours, the absence of mixed colors, the stark power of outlines reduced to their essentials, the clash of transections—by all of these and many other elements do the styles of the composer and the painter meet again, after many years of diverging paths.

"A closer description of the three movements is difficult to give because of the above-mentioned formal freedom, evolving without closely circumscribed themes. But these characteristics of construction could be mentioned:

"FIRST MOVEMENT: This is the weightiest of the three, both in size and content. The best name to describe its form would be 'toccata,' but the score indicates just the metronome marking of the speed. The normal symphonic instrumentation is enlarged by a piano which plays an important role in the middle section, forming by itself a 'concertino' against the rest of the orchestra.

"The thematic germs of this movement are of ultimate condensation. They consist of the interval of the minor third (with its inversion, the major sixth) and an ascending scale fragment which forms the background to the piano solo of the middle part. After an opening 'motto' in fortissimo unison, and its extension, the horns state the first of these thematic nuclei. This basic interval of the minor third then becomes the ostinato bass to a forward-driving rhythmical section and constitutes the backbone, either melodically or harmonically, of all of the following short groups which evolve in free toccata-like fashion. The tone of agitated power and the angular brilliance of sound come to an end when violas and cellos state it with short-lived tranquillity to lead into the central section of the movement. Here the solo piano takes over, and the orchestral tutti is reduced both in sound and size. With utmost inventiveness the thematic germs and constantly new a-thematic material are used in passages of increasingly polyphonic texture. A trio of two oboes and flute opens a soft codetta which makes use of intervals of high tension, suddenly interrupted by a repetition of the driving rhythmical ostinato from the first part. A recapitulation in reverse order follows, so that the motto of the opening is reached at the end, and with the extension of this motto transformed into elegiac chords, the brass instruments bring the movement to a soft close.

"SECOND MOVEMENT, Andante: Between the expansive orchestral forces of the outer movements this delicate intermezzo is written without trumpets, trombones, and percussion. The concertino is formed by harp and flute. An opening string motif which is associated with both Mozart's and Rossini's barber reaffirms Stravinsky's affinity to the classic style, and it accompanies the halting lyricism of these two solo instruments. Even the tender grace of this music bears the markings of the heaviness of this world and many of its passages continue the mourning song of the composer's recent 'Ode.' The dialogue of flute and harp is joined by strings and woodwinds alternately and in a modified three-part form the beginning is recapitulated. A short transitional bridge leads without interruption into the

"THIRD MOVEMENT, *Con moto*: The full orchestra opens with an introduction of psalmic elevation. It sets the scene for three distinct sections which could be classified as either 'variations,' as this term is understood in the ballet, or as preludes to the final fugue. The first of these sections, opening with a duet for two bassoons, contains already the hidden fugue theme; the second is based on a major-minor arpeggio figure which weaves around in strings and woodwinds; the third elaborates the material of the introduction of this movement. The subsequent fugal section opens with the theme stated by the trombone and piano. Its development is of the highest ingenuity and intricacy and it shows again how Stravinsky makes this prescribed form serve his stylistic intentions without becoming its slave. The fugal form never does become an end in itself; the composer even takes pains to disguise it in order not to obscure with any obviousness of procedures the free expressivity of the music. The driving impulse of a tutti coda that is a remarkable example of metrical spacing, creating a rhythm of silences within the rhythms of sound, leads the symphony to a sonorous ending."

Piotr Ilyich Tchaikovsky

1840-1893

A NY but the most exhaustive biography of the great Russian composer Tchaikovsky must confine itself to the more salient features of the life and character of the man. Little of his inward life was ever unveiled even to his intimates. Those who were closest to him were not able to penetrate the remoter recesses of his being, at least not beyond discovering that Tchaikovsky himself did not understand his own mind and heart. Thus the composer takes his place in music's hall of fame as one of its most mysterious personalities.

Piotr Ilyich Tchaikovsky was born on May 7, 1840 (according to the Gregorian, not the Russian calendar), at Votkimsk, in the province of Viatka, Russia. Young Piotr was given the conventional education of the better classes, his training including some study of the piano. He did not in his boyhood exhibit in music the precociousness which distinguished his accomplishments in other fields of learning. He obeyed with docility when at the age of ten he was sent to a school preparatory to study of the law, and at nineteen was graduated, drifting complacently into a government clerkship, and with somewhat more interest into the life of a young man of the world.

It was not long, however, until the aimlessness of his existence became apparent to the always introspective Tchaikovsky, and he discovered that the life of a law clerk was not for him. Music had always been his great pleasure; he had studied, though up to this time he had not, apparently, regarded the art with any great seriousness. Now it dawned upon him that it was for music that his restless soul yearned, and accordingly he set about studying seriously. With this decision came the necessity for giving up his government position and seeking a livelihood from some other source; so, in 1863, he deliberately chose the precarious existence of a musician. He undertook and in 1865 completed a rigorous course of instruction at the St. Petersburg Conservatory, graduating with honors. Here he had come into contact with Anton Rubinstein, whose personality so dominated and stimulated the languid Tchaikovsky that he put forth his best effort if only to please the master for whom he had conceived an affection bordering on adoration—a sentiment, which, by the way, was never reciprocated by Rubinstein.

Not long afterward Tchaikovsky was offered the post of professor of harmony at the newly organized Moscow Conservatory, and while teaching was distasteful to him, and the salary small, here was an honorable position in a musical atmosphere, with the pleasure and benefit of the society of other musicians. His new position gave the composer time to produce several important works, among them his First Symphony.

The next several years were devoted by Tchaikovsky to orienting himself in both his personal life and his position as a musician. He now came in contact with the group of young national musicians— among them Balakirev and Rimsky-Korsakov, who were then looked upon as musical radicals. Though doubtless influenced by them, Tchaikovsky could not sympathize with them completely, and indeed cannot himself be reckoned as strictly Russian in his music, as they sought to be.

During this period Tchaikovsky's financial resources were, as they had always been, at a low ebb. Information as to his troubles as well as his gifts and aspirations came to the ears of a wealthy widow, Nadejda von Meck. This generous woman was passionately devoted to music, and on learning many of the details of Tchaikovsky's life, she determined to assist him. With the utmost tact she managed to place herself in the position of patron, and established for him an annual income which greatly relieved his anxiety regarding money matters. The optimistic spirit of his Fourth Symphony, published soon after this happy event, must reflect the mental state that resulted from his liberation from material worries. When the income had to be discontinued, after thirteen years, because of Mme. von Meck's financial difficulties, there was a misunderstanding which saddened Tchaikovsky for the rest of his life.

The Fifth Symphony was written in a little country house where

Tchaikovsky had sought and found peace and quiet. Here he spent the happiest days of his life, albeit they were followed by his gloomiest season. The death of several friends and dear relatives, indifferent success of certain of his works, and homesickness caused by necessary travels outside Russia's frontiers preyed upon his sensitive soul and kept him constantly in mental misery. Success in conducting several of his own works in England brought him some cheer, however, and perhaps encouraged him in his projected journey to America. This was not interrupted even by the death of his beloved sister, and six concerts were given in the United States in the spring of 1891, in New York, Boston, Baltimore, and Philadelphia. All were extraordinarily successful.

In character and temperament Tchaikovsky was typically Russian. His music, however, while it does in truth portray some emotional phases of his personality, is not nationalistic. He was not steeped in the folklore and the folk music of his people as were Glinka and Balakirev and Mussorgsky and Rimsky-Korsakov. Rather, as he tells us himself, his devotion to the music of Mozart and his love for the Italian school dated from his sixth year. His thought is Russian, but its expression is colored with the richer hues of the South. The combination is a happy one, at least to cosmopolitan ears; it may, too, account for Tchaikovsky's more pronounced success in countries other than his own.

If durability is the criterion of the greatness of music, Tchaikovsky will probably always be ranked among the greatest composers of his time. His message has the quality of universality; it is eloquent, and it is beautiful. He expresses a sentiment which is probably felt at one time or another by every human being—the realization of the impotence of man, the ephemeral quality of his achievements, the certainty of death. While human nature remains unchanged, such feelings will occasionally arise to demand expression, and such music as Tchaikovsky's will express them more eloquently than any other means we now know.

Symphony No. 1 in G minor ("WINTER DAYDREAMS")

COMPOSERS, but more often critics, comment with scorn on the fact that conductors usually confine themselves to a few of the works of a given composer, neglecting those others which may be little known and which have not achieved popularity. Thus we have continually the Fourth, Fifth, and Sixth Symphonies of Tchaikovsky, with performances of the first three extremely rare; we have frequent performances of Schubert's Seventh and Eighth but rarely hear his lovely Fourth. Dvořák's Fifth ("New World") has endless performances, but his earlier works, in many ways almost as charming, are on the whole neglected. We hear all nine of Beethoven and most frequently those with odd numbers, but rare indeed is a performance of the "Jena" Symphony. On investigating this matter, as the author of this book had perforce to do, candor compels a word in defense of the conductor. The conductor's job is not only to conduct the orchestra but also to conduct the audience; to conduct it along both the highways and the byways of music wherever rewarding music has blossomed. A conductor who is also a sincere musician—and there are some—will play any music that seems to him good and worthy, and it can safely be believed that the unpopular works or the little-known works of any composer are, as a rule, unplayed and unpopular because they *are* unworthy: sometimes unworthy as music per se, sometimes unworthy as artistically adolescent products of the composer, and very often unworthy of the time and effort necessary to prepare them adequately.

It is probably safe to say that Tchaikovsky's symphonies grow in worthiness and in value exactly in their chronological order; but the First Symphony is not even a good *first* symphony. That is to say, if we judge it by the standards of Tchaikovsky's own best work, it could well be forgotten with no damage to the popularity or reputation of its composer. Mention of it is included in this book entirely for historical reasons. The reader is unlikely to encounter a performance of it, and if he should, is likely to be thoroughly disappointed and disillusioned. Records for the phonograph may make it available to those who wish to investigate it and to those who by some chance may find it satisfying.

Tchaikovsky himself came to think rather contemptuously of this symphony, though when it was first produced he found it difficult to accept the verdict of the public, which ultimately came to be his own.

The symphony was written about 1868, when the young Tchaikovsky was full of romantic notions—indeed, the subtitle of this symphony indicates that—and when his time was rather thoroughly occupied by his duties as a teacher in the conservatory or with his brief love affair with the singer, Desirée Artot. It was perhaps about this time that Tchaikovsky first gave evidence of that neuroticism that was to torment him during most of his life. His duties, his love affair, and his passionate determination to produce his First Symphony combined perhaps to bring about a state wherein creative impulses were seriously inhibited. When the symphony was at length finished, his impatience for a performance led him to request one, and his request was curtly refused by his former teacher, Anton Rubinstein. To any composer, and particularly to a man of such morbidly sensitive nature as Tchaikovsky, this was a crushing blow. He was by this time engaged to Artot, and naturally wanted not only to impress her in a profound way but probably needed some earnest of eventual success in order that he might marry her. This problem resolved itself, however, when Artot suddenly married a baritone in the same opera company of which she was a member.

Perhaps this was a kind of relief, for Tchaikovsky, after all his troubles with the rather invalid First Symphony, entered upon a period of activity and productivity. It is curious to observe that within two years of the production of the First Symphony he had written the infinitely superior, utterly different, and highly original fantasy overture *Romeo and Juliet.*

Nowadays few would dispute the judgment of Rubinstein in denying a hearing to the First Symphony. It has been said that Tchaikovsky never forgave Rubinstein, yet he could say of him, years later, "In him I adore not only a great pianist and composer but a man of rare nobility, frank, loyal, generous, incapable of petty and vulgar sentiments." And this after Rubinstein had told Tchaikovsky, rather pointedly, that it was not for the development of imbeciles that he took the trouble to teach composition. Tchaikovsky was grateful. Yet he also said of Rubinstein, "I have always regarded him as the greatest of artists and the noblest of men, but I shall never become his friend."

If Rubinstein gave the initial impetus not only to the public's indifference but to Tchaikovsky's distaste toward his First Symphony, Tchaikovsky, one reflects, could well have regarded him as a friend.

Symphony No. 2 in C minor ("LITTLE RUSSIAN")

PUBLISHERS are very strange people. Quite often they are used, put upon, or cheated by their authors. Not infrequently it is the author who comes out on the little end. This is to be accounted for no more by the eccentricity of creative artists than by the vagaries of publishers, who are not above (or shall we say below?) exercising an Olympian kind of censorship which permits them to receive a work with enthusiasm and then, out of irrational personal prejudices, refuse to publish it. How a publisher can encourage the completion of a work, accept it as fascinating and brilliant, and then forget or refuse to publish it is something which the creative artist has never yet been able to understand. Such things do happen.

Such a thing happened to Tchaikovsky with his Symphony No. 2 in C minor. A Russian publisher, Bessel, had agreed to publish this work, and since upon its first performance it had a success so definite as to require a repetition by general request, one would assume that the publisher would hasten to make the music accessible. Bessel, for some reason or other, did not observe his contract to publish the score, and Tchaikovsky laid it aside and perhaps forgot it for awhile. This was in 1872. Seven years later Tchaikovsky came upon the score in his library and decided to revise it. His revision was, we are told, quite drastic and in 1881 the version which we hear today was performed for the first time. Although one noted Russian critic, a colleague, friend, and quasi-biographer of Tchaikovsky, dissented, it appears that the revised version of the work was a decided improvement; at least Tchaikovsky thought so, for after the performance he wrote to his patroness, Mme. von Meck: "How I thank the fates that caused Bessel to fail in his contract and never print this score! How much seven years can mean when a man is striving for progress in his work! Is it possible that seven years hence I shall look upon what I write today as I look now at my music written in 1872? I know it is possible, because perfection, the ideal, is boundless, and in seven years I shall not yet be old."

FIRST MOVEMENT

Of the various titles which have been subscribed to Tchaikovsky's symphonies, only that of the Sixth—the *"Pathétique"*—had Tchaikovsky's own approval. This symphony is often called the "Little Russian," which subtitle was given it by the same Professor Kashkin who preferred the original to the revised version. This title is by no means improper since the very Russian character of the music is apparent even in the opening bars; and here and there throughout the work there are explicit quotations of typical Russian folk tunes. At the beginning the first horn asserts itself, but gently, in this characteristically Russian melody,

the contagiousness of which is presently felt by the solo bassoon accompanied pizzicato in the lower strings. The introduction of the movement is based on this engaging tune. Another melody of equally national character, not too far removed from a quite ancient Russian song called "Mother Volga," is made the chief thematic inspiration of the movement. It is presented tentatively in the woodwinds and then more explicitly in the strings, and it runs like this:

With great vigor the idea is developed into a climax, after which a contrasting and highly expressive thematic project is proposed by the oboe.

Here for the first time in the symphony one may observe a touch of the melancholy that later was to become almost the chief characteristic of Tchaikovsky's music. The composer does not linger in this mood, however, and from this point on indulges himself in a thorough elucidation of the melodic elements he has introduced. Indeed, the oboe theme noted above is seldom, if ever, discernible again, the composer apparently preferring to end the movement in the more characteristic and less sophisticated atmosphere created by the same haunting little tune that began it.

SECOND MOVEMENT

In this charming section of the work, *andantino marziale,* those who are familiar with the Sixth Symphony may find a vague resemblance between the basic theme of its third movement and the melody which is the first theme of the present movement.

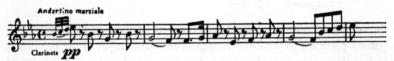

The truth is, however, that this bright tune, built up from a delicate pianissimo to a very sturdy forte, appeared originally in a wedding march in Tchaikovsky's opera "Undine," an unpublished work which he composed in 1869 and destroyed some time later. This melody together with a much smoother and sentimental one combine to form the thematic basis of the movement. The second melody, put forth with silken elegance by the violins, runs as follows:

The entire movement, for the most part, is devoted to the exploitation of these ideas together with a third of somewhat less importance; but the dominant one is always the pulsating marchlike motive with which the movement began.

THIRD MOVEMENT

There is certainly nothing of traditional Tchaikovsky melancholy here. The music is extremely lively in rhythm, gay in spirit, multicolored and highly ingenious in its use of orchestral resources, spirited and vigorous throughout. Sometimes the thematic material appears in the winds with a swiftly paced figure contrasting in the strings; then the position of the thematic material is reversed, with the accompaniment figure in the woodwind and the melody in plucked violins.

The movement as a whole is one of those charming little pieces which easily can be isolated from its setting and used as a separate entity. It is surprising that the conductors of "Pops" concerts have not come upon this gay little interlude so ideally suited to popular programs of the more intelligent type.

FOURTH MOVEMENT

Tchaikovsky turns once more to the folk song for the principal theme of the finale, and curiously enough the theme has, structurally, more than a little resemblance to the first theme of the second movement, though of course its time values and its orchestral color are different. This tune is almost literally borrowed from a peasant song of little Russia. Here it is:

The second theme of the movement is more characteristic of Tchaikovsky himself, and there seems to be no source for it other than the composer's own inventiveness.

The development of this thematic material is clear; it requires no profound study even by the uninitiated; the music is warmly romantic, brilliantly orchestrated and delightful to hear regardless of the degree of one's musical sophistication. It has been noted that Tchaikovsky himself had an especial fondness for this movement.

Symphony No. 3 in D major ("POLISH")

ROSA NEWMARCH, a most sympathetic commentator upon Tchaikovsky's music, asks a very pertinent question in connection with this symphony. "Certainly the symphony ends with an Allegro—*tempo di Polacca*," she says, "a very alien and artificial form of that genuine national dance, the polonaise; but since the second movement is *alla tedesca*, would it not be just as reasonable—and from internal evidence far more appropriate—to christen the symphony *The German?*" Another commentator suggests, perhaps even more pertinently, that it might be even more reasonable and more appropriate not to christen this symphony at all but to listen to it as the composer intended, simply as a symphony.

This is ingratiating music; it is not Polish, it is not German, it is not even Tchaikovsky at his best, but it is music that any sensitive, responsive listener can thoroughly enjoy. It does perhaps give the impression that it is assembled out of a number of disparate ideas. Its five movements have little or nothing in common, and one critic has ventured the opinion that any one movement could be omitted or the sequence of the movements altered without affecting the form or coherence of the whole. Tchaikovsky himself may have had some misgivings about the work, and he confessed in a letter to Rimsky-Korsakov that it could boast no new ideas; indeed, with his customary psychopathic anxiety he wondered if he had exhausted himself of musical ideas. It was perhaps characteristic of Tchaikovsky that, though his faith in the work was by no means invincible, he resented what seemed to him a lack of enthusiasm on the part of the critics who wrote of the work after its first performance. When we look back on these reviews, it is difficult to appreciate what quality in them aroused Tchaikovsky's resentment. Laroche, one of the leading St. Petersburg critics, was enthusiastic enough to write this:

"The importance and power of the music, the beauty and variety of form, the nobility of style, originality and rare perfection of technique,

all contribute to make this symphony one of the most remarkable musical works that has been produced during the last ten years. Were it to
be played at any musical center in Germany, it would raise the name of
the Russian musician to a level with those of the most famous symphonic composers of the present day."

César Cui, while perhaps more restrained than his colleague, was by
no means unkind and spoke warmly of the first three movements and
not too disparagingly of the others, although he found the allegedly
Polish movement weakest of all. "But we have a right to expect more
of Tchaikovsky."

The symphony was composed during the summer of 1875, and from
the first sketch to the finished orchestration required less than two
months—a fact which lends some credibility to the theory that Tchaikovsky made use of a variety of ideas which had lain gestating in his
mind for some time, and which he hoped he might combine into a coherent and viable work. The symphony was performed for the first time
on November 19, 1875, at a concert of the Moscow Musical Society
under the direction of Nikolai Rubinstein.

FIRST MOVEMENT

The emotional gamut explored by Tchaikovsky in this symphony is
indeed a wide one—so wide and so illogical, if considered with any expectation of continuity, as to give some substance to a charge that here
the composer was obviously straining for effect. The first movement
opens almost like a funeral march with this phrase, slow and lugu-
brious:

Yet within relatively few measures we are in the midst of an *allegro
brillante* of extraordinary aggressiveness and sonority based on this
idea, which is the fundamental musical idea of the movement:

Less than five minutes after the opening of the movement we are presented with another new idea, full of passionate longing and tender
melancholy. It sounds in the voice of the oboe and traces this line in
the score:

The entire movement is based on these powerfully contrasting and quite
unrelated ideas. One's interest is sustained more by the superb skill and
variety of orchestration rather than by any kind of musical logic that
would interrelate these themes. This is description and not disparagement of the music, for if one can discard momentarily the expectation
of a close-knit and musically logical structure, one can abandon himself to the sheerly sensuous pleasure of music skillfully fashioned and
eminently grateful to the ear.

SECOND MOVEMENT

The second movement gives as much occasion for describing the
symphony as the "German" as the fifth movement gives for identifying
the work as the "Polish" Symphony. The present section is in ¾ time,
allegro moderato, and is given the secondary title of *alla tedesca,* that is
to say, in German style. It has a certain resemblance to a German waltz
so far as its rhythm is concerned, but its melodic line is quite Russian,
quite Tchaikovskian. There are two melodic elements which are instantly conspicuous and almost always discernible in the music. The
first runs like this:

The second, which constitutes a kind of trill and which is decorated by a very rapid and somewhat complicated figure, is as follows:

THIRD MOVEMENT

With the beginning of the third movement Tchaikovsky seems to have accomplished a full emotional cycle, for here, in what he calls an *andante elegiaco*, he returns to the melancholy atmosphere of the introduction of the symphony. Here, perhaps, is the most authentic evidence of the Tchaikovsky that was to be, for this lovely melody

is put forward in the most expressive and richly combined voices of the orchestra, and in harmonies of a poignancy that is almost peculiarly Tchaikovsky's own. The composer is not concerned exclusively with this melody through the movement, however. There are contrasting ones of almost equal beauty and structural importance, culminating in a very broad and majestic treatment of the following:

FOURTH MOVEMENT

The fourth movement is one of the three in the symphony which Tchaikovsky himself felt was reasonably original and quite effective. Some of his critics found it trivial, but perhaps this was only because in their generation lightheartedness was not expected to be a characteristic of great music. Indeed, after the first light-footed passages for violins and flute alternately there is another melody, assigned to the trombone, which is of sufficient seriousness even for a Russian critic of Tchaikovsky's day.

In this movement Tchaikovsky really exercises his ingenuity, particularly in the Mozartian delicacy of the scherzo and again in the trio— a tour de force where, over what is tantamount to an organ point in the horns, the theme is presented in seven different tonalities.

FIFTH MOVEMENT

The finale of the work is responsible for its subtitle, the "Polish" Symphony, because of the rhythm and general style of the polonaise which Tchaikovsky makes the vehicle for his ideas in this section of the work. It was Sir August Manns who first applied the subtitle, when he directed a performance of the work in London in 1899. The brisk theme runs like this:

and is dealt with rather bombastically, but by no means unimpressively. Tchaikovsky's mastery of orchestration sometimes saves him from banality, and his music seems always infused with vital rhythm. These characteristics are more than evident in this final vigorous, and even brilliant, movement.

Symphony No. 4 in F minor

THE Tchaikovsky F minor Symphony is the first of what might be considered a cycle of symphonies—the composer's Fourth, Fifth, and Sixth —in which three differing aspects of his dark and mysterious personality are presented. Piotr Ilyich was a man of morbid sensitiveness, with pronounced leanings toward melancholy, sexual perversion and hypochondria, and a habit of introspection which carried to excess— as it was—contributed heavily to his gloomy and pessimistic outlook upon life.

Tchaikovsky's melancholia is exhibited in its most abject depths, its abysmal despair, its intolerable sadness, in his Sixth (*"Pathétique"*) Symphony. In the Fifth, there are indeed moments of poignant grief; there are passages shadowed by the dark wings of melancholy. But we find in the music a note of defiance, as well; a willingness to do battle against unfriendly fortune; and occasional moments of spiritual repose. In the present symphony, however, there is no overpowering gloom, no pervading melancholy, no despair or desolation. Its superb vitality leaves no room for morbid speculation and introspections. What gestures of an unkind fate are evident, now and again, are overpowered, crushed down, thrust aside, and treated with a vehement contempt and an outpouring of vigorous and virile utterance, and even with humor.

The symphony has fully come into its own only during recent years. The sentimentality of the Sixth, and the impressiveness of the Fifth brought them the more swiftly and forcibly to public attention; and their more obvious charms at once established them in the concert repertoire. The Fourth, however, by its wholesomeness, its soundness, its magnificent power and brilliance, its flashes of humor, and its marvelous orchestral coloring, has won its way to a point in the favor of concert audiences which places it on an equal footing with its successors. Present indications suggest that it may soon be even more popular than the Fifth and Sixth.

The symphony is dedicated, in Tchaikovsky's words, "to my best friend"—who could be no other than Mme. von Meck.

FIRST MOVEMENT

There is an introduction, in which the spirit of the movement as a whole is rather definitely forecast. Horns and bassoons give out a bold figure, somewhat military in character, somewhat ominous in significance, and treated with syncopation, a device of which Tchaikovsky

makes conspicuous use throughout the symphony. The brazen call of the horns is answered, at intervals, by a vigorous chord in full orchestra, and toward the end of the introduction, as the warning note becomes less insistent, suave utterances of the strings lead us gently to the presentation of the first theme of the movement.

Here Tchaikovsky sighs. It is not the suspiration of discouragement, defeat, and unutterable woe that breathes so unhappily in the long-drawn agonies of the *"Pathétique"* . . . nor yet the sign of weariness that comes, now and again, in the loveliest music of the Fifth. Here the theme seems to be relief, rather than resignation; peace, rather than pathos. The delicate motive appears at first in the violins and cellos, accompanied by the other strings and, faintly and occasionally, by the horn. Its progress upward to brighter planes of emotion is significant . . . and its subtly syncopated rhythm gives it vitality, motion, and grace. When it is presented, after a little, in the woodwind, it grows in emphasis, and a rather strong and insistent accompaniment in the strings gives it still more assertiveness. Its character changes, gradually but completely until we can scarcely recognize it as the underlying thought in the swelling torrent of tone to which it has given the initial impetus. There are fierce thrusts of sound from one section of the orchestra and another, driven along by an irregular, syncopated, but powerful rhythm. In this marked syncopation, and in the flying scales which the composer draws across and through the main texture of the orchestral utterance, we note two striking characteristics of Tchaikovsky's music which are frequently and most effectively exhibited in this symphony.

Another thought, a bit pensive, yet hopeful, detaches itself from the main body of the music toward the end of the first division of the movement. The clarinet utters it . . . the dryly humorous, half-pathetic, half-sardonic bassoon repeats it imitatively. More definite, as the second section begins, this idea takes shape as it is molded in tone once more by bassoon and clarinet. New fragments of loveliest melody mysteriously materialize from the nebulous and plastic material the composer puts before us. The clarinet diffidently intrudes with a gentle little song, strings supplying a diaphanous accompaniment in the background, and flutes, above, showering little cascades of glittering notes upon the curving outlines of the woodwind's song.

Two, and sometimes three, melodies are created, move, and have their being simultaneously; and so deftly the composer writes that while these lovely songs progress, while they are perfectly blended, one with the other, they nevertheless can be followed as certainly through the wondrous fabric of the music as one traces a bright thread through the warp and woof of a colorful tapestry.

Presently the composer abandons the somewhat elaborated counterpoint in order to demonstrate its antithesis. Now he permits us to hear one of the loveliest, and strangest, episodes in the symphony—a solo for strings, with contrasting woodwind, and accompaniment solely by timpani. Here is one of the most charming, and the most striking, ex-

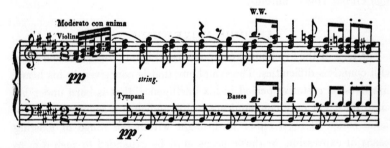

amples in all music of the subtlety, the versatility, and the eloquence of that frequently underestimated instrument, the kettledrum. The velvety quality of tone, the definite pitch, the inimitable rhythmic effect of this instrument, under the hands of an artist, are things to delight in and to wonder at.

The almost mesmeric calm invited by the preceding passage endures but briefly. Succeeding it after a space comes one of the thrilling climaxes of the symphony—a climax compounded of all the rhythmic and melodic elements that have been introduced; a climax that reaches its zenith in an awe-inspiring remembrance of the warning call that introduced the symphony. The trumpets put forth bright tongues of tone; the horns, somewhat veiled and ominous, repeat the figure in harmony. And the swift rhythm goes on once more.

Now thunderous basses urge the orchestra onward, fragments of melody are reviewed, impatiently discarded, discovered once more. Emotional intensity reaches a new degree of stringency. Striking through the whirling masses of tone, the warning of horn and trumpet leaps defiantly out from and above the combined might of a hundred instruments, yet finally the unbidden thought of terror and strife is thrust aside, and the peaceful if pensive song of the woodwind returns.

As the final section of the movement begins, the duet of strings and timpani, with the contrasting song in woodwind, appears again, but with a more agitated spirit than before, with the suggestion of disturbances to come, with the full mighty force of the orchestra lingering on the brink of utterance. Nor does this imminent utterance wait long. It bursts suddenly in a flood of tone, vigorous, strongly syncopated, compelling. There is a brief rehearsal of old thematic material, and the final climax slowly unfolds.

SECOND MOVEMENT

The task of the symphonic composer is a gigantic one, and one beset with countless difficulties. The symphony that is conceived in his heart, that lives its gestative period in his intelligence, that is born under his hand, must not only communicate to his audience a sequence of emotional states. It must either be brought within the range of existing means of expression, or those means must be expanded to such dimensions as to render them adequate to make clear his meanings. Again, the discipline that is the soul of art must be observed. Principles of structure are as necessary to music as to architecture, and by them the musical, as well as the material, edifice stands or falls.

No matter what storms of the spirit assail him, the composer must

coolly calculate to a nicety the degree of response he can exact from his
hearers. He must make his meanings clear if he wishes to create in his
audience the emotional state they have begotten in his own soul; he
must bring *this* idea into relief, subdue *that* one. And he must never ask
of his listeners the utmost of excitement for a period longer than they
can sustain it. It is natural, then, that the second movement of the symphony, after the prolonged and exigent spiritual demands of the first,
should be pitched on a lower and contrasting plane of emotion.

If the first movement represents, as it might, a temporary triumph
over, or a putting aside of, a troubled mood, the second may be considered as derived from a feeling of relief. Emotional tension is relaxed; there is weariness, almost lethargy, but yet a keen consciousness
of terrors held in abeyance. The pulse of the music, underlying the
larmoyant voice of the oboe as the movement begins, is measured and

slow and yet of such vitality that the strings presently themselves take
up the oboe's sweet lament. There comes a more cheerful, upward inflection of the violins, stronger as they are doubled with the other
strings; there is a growth in power and emphasis and sonority. And,
when the violas presently take up the suave opening strain, there are
gay little decorative figures in violin and woodwind.

The optimistic spirit grows in power until presently it is quite dominating. A more lively figure, like a grotesque sort of dance, appears
toward the end of the first half of the movement, its low-pitched but
lilting strain assigned to bassoon and clarinet, its rhythm to strings.
Presently the strings themselves sing the tune in smoother accent, and
the brighter woodwinds suggest even gayer spirits. Like spreading light
the melody and rhythm color all the orchestra, and a magnificent
growth in sonority accompanies the gradual addition of instrumental
forces until a splendid climax is reached.

The outburst of gay spirit is brief. The opening theme, weary but not
too sad, returns again, with flashes of brightness from the flute illuminating its otherwise shadowy colors. The movement closes in serenity.

THIRD MOVEMENT

Tchaikovsky's marvelous dexterity in the use of scales, in the invention of syncopated rhythms, and his love for the tone of the plucked string are given full play in the present symphony, and nowhere more than in the present movement. Here is one of the most charming, bright, and ingenious passages in all his music. There is scarcely a shadow in it; all is life, and brilliance, and humor.

The pizzicato string gives forth, or can give forth, a variety of emotional suggestions. In the third movement of the monumental Fifth Symphony of Beethoven, the string orchestra speaks ominously . . . suggests the restless pacing of some giant, incredible beast lurking in impenetrable shadows. In the second movement of the Schubert "Unfinished" it touches the depths of sadness and longing. In Tchaikovsky's own Fifth (at the close of the first movement) a progression of notes plucked, as if from reluctant strings, seems to mark the departure of loved ones into cavernous gloom. And here, Tchaikovsky uses the *same* device to mirror gaiety that is nothing less than exuberant.

Incidentally, here is a temptation that the merely virtuoso conductor rarely can resist, for the movement, if taken at a tempo much faster than that justified by judgment and good taste, is regarded by the uninitiate as an astounding tour de force. Indeed, to whip the rhythm and tempo to breathless speed does require technical facility of no mean order on the part of the orchestra—but consequent distortion of melodic line and burlesquing of the composer's intention constitute a price much too dear to pay for mere display. A properly tempered, restrained, and subtly molded playing of this movement is a joy to hear. The rhythm is quick, vital, and distinctly marked; impeccable intonation from the strings, beautifully rounded phrasing, and full justice to the subtle modifications of rhythm of which the movement is capable are all elements which can combine in one of the most delightful passages in symphonic music.

The opening theme is tossed about like a bubble in the hands of woodland sprites at play . . . dainty bits of melody flicker like will-o'-the-wisps, and are gone . . . and a lightfooted rhythm keeps the plucked notes flying like sparks. Up and down the scale, and up again, to rest for a moment on a shining note of the oboe. And this little pause is but the starting place for another lighthearted little song, such as might accompany children's games in the garden. Other woodwinds

join in the merry play and, after a space, the brass gives out a little subject that suggests toy soldiers marching across the grass, with a miniature fanfare of the piccolo to make them "stand up straight."

And in a moment the original pizzicato section returns, with more vigor and sparkle than ever, with even more subtlety of phrasing and nicety of accent. But now the strings invite brass and woodwind to join their own revel . . . and strangely, subtly, ominously almost, there is a sudden fierce climax that we are to encounter later as a striking feature of the final movement. In a moment, the vehement utterance passes; there is a parting flicker of humor as the brasses mimic and burlesque the tiny pompousness of toy soldiers; and the plucked strings end the movement in a lightfooted rush of notes.

FOURTH MOVEMENT

Nowhere in symphonic music is there a display of orchestral forces more magnificent than this overpowering movement. Here every instrument in the orchestra is asked for its utmost in dynamic contrast, in agility, in sheer power. Here, too, the outstanding characteristics of Tchaikovsky are exhibited with powerful emphasis and with brilliance of effort not to be found elsewhere in his writings.

Happily, his outstanding spiritual characteristic—melancholy—is not so exhibited. Did this symphony follow the lines of the Fifth and Sixth, we should have the joyous spirit of the preceding movement put to flight by a storm of baffled rage, an agony of melancholy, and an abandonment to despair. The fourth movement is, rather, the final justification and confirmation of the brightening spirits that have moved throughout the symphony ever since the close of the first section. In the first movement, the shadows, the warnings, the menaces that seemed to hang imminent over the music were ignored, thrust aside, forgotten. The second movement suggested rest after conflict; the third, carefree joy; and the fourth is a magnificent affirmation of the fact that triumph is complete, emphatic, and secure.

The entire orchestra bursts into a furious, a vehement utterance at the very opening of the movement. Strings and woodwind rush fiercely down long scales; brass and drum utter their boldest, and a mighty clashing of the cymbals is like a lancehead that flashes at the head of the great concourse of sound. Again the headlong rush of tone, and, after a tentative utterance of plucked cellos and basses, the first theme is given out in flute, clarinet, and bassoon. This theme is directly derived from an old Russian folk tune that every peasant knows. Its some-

what dark colors are fiercely denied by an antithetical outburst of the strings, and in sharp altercation the two instrumental groups lead once more to the all-powerful utterance that opened the movement. Now a new thought—a broader, still mightier phrase, rudely altering, by its syncopation, the prevailing rhythm of the music—enters and leads to a climax of stupendous sonority and power.

Stubbornly, yet with no emphasis other than that which a restrained and tempered utterance always carries, the little minor subject so brusquely thrust aside a few moments ago re-enters. The orchestra is held in check, as it were, listening. The contrasting subject presents itself in various guises—in oboe, thin and insinuating; in the pensive flute; in horn, in sonorous trombone, in mighty bass; in tearful woodwind once again; and ever the lighter strings deride, sneer, make sport of it, and at length convert it into a figure leading directly to another overwhelming pronouncement of the triumphant music that began the movement.

But, as the second section of the movement opens, we find that the disturbing thought of sadness, by its very persistence, has engaged the attention of the strings, too. Yet they rob it of melancholy suggestion; they make of it a suave and gracious utterance; they grow lyrical, and severe melodic lines are ornamented with glittering cascades of tone from the flute.

However the sad little theme is treated by the gusty fanfares of the orchestra, it persists; persists until, strangely, with a significance that gives pause, the dreadful warning that opened the whole symphony returns. There is a space during which the situation hangs in the balance. Will melancholy triumph? Have those magnificent outbursts of exuberance been premature, after all? But no . . . the horns subtly inject a recollection of the joyous music that began this movement. A few instruments catch the significance of this utterance. It is repeated, and its meaning permeates the whole orchestra. A powerful reminiscence of the mad music that occurred near the close of the third movement, and once more the entire orchestra plunges deliriously into the fury of joy and exaltation in which the final movement was born.

Symphony No. 5 in E minor

TCHAIKOVSKY'S Symphony No. 5 will probably always share honors with the Sixth, or *"Pathétique,"* as his most popular symphonic work, and with his Fourth and Sixth as his greatest. It embodies many of the qualities of the other two, yet is perhaps somewhat less clearly defined in emotional pitch than either of them. Its joy is never exuberant, like the mighty finale of the Fourth; its shadows of gloom are not so darkly painted as those of the *"Pathétique."*

The symphony presents several departures from conventional form, the most notable being the third movement. This part of the work is a waltz, rather than the classical scherzo, and is an interruption of and distraction from the emotional plane of the preceding and following movements. Tchaikovsky never sought bizarre efforts for their intrinsic appeal, nor did he violate accepted canons of form simply as a bold gesture; on the other hand, he did not hesitate to use whatever means his message seemed to require, regardless of convention.

FIRST MOVEMENT

Melancholy is in some respects the most beautiful of human emotions. Tchaikovsky alone of all the great composers seems to have fully understood and to have given most eloquent expression to its sad and mystical loveliness. Purified of ugliness and hatefulness in the marvelous alembic of his music, it is not the dull gloom that weighs down a soul by sheer oppressiveness; rather it glows, darkly and richly, as royal metal tried in the flame.

You feel this quality in the very first measures. The first subject, pronounced without prelude in the reedily sweet voice of the clarinets,

is sad, yet its continual gentle but firm movement suggests a driving force, temporarily vitiated, perhaps, but with a promise of a new influx of power. Viola, cello, and double bass accompany the first phrase of the theme, with the addition of the brighter second violin in the responsive sentence. There is something mesmeric in the mysterious association of stirring life and deadly gloom in these passages; it is as if a sleeper moved restlessly under the oppression of a dream of terror, then relapsed again into troubled slumber.

There is a subtle change in rhythm now, with the entire string section softly yet with ponderous weight intoning a swaying figure like the stealthy pacing of some huge and menacing creature. Against this new rhythm the clarinet appears with a second theme, now reinforced yet shadowed by the somber note of the bassoon. With delicate syncopa-

tion, and an always upward inflection, the new subject proceeds with growing brightness. Presently the flutes are added, doubling with the clarinet for a phrase or two, whereupon the subject is transferred to the strings with bright and pathetic figures of the flute, like coursing tears, playing over it. Now the struggle begins as the somnolent spirit writhes and heaves under the incubus of melancholy. Between crushing masses of tone that seem to strike at each other from different sections of the orchestra the simple syncopated subject persists and cannot be entirely obliterated in the furious duel raging about it. From horns and again from the strings it comes with increasing boldness, to disappear only at the pinnacle of the climax for which preparation is being made.

The vehemence that marks the composer's utterance here is not like the wildness of despair that so often rings out in the almost intolerably sad measures of the *"Pathétique"*; rather we have here a war cry, an expression of resentment and fierce defiance of the powers of darkness almost explosive in its violence. Enfolded in the warm, dark robes of melancholy, the spirit had almost failed, but now, with a heroic effort, it rouses itself in a thrilling, almost frenzied burst of energy as it tears and disentangles itself from the trailing weeds of woe.

Hardly has the orchestra, the full powers of which are required in the first few measures, given forth its message of defiant courage when a moment of pure lyric feeling appears. The first violins, accompanied by the remainder of the string choir, intone a lovely if fragmentary melody, with bassoon and clarinet in the antiphonal phrase against a descending scale on pizzicato strings. There is some development of this idea, with more and more brilliance and then a sudden fading of light as the ghostly voices of the horns come uppermost. But an incisive chord is plucked from the whole string section, ushering in a new figure for the woodwind—a figure that suggests the quick-drawn, panting breath of a desperate warrior struggling for very life. Presently, in clear contrast, there is an answering sentence in the strings, the string and woodwind figures alternating in two-bar passages until at last the violins become uppermost in a beautiful cantabile.

The present portion of the work is one of swiftly moving episodes. Panting weariness, awakening, defiance, travail, and momentary surcease have hitherto been depicted in musical color; presently the struggle is resumed with renewed vigor. It is as if the spirit beat with bruised wings against the impregnable barriers of time and circumstance—vainly, but never entirely without hope. Masses of tone almost terrible in might and splendor come swiftly, and toward the end there are combinations as well as separate appearances of several subjects already heard in the movement, notably the marchlike rhythm against a figure based on the principal theme, and the short sentence for the horns which has been put forward at intervals. A return to the principal theme is intimated as the music proceeds, such a return being of course in consistency with the sonata form.

Its statement and the development of figures contingent upon and succeeding it are much the same as in the first section. Yet there is more energy, more decision, as the chief theme is resumed; its elaborations are stated with greater determination than before. Phrases of contrasting color and emotional character—one bold, powerful, vivid, the other gentler and in the pastel tints of the woodwind—are now heard alternately, and then the entire orchestra, as if in impatience, rushes headlong into the swift, marchlike rhythm which has appeared several times in preceding portions of the movement.

The eerie voice of the faintly blown horn utters once more its soft complaint, and again is answered tremulously by the strings. Then from the very hearts of the violins, from first to double bass, is plucked a single chord—the signal for a new burst of life and vigor in the entire orchestra. Pizzicati flutter for a moment like shining wings, and wind and stringed instruments are again engaged in a strange dialogue, the utterances of the former in labored suspirations, the latter sure and smooth and confident in their brief antiphonal.

From this point onward the music rises to a repetition of a climax terrible in its intensity and sheer power. At the end, the deep and ominous mutterings of the double bass cast a shadow over all.

SECOND MOVEMENT

Seven measures of harmonies deep and rich and solemn in the strings prepare for the utterance, as an important subject of the second movement, of one of music's loveliest melodies—one of the rare songs that pierce the inmost places of the heart; a languishing melody, burdened with nameless longings, poignant with yearning, yet having within itself the element of joy and courage and hope, in the midst of sadness, that is the emotional keynote of the Fifth Symphony. To the weirdly beautiful voice of the horn the exquisite song is given; ethereally it

floats above the gentle intonations of the strings like moonlight over misty waters, with now a flicker of light, now a pale ephemeral glow, and always with life and motion.

We have learned to seek and find in the drama the assuagement of the grief and terror of the protagonist, and the purgation of those emotions as they are produced in the soul of the spectator. Tchaikovsky in the present work, and particularly in the present movement, achieves an analogous effect. The utter longing, the bittersweetness of melancholy, are expressed in eloquent accents, albeit without the astonishing candor of the Sixth Symphony's complete surrender to despair. Here Tchaikovsky is more reticent, more reserved, and therefore even more eloquent—yes, the note of sadness is keener than in the *"Pathétique,"* if only because of the contrasting note of hope.

The antithesis of the first theme appears now, after a short transitional passage, in the first violins, with the other strings and the entire

woodwind section in the accompaniment. Presently certain sinister utterances of the bass presage changes in the prevailing sentiment—changes which the following section of the movement will reveal.

That a climax is imminent is suggested in the more powerful movement, the increasing agitation, the more emphatic voices of the orchestra. Woodwind and strings in turn color with their various interpretations a figure much like that first heard in the clarinet and again in the bassoon, and in the midst of this exposition the first violins interrupt with delirious spirals of tone that whirl upward, through and above the heavier masses of sound, hesitating and again circling upward as if seeking a moment's resting place. Nor indeed is that resting place found, for after a few chromatic phrases, the brass, so long restrained, bursts the bonds of silence and speaks suddenly and with fierce emphasis, obliterating the thin voice of the strings in its commanding power and majesty. The full powers of the orchestra are now invoked; the war cry of the powers of darkness, the demoniacal laughter of the spirits of mad despair, ring brazen in defiant finality.

But it is not finality for the irrepressible spirit of hope that can be felt in nearly every measure of the symphony's first two movements. There is a sudden pause, a hesitation in a slow and terrible march of tremendous notes in both lighter strings and double bass, that conjures up again the vision of some Gargantuan creature striding toward its victim. A pause, and the exquisite melody of hopeful longing returns; a melody that sings a "pleasure that is all but pain"—now in the vibrant strings, with the tearful oboe in the answering cadence above. In the background, yet full of menace, comes the heavy pulse of the plucked double bass, the cello, the viola, and the violins of the second section, yet bravely the first violins sing on, carrying their melody aginst both the threat of the dark utterances in the bass and the glitter of tears dropped by the woodwind from above. Almost imperceptibly the chief elements of the present portion of the movement are being gradually combined, until of a sudden we are led into passages of most skillful counterpoint into the texture of which the colors of the horn, the bassoon, the oboe, and clarinet, and the violins have been marvelously woven. Here, Tchaikovsky has not only artfully combined the voices of a variety of instruments, but at the same time has presented simultaneously the motives of gently persistent hope, of tears and temptation to despair, and of menace and terror that would crush hope— all engaged in a quietly fierce struggle, the outcome of which for a time remains in doubt.

There is a session of stormy music. Rising to a climax of almost terrifying power the tempest of tone pours out its final violence on a quick succession of chords that hesitate and then are silent; a small voice from the woodwind gives evidence that the brighter theme still survives, and presently we hear, more gentle and more appealing than ever, the last statement of the chief theme of the movement. The string choir divides into three sections, one composed of violins and violas entering into the theme in canon form, with the second section—cellos and second violins—giving back the same figure in their deeper voices, while underneath all, the third section, composed of double basses alone, sends forth deep but plangent notes from its gently plucked strings. The brass is silent in defeat, but the woodwind chants softly in rhythmical triplets.

Like one falling into the sleep of exhaustion, the melody sinks into deeper and deeper tones; its final phrase is sung once by each section of the string choir, violin, second violin, viola, cello, until it reaches the sonorous double bass. Here, after a final flicker of lambent light from the clarinet's mellow reed, it ends in silence.

THIRD MOVEMENT

The emotional exhaustion suggested in the latter part of the preceding movement is something more than a mere figure of speech. The heartstrings, like nerves, become fatigued and unresponsive if too violently or if incessantly played upon. Tchaikovsky, therefore, at the precise moment when he is suggesting exhaustion as well as causing it in sensitive listeners by the sustained intensity of the second movement, now provides a welcome and charming distraction in the third. The use of the waltz rhythm in symphonic writing is not common, chiefly because it does not readily lend itself either to the classical sonata form or to the expression of profound feeling, but these very facts provide reasons for its introduction here in the third movement of the symphony. There is no attempt to invest the waltz—and it is nothing more —with any deep significance, there is no spur to the emotions, already jaded after the soul struggles of the second movement.

Contrarily, the urbanity of the principal theme, introduced without prelude as the movement opens, is soothing to the senses and gently stimulating intellectually. Strings, horns, and bassoons appear in the first presentation of the melody—the theme itself being assigned to the

first violin, with the other strings supplying a pizzicato accompaniment, and woodwind punctuating the measure with gently blown chords.

Though always the swaying three-beat rhythm is maintained, the composer brings to it a variety of orchestration and a skillful play of internal movements that are really fascinating.

So it is that the first arrangement of the thematic material and its accompaniment does not endure for long. The viola presently has a fragment, the woodwind answers in countermelodies, and then oboes, with horns, doubled, have a short solo—all these episodes based on the first melody of the movement.

The nervous intensity produced in the first and second movements has now been thoroughly relaxed. Such was the primary purpose of the present portion of the symphony—but there was a further one, and that was to prepare for the final movement, not only by distracting the attention for a moment from the emotional stress of the first movement, but to suggest, without intruding, the somber thought that underlies the whole work.

Just as in the merriest rout it is always possible to detect a hidden note of melancholy; just as in the happiest moments there sometimes come the ghosts of griefs, more anguishing for the contrast, so, near the end of this pleasant space in the symphony, the first important theme of the entire work, taken from the first movement, insinuates itself into the music, the clarinet shrouded in the shadowy tones of the bassoon. For a moment the lilt of the waltz seems distant, faint, unreal, as the sober reminder of the troubled past hangs nebulously above it— now somewhat brighter in rhythm, to be sure, and in the major mode where first it came in the minor, but awful in its significance, nevertheless. There is but a moment of gloomy retrospection, however. Subtly the intoxicating rhythm of the waltz reasserts itself; a few bars of chords, quaintly syncopated, and then a final fanfare that speaks of determined cheerfulness. So the movement ends.

FOURTH MOVEMENT

The final movement of the Fifth Symphony presents a number of interesting features, some of them entirely new, some the resultants of what has gone before. In the first section of the movement at least, there is a complete change in the character of the music, in spite of the fact that the opening theme is nothing but the principal subject of the first movement. It appears disguised somewhat in a new orchestration, and brightened by transposition from the minor to the major mode. The change from the minor to the major effects a wonderful transformation in the significance of this theme. Where first it spoke of soul desolation

and melancholy, those emotions now seem in the heat of the struggles which have passed to have been purified, sublimated into a calm religious joy. Even the underlying slow march, that once suggested the irresistible advance of a destroying monster, has now become a solemn ecclesiastical rhythm, marking the slow procession of peaceful thought that moves across the scene.

The orchestration, too, has been subtly altered to lend the appropriate color to the present moment. Where once were crawling shades of gloom, now falls "a dim religious light." Even in the rhythms one feels subtle but significant changes—the development of the latent vitality dimly perceptible in the original theme at its very first appearance.

In its most solemnly joyous moments the music is nevertheless undergoing a continual change. There is a feeling that the relief and joy, after the emotional stress of the first two movements, are too new, too powerful, too exuberant to be contained within the stately measures of the present portion of the work. Even while the brass calls out a summons to thanksgiving and prayerful utterance, a brighter, more thrillingly vital motive is taking form from the elements already introduced into the symphony. The heavy dignity of the dominating religious note keeps down the less serious thought for a while, but after a period filled with alternating long-drawn chords in brass or woodwind, or both, against tripleted figures in the strings, there is a return to the key of E minor. In keeping with the structural laws of symphonic writing, the music has returned to the original tonality of the first movement, but not to the depressed spirit of that portion of the work. On the contrary, the bright, almost dancelike subject introduced with the change in key persists in its exhilaration and vitality.

All the barbaric splendors of Tartary burst forth in blazing color and exotic rhythms, as vivid and irregular in form as a gigantic pyrotechnical display against a midnight sky, as the second section of the final movement unfolds. Little of the orchestra's resources are left unexplored in the first few bars—utterances of seemingly blind and unreasoning jubilation which, notwithstanding their superficial indefiniteness of form and structure, can be found on a closer examination to embody the basic idea of the symphony as it was elucidated in the first important theme of the work and at intervals throughout its exposition. In fact, the electrifying sweep of fiery brilliance here is but the prelude to another pronouncement of this theme in its revised and triumphant form. Soon one hears it blown upon the majestic brass, now in magnificent broad phrases, again quickly and with nervous emphasis. Above it the woodwind delivers itself of ecstatic scales, frenetically joyful.

The essential difference of Tchaikovsky's Fifth from his perhaps more famous Sixth Symphony ("*Pathétique*") becomes perfectly apparent now. In that paean of pessimism were embodied the cardinal tenets of his gloomy creed that effort is vain, that hope is vain, that all is vain. And at the end despair conquers. But here the composer must have written in one of those rare moments when, after spiritual storms, life seemed brighter and cleared of the clinging mists of melancholy; a moment in which, perhaps, he experienced in regard to his creed, such as it was, the uncertainty that must sometimes come to every introspective mind that subscribes to dogma. There is always the possibility of error, and let us suppose that here Tchaikovsky happily doubted his belief that spiritual courage, hope, and energy cannot prevail against the stern realities of life. Here, certainly, he bears arms bravely against the dark spirits which at moments throughout the symphony have seemed invincible.

The final section of the fourth movement is one of the greatest pieces of bravura writing in the orchestral form which we have from the hand of Tchaikovsky. The atmosphere is distinctly Oriental in the first few bars, with bizarre tonal effects and syncopated rhythms. The music has not progressed far, however, before we come once more upon a derived form of the principal theme of the symphony, following the exploitation of a more joyous subject in strings and woodwind. The brass puts forth tongues of shining tone, illuminating the once somber phrase with golden light. A constantly accelerated fuguelike figure climbs swiftly upward from beneath, and still above the deep mutter of the double bass the aureate tones of the trumpet and trombone ring clearly. There is a reminiscent touch of the religious triumph. Now a figure based on the first short introductory theme of the opening movement is combined with the new form of that movement's principal subject; practically the whole symphony is recapitulated in this closing section of the final movement.

The Fifth Symphony is in many respects the most satisfying of Tchaikovsky's works in the larger forms. Its structure is not so close an approach to the classical, perhaps; the third movement, a simple waltz, is not a detail which commends the work particularly to the pedant and the purist. Its emotional content is not as great, nor is it as intense, as that of the Fourth or Sixth Symphonies, yet here the emotion is disciplined, restrained; there is a more severe artistic reticence. The theme is the eternal struggle between hope and despair, and its development is so reasonable, so logical in its processes, and so definite in its conclusion that those whose belief in the power of the human soul to triumph over the vicissitudes of life has wavered or perhaps has been destroyed, as well as those happier ones who, though knowing human weakness and fallibility, still bravely face the world's cruel realities, alike should be satisfied.

Symphony No. 6 in B minor ("PATHÉTIQUE")

WHETHER or not he so intended, this is Tchaikovsky's last musical utterance, his farewell to the world. The strange circumstances surrounding its composition and performance, its agonizing melancholy, its inclusion of certain unmistakably significant passages, have given rise to the suspicion that Tchaikovsky wrote it as his "swan song," and committed suicide. It has even been called, rather cruelly, "the suicide symphony." There is much external evidence to disprove the suicide theory. Tchaikovsky, perhaps like every introspective and pessimistic man, meditated suicide at one time or another; but to speculate upon such an act is far from committing it. Tchaikovsky would doubtless have appreciated the melancholy dramatic possibilities of such an act after the first performance of music so intolerably sad—but like most who contemplate self-slaughter, he might have been deterred by the realization that he would not be present to enjoy the drama. The composer was sensitive to adverse criticism, and this symphony was not well received—not even appreciated by the musicians in the orchestra. But he was not so sensitive that the cool reception of his work would have driven him to suicide; if he had been, his career as a musician would have ended long before it did.

The fact remains that this music laments such woes as few have ever suffered, and though there is probably no connection between it and the death of the composer, it could, without too much exercise of the imagination, be regarded as suggesting the bitter griefs of life, an attempt to overcome them by a forced and unreal gaiety, a vigorous and manly struggle against despair, and, finally, surrender and death.

The symphony was completed in October, 1893, and performed for the first time at St. Petersburg, October 28, 1893, under the direction of the composer. It was a *succès d'estime,* and, of course, Tchaikovsky was not satisfied. A few weeks later it was played again—but the composer was not there to witness the enthusiasm. He was dead.

This work is one of the few pieces of absolute music which has been acceptably named by a person other than the composer. Tchaikovsky had thought of calling it a "Program Symphony," but quite reasonably asked himself, "What does 'program symphony' mean when I will give it no program?" His brother Modest suggested "Tragic," but the composer rejected this. Later, as an afterthought, Modest proposed "Pathetic"—and Piotr Ilyich agreed with enthusiasm.

FIRST MOVEMENT

A melancholy that is almost gruesome is exposed in the ominous phrases of the solo bassoon that crawl like serpents in shadow from

the darkest tonal recesses of the orchestra. The last section of the bassoon's utterance is taken from it by protesting strings, the violas laying on an intolerant accent in the middle of their phrase, above the sustained and pianissimo background of cellos and basses. The introductory measures are repeated; then the violins, with nervous impatience, hurriedly put forth a contrasted version of the introductory phrase, and the movement proper begins.

The melodic fragment, first introduced in a spirit of unhealthy lethargy, has now become completely transformed. It flickers briefly in strings and woodwinds; appears here and there in the orchestra, now powerful and dominating, now furtive and feeble. The flute disguises it with brilliant and determinedly—and pathetically—gay elaborations, like one who speaks and tries to smile through bright tears. Other woods and strings seize upon this fragment of woe and terror, refusing to let it rest, refusing its melancholy assertions, parrying its persistence, and masking its every appearance with their varying colors and rhythmic mutations—yet this condensed version of the orchestra's first ominous pronouncement tinctures the whole body of the music like a single drop of poison in a cup of rich and heady wine. At length the orchestra grows weary of the struggle to ignore, to hide, to fend off the hateful thought, and with a monotonous repeated figure in the cellos, a weary and tremulous sigh fading in the thinner, upper tones of violas, there comes a pause.

The violins, muted and soft, assure us that "there is a balm in Gilead." A soothing, a warm, and comforting melody is drawn from them—and from the cellos, too. Here is one of the saddest and sweetest, one of the most pathetic and consoling, melodies from the fluent pen of

this composer. It is not, at the outset, as passionate as it is resigned; but after the flute inserts a brighter fragment (shadowed by the mockingly imitative bassoon), there is a growth in intensity of expression, and the smooth melodic contours are troubled by more vehement ejaculations. These, too, pass; and the lovely song of the strings returns, now clear and *senza sordino,* but still not concealing the restless rhythmic figure that moves through the other sections of the orchestra. Almost imperceptibly the melody seems to lose its element of courage, its strength, and the impetus of its rhythm; transferred to the sweetly sad voice of the clarinet, ever *dolce* and diminuendo, it falls just short of silence. The last four notes hang imminently in the low range of the bassoon—and suddenly we are assaulted by a mighty, a fierce, and incontinent discord, torn violently from the whole orchestra, and instantly crushing down all possible thoughts of complacence and of peace.

There is a resistless outpouring of orchestral power, a forcible seizure of attention, and suddenly, condensed but (as the composer marks it in the score) ferociously, the opening theme returns with its ominous significance magnified by its vehemence. Violent is the fierce discourse that now succeeds. The theme rages through the orchestra; masses of tone are hurled like missiles; woodwinds and strings shriek question and protest; trumpets put out hot and quivering tongues of flaming tone. Sonorous brasses in grisly suggestion intone a fragment of the Russian liturgy for the dead. A climax is reached after a period of passionate agitation that is almost painful. There are sad recollections of past themes, like half-forgotten songs, like words of a departed loved one; and presently we come upon one of the loveliest, most intimately and poignantly touching passages in all Tchaikovsky's music. The strings, pizzicato, move softly and ever downward; above them sounds the brass in a mournful, yet tender and somehow noble

phrase. Again and again it is repeated, with the strings ever descending more deeply, more softly, into the depths and into silence. Who, listening to this music, can escape the recollection of Omar's lines of sweet resignation:

> *For some we loved, the loveliest and the best*
> *That from his vintage rolling Time hath pressed,*
> *Have drunk their cup a round or two before*
> *And one by one crept silently to rest.*

SECOND MOVEMENT

The curious and somewhat unnatural rhythm of this movement is significant. It is as if the conscious gaiety of the movement were under constraint, directed not by careless joy but by a determination to be joyful, *quand-même*. It is a waltz that is not a waltz—for it lacks a rhythmic member; it limps and falters. The smooth and gracious, though low-pitched, melody that moves about the 5/4 rhythm, first in cellos, then in woodwind against pizzicato strings, has a ghostly and unreal life; and it is not untouched by accents of pathos that seem to grow directly from its efforts to be gay.

The first theme is succeeded by a second melody, descending toward the persistent beating of the timpani. Happiness is still elusive, and the memory of tragedy persists. Later the two chief ideas of the movement are brought to bear simultaneously, and in brief antiphonal phrases, upon the orchestra. The result is always the same—a pensive and pathetic grieving that will not be comforted.

THIRD MOVEMENT

Here we may feel that Tchaikovsky has thoroughly aroused himself, for once, from the soul weariness, the lethargy of melancholy, that so persistently beset him. Here he "takes arms against a sea of troubles," and temporarily at least, "by opposing, ends them." Here is a fierce and apparently triumphant struggle; the hosts of human courage and vitality march with a quick and ever more determined step toward a blazing and frenetically joyful victory.

There is a busy rustling in the orchestra, a gathering of orchestral forces at the sound of an imperative summons, first proclaimed in the small but penetrating voice of the oboe, then gathering power and authority in the succeeding voices of sonorous brass. It is this trumpet-like call that vitalizes the whole movement, urges it on from its little, secretive beginnings, and drives it to the mighty climax. Always there is a quick and nervous rhythm; always a growth in power, until the entire orchestra, urgently driven along, bursts fortissimo into the bold rhythm. The theme is surrounded, as with a halo of flames, by a blaz-

ing fury of scales; splendid clashings of cymbals seem to strike fire from the orchestra, and the drums resound.

FOURTH MOVEMENT

So, all triumph is empty, all effort is vain; the end of life is a brief lamentation, a last despairing cry, and oblivion. There, very obviously, is the meaning of this movement. No one has ever wrenched from the orchestra cries of such complete, such abject, despair; no one, in musical language, has ever said so clearly and so finally, "All is lost." Even Tchaikovsky, never far from morbidity in his preoccupation with melancholy thoughts, has not elsewhere so abandoned himself to woe.

The movement is a succession of pleading, of bitter and tearful lamentations; but they are richly garbed in tone, for this is the very luxury of grief. The massed strings pour out their larmoyant plaint;

the bassoon follows with hopeless confirmation. Again, violins and cellos sing of nameless dolors and hearts that break; they rise, finally, through a prolonged access of passion, to a vehement climax. From this the orchestra descends, with increasing violence and in a headlong rush, into dark depths; there is a sudden burst of tone. It is the end. A single stroke upon the cymbal announces the passing of a soul; and the orchestra's brief requiem fades into silence.

It is this rushing passage which really gives the clue to the movement. It is violent, not valiant; it is surrender, and not a sortie against death and despair. With a gesture that cannot be misunderstood, the composer abandons all—his struggles, his sorrows, and his grieving. He rushes toward death not as toward a powerful enemy that must bravely be met, but rather as to a welcome relief from the necessity for effort and fortitude of soul. The movement is not really the apotheosis of sorrow, but a declamation of despair. If the opulent richness of its presentation suggests insincerity, let us not forget that it was perfectly possible for the neurotic Tchaikovsky to view his woes quite objectively; to appreciate their possibilities as musical inspiration; to separate his artistic from his personal self, without for a moment abandoning either. He was happiest when he was sad.

Manfred Symphony

*[Symphony in Four Pictures After the Dramatic Poem of
George Gordon, Lord Byron]*

BYRON's dramatic poem has been the inspiration of two important musical works, one by Robert Schumann and the other by Tchaikovsky. These two works in turn have certain qualities in common with two others, the *Fantastic Symphony* of Berlioz and the *Faust Symphony* of Liszt. It is not improbable that the Faust legend is the remote progenitor of *Manfred* and the various musical treatments that have been given this story, and this is particularly true with reference to the Tchaikovsky musical setting. It is perhaps of particular interest to remember that Lord Byron explicitly required the reinforcement of music for his dramatic poem, and it is still debatable whether the Schumann *Manfred* or the Tchaikovsky more adequately reinforces the poet's lines. In Germany before World War II, the Schumann *Manfred,* which was usually presented in dramatic form, appeared with relative frequency; outside of Germany performances of either the Tchaikovsky or Schumann are rare indeed.

Tchaikovsky's setting of the dramatic poem is called, in this score, "a symphony in four pictures, or scenes (*en quatre tableaux*), after Byron's dramatic poem." It does not appear among Tchaikovsky's numbered symphonies, but in the chronological order of composition it would come between the Fourth and the Fifth.

Byron himself, in a note to his publishers describing his work, perhaps provided a concise program note for Tchaikovsky's music. It follows: "It is in three acts, of a very wild, metaphysical and inexplicable kind. Almost all of the persons . . . are spirits of the earth and air, or the waters; the scene is in the Alps; the hero is a kind of magician, who is dominated by . . . remorse. . . . He wanders about invoking these spirits . . . and at last goes to the very abode of the Evil Principle to evocate a ghost. . . . In the last act he is found dying in a tower, where he had studied his art."

It is interesting to discover that the idea of providing a musical setting for Byron's rococo poem was not original with Tchaikovsky but was suggested to him by his friend, Balakirev, who was very definite, even to the extent of laying out a dramatic scheme for the work. Balakirev's directions required that there be a specific musical motive

identifying Manfred, the hero; that the first movement should be associated with Manfred's wandering through the Alpine hills; the second should suggest the pastoral life of the Alpine mountaineers; the third, a hallucination of a fairy dancing in a waterfall; and the finale, a kind of *Walpurgisnacht* in the cave of Arimanes; the appearance of Astarte, whom Manfred loved and lost.

It seems that Tchaikovsky was none too willing to undertake the work, although he had promised to do so. His conscience must have troubled him, for years after his discussion of the matter with Balakirev he wrote to a friend that he had undertaken the work in order to redeem a "promise so rashly given to Balakirev." Though Tchaikovsky did not in every detail follow the prescription of Balakirev, he did so inasmuch as essentials are concerned, the only notable deviation being a change in the sequence of movements. It is impossible to find that the composer entered into the work with great enthusiasm, or regarded it too happily after it had been completed. It appeared that he felt somewhat handicapped by writing to a program, although in fact he had often done so in his ballet music and other works. He remarked, in connection with *Manfred,* "It is a thousand times pleasanter to compose without a program." Later on he gives a hint, in a letter to his patroness, Madame von Meck, that he was not completely at ease mentally: "The work is so difficult and complicated that I myself am for the time being Manfred."

FIRST MOVEMENT

Tchaikovsky's reluctance to write to a program is rather quaintly evident in the fact that he causes to be printed in the score a program for the music, and in the next breath says in a foreword that the music is not descriptive of reality. "It is the soul of Manfred that the composer wishes to portray." Hopelessness and restive seeking for Nirvana seem to be compulsions that move this music through its course.

The portentous phrase in the dark tones of bass clarinets and bassoons is intended to identify the hero. "Manfred wanders in the Alps. Tortured by the fatal anguish of doubt, racked by remorse and despair, his soul is a prey to sufferings without a name. Neither the occult sciences, whose mysteries he has probed to the bottom, and by means of which the gloomy powers of Hell are subject to him, nor anything in the world, can give him the forgetfulness for which alone he yearns. The memory of the fair Astarte, whom he has loved and lost, eats his heart. Nothing can dispel the curse which weighs on Manfred's soul; and without cessation, without truce, he is abandoned to the tortures of the most atrocious despair."

There is a subsidiary theme apparently intended to suggest the hero's restlessness and longing for the peace of forgetfulness. These two themes constitute the basis of the movement, and a third, heard in strings *con sordino,* is intended to suggest the loveliness and the seductiveness of Astarte. A violent projection of the Manfred theme ends the movement.

SECOND MOVEMENT

"The Fairy of the Alps appears to Manfred beneath the rainbow of the waterfall." One can find in Byron's poem lines that might have suggested this movement.

It is not noon: the sunbow's rays still arch
The torrent with the many hues of heaven,
And roll the sheeted silver's waving column
O'er the crag's headlong perpendicular,
And fling its lines of foaming light along.
—   —   —   *No eyes*
But mine now drink this sight of loveliness.

The movement is entrusted almost entirely to strings and woodwind. The play of waters and the iridescence of the rainbow that arches above the waterfall are vividly suggested in the deft use of violins and the less aggressive wind instruments, with only an occasional note of the horn to give substance to the diaphanous quality of the music. The middle section of the movement presents a lovely song in the violins with accompaniment from the harp, and there are references to the Manfred motive of the preceding movement.

THIRD MOVEMENT

"Pastorale. Simple, free, and peaceful life of the mountaineers." As far as the dramatic action of Byron's poem is concerned, this music seems to have no particular reference, unless, perhaps because of its pastoral quality, you might recall the lines:

The Shepherd's pipe in the distance is heard.
The natural music of the mountain reed
Mix'd with the sweet bells of the sauntering herd.

A quite obviously pastoral melody, voiced by the oboe, establishes the atmosphere of the movement which endures in pastoral simplicity until we are reminded of the Manfred theme. This initiates a period of some excitement, rising to a climax of marked dramatic impact; but in almost conventional style the sound of distant bells and reappearance of the pastoral theme of the opening bring about a return of the serene atmosphere in which the movement began.

FOURTH MOVEMENT

"The underground palace of Arimanes. Manfred appears in the midst of a bacchanal. Invocation of the ghost of Astarte. She foretells the end of his earthly woes. Manfred's death."

The final scene of Tchaikovsky's musical setting has no direct connection with the text of Byron's poem. Tchaikovsky introduces Manfred into a wild bacchanalian scene in the palace of Arimanes, whereas in the Byronic version Arimanes is seated in majesty on his glowing, fiery throne surrounded by ethereal characters chanting in his praise. There is indeed a kind of chant in Tchaikovsky's finale, and this is interrupted by an extremely aggressive outpouring of Manfred's own theme as he enters upon the scene. He is commanded as a mortal to bow down and worship, which he refuses to do. Because of his daring he is condemned, and the ghost of the lost Astarte appears to inform him of his imminent end. Organ and orchestra join in a vivid and sonorous climax, and there is a vague but perceptible reference to that wonderful melody from the liturgical Requiem Mass of the Roman Church, which has inspired so many composers—the *Dies Irae*. This music, so grim, so fateful, and yet somehow consoling, is not without meaning if we remember the closing line which Byron puts into the mouth of Manfred in the play: "Old man! 'tis not so difficult to die."

Randall Thompson

BORN 1899

R ANDALL THOMPSON is an American musician who has made important contributions to the art in various capacities and directions
—creative, musicological, and pedagogical. He was born in New York
of an old down-East family. He was graduated from Harvard College
in 1920, and two years later took his master's degree at the University.
He studied under Professors Spalding and Hill at Harvard, and later
with Ernest Bloch in New York; he was a Fellow of the American
Academy in Rome and later was awarded a Guggenheim Fellowship.
He has held numerous important musical posts, such as Assistant
Professor of Musical Theory, organist, and director of choral music at
Wellesley College; lecturer at Harvard; conductor of the Dessoff
Choirs, and of the University Chorus of the University of California.
In 1939 he became Director of the Curtis Institute of Music, which post
he occupied for several years. In 1941 he became head of the depart-
ment of music at the University of Virginia, and remained there until,
in 1945, he joined the music department at Princeton University. Mr.
Thompson has written an opera, two symphonies, a symphonic poem,
a string quartet, and many smaller works, both for instrumental and
vocal performance. One of his notable works is *The Peaceable King-
dom* for chorus unaccompanied, which was commissioned by the
League of Composers and presented for the first time by the Harvard
Glee Club and the Radcliffe Choral Society in New York in 1936.
More recently his *Testament of Freedom*, a work for male chorus and
orchestra, with text excerpted from the writings of Thomas Jefferson,
was given its first performance by the Boston Symphony Orchestra on
April 6, 1946.

Mr. Thompson's Second Symphony was performed for the first time
at a concert of the Rochester Philharmonic Orchestra, March 24, 1932,
Howard Hanson conducting.

Symphony No. 2

THOUGH Randall Thompson has written a number of successful works, unquestionably his most important and most successful is this symphony, which in a relatively short time has become an accepted part of the standard American orchestral repertoire. It has had an impressive number of performances outside of the United States as well, particularly in England, Italy, and Germany. Its contemporary and American qualities are emphatically present and yet less self-conscious than in most works of present-day American composers. Mr. Thompson is not afraid to be happy, to write melody, to fit his very notable rhythmic feeling into conventional time indications. He uses a large orchestra but not an unconventional one, and he uses it judiciously and seldom with the instruments all playing at one time. He has a feeling for line, for color, for rhythm, and for climax, all of which are superbly exemplified in this genuinely interesting, sincere, and convincing music. Mr. Thompson himself has written of this music: "I wanted to write four contrasting movements, separate and distinct, which together should convey a sense of balance and completeness." It appears to many musicians that Mr. Thompson has emphatically succeeded. One can hardly get a clearer idea of this music than by reading the analytical sketch supplied by the composer himself. He writes as follows:

"It is based on no program, either literary or spiritual. It is not cyclical.

"I have used the ordinary full orchestra by threes. I have not used all the instruments in every movement. Limiting the percussion to cymbals and kettledrums may seem to be a curious twist for a contemporary composer. I have been sparing in my use of percussive punctuation in an attempt to make the music itself intrinsically rhythmic. The kettledrums are used only in the first two movements; the cymbals only in the last two. The orchestra is greatly reduced in the second movement. The brass in the scherzo is limited to horns and one trumpet. The trombones and tuba are employed only in the last movement."

The analysis that follows is from the pen of the composer:

I. Allegro, E minor; 2/4 time. The principal theme is announced

immediately by the horns, forte, and answered by the trumpets. From
this motive is derived a series of rhythmic figures which form the

toccata-like background of the entire movement. The subsidiary theme
(G minor, oboes, English horn, and bassoon) is of a more reticent
nature, but the violoncellos accompany it in persistent rhythm.

The development section begins quietly, and forms a gradual crescendo, at the apex of which the first theme returns in an ominous
fortissimo against a counter-rhythm on the kettledrums. A more extended transition leads to a sinister presentation of the second theme
(C minor, muted trumpets answered by bassoon and clarinets antiphonally). At the close, a major version of the second theme in augmenta-
tion is sounded fortissimo by the horns and trumpets against the
continuous pulse of the strings. The movement subsides, apparently to
end in the major. An abrupt minor chord brings it to a close.

II. Largo, C major; 4/4 time. The violins play a warm, quiet

melody against pizzicato chords in the violoncellos. A contrasting melody is sung by the oboe. The movement is not long, but its mood is

concentrated. It ends simply, on a C major chord with lowered seventh.

III. Vivace; 7/4 time. Scherzo with trio. The first section begins in
G minor and ends in D minor. The trio (*Capriccioso,* 6/8 and 9/8
time) progresses from B major to G major. The first section returns
transposed. Now beginning in C minor and ending in G minor, it

serves as a kind of extended "subdominant answer" to its former presentation. There is a short coda making intensified use of material from the trio.

IV. *Andante moderato—Allegro con spirito—Largamente*, E major. The slow sections which begin and end this movement serve to frame the Allegro, a modified rondo.

The theme of the Allegro is a diminution of the theme of the first and last sections. The *Largamente* employs for the first time the full sonorities of the orchestra in a sustained assertion of the principal melody.

Ralph Vaughan Williams

————————————— BORN 1872 —————————————

RALPH VAUGHAN WILLIAMS was born at Down Ampney, Gloucester-shire. He prepared for college at Charterhouse and studied simultaneously at Cambridge and at the Royal College of Music. At the University he earned both his master's degree in arts and his doctorate in music, and later pursued his music studies with Max Bruch. Through the following years he studied with many teachers, but not one has either imposed identifiable influence or devitalized Williams' own musical personality. He is a master in his own right and nobody's disciple. He has not hesitated to do violence to accepted canons of harmony when in doing so he accomplished an end that seemed to him desirable. His music is modern in the sense that it is contemporary, but it often involves medieval tonalities and modalities and archaic ideas of counterpoint when these suited his purpose. This independence might have been stimulated by his interest in English folk song and the music of England generally from the time of the Tudors to that of Purcell.

Williams joined the colors at the beginning of the First World War and later was commissioned as an officer in the artillery. He acquitted himself with distinction and after the end of the war devoted himself to composition and to his activities as professor in the Royal College of Music.

While Williams has given evidence of an acute and penetrating interest in the folk music of his native islands, he has not by any means been lacking in sheer melodic invention, and the combination of his own inventiveness plus the curious and interesting method of employing chords rather than melodies in counterpoint has resulted in a highly distinctive, logical, interesting, and gratifying style. It is certainly true, as has been remarked, that Williams has moved far to the left of old-fashioned scholasticism; but it is equally true, one may reflect, that the solidity and logic of old-fashioned scholasticism have been applied to his music with salutary effect; nor has the composer yielded to the temptation, suggested by the freedoms granted by the eclecticism and formlessness of modern composition, to create shocking dissonances and deliberately awkward melodic contours for the sake of being recognized as a contemporary.

His more recent works reveal some exceedingly interesting and often quite novel tonal evolutions. His approach to the implicit and potential miracles of counterpoint that lie fallow at the end of every writer's pen is rather original, since he conceives his counterpoint not so much in the melodic or uni-vocal sense, but rather as a kind of solidified polyphony which moves in chords rather than in melodies. This results in an exceedingly rich, colorful, sometimes startling but always justifiable tonal texture. From this fabric he has fashioned some of his best and most durable works.

Symphony in F minor

THE music of Vaughan Williams asks of its hearers a cultivated taste and a sympathetic attitude. Its moods are often so ephemeral, so delicately suggested, so independent of accepted canons and forms of musical structure that they can and often do escape the casual listener. Furthermore, in Williams' instrumental music there is seldom anything in the material world to which the music can be attached, which is discouraging to listeners who hope for and look for programmatic significance in any and all music.

The F minor Symphony is purely abstract and is susceptible of no interpretation, requiring little comment other than what can be supplied by the musical intelligence and responsiveness of the listener. It has certain characteristics, however, that might make one's responses more understanding. The symphony was performed for the first time at a concert of the British Broadcasting Company Orchestra at London, April 10, 1935, under the direction of Sir Adrian Boult. The Cleveland Orchestra was the first to give the work in America, the performance taking place at Cleveland December 19, 1935, Artur Rodzinski conducting.

FIRST MOVEMENT

A single hearing of this work certainly cannot reveal its profoundest beauties but will, to the attentive listener, display a quality of unity and integration that is quite uncommon in the compositions of Williams and other contemporary musicians. Further hearing of the work tends further to solidify this unity and make the symphony seem almost like a single rhapsodic utterance. The movements are very definitely interrelated by means of common thematic material. Two themes, both of them appearing within the first few minutes of the opening movement, are basic to the whole work. One of them is of further interest in that

it is not too far removed from a musical phrase devised upon the name BACH.* The second basic idea of the movement appears not long after the first and is projected by both woodwind and strings in an ascending figure. There are subsidiary passages of more or less

structural importance and a more or less circular return to them after their various explorations and mutations.

SECOND MOVEMENT

The second movement is bound to the first by means of the opening bars and its own basic idea is not presented until, shortly after the beginning, we hear it given out by the violins. There is a wandering flute solo culminating in a shining and flowing cadenza against which, surprisingly, is contrasted and rather explicitly stated the main idea of the first movement, coming now from the muted trombones.

THIRD MOVEMENT

Still the influence of the first movement persists. To accomplish the lightness and pace of a scherzo through the use of some of the lowest

* "H" in the older musical notation would correspond with B flat, which various composers have used as a basis for variations and other developments.

and heaviest voices of the orchestra is craftsmanship of the first order, both in composition and in playing. Williams has done his part in the opening passages of the scherzo, where a swift-moving figure is given to the basses and bassoons. There are references back to the first movement and what is perhaps the most interesting section of the movement comes about in a *fugato*, lively in tempo and vigorous in spirit involving prominently both tuba and bassoon. There is no interruption between it and the

FOURTH MOVEMENT

which stems from the third. Considerable sonority is required here, perhaps more than at any other moment in the symphony. The almost cyclic character of the work is once more re-emphasized by the employment of material developed from the closing passages of the first movement and there is a kind of peroration in which a good many of the basic ideas of the entire work are re-stated and re-argued. The integrating element of the whole symphony is the BACH theme or something very like it, and further exploration of it constitutes a large section of the finale in both simple and inverted form. It is combined and contrasted with other themes but in itself dominates the closing passages of the work.

A London Symphony

DR. ALBERT COATES, who was entrusted with the first performance of this symphony and was closely associated with the composer, supplied the following programmatic description of the work:

"The first movement opens at daybreak by the river. Old Father Thames flows calm and silent under the heavy gray dawn, deep and thoughtful, shrouded in mystery.

"London sleeps, and in the hushed stillness of early morning one hears 'Big Ben' (the Westminster chimes) solemnly strike the half-hour.

"Suddenly the scene changes (Allegro).

"One is on the Strand in the midst of the bustle and turmoil of morning traffic. This is London street life of the early hours—a steady stream of foot passengers hurrying, newspaper boys shouting, messengers whistling, and that most typical sight of London streets, the coster-monger (Coster 'Arry), resplendent in pearl buttons, and shouting some coster song refrain at the top of a raucous voice, returning from Covent Garden Market, seated on his vegetable barrow drawn by the inevitable little donkey.

"Then for a few moments one turns off the Strand into one of the quiet little streets that leads down to the river, and suddenly the noise ceases, shut off as though by magic.

"We are in that part of London known as the Adelphi, formerly the haunt of fashionable bucks and dandies about town, now merely old-fashioned houses and shabby old streets haunted principally by beggars and ragged street urchins.

"We return to the Strand and are once again caught up by the bustle and life of London—gay, careless, noisy, with every now and then a touch of something fiercer, something inexorable, as though one felt for a moment the iron hand of the great city—yet, nevertheless, full of that mixture of good humor, animal spirits, and sentimentality that is characteristic of London.

"In the second movement the composer paints us a picture of that region of London which lies between Holburn and the Euston Road, known as Bloomsbury. Dusk is falling. It is the damp and foggy twilight of a late November day. Those who know their London know this region of melancholy streets, over which seems to brood an air of shabby gentility—a sad dignity of having seen better days. In the gathering gloom there is something ghost-like. A silence hangs over the neighborhood, broken only by the policeman on his beat.

"There is tragedy, too, in Bloomsbury, for among the many streets between Holburn and Euston there are alleys of acute poverty and worse.

"In the front of a 'pub,' whose lights flare through the murky twilight, stands an old musician playing a fiddle. His tune is played in the orchestra by the viola. In the distance the 'lavender cry' is heard: 'Sweet lavender; who'll buy sweet lavender?' Up and down the street the cry goes, now nearer, now farther away.

"The gloom deepens, and the movement ends with the old musician still playing his pathetic little tune.

"In this movement one must imagine oneself sitting late on a Saturday night on one of the benches of the Temple Embankment (that part of the Thames Embankment lying between the Houses of Parliament and Waterloo bridge). On our side of the river all is quiet, and in the silence one hears from a distance, coming from the other side of the river, all the noises of Saturday night in the slums. (The 'other' side, the south side of the River Thames, is a vast network of very poor quarters and slums.)

"On a Saturday night these slums resemble a fair; the streets are lined with barrows, lit up by flaming torches, selling cheap fruit, vegetables, produce of all kinds; the streets and alleys are crowded with people. At street corners coster girls in large feather hats dance their beloved 'double-shuffle jig' to the accompaniment of a mouth-organ. We seem to hear distant laughter; also every now and then what sound like cries of suffering. Suddenly a concertina breaks out above the rest; then we hear a few bars on a hurdy-gurdy organ. All this, softened by distance, melted into one vast hum, floats across the river to us as we sit meditating on the Temple Embankment.

"The music changes suddenly, and one feels the Thames flowing silent, mysterious, with a touch of tragedy. One of London's sudden fogs comes down, making Slumland and its noises seem remote. Again, for a few bars, we feel the Thames flowing through the night, and the picture fades into fog and silence.

"The last movement deals almost entirely with the crueler aspects of London, the London of the unemployed and unfortunate. After the opening bars we hear the 'Hunger March'—a ghostly march of those whom the city grinds and crushes, the great army of those who are cold and hungry and unable to get work.

"We hear again the noise and bustle of the streets (reminiscences of the first movement), but these now also take on the crueler aspect. There are sharp discords in the music. This is London as seen by the man who is 'out and under'; the man 'out of a job,' who watches the other man go whistling to his work; the man who is starving, watching the other man eat—and the cheerful, bustling picture of gay street life becomes distorted, a nightmare seen by the eyes of suffering.

"The music ends abruptly, and in the short silence that follows one again hears 'Big Ben,' chiming from Westminster tower.

"There follows the epilogue, in which we seem to feel the great deep soul of London—London as a whole, vast and unfathomable—and the symphony ends as it begins, with the river—old Father Thames—flowing calm and silent, as he has flowed through the ages, the keeper of many secrets, shrouded in mystery."

* * * * *

A London Symphony was composed during the years 1912 and 1913. Dr. Williams had not been the first to associate music with the British metropolis. In 1902 Sir Alexander Campbell MacKenzie had produced his suite for orchestra, *London, Day by Day,* and also in that year Sir Edward Elgar had brought out his "Cockaigne" overture. The performance of the symphony took place at an orchestral concert given by F. B. Ellis at Queen's Hall, London. Other works on the program were Balakirev's *Thamar; In a Summer Garden* by Delius; Ravel's *Valses nobles et sentimentales;* Ellis' version of César Franck's *Pièce Héroique,* and three songs by Arnold Bax, which were sung by Miss Dilys Jones. The new symphony and Balakirev's symphonic poem were conducted by Geoffrey Toye; the remainder of the program by F. B. Ellis.

After this first production of the symphony—which took nearly an hour to interpret—Vaughan Williams made a revision of the work, and this was played under the direction of Sir Adrian Boult. Still other changes were made, and a third and final version was given to the public under the direction of Albert Coates, at one of the British Music Society's concerts, Queen's Hall, London, with the London Symphony Orchestra, May 4, 1920. The first performance in America was done under the direction of Dr. Coates on the occasion of his first appearance in the United States with the New York Symphony Society, December 30, 1920.

FIRST MOVEMENT

The introduction to the first movement is somewhat misleading in its atmosphere of rich melancholy created by the colors of muted strings and woodwinds and horns gently blown. The pulse of life moves through the music, making itself more definitely felt as the moment of full awakening approaches—a moment signalized with brazen brilliance first by horns, then trumpets, then trombones.

Now the allegro begins, and with it the main body of the movement.

While the music is strikingly episodic, the lyrical line is generally maintained as if the description of London at dawn were sung rather than recited. There is a possible reference to the quasi-Oriental atmosphere of certain sections of the London waterfront in the tentative use momentarily of the pentatonic scale, but for such atmospheric details one may with profit look back to Dr. Coates' description of the music.

SECOND MOVEMENT

The second movement is full of the singularly gentle, somewhat cynical and tolerant humor which the English have made rather peculiarly their own. As the program note points out, this section of the work is intended to recall the decayed and musty elegance of Bloomsbury and the sad, ridiculous pride with which that depressing section of London wears its air of having seen better days. An old street fiddler makes his unhappy music at the door of a pub, and he is represented in the score by a solo viola; here, perhaps, is a sly reference to the musical tradition that decadent violinists take up the viola.*

There are less tranquil suggestions here and there through the movement and bursts of passionate emotion as if one looked for a moment behind the dull, respectable housefronts of Bloomsbury's Victorian respectability and glimpsed for a moment the little, drab tragedies of human life that might transpire there. But at the end the fiddler is still bravely and lonesomely playing in front of the pub.

THIRD MOVEMENT

In some respects this music is both ironical and compassionate. It suggests at once the forced and tawdry gaiety of a Saturday night in the London slums and likewise reminiscences of the day when England was the land of folk song and folk dance. Indeed, in the studied vulgarity of some of the dance tunes and rhythms introduced here there are vestigial remains of the happy and innocent dance music of medieval England—the very music in which Vaughan Williams has found some of his happiest inspiration. We cannot read into this music the "simple

---

* A certain Briton named William Primrose, who has so brilliantly disproved this theory and who is himself a friend of Vaughan Williams, will forgive our mentioning the matter here.

annals of the poor," but rather, the viciousness, the greed, the raw, undisguised wolfishness that poverty engenders in the poor even during those brief intervals when they are supposed to be having a good time. This is a Saturday night under the murky light of reeking kerosene torches, a light that reveals crowded streets even more crowded with whores, hucksters, coster-mongers, fish-and-chips peddlers, and every type of catch-penny merchant, male and female. One views this pathetic spectacle as from a distance, from a point where the myriad sounds of the teeming slums become one great confused sound reflected from the dark bosom of the Thames. Suddenly a fog descends, mercifully concealing the garish spectacle and as mercifully shutting out its strident sounds.

FOURTH MOVEMENT

There is something peculiarly significant in the disorganization of this movement. It is a studied, clever, planned, and deliberate disorganization because the music is intended to portray London as seen by what, in our present economy, is called the common man; the stupid, faceless, voiceless, soulless automaton that our emasculated Communists would like to have use believe represents the typical man of our country, just as the political *castrati* who at present ride side-saddle on the warhorses of England would have one believe a similar invertebrate represents the soul of Britain. The entire movement is at the same time a picture of frustration and an example of it. The man is trying to portray musically the dreadful bitterness of the ordinary Englishman during the depression years; but the composer can no more detail the sense of helplessness, impotence, and frustration than can the poor victim of the same circumstances put into words his feeling of maddened ineptitude. The fourth movement of this work is by far its weakest and most insignificant, perhaps because the composer was shaken by feelings far too deep and powerful for his own talents to translate. In trying to present the feelings of what we are now told is "the common man," Mr. Williams fails utterly; perhaps because nobody has the right to speak for the common man. The ultimate explanation of this lies in the fact that there is no common man; that every man is a man unto himself, a world unto himself, a law unto himself;

and that those characteristics which are common to all men—the high, the middle, and the low—are not the denominators by which any man may, can, or should be judged, but are only the detritus, the waste matter which is left over after the creation and development of any Homo sapiens.

From a philosophical point of view, the fourth movement of Vaughan Williams' *London Symphony* is a colossal failure, but a very distinguished one. From this aspect it is a good try and a complete flop. In the abstract sense it is ingeniously and ably constructed music; from a contemplative point of view it is sounding brass and tinkling cymbal— signifying nothing. Yet it is not lightly to be discarded, for it is the honest effort of an honest man to put into music (which is to say, into an articulate and universally understood voice) the stupidities and the horrors with which the ordinary man is today surrounded; and in addition to this, it is a prayer and a hope for the amelioration of these conditions. It would be pleasant to think that a composer—a man sensitive to human sensibilities, human sufferings, human shortcomings, and human virtues—could influence and bend in the direction of decency the course of human history. This does not seem probable or possible or imaginable; if it did, such people as Vaughan Williams rather than the primates who at present guide our destiny might (and to our indescribable advantage) be the leaders of the world.

Pastoral Symphony

A CRITIC writing in the *London Times* on the occasion of the first performance of this work remarked that there is nothing in the *Pastoral Symphony* but music—a soft impeachment which the composer could and did admit without embarrassment. It is not difficult to discern that this music had its germinal origin in the lovely countryside of England, and its mood and atmosphere are often suggested and sustained by melodic ideas which certainly had their beginnings in the folk music of Britain; but there is no program, there are no subtitles, there is no imitation of nature or painting of pictures. There is only a profound stimulus to the listener's imagination, an eloquent evocation of the lights and shadows, the mood and spirit of the loveliest pastoral land we know.

Certain British commentators have "concocted" a program for this symphony; but this the composer repudiates, preferring, as he has said, to let the music suggest whatever images come to the individual mind. The symphony was performed for the first time by the Royal Philharmonic Society in London under the direction of Sir Adrian Boult on January 26, 1922. America heard it for the first time at the Festival of the Litchfield County Choral Union, Norfolk, Connecticut, Ralph Vaughan Williams conducting.

Vaughan Williams has lavished years of study and devotion upon the rich treasury of English folk music, and it is hardly surprising that out of this devotion there should develop in his own music a unique quality having its origin in the folk songs of his native land. It is perfectly logical that this influence should be felt more in this very English work than in any other. That is not to say that there is anywhere in the *Pastoral Symphony* a literal quotation of any folk song. There are, indeed, traces of many. One is a famous song, called originally either "Green Briars" or "Bushes and Briars." It is, like most British folk songs, modal in character; that is to say, it is derived from and in general follows the pattern of the characteristic intervals of medieval church music. Most British folk songs of any considerable antiquity fall into this pattern and, generally speaking, employ one of the three most familiar church modes—the Dorian, the Aeolian, or the Mixolydian. Mr. Williams feels that the Mixolydian and Dorian modes are more frequently found in country districts, while the Aeolian mode often can be observed in the somewhat more sophisticated tunes popular in towns.

The tune of "Bushes and Briars" was collected by Mr. Williams in Essex, and was sung to him by an old shepherd of the county, a Mr. Pottipher. Here is the first verse:

> Through bushes and briars of late I took my way,
> All for to hear the small birds sing and the lambs to skip and
> play;
> I overheard my own true love, her voice it was so clear,
> "Long time I have been waiting for the coming of my dear."

Strangely enough, the shepherd sang exactly the same tune to another ancient ditty called "Willy on the Wagon-Train."

The tune is in the Aeolian mode.* It was published in the journal of the Folk-Song Society in 1906 and, commenting upon this and other songs, Mr. Williams expressed his sympathetic attitude toward "that precious heritage of beautiful melody which is being allowed to slip through our hands through mere ignorance and apathy. I could imagine a much less propitious way of spending a long winter evening than in the parlor of a country inn taking one's turn at the mug of 'four-ale' (surely the most innocuous of all beverages), in the rare company of minds imbued with that fine sense which comes from advancing years and a life-long communion with nature—and with the ever-present chance of picking up some rare old ballad or an exquisitely beautiful melody."

FIRST AND SECOND MOVEMENTS

It would be misleading to suggest that the composer makes a fetish of modality or slavishly copies from the treasury of British folk melody. True, at the very beginning of the *Pastoral Symphony* we find the first theme in the Mixolydian mode, a very irregular rhythm moving a thoughtful subject for basses and harp. What is accomplished by this is

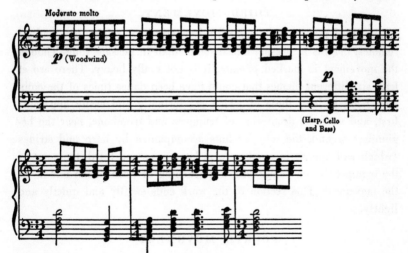

to suggest an atmosphere of serenity, the ancient lovely complacence and benignity of medieval and pastoral England now so irrevocably in

* The ninth of the ecclesiastical modes, fifth Authentic.

the past. The extraordinary suggestions of time, of distance, of remoteness, and even of silence accomplished by this first theme are extraordinary and beautifully effective; but from here on the mood is sustained and intensified by other means—means which a few years ago we might have called "modern" but which, after listening to some of our contemporary masters, seems as innocent as, and no more shocking than, Debussy. The restraint and gentleness of the whole movement is broken only once by a fortissimo; and we are startled only once by some extraordinary high trumpet playing. It is perhaps a little unconventional to regard the first and second movements as a unit, but indeed, one is the outgrowth of the other and they are closely related in feeling though not in thematic material. The second is actually an intensification of the first and, as one reviewer has remarked, "You think you have had 'contemplation' in the first movement, and, judged by the commoner standards, you have. But what Vaughan Williams means by 'contemplative mood' you will only know when the second is reached. . . . It seems to be an easy expression of those vaguer emotions which Fiona Macleod struggled to express in words."

THIRD MOVEMENT

The third movement is a modified scherzo that might have had its remotest origins in peasant dance rather than in peasant song. Though the movement is marked *pesante*, it is not really heavy. There are at least six different themes that could have been dance tunes of the common man, at least three of which are instantly and easily apparent: first, and with the decoration of trumpets and trombone, near the beginning; second, the solo for flute accompanied by harp and strings (which will appear in another form later on); and third, the song of the trumpet, which comes with a quickening of pace in the middle of the movement. This section of the work ends swiftly and quietly and lightly.

FOURTH MOVEMENT

The fourth movement is perhaps the loveliest, the most subjective, most contemplative, and the one which comes nearest to evoking a sense of the wholesome, healthy, human peace that lay over England's fields for generations. As Lawrence Gilman * has remarked, "It is the feature of the work—one of the remarkable symphonic movements of our time: a thing saturated in the stuff of poetry, full of a kind of speechless and musical beauty, a sense of 'evening hush, broken by homing wings,' though it has accents of passionate feeling."

The score calls for a voice without words singing in the distance, though ordinarily in performance this part—a melody of poignant loveliness—is sung by the clarinet. If we refer back to the flute solo in the preceding movement we will see that this wordless voice had its inspiration there. This is not the principal theme of the movement, however. We must wait a little until the tempo changes, and we hear in woodwind and horns the basic idea on which the movement is built. The cellos recall the melodic line of the wordless voice, and a curious

effect is brought about by scoring the strings and woodwind either in unison or an octave apart, with no harmony in between. The wordless song finally makes its way once more through the orchestra, appearing and disappearing among tonal shadows until at length all is quiet.

* In his program notes of the Philadelphia Orchestra.

William Walton

BORN 1902

Among various intelligent and constructive steps which English custom approves is the practice of providing to a choir boy his general education as well as a very solid musical training. William Walton was a beneficiary of this sane idea. When he was a lad of ten he read in the pages of the *Manchester Guardian* that there was an opportunity for a chorister at Christ Church, Oxford. He entered into competition for the position and won it. Three years later he attracted the attention of the Dean of Christ Church cathedral, and through the influence of this right reverend gentleman he was awarded a scholarship. In less than three years he had won his degree of Bachelor of Music. Following this accomplishment he had some instruction from Sir Hugh Allen and the eminent musicologist Edward J. Dent, but apart from the help that these gentlemen gave, his progress in music from that time to this has been entirely the result of his own unaided, unguided efforts.

Walton's works are fairly numerous, but what is more remarkable is that they have almost without exception been phenomenally successful. There is a notable quartet for piano and strings, written when Walton was only sixteen years old; there is the genuinely original *The Passionate Shepherd* for tenor and small orchestra; there is the highly entertaining and fashionable though frivolous *Façade* for speaking voice, flute, clarinet, saxophone, trumpet, cello, and percussion—a work done on a series of verses by Edith Sitwell; there is the handsome overture *Portsmouth Point;* the viola concerto; and the oratorio, *Belshazzar's Feast,* all of which are works of very definite importance.

Symphony No. 1

Sir Hamilton Harty, that genial and enormously talented Irishman who for a generation had a healthy and very important influence upon the progress of music in the British Empire, had also much to do with the success of Walton's music. Sir Hamilton presented the First Symphony of William Walton in very distinguished company, and did so deliberately with the compliment that it naturally implied. The symphony was performed for the first time on November 6, 1935, by the BBC Orchestra under Sir Hamilton Harty's direction, in company with Strauss' *Don Juan*, the Chopin E minor concerto with Josef Hofmann, and the Mozart Divertimento No. 17.

FIRST MOVEMENT

If music can be malicious, then Walton's music is, one may suspect, amusingly so. This quality is evident not only here but in other works of this composer, particularly his *Façade*. It is a quality akin to that one detects in Noel Coward's writing for the stage, or perhaps in certain outgivings of the Sitwells. In spite of the highly personal quality that informs this symphony, the form is chaste without brummagem distractions, although in truth it is not strict or strait-laced. The essence of the whole movement is contained in these few bars, with timpani (not indicated here) in the background.

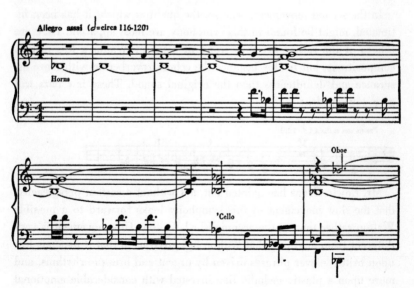

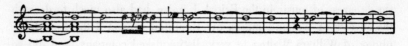

In contrast to what has just been quoted, we have presently in the violins a quite different utterance:

How this music is transfigured and twisted this way and that and ironically commented upon by means of fragmentary ideas plucked from the essence of the symphony itself one must really hear to understand, but there is no occasion for meticulous analysis. The music speaks for itself —and perhaps that is the best one can say of any music.

SECOND MOVEMENT

In the second movement, scherzo, the qualities which, it has been intimated, might be found in this symphony are most apparent. Here are echoes of the rather precious irony of some of Walton's less mature compositions, but in this instance the echoes reverberate with more assurance and definiteness than the original sound. These few bars will give you an idea:

Mr. Edwin Evans has pointed out, not without a certain perspicacity, that the slow movement of this symphony looks forward to a possible Walton rather than to the accomplished Walton. This movement is very different from anything that Walton has given us in that it depends less upon brittle, clever phrases driven by urgent and brusque rhythms, and more upon a plastic melodic line invested with considerable emotional

significance. Yet, curiously enough, it is not stretching imagination to
find in this movement a certain affinity (thematically considered) with
the first movement. There is a richness of thematic ideas, and perhaps
the most typical would be the following:

The whole atmosphere is one of restive melancholy.

THIRD MOVEMENT

The final movement is built upon a rather grand scale, full of contrasts, and is for the most part free, vigorous, and almost rhapsodic.
The composer makes his bow to formality by developing his final idea
in almost fugal style, with this tune as the basis for his contrapuntal
experiment:

He ends his excursion in abstract satire by referring to the rather pompous attitude of the opening part of the movement, but here even more
pompous, more declamatory, and more sonorous.

GLOSSARY

Accelerando: A gradual speeding up of tempo.

Accidental: A chromatic alteration; a semi-tone or fractional division of a whole tone in the scale.

Adagio: Very slow.

Ad libitum: At will as regards tempo and expressiveness.

Alla marcia: Like a march.

Allegro: A time indication meaning quickly.

Andante: A time indication meaning moving at a moderate pace.

Arpeggio: Playing the components of a chord individually instead of as a unit of harmony; a characteristic of the harp.

Bravura: Showy; calculated to display technical facility and power.

Cadenza: A brilliant display passage designed to reveal dexterity and, in some cases, invention.

Cantabile: A songlike, or singable, passage.

Cantilena: See cantabile.

Chaconne: Anciently a dance form in three-beat rhythm, practically identical with *passacaglia*. Developed as a variation form, the *chaconne* usually has the subject in the bass, with variations in the middle and upper voices.

Coda: Literally, a tailpiece; the concluding passages of a movement.

Col legno: A direction for string players, meaning "with the wood"; to play with the wooden part of the bow.

Concerto grosso: A music form in which a group of instruments is used as a unit in contrast with the remainder of the orchestra.

Con sordino: With the mute, an attachment for altering the tone of various instruments.

Counterpoint: Horizontal harmony; distinguished from chords, which are vertical harmony. In counterpoint two individual melodies are opposed and harmonized, whereas in a chord individual notes are similarly treated.

Crescendo: A gradual increase in sonority.

Diminuendo: A gradual decrease in sonority.

Dolce: Sweetly and tenderly.

Embouchure: (1) The mouthpiece of a wind instrument. (2) The arrangement of the mouth and other vocal organs for producing musical tone on a wind instrument.

Finale: Concluding section or passage.

Forte: Powerfully.

Fortissimo: With all possible power.

Fugato: In the style of a fugue.

Fugue: A musical form in which a given theme in one voice is announced in others and developed in counterpoint.

Glissando: A sliding.

Largo: In very slow tempo and broad phrase.

Legato: Connected; smooth and flowing.

Leitmotiv: A musical phrase used to represent a particular person, thing, or situation.

Motive: A significant but abstract phrase, less important than a theme but similar in character.

Passacaglia: Virtually the same as *chaconne*, but a somewhat less rapid form, in which the subject may appear not only in the bass, but in any part of the musical structure.

Pianissimo: Softly as possible.

Piano: Softly.

Pizzicato: Plucked; applied to strings.

Prestissimo: As rapidly as possible.

Presto: Very rapidly.

Rondo: A musical form analogous to the rondeau in verse, in which the subject matter invariably returns after each introduction of new material.

Roulades: Brilliant running passages on piano or harp.

Saltando: With bouncing bow.

Scherzo: In lively and playful style; a symphonic movement in a lively mood, usually with a middle section more restrained in character.

Sforzando: With a sudden outburst of power.

Solfège: General musical exercise and study; specifically, voice training by singing certain syllables on various tones.

Spiccato: To play sharply and crisply: detached.

Staccato: With a short, sharp accent, the notes clearly detached.

Sul ponticello: A direction to string players indicating that the passage is to be played close to the bridge. A peculiar tonal effect is produced.

Tempo: Time, in the sense of pace, or speed.

Theme: The musical sentence or subject on which a movement is constructed.

Timbre: Quality of tone.

Tremolando: See tremolo.

Tremolo: An alternate partial extension and re-enforcement of a tone, producing a trembling or vibrating effect.

Tutti: All together.

Vibrato: A rapid alternate flattening and sharpening of pitch, by which a trembling effect results.

Vivace: Lively and bright.

Vocalise: Strictly a melodious and wordless exercise for the voice; a passage or piece of music in similar style.

DISCOGRAPHY

BEETHOVEN

Symphony No. 1 in C: *Toscanini—B.B.C. Symphony Orchestra*: $7.25, DM–507.

Symphony No. 2 in D: *Koussevitzky—Boston Symphony Orchestra*: $6.00, DM—625.

Symphony No. 3 in E Flat ("Eroica"): *Toscanini—NBC Symphony Orchestra*: $9.75, DM–765. *Koussevitzky—Boston Symphony Orchestra*: $9.75, DM–1161.

Symphony No. 4 in B Flat: *Toscanini—B.B.C. Symphony Orchestra*: $6.00, DM–676. *Beecham—London Philharmonic Orchestra*: $6.00, DM–1081.

Symphony No. 5 in C Minor: *Toscanini—NBC Symphony Orchestra*: $6.00, DM–640. *Furtwangler—Berlin Philharmonic Orchestra*: $7.25, DM–1226.

Symphony No. 6 in F ("Pastoral"): *Toscanini—B.B.C. Symphony Orchestra*: $7.25, DM–417. *Stokowski—New York City Symphony Orchestra*: $7.25, DM–1032.

Symphony No. 7 in A: *Toscanini—Philharmonic Symphony Orchestra of New York*: $7.25, DM–317.

Symphony No. 8 in F: *Toscanini—NBC Symphony Orchestra*: $4.75, DM–908. *Koussevitzky—Boston Symphony Orchestra*: $4.75, DM–336.

Symphony No. 9 in D Minor ("Choral"): *Koussevitzky—Boston Symphony Orchestra—Shaw—Berkshire Music Festival Chorus—Yeend—Alberts—Lloyd—Pease*: $11.00, DM–1190.

BERLIOZ

Symphony fantastique: *Monteux—San Francisco Symphony Orchestra*: $8.50, DM–994.

Symphony, Romeo and Juliet (Excerpts): *Toscanini—NBC Symphony Orchestra*: $4.75, DM–1160.

BERNSTEIN

Symphony, "Jeremiah": *Bernstein—St. Louis Symphony Orchestra—Merriman*: $4.75, DM–1026.

BIZET

Symphony No. 1 in C: *Goehr—London Philharmonic Orchestra*: $6.00, DM–721.

BORODIN

Symphony No. 2 in B Minor: *Defauw—Chicago Symphony Orchestra*: $4.75, DM–1225.

BRAHMS

Symphony No. 1 in C Minor: *Toscanini—NBC Symphony Orchestra*: $7.25, DM–875. *Stokowski—Hollywood Bowl Symphony Orchestra*: $11.00, DV–4 (*Deluxe, non-breakable records*).

Symphony No. 2 in D: *Monteux—San Francisco Symphony Orchestra*: $6.00, DM–1065.

Symphony No. 3 in F: *Koussevitzky—Boston Symphony Orchestra*: $6.00, DM–1007.

Symphony No. 4 in E Minor: *Koussevitzky—Boston Symphony Orchestra*: $7.25, DM–730.

BRUCKNER

Symphony No. 4 in E Flat ("Romantic"): *Bohm—Saxon State Orchestra*: $11.00, DM–331.

Symphony No. 9 in D Minor: *Hausegger—Munich Philharmonic Orchestra*: $9.75, DM–627.

CHAUSSON

Symphony in B Flat: *Stock—Chicago Symphony Orchestra*: $6.00, DM–950.

CHÁVEZ

Sinfonia de Antigona
Sinfonia India   : *Chavez—Symphony Orchestra of Mexico*: $6.00, DM–503.

D'INDY

Symphony on a French Mountain Air: *Monteux—San Francisco Symphony Orchestra—Schapiro*: $4.75, DM–913.

Symphony No. 2 in B Flat: *Monteux—San Francisco Symphony Orchestra*: $7.25, DM–943.

DVOŘÁK

Symphony No. 1 in D: *Talich—Czech Philharmonic Orchestra*: $7.25, DM–874.

Symphony No. 2 in D Minor: *Talich—Czech Philharmonic Orchestra*: $7.25, DM–663.

Symphony No. 4 in G: *Talich—Czech Philharmonic Orchestra*: $7.25, DM–304.

Symphony No. 5 in E Minor ("From the New World"): *Iturbi—Rochester Philharmonic Orchestra*: $7.25, DM–899.
Stokowski and his Symphony Orchestra: In Preparation.

FRANCK

Symphony in D Minor: *Monteux—San Francisco Symphony Orchestra*: $7.25, DM–840.

GLIÈRE

Symphony No. 3 in B Minor ("Ilya Mourometz"): *Stokowski—Philadelphia Orchestra*: $8.50, DM–841.

HANSON

Symphony No. 1 in E Minor ("Nordic"): *Hanson—Eastman-Rochester Symphony Orchestra*: $4.75, DM–973.

Symphony No. 2 ("Romantic"): *Hanson—Eastman-Rochester Symphony Orchestra*: $6.00, DM–648.

Symphony No. 3 in A Minor: *Koussevitzky—Boston Symphony Orchestra*: $7.25, DM–1170.

HARRIS

Symphony No. 3: *Koussevitzky—Boston Symphony Orchestra*: $3.50, DM–651.

HAYDN

Symphony No. 88 in G: *Toscanini—NBC Symphony Orchestra*: $4.75, DM–454.

Symphony No. 92 in G ("Oxford"): *Walter—Paris Conservatory Orchestra*: $4.75, DM–682.

Symphony No. 94 in G ("Surprise"): *Koussevitzky—Boston Symphony Orchestra*: $4.75, DM–1155.

Symphony No. 96 in D ("The Miracle"): *Walter—Vienna Philharmonic Orchestra*: $4.75, DM–885.

Symphony No. 97 in C: *Beecham—London Philharmonic Orchestra*: $4.75, DM–1059.

Symphony No. 98 in B Flat: *Toscanini—NBC Symphony Orchestra*: $6.00, DM–1025.

Symphony No. 100 in G ("Military"): *Walter—Vienna Philharmonic Orchestra*: $4.75, DM–472.

Symphony No. 101 in D ("The Clock"): *Toscanini—NBC Symphony Orchestra*: In Preparation.

Symphony No. 102 in B Flat: *Koussevitzky—Boston Symphony Orchestra*: $4.75, DM–529.

Symphony No. 104 in D ("London"): *Fischer and his Chamber Orchestra*: $4.75, DM–617.

Toy Symphony: *RCA Victor Concert Orchestra*: $0.60, catalogue number 20215.

HINDEMITH

Mathis der Maler: *Ormandy—Philadelphia Orchestra*: $4.75, DM–854.

KALINNIKOFF

Symphony No. 1 in G Minor: *Sevitzky—Indianapolis Symphony Orchestra*: $6.00, DM–827.

MAHLER

Symphony No. 2 in C Minor: *Ormandy—Minneapolis Symphony Orchestra*: $14.75, DM–256.

Symphony No. 9: *Walter—Vienna Philharmonic Orchestra*: $13.50, DM–726.

McDONALD

Symphony No. 1 ("The Santa Fe Trail"): *Ormandy—Philadelphia Orchestra*: $4.75, DM–754.

MENDELSSOHN

Symphony No. 3 in A Minor ("Scotch"): *Iturbi—Rochester Philharmonic Orchestra*: $6.00, DM–699. *Rodzinski—Chicago Symphony Orchestra*: In Preparation.

Symphony No. 4 in A ("Italian"): *Koussevitzky—Boston Symphony Orchestra*: In Preparation.

Symphony No. 5 in D Minor ("Reformation"): *Beecham—London Philharmonic Orchestra*: $6.00, DM–1104.

MOZART

Symphony No. 26 in E Flat (K. 184): *Koussevitzky—Boston Symphony Orchestra*: $1.25, catalogue number 11–9363.

Symphony No. 29 in A (K. 201): *Koussevitzky—Boston Symphony Orchestra*: $7.25, DM–795.

Symphony No. 34 in C (K. 338): *Koussevitzky—Boston Symphony Orchestra*: $7.25, DM–795.

Symphony No. 35 in D (K. 385): *Toscanini—NBC Symphony Orchestra*: $4.75, DM–1172.

Symphony No. 38 in D (K. 504) ("Prague"): *Golschmann—St. Louis Symphony Orchestra*: $4.75, DM–1085.

Symphony No. 39 in E Flat (K. 543): *Walter—B.B.C. Symphony Orchestra*: $4.75, DM–258.

Symphony No. 40 in G Minor (K. 550): *Toscanini—NBC Symphony Orchestra*: $4.75, DM–631.

Symphony No. 41 in C (K. 551) ("Jupiter"): *Toscanini—NBC Symphony Orchestra*: $6.00, DM–1080.

PROKOFIEFF

"Classical" Symphony in D: *Koussevitzky—Boston Symphony Orchestra*: In Preparation.

Symphony No. 5: *Koussevitzky—Boston Symphony Orchestra*: $7.25, DM–1095.

RACHMANINOFF

Symphony No. 2 in E Minor: *Mitropoulos—Minneapolis Symphony Orchestra*: $8.50, DM–1148.

Symphony No. 3 in A Minor: *Rachmaninoff—Philadelphia Orchestra*: $7.25, DM–712.

RIMSKY-KORSAKOV

Symphony No. 2 ("Antar") : *Monteux—San Francisco Symphony Orchestra*: $4.75, DM–1203.

SAINT-SAËNS

Symphony No. 3 in C Minor: *Coppola—Symphony Orchestra*: $6.00, DM–100.

SCHUBERT

Symphony No. 4 in C Minor ("Tragic") : *Barbirolli—Philharmonic-Symphony Orchestra of New York*: $6.00, DM–562.

Symphony No. 5 in B Flat: *Koussevitzky—Boston Symphony Orchestra*: $4.75, DM–1215.

Symphony No. 6 in C: *Beecham—London Philharmonic Orchestra*: $6.00, DM–1014.

Symphony No. 8 in B Minor ("Unfinished") : *Koussevitzky—Boston Symphony Orchestra*: $4.75, DM–1039.

Symphony No. 9 in C (Old B. & H. No. 7) : *Toscanini—NBC Symphony Orchestra*: $8.50, DM–1167.

SCHUMANN

Symphony No. 1 in B Flat ("Spring") : *Koussevitzky—Boston Symphony Orchestra*: $6.00, DM–655.

Symphony No. 2 in C: *Ormandy—Philadelphia Orchestra*: $7.25, DM–448.

Symphony No. 3 in E Flat ("Rhenish") : *Mitropoulos—Minneapolis Symphony Orchestra*: $6.00, DM–1184.

Symphony No. 4 in D Minor: *Goossens—Cincinnati Symphony Orchestra*: $4.75, DM–1124.

SHOSTAKOVICH

Symphony No. 1: *Stokowski—Philadelphia Orchestra*: $7.25, DM–192.

Symphony No. 5: *Stokowski—Philadelphia Orchestra*: $8.50, DM–619.

Symphony No. 6: *Stokowski—Philadelphia Orchestra*: $7.25, DM–867.

Symphony No. 9: *Koussevitzky—Boston Symphony Orchestra*: $4.75, DM–1134.

SIBELIUS

Symphony No. 1 in E Minor: *Ormandy—Philadelphia Orchestra*: $6.00, DM–881.

Symphony No. 2 in D: *Koussevitzky—Boston Symphony Orchestra*: $8.50, DM–272.

Symphony No. 4 in A Minor: *Beecham—London Philharmonic Orchestra*: $9.75, DM–446.

Symphony No. 5 in E Flat: *Koussevitzky—Boston Symphony Orchestra*: $7.25, DM–474.

Symphony No. 6 in D Minor: *Schneevoigt—Finnish National Orchestra*: $9.75, DM–344.

Symphony No. 7 in C: *Golschmann—St. Louis Symphony Orchestra*: $4.75, DM–922.

STRAUSS, RICHARD

Sinfonia domestica: *Ormandy—Philadelphia Orchestra*: $7.50, DM–520.

TCHAIKOVSKY

Symphony No. 1 in G Minor ("Winter Daydreams"): *Sevitzky—Indianapolis Symphony Orchestra*: $7.25, DM–1189.

Symphony No. 2 in C Minor: *Goossens—Cincinnati Symphony Orchestra*: $6.00, DM–790.

Symphony No. 3 in D ("Polish"): *Kindler—National Symphony Orchestra*: $7.25, DM–747. *Beecham—Royal Philharmonic Orchestra*: *In Preparation.*

Symphony No. 4 in F Minor: *Stokowski—NBC Symphony Orchestra*: $7.25, DM–880.

Symphony No. 5 in E Minor: *Koussevitzky—Boston Symphony Orchestra*: *$8.50, DM–1057.*

Symphony No. 6 in B Minor *("Pathétique")*: *Stokowski—Hollywood Bowl Symphony Orchestra*: *$8.50, DM–1105.*

Manfred Symphony: *Sevitzky—Indianapolis Symphony Orchestra*: *$9.75, DM–940.*

VAUGHAN WILLIAMS

Symphony in F Minor: *Vaughan Williams—B.B.C. Symphony Orchestra*: *$6.00, DM–440.*

London Symphony: *Goossens—Cincinnati Symphony Orchestra*: *$7.25, DM–916.*

A Note About the Author

CHARLES O'CONNELL'S *phenomenal career began more than a quarter of a century ago when he joined the staff of a New England newspaper. In 1924, he went to Victor Talking Machine Company (now RCA-Victor Division of the Radio Corporation of America), and was with them, in various key positions, until 1944. Since then he has been engaged in supervisory and consultative capacities with other recording organizations. He was an important figure in the comeback of records in the early 30's, his audacity in testing market response with a recording of Schönberg's vast* Gurrelieder, *with Leopold Stokowski and the Philadelphia Orchestra, being still pointed to with pride. As manager of red seal artists and repertoire for RCA Victor, Mr. O'Connell supervised the artistic creation, in all its aspects, of that company's vast output of records for twenty years. Yet, recording music has represented but one side of Mr. O'Connell's activities. A finely trained musician and accomplished organist, he has conducted major orchestras the country over. In addition, his ability as a writer is attested to by the success of* The Victor Book of the Symphony, *which has been a best seller of many years standing, and by the more recent* The Other Side of the Record.